St. Helena Library
1492 Library Lane
St. Helena, CA 94574
(707) 963-5244

Cheers to the
Napa Valley Vintners,
Sponsors of Bookmark
Napa Valley 2016.

napa valley vintners From Friends & Foundation

THE WAY
TO THE
SPRING

THE WAY
TO THE
SPRING

LIFE AND DEATH IN PALESTINE

BEN EHRENREICH

PENGUIN PRESS

NEW YORK

2016

PENGUIN PRESS
An imprint of Penguin Random House LLC
375 Hudson Street
New York, New York 10014
penguin.com

Portions of this book appeared in different form in *The New York Times Magazine*.

Excerpt from "On the Slaughter" from *Songs from Bialik: Selected Poems of Hayim
Nahman Bialik*, translated by Atar Hadari (Syracuse University Press, 2000).

ISBN 9781594205903 (hardcover)
ISBN 9780698148192 (e-book)

Printed in the United States of America
1   3   5   7   9   10   8   6   4   2

Designed by Meighan Cavanaugh
Maps by Jeffrey L. Ward

For my mother

The dawn is breaking. The dawn is breaking persistently.
The dawn is breaking in all the stories of this book.

—Viktor Shklovsky

DRAMATIS PERSONAE

NABI SALEH

Bassem Tamimi: leader of the village protest movement; Fatah activist from early youth; designated a "Prisoner of Conscience" by Amnesty International following his arrest in March 2011; married to Nariman.

Nariman Tamimi: popular resistance activist and leader in the village protest movement; married to Bassem; sister of Rushdie Tamimi, who was shot by an Israeli soldier on November 17, 2012, and died in the hospital two days later.

Waed Tamimi: eldest son of Bassem and Nariman.

Ahed Tamimi: daughter of Bassem and Nariman.

Mohammad "Abu Yazan" Tamimi: middle son of Bassem and Nariman.

Salam Tamimi: youngest son of Bassem and Nariman.

Bilal Tamimi: videographer; former prisoner and Fatah activist during the First Intifada; employed as a graphic designer with the Palestinian Authority Ministry of Public Health; married to Manal.

Manal Tamimi: popular resistance activist and a leader in the village protest movement; married to Bilal.

Osama Tamimi: eldest son of Bilal and Manal.

Mohammad "Hamada" Tamimi: middle son of Bilal and Manal.

Rand Tamimi: daughter of Bilal and Manal.

Samer Tamimi: youngest son of Bilal and Manal.

Naji Tamimi: a leader in the village protest movement; former prisoner and Fatah activist; employed with the Palestinian Authority's Anti-Wall and Settlement Commission; cousin to Bassem; married to Boshra.

Boshra Tamimi: popular resistance activist, married to Naji.

Marah Tamimi: daughter of Naji and Boshra; cousin and closest friend of Ahed.

Mohammad "Hamoudi" Tamimi: youngest son of Naji and Boshra.

Abd al-Razzaq Tamimi: taxi driver; father of Mustafa Tamimi, who died at twenty-eight after being shot in the face with a tear gas canister on December 9, 2011.

Ekhlas Tamimi: mother of Mustafa Tamimi.

Odai Tamimi: younger brother of Mustafa Tamimi, twin to Loai.

Loai Tamimi: younger brother of Mustafa Tamimi, twin to Odai.

Bahaa Tamimi: Mustafa Tamimi's best friend; writer of plays and songs; leader of Nabi Saleh's *dabke* troupe.

Mohammad Ataallah Tamimi: founder of Tamimi Press, Nabi Saleh's media team.

Bashir Tamimi: owner of the land around 'Ein al-Qoos spring; active in the village demonstrations; head of Nabi Saleh's village council.

Said Tamimi: prisoner; friend to Bassem and Bilal; jailed in 1993 for the murder of Chaim Mizrahi.

Abir Kopty: activist, organizer, and spokesperson for the popular resistance movement; born in Nazareth; lived in Ramallah.

Mariam Barghouti: activist; blogger; student at Birzeit University; lives in Ramallah.

"Shireen": activist; friend to Bassem and Nariman, and to Bahaa and the village youth; lives in Ramallah.

Irene Nasser: journalist and documentary film and television producer; lives in Jerusalem.

Jonathan Pollak: Israeli activist, cofounder of Anarchists Against the Wall.

Renen Raz: Israeli activist.

HEBRON

Issa Amro: popular resistance activist; teaches electrical engineering at a local technical college; cofounder and leader of Youth Against Settlements (YAS).

Ahmad Amro: Issa's brother; trained as a veterinarian; activist and volunteer at YAS.

Mufid Sharabati: former merchant; ex-prisoner; volunteer with YAS; brother to Zidan.

Zidan Sharabati: my host in Hebron; unemployed laborer; volunteer with YAS; Mufid's brother.

Jawad Abu Aisha: popular resistance activist; volunteer with YAS; municipal employee; nephew to residents of the "cage house" of Tel Rumeida; grandson to the business partner of Jacob Ezra, the last Jewish inhabitant of Hebron prior to the 1967 occupation.

Ahmad Azza: student; YAS volunteer; lives in Tel Rumeida.

Imad al-Atrash: metal worker; activist; cousin of Anas al-Atrash, who was killed by an Israeli soldier at the Container checkpoint on November 7, 2013.

Tamer al-Atrash: popular resistance activist; cousin of Anas al-Atrash.

Fouad al-Atrash: shoemaker; father of Anas al-Atrash; lives in Hebron's Abu Sneineh neighborhood.

Najah al-Atrash: mother of Anas al-Atrash.

Ismail al-Atrash: brother of Anas al-Atrash.

David Wilder: New Jersey–born spokesman for Hebron's Jewish settlers; lives in Beit Hadassah.

Tzipi Schlissel: Tel Rumeida settler; granddaughter of Rabbi Abraham Isaac Kook, first Ashkenazi chief rabbi of Israel; daughter of the murdered Rabbi Shlomo Ra'anan.

Baruch Marzel: Boston-born leader of Tel Rumeida settlers; disciple of ultranationalist rabbi Meir Kahane; founder of the far-right Jewish National Front party; perennial Knesset candidate.

Anat Cohen: settler; daughter of Jewish Underground member Moshe Zar and sister of Gilad Zar, who was killed by Palestinian gunmen in 2001; notorious for attacks on local Palestinians and foreign activists.

Eran Efrati: Israeli activist and former soldier.

Haim Hanegbi: cofounder of the socialist, anti-Zionist Israeli political party Matzpen; son of Haim Bajayo, the leader of Hebron's Jewish community before the 1929 massacre.

Umm al-Kheir

Eid Suleiman al-Hathalin: sculptor; vegetarian; searcher for unexploded munitions.

Tariq Salim al-Hathalin: student; Eid's cousin.

Khaire Suleiman al-Hathalin: shepherd and seasonal worker inside Israel; Eid's half-brother.

Mo'atassim Suleiman al-Hathalin: Eid's younger brother; also a shepherd and sometime migrant worker in Israel.

Bilal Salim al-Hathalin: Tariq's older brother; Eid's cousin; also a shepherd and migrant worker.

Mohammad Salim al-Hathalin: Tariq's older brother; Eid's cousin; suffered extensive brain damage in 2004 after being beaten by a resident of the neighboring settlement of Carmel.

Suleiman al-Hathalin: Eid's father; shepherd; the current patriarch of Umm al-Kheir.

Hassan al-Hathalin: teenage shepherd; Eid's cousin.

Ezra Nawi: Israeli activist; born in Jerusalem to Iraqi-Jewish parents; ex-plumber.

GLOSSARY OF ARABIC TERMS

arghile: a water pipe or hookah through which tobacco is smoked

dabke: a traditional dance practiced throughout the Levant

diwan: a room or freestanding building used for meetings, gatherings, and the reception of guests

galabiya: a long, loosely fitting robe traditionally worn by Arab men

hadith: a story or saying attributed to the Prophet Mohammad but recorded outside of the Koran

intifada: literally, a "shaking off," a popular uprising; the First Intifada lasted from 1987 to 1993 and the Second Intifada from 2000 to 2005

jeish: army

keffiyeh: traditional Palestinian checked cotton scarf

mukhabarat: secret police or intelligence officers

muqata'a: generically, an administrative center or government headquarters; the word is often used specifically to refer to the presidential compound in Ramallah, and metonymically to the government of President Mahmoud Abbas

Nakba: literally, "catastrophe," the term refers to the displacement of more than 700,000 Palestinians during the foundation of the Israeli state in May 1948

qatayef: a dessert popular during Ramadan made of a small pancake stuffed with cheese or nuts and drenched in a sweet syrup *shebab*: literally, "youth"; the word is used to refer collectively to the unmarried young men and adolescent boys of a particular locale; in the text I have used the English word *guys* as an approximate equivalent

tawjihi: the matriculation exam taken by all Palestinian students in their final year of secondary school

za'atar: a sharply flavored wild thyme; eaten with bread and olive oil as a staple of the Palestinian diet

LIST OF MAPS

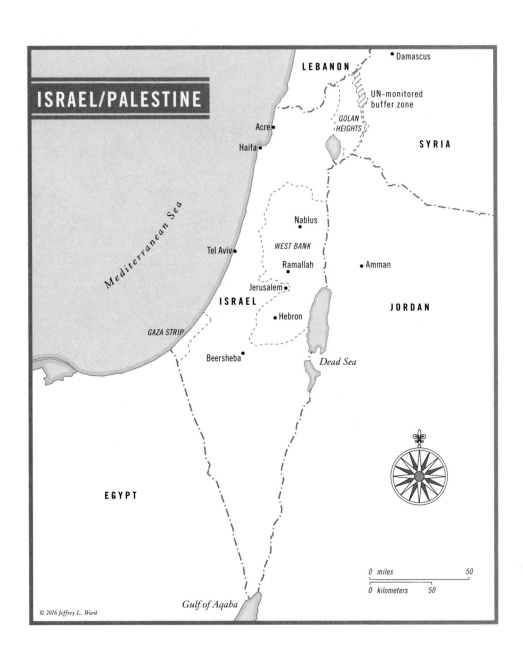

ISRAEL/PALESTINE

• Damascus

LEBANON

UN-monitored
buffer zone

Acre •

GOLAN
HEIGHTS

Haifa •

SYRIA

Mediterranean Sea

Nablus
•

WEST BANK

Tel Aviv •

Ramallah
•

• Amman

Jerusalem •

ISRAEL

JORDAN

• Hebron

GAZA STRIP

Beersheba •

Dead Sea

EGYPT

0 miles   50

0 kilometers   50

Gulf of Aqaba

© 2016 Jeffrey L. Ward

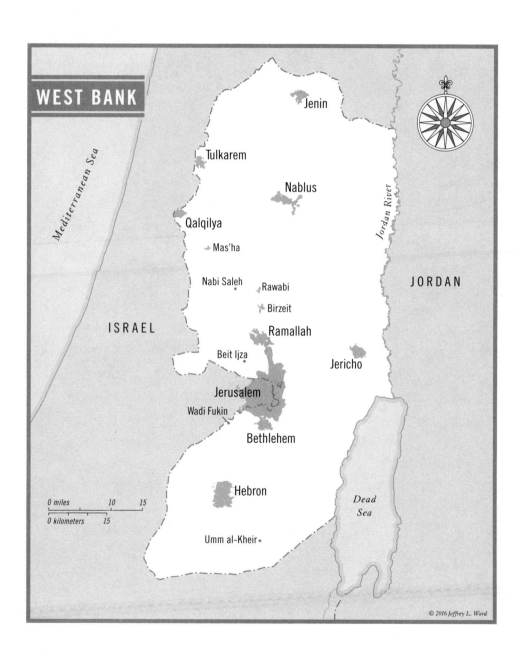

WEST BANK

Mediterranean Sea

Jenin

Tulkarem

Nablus

Qalqilya

Jordan River

Mas'ha

JORDAN

Nabi Saleh

Rawabi

Birzeit

ISRAEL

Ramallah

Beit Ijza

Jericho

Jerusalem

Wadi Fukin

Bethlehem

Hebron

Dead
Sea

0 miles   10   15

0 kilometers   15

Umm al-Kheir

© 2016 Jeffrey L. Ward

CONTENTS

INTRODUCTION

I'm scared of a history that has only one version. History has
dozens of versions, and for it to ossify into one leads only
to death.

—Elias Khoury

stepped onto the path that led to this book in 2011, when I traveled to the
West Bank on an assignment for *Harper's* magazine and spent a Friday in
the village of Nabi Saleh. I had no plans then to return, but one year later
I was back, this time for *The New York Times Magazine*. Palestine has a way
of enchanting people. I have seen it happen to many others since. Perhaps it
is the intoxicating proximity there of grief to joy and love to fury, the scale
and the awful clarity of the injustice, people's resilience in the face of it. I
can remember the moment that I knew it had caught me. I had just left
Hebron and was about to turn north toward Jerusalem. It was late in the
day and the light was soft, the harshness of the landscape briefly transformed. The car was stopped at a traffic light with fields and orchards on
all sides. A teenage boy stood alone at the intersection, waiting, presumably,
for a ride, and passing the time by singing an old Lebanese pop song. He
was singing for himself and took no notice of us in the car idling beside
him. The words were in English: "Do you love me? Do you? Do you?"
Somewhere beyond the fields a gunshot echoed. It wasn't far, but the boy
did not pause in his singing: "Do you love me? Do you? Do you?" The light
changed. We turned the corner. Four months later, I moved to Ramallah.

It is perhaps unavoidable and surely unfortunate that any book about the region between the Jordan River and the Mediterranean Sea requires introduction, and some small degree of defensiveness on the part of the author. Such is the current atmosphere, and the state of the debate, if that is not too genial a term. With this work I hope to correct, or to begin to correct, an imbalance of long standing, one that has already exacted far too great a cost in lives. The world—the human part of it anyway—is made not only of earth and flesh and fire, but of the stories that we tell. It is through narrative, stories woven into other stories, that we conjure up the universe and determine together its present contours, the shape of the past, and of our future. The exclusion of discomforting and inconvenient narratives, the near exclusive favoring of certain privileged perspectives and the tales that affirm them, this sets the world off balance. It makes it false. It is the task of the writer, and my task here, to battle untruth and the distortions it wreaks on our lives. All of our lives, on all available sides.

Telling the stories that I am telling, choosing certain stories and not others, means taking a side. This is unavoidable, and only a sin to those standing on the other side. "No spectators at chasm's door," wrote the great Palestinian poet Mahmoud Darwish, "and no one is neutral here." Not anywhere, but especially not in Palestine. I do not aspire in these pages to objectivity. I don't believe it to be a virtue, or even a possibility. We are all of us subjects, stuck fast to bodies, places, histories, points of view. Insistence on objectivity is always, Frantz Fanon observed more than half a century ago, "directed against" someone. (For Fanon, that someone was the colonized, the marginalized, and the oppressed.) The truth of this soon becomes clear to any journalist—or any morally sensitive individual—who chooses to work and live in the West Bank. Simply to refer to it by that name rather than as "Judea and Samaria," to call it Palestine rather than Eretz Israel, is to already be involved. And to base oneself there rather than in Tel Aviv or West Jerusalem, or Washington or New York, is to enter the conflict, whether one wishes to or not. If the nature of this choice is at first not obvious, the soldiers at the checkpoints can be counted on to quickly make it so.

I aspire here to something more modest than objectivity, which is truth. It is a slippery creature, and elusive, one that lives most of the time in contradiction. Its pursuit requires not only the employment of rigorous doubt and thorough research but the capacity for empathy and discernment, qualities available only to individuals embedded in bodies, places, histories, and points of view. There is blood in us, to paraphrase Eid Suleiman al-Hathalin, whom you will meet, and spirit and a heart. This is not a handicap but a strength, and the source of our salvation. I brought a lot with me when I set out to write this book. You carry no less as you set out to read it. If our meeting is fruitful, and I pray that it is, it will be because of what we both brought to it, and not in spite of that.

There are surely arguments contained in its pages, but I do not intend this work primarily or even secondarily as a polemic. The arguments it makes, it makes along the way. It is first of all a collection of stories about resistance, and about people who resist. My concern is with what keeps people going when everything appears to be lost. These pages represent an attempt to understand what it means to hold on, to decline to consent to one's own eradication, to fight actively or through deceptively simple acts of refusal against powers far stronger than oneself. It is also a reckoning with the consequences of such commitment, the losses it occasions, the wounds it inflicts.

This is therefore not an attempt to explain Palestinians to an English-speaking audience. They are more than capable of explaining themselves. One must only trouble oneself to listen. Nor is it an effort to "humanize" them, a favor they do not need from me. It is certainly not an attempt to speak for them. Or for anyone. I make no effort here to be comprehensive. Though I spent time in Jerusalem, in Israel, and, briefly, in Gaza, I chose to focus on the West Bank, if only because I knew my research had to have some limits. Even within the West Bank, I made only fleeting visits to the refugee camps, which are their own reality. For reasons of both access and affinity, I spent little time among adherents of political Islam. However much and with however much sadness I may have come to understand

Israeli perspectives, I make no attempt here to describe these events through the eyes of Israelis. Except when their presence was an intimate and immediate part of the world I was describing, as in Hebron, you will not find their voices here.

When I began traveling to Palestine, I had a strong conviction that something had to happen, that such a state of affairs could not persist indefinitely. I'm not sure that I was right, but something did happen. This book is also a chronology of the events leading up to that awful something, Israel's catastrophic assault on the people of Gaza in the summer of 2014. It is thus by no means a happy story. There is nonetheless a great deal of joy in it, and also of laughter, and of love. I do believe that this book is a work of optimism, and of hope. Not because I see any imminent "solution" to the Palestinian "problem," or the easy advent of something called "peace." On the contrary, I am optimistic because even in their despair, with no reason to hope, people continue to resist. I cannot think of many other reasons to be proud of being human, but that one is enough.

PART ONE

NABI SALEH

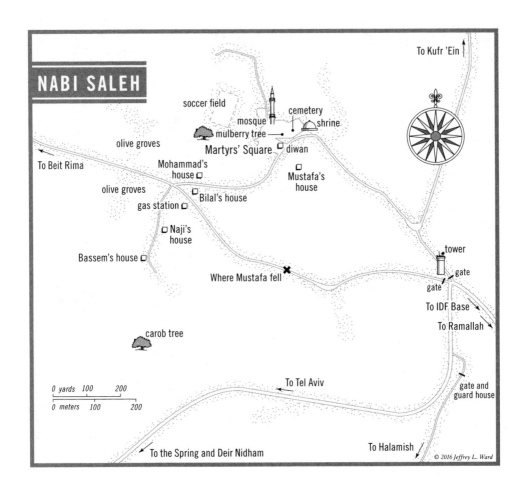

NABI SALEH

To Kufr 'Ein

soccer field

mosque
cemetery
shrine

olive groves
mulberry tree
Martyrs' Square   diwan

To Beit Rima
Mohammad's
house
Mustafa's
house

olive groves
Bilal's house

gas station

Naji's
house

Bassem's house

tower

Where Mustafa fell   gate

gate

To IDF Base

To Ramallah

carob tree

0 yards 100   200

0 meters 100   200

To Tel Aviv

gate and
guard house

To the Spring and Deir Nidham

To Halamish

© 2016 Jeffrey L. Ward

PROLOGUE

Ramallah, Tel Aviv, Nabi Saleh

And the nations' roads to the same old springs are endless!

—Mahmoud Darwish

In retrospect it all looks very different. It's hard to remember now, hard to push aside the intervening dread and the images that have lodged in the mind, but in those days the uncertainty was still intoxicating. No one knew that it wasn't really spring. No one understood that it was autumn. The air was crisp and cool and terrifically clear, the trees a riotous delight of colors so bold that they blinded us to every signal that winter was approaching. The past was mainly rotten, but it appeared to have passed. The present was pure ebullient collapse. And the future? It hadn't happened yet. For a few weeks in early 2011, hope felt almost material in its sweetness, like you could cut a slice from the air and taste it.

In Tunis, a fruit vendor named Mohammed Bouazizi, humiliated one time too many by the police, determined at least to die with dignity. He doused his clothes and skin and hair with paint thinner and lit himself ablaze on the steps of city hall. It took more than an hour for the ambulance to arrive. Within a week the streets were burning. Within a month President Zine al-Abidine Ben Ali, who had ruled Tunisia for twenty-two years, had fled the country. Within two months, the flames had spread to Egypt and Hosni Mubarak had stepped down after thirty years of uninterrupted rule. The fire jumped to Morocco, Algeria, Jordan, Yemen, Bahrain, Oman, even Saudi Arabia. Libya rose in open, armed revolt. By mid-March, only Syria was still quiet. And Palestine.

I arrived in Ramallah for the first time on March 15, 2011. Nowhere else in the Middle East had the oppression and violence seemed so intractable for so long. The worst days of the Second Intifada had ended several years before, but nothing whatsoever had been resolved. Peace talks between Israel and the Palestinian Authority had collapsed in 2010. Only the Americans seemed to mourn them. To most Palestinians, the previous twenty years of on-again-off-again negotiations had been one long charade, a glitzy show for the cameras that served mainly to hide the grinding and ever-escalating humiliations of life under occupation. What Israelis experienced as relative calm, Palestinians lived out as a slow and steady exercise in annexation: more settlements, more prisoners, more evictions and home demolitions, more land lost to the path of the wall. The number of Israeli settlers living in the West Bank had more than tripled since the first Oslo agreement was signed in 1993. Assaults on Palestinians by soldiers at checkpoints, or by settlers anywhere else, were so common that they rarely made the news. But things were changing. Elsewhere, entire populations were taking to the streets. Tyrannies that had seemed destined to last forever were collapsing left and right. The air seemed crisp and clear. Palestine had seen major uprisings in each of the two previous decades. Surely, if it could happen in the comparatively placid political climes of the Maghreb and the Gulf, Palestine would not be long in rising up.

But whom to rebel against? Ostensibly at least, the cities and towns of the West Bank were governed by the Palestinian Authority, which was controlled by Fatah, the secular nationalist party established in 1959 by Yasser Arafat and currently led by Mahmoud Abbas. The Gaza Strip was ruled by Hamas, an offshoot of Egypt's Muslim Brotherhood founded during the First Intifada, in the late 1980s. Elections had not been held since 2006. Hamas had won, but Fatah, with covert encouragement and support from the Bush administration and the Israelis, had tried to push them from power. Hundreds died in factional fighting. The plan failed. Since 2008, Hamas had held on to Gaza and Abbas had ruled the West Bank, though his term as president officially expired in January 2009. The legislature had not convened since 2007. Each faction persecuted and imprisoned the other's loyalists in the territory under its control. There was, in other words, no legitimate government in place. And then there was Israel, whose troops occupied the West Bank, directly governing more than 60 percent of it and imposing their will on the remainder through a variety of less-than-subtle means. Gaza they merely bombed and blockaded.

Where to begin—with the glove or the hand inside it? That was the question facing a small group of young activists—mostly women, mostly the children of the urban professional middle class, English-speaking and technologically astute. They decided to start with the glove, and to do so gently, discreetly, not by criticizing their leaders but by urging them to end the division that for half a decade had cleaved Fatah from Hamas and the West Bank from Gaza. Challenging the PA was impossible, one young activist told me; they would all land in jail. By focusing on the inoffensively patriotic demand for unity, he hoped, activists could open a space for dissent without spooking the leadership. To get the movement going, they called for simultaneous demonstrations in the West Bank and in Gaza on March 15, 2011.

The leadership, though, was wilier than the young activists gave it credit for. Both ruling factions correctly understood the demonstrations as a challenge to their authority. The response in Gaza was direct: Hamas repressed the protest there with beatings and arrests. In Ramallah, the PA was more subtle. The authorities first tried to coopt the event by flooding al-Manara, the traffic circle that functioned as the city's central square, with Fatah supporters and Fatah speakers, broadcasting Fatah songs, shouting Fatah chants. Late in the afternoon, the Fatah crowd abruptly withdrew, leaving perhaps a hundred protesters and an almost equal number of plainclothes policemen and intelligence agents, or *mukhabarat*. The beatings began after dark. Not all at once: one here, another there, as if fights were breaking out spontaneously. Before the end of the night I would see seven activists carried off in ambulances.

I spent much of the evening scanning faces, trying to spot the *mukhabarat*. It was easy, even when they weren't muttering into the collars of their coats. They were the watchful ones, the ones who looked like they didn't want to be there. But there was one small-framed man in a leather jacket whom I couldn't place. He stood apart, a point of stillness in the uproar of the crowd. He looked wary, distant, tense, but without the heaviness and suppressed violence that, no matter how cool they try to look, always characterizes the posture of police.

The man's name was Bassem Tamimi. He was, the friend who introduced us said, a leader in the protest movement in Nabi Saleh, a tiny village about twenty-five minutes northwest of Ramallah. For a little more than a year, the people of Nabi Saleh had been holding a march every Friday after the midday prayer. And every Friday Israeli soldiers beat them back with tear gas, stun grenades, and rubber-coated bullets. In the chaos of the square that evening, Bassem wore a strange, stiff sort of calm, as if his long face and blue eyes were directed at some other world than the tumultuous one surrounding us. Looking back, I can imagine a few reasons that he might have felt out of place, but perhaps it was just exhaustion. He had not been home for days. "I am wanted," he explained, and smiled sadly.

WE MET AGAIN a few days later in a small and smoke-filled coffee shop. Images of the walled old city of Jerusalem coated in snow hung above us, and a photo of a martyr—a young man presumably fallen in the Second Intifada, posing proudly with his Kalashnikov—was displayed on a far wall. Bassem sat erect, puffing at an *arghile*. Twelve days earlier, an hour or two after midnight, the Israeli army had visited Nabi Saleh. They started at the house of Bassem's cousin Naji Tamimi. (All of Nabi Saleh's six-hundred-odd residents belong to the same extended family, and nearly all share the surname Tamimi.) The soldiers woke Naji in his bed, blindfolded and handcuffed him, and took him away. They went to Bassem's house next. His wife, Nariman, came to the door. Bassem wasn't home, she told them. Anticipating trouble, he had slept outside the village. The soldiers came in anyway and spent an hour searching the house, waking his four children and his elderly mother, turning everything upside down. He hadn't been home since.

"I will tell you the whole story," he began. "You can write what you want."

"I was born in 1967," Bassem said, the year that Israel occupied the West Bank, East Jerusalem, Gaza, the Sinai peninsula,* and the Golan Heights. "For me the Israeli was just a soldier at a checkpoint, searching houses, shooting, killing, injuring people, the jailer in the jail, the woman translator in the court."

His sister, he said, died in 1993 when a translator at the Israeli military court in Ramallah pushed her down a flight of stairs. (Translators in the military legal system are uniformed soldiers, as are the judges and prosecutors.) She broke her neck in the fall. She was there to visit her son Mahmoud, who was twelve or thirteen at the time, and had just been arrested. Bassem was in prison too, accused along with three others from Nabi Saleh of murdering an Israeli named Chaim Mizrahi near the settlement of Beit El, just outside Ramallah.† While questioning Bassem, an interrogator from Israel's General Security Service, also known as the Shin Bet or Shabak, shook his head back and forth so hard and for so long that he lost consciousness. "I felt as if my brain was rolling around loose in my head," he told Human Rights Watch investigators at the time. "I thought my head

---

*Israel withdrew from the Sinai in 1982.

†Mizrahi was abducted while on his way to buy eggs from a Palestinian farmer. He was stabbed to death and his car, with his body in it, was burned. He was thirty years old and left behind a pregnant wife. In response to his killing, mobs of thousands of settlers blocked roads around Ramallah and burned as many as fifty Palestinian homes.

was going to explode, it hurt so much." He woke up paralyzed, with sixty-three stitches in his head, his bed surrounded by soldiers. "They gave me a newspaper," he recalled, "a Hebrew newspaper. There was my photo, and my cousin's photo. It said that I was a killer, that we killed a settler." He noticed the newspaper's date. Days had gone by that he could not account for: he had been in a coma and had undergone surgery to relieve pressure on his brain caused by a cerebral hemorrhage. He was released without charge on the day of his sister's funeral. Weeks passed before he regained the full use of his limbs. Bassem pointed to a nickel-size dent on his right temple and parted his short, graying hair to reveal the scars on his skull.* His hands, pale and delicate, seemed to belong to another man.

"During my life, I was arrested ten times," Bassem continued. In most of those arrests, he said, he was not charged or tried, but confined under what is blandly referred to as "administrative detention," a legal leftover from British colonial rule that permits Israeli authorities to jail an individual considered a threat to Israel's security without charge and without presenting evidence to the accused.† Altogether, Bassem had spent three years of his life in Israeli prisons without ever being convicted of a crime. "My wife," he added, "was arrested in 2010 at the second and third demonstrations. My son, thirteen years, was wounded, my wife was wounded by rubber-coated bullets, and my small child, seven years, was wounded with rubber bullets and tear gas."

Nabi Saleh's troubles began in 1976, when Israelis belonging to the messianic nationalist group Gush Emunim ("Bloc of the Faithful") established themselves on the hilltop opposite the village in an old stone fort erected by

---

*In June 1994, eight months after Bassem's arrest, a Human Rights Watch investigation concluded that "the extraction of confession under duress, and the acceptance of such confession into evidence by the military courts form the backbone of Israel's military justice system."

†During the brief period prior to the establishment of the Israeli state when the British Defense Regulations of 1945 were also applied to Jews, one future Israeli high court justice complained, "The laws contradict the most fundamental principles of law, justice and jurisprudence." Dov Yosef, who would twice serve as Israel's minister of justice, called the laws "officially licensed terrorism."

the British as a police station. The settlers, Bassem said, soon began clear-
ing trees and building homes. Residents of Nabi Saleh and the neighboring
village of Deir Nidham took the settlers to court, accusing the settlers of
stealing their land. The court ruled in the villagers' favor—the land immediately around the police station belonged to the state, but the fields around
it were private. The settlers left, but in May 1977, the right-wing Likud
Party won Israel's legislative elections, ending three decades of center-left
rule by the predecessors of today's Labor Party. Menachem Begin replaced
Yitzhak Rabin as prime minister. The settlers returned. The following
year, the state seized nearly 150 acres of the village's land for "military
needs" and gave them to the settlers, whose community would ultimately
become known as Halamish. It now has a population of about 1,200, almost
twice that of Nabi Saleh.

The problem became worse, Bassem said, during the Second Intifada,
the bad, hard years of the early 2000s. The Israeli army declared the land
directly downhill from the settlement a closed military zone. Soldiers, he
said, "attacked anyone they saw on the land." Palestinian farmers could no
longer work their fields. Settlers began to farm them. More land was lost,
and more after that.* Forty percent of the village's land, Bassem said, "is
under the control of the settlers. We can't use it. We can't farm it. They
keep it empty for the settlement to expand."

Just south of the village and down the hill from the settlement, a spring
bubbles from a low, stone cliff. The people of Nabi Saleh called it 'Ein al
Qoos, or the Bow Spring. The farmers who worked the fields beside it
relied on its waters for longer than anyone could remember. In the summer
of 2008, the youth of Halamish dug a hole and poured cement to construct
a pool that would collect the waters of the spring. The settlers seeded the

---

*In March 2007, the Israeli NGO Peace Now reported that 32 percent of the land registered
to West Bank settlements was "effectively stolen" from private Palestinian owners. In
Halamish, the figure—which does not include land judged to be "State Land"—was 33
percent.

pool with fish and built a bench, a swing, more pools, an arbor for shade.*
They gave the spring a Hebrew name—Ma'ayan Meier, or Meier's Spring,
after one of the settlement's founders. When Palestinians came to tend
their crops in the fields beside it, Bassem said, the settlers chased them
off—"hitting them, beating them, threatening them, scaring them." The
army, which had long since established a base in the old British police station, was always a few steps behind them.

One Friday in December 2009, the people of Nabi Saleh marched to
the spring, "to tell the world," Bassem said, "that we have the right to work
our land." A group of armed settlers came down from Halamish. ("They
are always with guns. They don't walk without their guns.") They began
shooting, Bassem said, and throwing stones. Soon the soldiers joined them,
firing tear gas and rubber-coated bullets. Twenty-five people, Bassem said,
were injured. The villagers—men, women, and children—came back the
next Friday, and every Friday after that, joined by increasing numbers of
foreign and Israeli activists and by the press. The soldiers hadn't let them
near the spring since, but taking it back, Bassem insisted, had never been
the goal. The idea was to challenge the entirety of the occupation, the
almost infinitely complex system of control that Israel exercised over Palestinians throughout the West Bank: not just the settlements and the soldiers
in their hilltop bases, but the checkpoints, the travel restrictions, the permits, the walls and fences, the courts and the prisons, the stranglehold on
the economy, the home demolitions, land appropriations, expropriation of
natural resources, the entire vast mechanism of uncertainty, dispossession,
and humiliation that for four decades has sustained Israeli rule by cur-
tailing the possibilities, and frequently the duration, of Palestinian lives.
"The spring is the face of the occupation," Bassem said. "The occupation is
illegal and we have the right to struggle against it."

---

*Years later, the settlers retroactively applied for a building permit, which Israeli courts
refused to issue, ruling that "the applicants did not prove their rights to the relevant land."

The army, in the meantime, had begun to bring the fight inside the village, throwing tear gas grenades into people's homes, returning at night to search houses and make arrests. Bassem rattled off the numbers: in the fourteen months since the protests began, 155 residents of Nabi Saleh had been injured, 40 of them children. A thirteen-year-old boy from a neighboring village had spent three weeks in a coma after being shot in the head with a rubber-coated bullet. Nearly every home in Nabi Saleh had been damaged. Gas grenades had sparked fires in seven houses, igniting curtains, rugs, and furniture. Seventy villagers had been arrested, 29 of them children. The youngest was eleven years old. Another 40 or so foreign and Israeli activists had been arrested as well. Fifteen villagers were still in prison. Six, Bassem included, were in hiding.

I ASKED BASSEM what he thought about the unity demonstration in al-Manara square. "It's good," he said. "Our main enemy is the occupation. When we target the division [between Fatah and Hamas], we take a step to go directly against the occupation." It turned out to be a very short step. The March 15 movement, as it would later be called, didn't survive past March 15. The activists kept meeting and strategizing, but they failed to attract any significant following, and soon went their separate ways. In Palestine, at least, spring would have to wait.

FIVE DAYS AFTER we talked in Ramallah, Bassem risked a visit to his family. His mother was ill and he didn't think it would be hard to slip in and out of the village unnoticed. "I'm not Osama bin Laden," he joked to the cousin with whom he was staying as they got in the car. He had been home for just ten minutes when soldiers arrived at his door.

The following Friday, I visited Nabi Saleh for the first time. I was staying in Tel Aviv, and caught a ride with a group of young Israeli activists.

They were theatrically cautious: my contact instructed me to wait on a street corner in the southern part of the city. Only after I had been standing there for a few minutes did a text message arrive with the address of the real meeting place a few blocks away. Most of the activists were in their early twenties: pale, pierced, straight-edge kids in faded black jeans, black boots, black backpacks. The majority were anarchists, as opposed in principle to militarism and the state as they were to any specific actions of the Israeli army in Nabi Saleh or anywhere else. A few had been participating in protests against the construction of the separation barrier (Israelis call it the "security fence"; Palestinians prefer "Apartheid wall") through West Bank villages since the early 2000s, and were among the founders of a loose confederation of activists called Anarchists Against the Wall. They were an earnest and sometimes dour lot, quick to lecture, slow to laugh. Their commitment, though, was impressive: their politics had made most of them outcasts in Israeli society, some of them in their own families. Nearly all of them had been arrested—some of them dozens of times—and beaten and gassed and shot at, and Friday after Friday, they kept going back. With a few notable exceptions, the anarchists were—and remain—the only Israelis who regularly cross the Green Line into the West Bank to stand in solidarity with Palestinians protesting the occupation. Gathered together, they could all fit in a single city bus. Two buses tops.

Five of us piled into a red Suzuki compact. As we drove east out of the city, an eager fellow with a patchy, reddish beard prepped me on Nabi Saleh. "It's a very strong village," he enthused. "Nothing is more Asterix than this village—you know Asterix, right?" I did. I had grown up on the French comic books about the indefatigable Gauls cheerfully fighting their Roman occupiers. In the books, the Gaulish druid Getafix brewed up a magic potion that made the villagers invincibly strong, capable of pummeling entire legions of Roman soldiers with their bare fists. Nabi Saleh had no druid, and no potion. "It's the most resilient village," my new friend assured me. "It's weak now, but it will never stop. Never."

By the time we got there, a jeep and four soldiers had blocked the main road leading into Nabi Saleh. We parked beside the spring, and climbed a steep and rocky hill. The clouds were low and gray. It was raining a little. The red-roofed homes of Halamish hunched on the hilltop behind us. The demonstration began a few minutes after noon. The idea, as always, was to march from the square at the center of the village to the spring. There were maybe fifty of us. About half were from the village—men and boys and a few women. The rest were solidarity activists—the Israelis I had met in Tel Aviv plus another dozen or so college-age Europeans. We could see the soldiers' jeeps parked at the bottom of the hill when we set out along the road and then down across a sharply sloped field of thistles and wild-flowers. One of the older boys shouted chants into a megaphone. "We are not afraid," he yelled in Arabic, and everyone clapped as they marched and echoed his words back to him. Three donkeys wandered over to check us out, then apparently thought better of it and trotted off.

We were barely halfway down the hill, the spring still a few hundred yards away, when, four minutes after the march began, the first tear gas grenades streaked through the sky above us. The next volleys were lower— one whizzed a foot above my head—and soldiers were advancing up the hill from the right and left. The chants gave way to shouts and soon we were all running, ducking, and scattering as the grenades whistled past and the gas drifted in slow, sour clouds around us. I watched three soldiers at the base of the hill fire grenade after grenade, not lobbing them but aim-ing at the level of our heads and chests, and suddenly there were more soldiers above us, shooting down at us from the center of the village.

I took refuge with about a dozen activists crowded into the front room of a home that I would later know as Mustafa's house. It belonged to a taxi driver named Abd al-Razzaq Tamimi, his wife Ekhlas, their daughter and four sons, the eldest of whom was named Mustafa. When the rain had let up and the soldiers had withdrawn, I went outside again. Word came down that a teenager had been arrested, one of Ekhlas's sons. Ekhlas ran to the center of the village, howling with grief. Two veteran Israeli activists—Jonathan Pollak and Kobi Snitz—were arrested also, as was Bilal Tamimi,* Nabi Saleh's resident videographer, who filmed every protest, documenting almost every interaction the villagers had with the army. That day they blindfolded Bilal and locked him in the back of a jeep parked on the edge of the town square. The Israelis and internationals linked arms and sat down in the jeep's path. The village kids began tearing up cardboard so the activists wouldn't have to sit on the cold, wet asphalt. Soon an Israeli officer in the gray uniform of the Border Police was tugging up the seated protesters' chins and pepper-spraying them in the eyes, and their friends were rushing to help them. Two activists clung to each other on the hood of the jeep as the soldiers drenched them with pepper spray, and they stumbled off spitting and retching with their swollen eyes squeezed shut as the soldiers cleared the square with stun grenades† and more tear gas until finally, as suddenly as it had erupted, the chaos subsided and a strange, lighthearted calm prevailed.

The sun came out. The square was empty but for the soldiers with their body armor and assault rifles and a half dozen little boys running giggling in circles, punting spent grenades like soccer balls. The boys lined up in front of the soldiers, arms around one another's shoulders. They danced, kicking their legs high in the air, hooting with glee. A red-headed kid with Down syndrome blew into a battered trumpet missing both mouthpiece

---

*The consequences for Israelis and Palestinians arrested at West Bank protests differ vastly, even when they are arrested under identical circumstances. Israelis are rarely charged, and when they are, the proceedings occur in civilian courts. Jonathan Pollak had lost count of the number of times he had been arrested. "More than fifty," he once told me. But for all his arrests, he had only been sentenced to prison once, and was released after two months. If they are processed and charged, Palestinians arrested at demonstrations will be tried in military courts and can expect to spend anywhere from a few days to many months in jail.

†Also known as "sound bombs," stun grenades are designed to disperse crowds with loud noises and to otherwise be harmless. If they explode too close to your head, though, they can damage the inner ear. Every rare now and again a metal fragment of the mechanism flies off and causes a more serious injury.

and valves. The sound was almost unbearable. He kept blowing until the other boys snatched the trumpet from his hands and egged him into tossing a rock. It banged against a metal fencepost fifteen feet from the soldiers. Three of them chased him anyway, barreling after him with their rifles, barking threats.

BASSEM WOULD ULTIMATELY be charged with "incitement," "organizing and participating in unauthorized processions," "solicitation to stone throwing," and "disruption of legal proceedings."* The latter charge, for allegedly coaching the village youth on how to behave under interrogation, was not without its ironies: the bulk of the evidence against him was drawn from the testimony of two teenage boys arrested in Nabi Saleh and questioned for hours under duress without the presence of a lawyer or their parents, as is required by Israeli law.

The trial did not begin until June. In the courtroom, which was part of the Ofer military prison complex just outside Ramallah, Bassem was defiant. He read from a prepared statement: "International law guarantees the right of occupied people to resist occupation," he said.† "In practicing my right, I have called for and organized peaceful popular demonstrations . . . in order to defend our land and our people. I do not know if my actions violate your occupation laws. As far as I am concerned, these laws do not apply to me and are devoid of meaning."

---

*Israel's Military Order 101, issued two months after the 1967 occupation of the West Bank began, criminalized any "procession, gathering, or rally . . . held without a permit issued by a military commander," and defined a "procession" or "rally" as "any group of ten or more persons" gathered "for a political purpose or for a matter that could be interpreted as political." "Incitement" is outlawed in the same order and defined as "orally or in any other way attempt[ing] to influence public opinion in the region in a way that is liable to disturb public peace or order."

†The 1977 Geneva Protocol I, Article I, paragraph 4 recognizes the recourse to "armed conflicts in which peoples are fighting against colonial domination and alien occupation against racist regimes" as part of "the exercise of their right of self-determination."

He went on: "The civil nature of our actions is the light that will over-come the darkness of the occupation, bringing a dawn of freedom that will warm cold wrists in chains, sweep despair from the soul, and end decades of oppression. These actions are what will expose the true face of the occupation."

The judge cut him off. The trial was not political, he said, and a court-room was no place for such speeches. It was no place for much of anything: in 2010, the last year for which records were made public, 99.74 percent of Palestinians tried in the military court system were convicted. Bassem would be found guilty of two of the charges and sentenced to thirteen months in prison and an additional seventeen months during which he would be forbidden from all "violations of public order." That, of course, was the point—to violate, challenge, and ultimately upend an order that he was unwilling to accept.

1.

LIFE IS BEAUTIFUL

Nabi Saleh, Ramallah

One does so rejoice in a spring!

—T. E. Lawrence

I met Bassem again, stiff-backed as always, in the same Ramallah coffee shop beneath the same framed photos of Jerusalem rimmed with snow. It was 2012; more than a year had passed. Bassem had been released from prison a few weeks earlier. He caught me up a little as we walked together to the taxi station. He was no longer a hunted man and seemed more at ease than when I had seen him last. But things were not going well. While I was gone and he was locked up, his mother had suffered a stroke that had left her mostly paralyzed. The paralysis was general. "This is the worst time for us," he confided. In Nabi Saleh and outside it, the popular resistance was losing momentum. The land was vanishing beneath their feet, but few Palestinians were choosing to fight back. And the protest movement in Nabi Saleh had suffered its first martyr. On December 9, 2011, Mustafa Tamimi, in whose home I had briefly sought shelter the year before, had been shot in the face with a tear gas canister fired at close range from the back of an Israeli army jeep. He was twenty-eight.

I had come back because I wanted to see some less cartoonish version of the heroic village that had been painted for me one year before—the stalwart, semimagical place that would fight and fight and never, ever despair, no matter the odds and the losses. It was there, that place. It did exist. But there was another village too, one that was at first harder for me to see. I didn't know enough then to understand that a sure conviction that things were worse than bad could coincide with an optimism that was neither fragile nor delusional. In the taxi, Bassem asked me something strange. "What do you believe?" he said. I was taken aback by the question's intimacy. I didn't know how to answer, or what exactly he was asking. Did he want to know if I was a Jew, or if I was religious at all, or where my politics fell? I told him I believed in struggle. I don't remember how much I stuttered on. I might have even said that I believed that God *was* struggle, the tension and conflict at the root of all things that pushes the universe onward, not consciousness or will so much as an infinitely echoing demand. Probably I didn't say that much. Whatever I said, Bassem nodded, and never brought it up again.

The taxi sped through the rocky West Bank hills, terraced with ancient walls of stone in some places and in others ridged by horizontal veins of rock so that it was often hard to tell from a distance where they had been transformed over slow centuries by the hands of men and women and where they had not. It was summer and the hills, green with winter rains the last time I had been there, were dry and brown.

The home that Bassem shared with his wife Nariman, their four children, his mother, and, for a little while, me, was the last house on the northwestern edge of Nabi Saleh, just beneath the crest of the hill that stretched down to the spring. What a joyous wreck their garden was. There were a couple of olive trees, a young pomegranate bearing a few small and still-green fruit, and a mulberry that in the summer bore the sweetest, plumpest berries I could ever hope to eat. Beneath it, the nettles and weeds were littered with plastic bags and plastic bottles, cigarettes butts and stray shreds of paper, the remains of broken lawn chairs, here and there a black rubber fragment of a tear gas grenade, or a circle of char where one had sparked the weeds aflame. On the wall of the house just outside the door, someone had spray-painted a golden *W* and two blue hearts.

Waed, Bassem's oldest boy and the likely author of that *W*, was watching cartoons when we arrived at the house. He was fifteen then but looked much younger. Except for his face, which was somehow both young and old, at once exhausted and perpetually surprised, lips pursed in boredom, eyebrows always raised. I sat beside him on the sofa while Bassem made a phone call. Waed pointed to a neat divot carved out of the flesh of his calf. It was about the size of a half-dollar coin. "From a rubber bullet," he said.

Bassem frowned, and interrupted his call to correct his son: "Rubber-coated *steel* bullet."

Waed poked his finger at the shiny circle of scar.

The moment their father pronounced the words "rubber-coated steel bullet," Bassem's other two boys, Salam and Abu Yazan, scurried into another room and reappeared with a heavy ball of metal coated with a thin layer of black plastic. It was about the size of a marble. They dashed off again and came back with two bronze .22 caliber shells. Salam clutched them in his little fist. He was six then, chubby-faced and cherubic, his hair shorn into a near-perfect bowl cut. Abu Yazan was eight and already a hurricane. His hands and usually his face were always sticky with some new mess, his green eyes at once wounded and infinitely defiant. Almost anytime there was trouble anywhere in the village it wasn't long before an angry voice rang out: "Abu Yazan!" The boys pulled me into another room to show me the bullet hole in the aluminum frame of one of the windows, a matching perforation in the Palestinian flag on the table beside it, and a scar on the stone wall opposite the window.

Nariman, Bassem's wife, emerged from the back of the house with their one daughter, Ahed, a thin, blond slip of a girl with her mother's bright green eyes. Nariman smiled a greeting and sat down to comb the knots from her daughter's hair. Ahed, who was eleven then, winced and tugged against the brush. She was reserved and almost always quiet, but she was not shy exactly. Even at rest something stayed taut in her, like a wire stretched along her spine. Salam and Abu Yazan dragged my bags into the room in which I would be staying and opened the door of a standing closet, the room's only furnishing other than a narrow bed. Together, with great seriousness, they began unpacking my clothes, hanging each item—shirts, jeans, underwear, everything but the socks—on a separate clothes hanger, standing on tiptoes to hang it in the closet until they ran out of hangers and, satisfied that they had done their duty, left me there to rest.

Later that evening, I stood outside with Nariman. After dinner each night when the weather allowed, she sat on the patio and smoked an *arghile.* Sometimes she read in the harsh light cast by the bare bulb above the door. That summer, she was reading Dan Brown in Arabic translation. Sometimes she would just sit and smoke in silence and wander far away until something jarred her back—a thought, or a word from one of the children, or a neighbor, or her husband—and she would meet the moment with an energy and intelligence that could be fierce and with a sharp laughter that bubbled up out of her compact frame like smoke through the *arghile.* That evening Nariman pointed down into the darkness at the bottom of the hill. There were two lights on the guard tower, a concrete pillbox about twenty feet high adjacent to the swinging metal gates the Israeli army had erected to block the road during the Second Intifada. One of the gates had been closed for all the years since, forcing drivers to take the long way around. The other was usually open, but the chain of red brake lights beside it indicated that the soldiers were stopping every car that passed. "It's been like that every night this week," she said.

THE NEXT DAY was a Friday. It was after the morning quiet passed and after the first visitors arrived, two Amnesty International researchers who seemed to already know Bassem well, after Nariman had prepared coffee and breakfast, and just after the midday prayer sounded from the mosque in the middle of town, that Waed emerged from his bedroom wearing shorts and a tank top, a medallion in the shape of Palestine hanging from his neck. He pulled on his socks, tied his shoes, and wrapped a keffiyeh around his head and face. Then he thought better of his outfit and exchanged the tank top for a black Real Madrid jersey bearing Ronaldo's number 7.

I followed the others down the road toward the village square. The windows of most of the houses were covered with crude steel screens to keep projectiles out. More boys with scarves or T-shirts tied over their faces joined us as we walked. Some had slingshots stuffed into the back pockets of their jeans. Beside the square a few dozen people had already gathered in the shade of an old mulberry tree. There were men, women, and children from the village, and a handful of activists from Ramallah, most of them young women, some of their faces familiar from the March 15 protests the year before. Another handful of journalists, most of them Palestinian, mingled with them, as did perhaps a dozen twenty-something European and American activists. These were not mere spectators, or participants like the others. They might come once and never return, but it was their presence, no matter how shallow their understanding or fleeting their concern, that turned these demonstrations into something that stretched beyond this tiny, one-street village. Being shot at can have a profound effect on people. It makes things suddenly concrete, urgent, real. It makes you choose a side, or better put, chooses one for you. The journalists would file their stories and the activists would tweet and write blog posts and fly home to give talks to campus solidarity groups. They would tell people what Bassem said, what Nariman said, how brave the children were. They would organize boycott campaigns and write letters to politicians. Some would return, and stay involved for years. If enough of them came, and kept coming, and kept spreading the word, Nabi Saleh would have worked a form of magic no less potent than a druid's secret potion. That, at least, was the idea.

Jonathan Pollak and a few of the anarchists I had met the year before were there as well. Tall, gruff, invariably wearing all black and a skeptical half smile, Jonathan would be in Nabi Saleh nearly every Friday. So would about half a dozen others. However small their numbers and however politically marginal they were inside Israel, they too fulfilled a vital function. They knew how to navigate the Israeli system and could coordinate publicity and legal help if people were injured or arrested. And they were witnesses. Even if the soldiers scorned them as traitors, the Israeli activists' presence meant that each soldier knew that there were people watching him who might sit next to him one day on the bus or in a café or a park, people whose cousins or siblings might work with or even marry his cousins or siblings. Israel is a small country. So long as the activists were there, the soldiers knew that what the army did in the West Bank might find its way back across the Green Line, to their families, and their homes. Perhaps this sometimes gave them pause.

Finally the midday prayer let out. A few more men ambled over from the mosque and together we headed down the road, the villagers chanting as they clapped, the photographers strapping on their helmets and jogging ahead for better shots. Bassem and Nariman's son Abu Yazan, licking a popsicle, marched at the back of the crowd.

That, by the way, was not his real name. His real name was Mohammad, but there were about three dozen Mohammads in Nabi Saleh, all of them surnamed Tamimi, so for simplicity's sake most went by one nickname or another. Abu Yazan won his odd sobriquet as a toddler, when his waddling gait recalled that of a portly old man from a neighboring village. The moniker stuck.

Just past the gas station, the marchers stopped. A few began rolling heavy stones onto the asphalt to keep the jeeps out of the village, or at least to slow them down. But instead of proceeding along the road as they usually did, the demonstrators cut straight down the hillside. Bashir Tamimi, a thin man of sixty with a heavily lined face, led the procession down the rocky slope, waving a Palestinian flag as he climbed through the boulders and the brambles. Bashir was the owner of the land around the spring. On all sides the earth was littered with spent tear gas canisters and patches of burned brush. At the base of the valley we crossed the road. Strangely, no one stopped us.

Two jeeps were parked in the dirt lot beside the spring. Four soldiers stood around them, clutching their weapons. They looked bewildered. The marchers were also confused, but happily so: how had they made it this far? Usually the shooting began while they were still hundreds of meters from the spring. The soldiers held up their hands to stop them, but the marchers walked past them up the path to the spring, where they surprised another group of soldiers eating their lunch in the shade. Three were still wet from a dip in the pool. One wore only soggy briefs and a rifle slung over his chest.

Abu Yazan and three other boys ran up, panting, their eyes enormous. His sister Ahed raced in behind them. The adults milled about as if at a picnic, chatting in the shade while the children splashed from pool to pool. More soldiers arrived in their body armor and riot helmets, bristling with weapons, antennae, and gear. Waed kicked a soccer ball over the pools with Abu Yazan until another boy spotted a bright orange carp and Abu Yazan and his friends rushed over to try and catch it, squealing with delight, splashing until the water went cloudy and the carp disappeared.

Four young men in dark sunglasses appeared on the ledge above the spring. One carried a rifle, the same kind the soldiers had. They were settlers. They looked unhappy. Below them, the one Israeli officer present—a sturdy, bald man, helmetless—was arguing with Jonathan.

"I let you come," he said. "Now you have to go."

Jonathan disagreed.

The settler with the gun climbed down from the ledge and stood in the shade among the protesters, his eyes hidden behind his glasses.

"This is Palestinian land," shouted one of the women from Ramallah. "No weapons allowed."

"Go to Syria," the settler muttered.*

---

*This was June 2012. Antigovernment protests in Syria had long since given way to civil war. Every day brought some fresh massacre.

Another young woman yelled out a question. "Where are you from?" she asked.

"I was born here," the settler answered.

"I was born here too," she said.

It went on like that for a while until the settler got bored and climbed back up to join his friends.

Behind the last of the pools, the children found a swing. It was the kind you might find in a suburban backyard, a high-backed bench suspended from a metal frame. Eight kids were squeezed in and swinging furiously, singing and laughing, stretching their legs to the sky. Ahed sat in the middle. Abu Yazan stood balanced atop the back of the bench behind her, clutching the chains, a grin splitting his face. A few yards distant, the youngest of the settlers—he was probably in his early twenties—argued with the officer.

"They have another ten minutes," the officer was saying. "What difference does ten minutes make?"

"Every ten seconds makes a difference," the settler said.

But before those ten minutes were up, one hour after they arrived at the spring for the first time in two and a half years of weekly marches, the protesters gathered the children and left as they had come, clapping and chanting. Their voices were lighter than before, their defiance now buoyed by victory. The soldiers were close behind. A Border Police* jeep had joined them, and two armored cars. Ahed, her blond hair in a long braid, had scampered to the front of the procession with her cousin Marah. Several very tall Border Police officers ran ahead, barking orders, shouting at the marchers to get off the road. Ahed walked faster, clutching Marah with one arm as two women, activists who had come that afternoon from Ramallah, jogged alongside, hugging the girls to protect them from the soldiers. Their

---

*Despite its semicivilian character, the Israeli Border Police is a thoroughly militarized force. I will often refer to Border Police officers generically, as Palestinians do, as "soldiers," without distinguishing them from their green-uniformed colleagues in the IDF.

names were Abir Kopty and Mariam Barghouti. Neither of them was
much taller than Ahed and Marah. Soon the soldiers were shoving at them
and at anyone with a camera until everyone, soldiers and marchers and
journalists alike, was sprinting to keep up with the two little blond girls and
their not-much-larger escorts, the soldiers towering above them, grabbing
and shouting as they ran. We were about a hundred feet from the settlement's driveway when one of the Border Police officers tossed a stun grenade at the girls' feet, and then another, and another, and then we were all
jumping and falling over the guardrail and scrambling through the rocks
up the hill, the tear gas grenades streaking through the sky above our heads.

Five jeeps were parked on the road beneath the concrete watchtower at
the base of the village. A white tanker truck idled behind them, a thick
screen of wire mesh welded to its windshield and a sort of cannon mounted
on its roof. About fifteen slender figures had spread out in a long line on
the hill above the road. The guys.* They wore skinny jeans and tank tops
and covered their faces and their short, spiky hair with scarves or masks or
T-shirts. Every few seconds one or another of them would run out from
behind a low stone rise to hurl rocks at the soldiers before dashing back
again. They threw the stones with their arms, with slingshots made from
forked twigs and braided rubber bands, with slings crafted out of shoelaces
threaded through square scraps of cloth. It's not quite right to say they
threw them *at* the soldiers, though that was surely their intention. More in
their general direction. The soldiers stood too far off to hit with a naked
arm or slingshot, and the slings, though their range could be impressive,
were of highly limited accuracy. But the guys kept at it, stone after stone
after stone, and the soldiers answered with rubber-coated bullets and with
tear gas in hard rubber grenades and harder steel canisters, the former
thrown by hand or fired through attachments to their rifles, the latter shot

---

*I use the word as an approximation of the Arabic *shebab*, which literally means "youths" but
is used to refer collectively to young, unmarried men and older, adolescent boys.

singly from handheld launchers or in salvos of seven at a time from the roofs of their jeeps.

Then there was that truck, the white one idling behind the jeeps, a clear liquid dribbling from the cannon on its roof. The skunk truck, it was called. The liquid it so violently emitted was called skunk water. The Arabic term was less polite and more accurately descriptive: shit water. No one knew what chemicals it contained or what effect exposure to it might have.* But everyone knew what it smelled like. It smelled like feet that hadn't seen soap for years. It smelled like dead dog in a Dumpster in August. Mainly, it smelled like shit. And no matter how many times you scrubbed your hair and your clothes, the scent would linger for days, even weeks.

The truck let off the occasional putrid spurt, but the stone throwers stayed out of its range. Every now and again a few soldiers would charge up the hill. The guys would scatter, or the gas would push them back. Within seconds, they would regroup and start again where they had left off. So it went. Abu Yazan panted past me on a supply mission, hauling a bucket filled with stones.

The village videographer, Bilal Tamimi, was filming all of it, or as much of it as he could fit into the camera cradled in his palm. Shots were ringing out and gas grenades landing right and left, but Bilal did not flinch. He might as well have been birdwatching and, notwithstanding the bicycle helmet protecting his head, he looked the part. He wore bottleglass-thick glasses, khaki trousers, a reflective vest over a short-sleeved plaid shirt. He was unshaven and his wiry hair was mainly gray. Bilal was a warm, unflappably good-humored man with something of the air of an absent-minded middle school math teacher—the kind who never remembered to check homework and always dropped the lowest grade. Not counting the first two or three, when he didn't yet have a camera, he had filmed every dem-

---

*One IDF officer told me it was "yeast based." An army spokesman demurred in an e-mail that he was "unable to provide more background about *the skunk system*, as that falls under the category of operational specifications." Italics mine.

onstration in the village but one. Most weeks, he uploaded an edit of his footage to YouTube and posted the link to Facebook. When the soldiers came at night, he dragged himself from bed and jogged over to whatever house they were raiding. "I try to be everywhere the soldiers are," he said, and added, laughing, "They don't want me there. They kick me, they shoot at me." They arrested him a lot too. When I had first come to Nabi Saleh the year before, we hadn't met—he spent most of that Friday locked in a jeep. The last time they arrested him, two months ago, they took him to Ofer, the military prison just outside Ramallah, and held him for four days before releasing him without having charged him with a crime. Bilal told the story with a vague smile, as if it had been funny, and had happened to someone else.

A few yards off, eight soldiers rested in the shade. A rock bounced and hit my ankle. The guys had moved uphill—we were no longer standing behind the soldiers, but between them and the village youth. The soldiers roused themselves and fired a few more rounds of gas. I followed Bilal and took cover behind some trees. Another rock glanced off my hand. The soldiers appeared to be leaving.

"That's the end?" I asked Bilal.

"I don't think so," he answered.

He was right. The guys poured down from their perches on the hillside, raining rocks at the retreating soldiers. They ran after a jeep in the road, pelting it with stones. The sun began to sink, and the dry grass and thistle looked almost soft in its light. The clashes moved to the other side of the village. Shots echoed through the valleys and the gas drifted in loose, dissolving clouds. The younger kids combed the hills, collecting tear gas canisters to sell for the scrap metal. The boys rattled as they ran past, their pockets and shirts stuffed with clanking shells. The demonstration had been going on for more than six hours. It was after seven and still hot. Finally the guys were leaving the hills. They walked by, red-faced, their shirts wet with sweat. One of them smiled. "Enough," he said.

Ten minutes later, shots rang out again.

NABI SALEH'S STRATEGY was not new. Unarmed "popular resistance"— as opposed to the military kind, which has dominated headlines about Palestine since the 1960s—has been a local tradition at least since the years after the First World War and the collapse of the Ottoman Empire, when the colonial powers of France and Great Britain divided the Arab territories of the Levant between them. As the region was then "inhabited by peoples not yet able to stand by themselves under the strenuous conditions of the modern world," the great powers in their benevolence agreed that "the tutelage of such peoples should be entrusted to advanced nations." The quotes are from Article 22 of the Covenant establishing the League of Nations. Then, as now, nations were not for everyone. Some people deserved to govern themselves. Others did not. "In the case of Palestine," wrote the British foreign secretary Lord Arthur Balfour to Prime Minister David Lloyd George in 1919, "we deliberately and rightly decline to accept the principle of self-determination." Until its inhabitants could demonstrate sufficient maturity, the magnanimous British would shoulder responsibility for Palestine's well-being. To complicate matters, Balfour had made a competing commitment while the war was still on to a people who did not, for the most part, currently reside in the region. Balfour had promised that "His Majesty's Government" would "use their best endeavors" to facilitate "the establishment in Palestine of a National Home for the Jewish people."* Thus, out of overweening imperial charity, was a century of conflict born.

By the mid-1930s, British policies favoring the quickly growing and largely urban Jewish population† and the small elite of wealthy Palestinian landowners had decimated the rural economy, displacing thousands and

---

*There were at the time about 60,000 Jews in Palestine, out of a total population of 800,000.
†By 1931, the Jewish population of Palestine had jumped to 174,610. Hitler's rise dramatically increased the flow of emigrants—62,000 arrived in 1935 alone.

flooding the cities with the dispossessed. In April 1936, Palestinians called
a general strike, forming committees in every major town from Nablus
and Tulkarem in the north of what is now the West Bank, to Haifa, Jaffa,
and Gaza on the Mediterranean coast. They declared a boycott of British and Jewish goods and institutions. They held marches and demonstrations, and in May called a tax strike too. Women led protests in Gaza,
Jaffa, Haifa, Jenin, Jerusalem, Hebron, and Beersheba. The British responded to this early outbreak of popular resistance, writes historian Gudrun Krämer, with "house searches without warrants, night raids, preventive
detention, collective punishment, caning and flogging, deportation, the
confiscation or destruction of the homes of actual or presumed rebels, and
in some cases even the torture of suspects and prisoners." Demonstrations
were met with "massive force, . . . causing numerous casualties." In June,
the Royal Air Force destroyed large parts of Jaffa's old city in an aerial
bombardment. The following year, the British established a military court
system. (With the sole exception of caning, all of these tactics had, by the
end of the Second Intifada, become standard practice in Israel's management of the occupied territories.) By the time the boycott was called off that
October, more than one thousand Palestinians had been killed. All open
and nonviolent protest had been effectively crushed. Only the clandestine
and violent sort remained. The Arab Revolt, as it would be referred to in the
history books—to Palestinians, it was the *Thawra*, or revolution—became a
guerrilla war. The men of Nabi Saleh took part. The villagers had only six
rifles, Bassem told me, but they managed to steal a machine gun from the
British. By early 1939, when the insurrection was finally defeated, as many
as five thousand Palestinians had died.

The British soon decided that Palestine was more trouble than it was
worth. During the Arab Revolt, the underground Zionist militia known as
the Irgun had announced itself with an extensive terror campaign against
Palestinian civilians, planting bombs in Arab markets, hurling explosives
at Arab buses and cafés. In 1944, the Irgun began assassinating British
soldiers, police, and colonial officials. In February 1947, Britain, which at

that point had more troops in the tiny region—"petty Palestine," Winston Churchill called it—than in all of the Indian subcontinent, announced that it would entrust its mandate to the care of the United Nations. The war that began the following year, and that arguably has not ended, saw nearly three quarters of a million Palestinians expelled from what became the state of Israel. Israelis would remember it as the War of Independence, Palestinians as the *Nakba*, or catastrophe. The West Bank went to Jordan, the Gaza Strip to Egypt, and the Golan Heights to Syria. The Irgun was integrated into the new Israeli army. Two of its members, Menachem Begin and Yitzhak Shamir, later became prime ministers of Israel.

Nearly four decades would pass before the next major uprising. By then the British Empire had crumbled, Israel had occupied Gaza and the West Bank during six days of fighting in June 1967, and Israeli troops were garrisoned in the old stone forts the British left behind. Resistance continued, but most of it was organized from abroad. The 1967 war had pushed the leadership of the Palestine Liberation Organization into Jordan, from which the *feda'yeen*, as the Palestinian fighters were known, launched guerrilla attacks on Israeli targets until they were forced to flee again—to Beirut this time—after a brutal crackdown by Jordan's King Hussein. A decade later, the Lebanese civil war uprooted them once more, this time to Tunisia. The uprising that broke out on December 8, 1987, when an Israeli tank transporter crashed into a string of cars and killed four Palestinians waiting at the main checkpoint between Israel and Gaza, began as an entirely local affair. The following day, Israeli soldiers opened fire on demonstrators in Gaza's Jabalya refugee camp, killing seventeen-year-old Hatem al-Sisi and wounding two others. The camps exploded, first in Gaza, then in the West Bank. The protests leaped to the villages, cities, and towns. The First Intifada—the Intifada of the Stone, it would be called, after the primary weapon used by the Palestinian side—had begun.

In the beginning, participation was almost universal. Organizing committees sprang up village by village and neighborhood by neighborhood. Women played a leading role. Many of the combatants, if that is the right

word, were children, the "children of the stones" celebrated in Nizar Qabbani's poetry, who brought "rain after centuries of thirst . . . the sun after
centuries of darkness . . . hope after centuries of defeat." After a month of
purely local coordination, an anonymous Unified National Leadership
began issuing communiqués, calling on merchants to close their shops, land-
lords to cease collecting rents, taxi and bus drivers to block the roads, consumers to boycott Israeli goods, employees of Israel's occupation government
to resign from their posts, Palestinians who worked in Israel to stay home,
everyone to stop paying taxes. Only pharmacies, clinics, and hospitals were
to stay open on strike days—someone had to care for the wounded. In the
first year of the Intifada, 390 Palestinians were killed—nearly half of them
children and teens—and not a single Israeli soldier.

The idea was unarmed civil disobedience on a massive scale. The occupation, like any effective system of control, functioned through complicity—
Palestinians worked in Israel, paid taxes to Israel, ate food and wore clothing
imported from Israel, paid court fees, licensing fees, and fees for permits to
the Israeli authorities. The Intifada—literally, *shaking off*—represented a
refusal on the part of Palestinians living under occupation to participate in
their own oppression. It was, for those who lived through it, an experience
of radical solidarity. The foundations had already been laid: Fatah and the
three main left-wing Palestinian political parties* had been quietly building
grassroots networks of youth organizations, trade unions, and women's
committees since the mid-1970s. Once the uprising began, those networks
adapted themselves into a web of autonomous institutions, providing services that the occupation authorities would not. Bassem, who had headed a
Fatah youth group while in high school and formed a youth committee in
Nabi Saleh before the Intifada, became one of the main regional coordina-
tors for the area around Ramallah, moving from village to village and working with local popular committees, often sleeping in the hills to avoid arrest.

---

*The Palestine Communist Party, the Popular Front for the Liberation of Palestine (PFLP),
and the Democratic Front for the Liberation of Palestine (DFLP).

The motivations were strategic as much as they were ideological—if the boycott forbade the purchase of Israeli produce, agricultural committees could make up the difference; when the military closed the schools,* villages and refugee camps were ready with educational committees to teach their own children; if the curfews and closures imposed by the army prevented the sick and injured from reaching the hospital, health committees could provide treatment; if the Israelis arrested all identifiable leaders, the leadership would remain collective, anonymous, and decentralized. The result was revolutionary. For the first two years of the Intifada, Gaza and the West Bank governed themselves on de facto anarchist lines. Power was communal, democratic, diffuse.† Not only Israeli institutions but the traditional power relations of Palestinian society were overturned. The patriarchs of the elite landowning families were no longer relevant.‡ Authority—based on courage, capability, and commitment—could be held by women, the young, the poor, and the unpropertied.

It didn't last. After 1990, power shifted from the grassroots leadership that had arisen within Palestine to the centralized command of the PLO's government in exile in Tunisia. Peace talks began in Madrid. Oslo happened. The PA happened. In retrospect it looks less like peace and nation building than reaction and counterrevolution. The grassroots leaders were shoved aside. A pattern would be established: the people fight, their leaders fold. The revolution, still incomplete, was snatched away. It was not, however, extinguished. The explosion came in late September 2000, when Ariel Sharon entered the compound of the al-Aqsa mosque, Islam's third

---

*In February 1988, Israel shuttered nine hundred schools and six universities. Birzeit University, where Bassem was studying economics, would not be allowed to reopen for four and a half years.
†This may help explain the affinity between Israeli anarchists and the Palestinian popular struggle: most of the current leaders of the popular resistance came of age during the First Intifada.
‡From Qabanni's *Trilogy of the Children of the Stones*: "The most important / thing about them is that they have rebelled against the authority of their fathers, / That they have fled the House of Obedience. . . ."

holiest site, provoking riots in Jerusalem's old city. By the end of the next day, seven Palestinians had been killed by Israeli security forces. The clashes spread to Gaza and to the West Bank. A second intifada had begun. For the first few weeks, it appeared to be following the model of the first one: demonstrations, stone throwing, a general strike. The Israeli response was severe. In the first five days, nearly 50 Palestinians were killed and more than 1,800 wounded. The next month, 121 died, and 123 the month after. In Nabi Saleh, there were clashes almost every day. The Israeli army took over a house inside the village. When trucks came to resupply the soldiers, the guys threw stones to chase them off. Children tossed snakes, scorpions, and what Bassem politely called "waste water" through the windows. After twenty-nine days, the soldiers withdrew, but the roads to the village stayed closed for the remainder of the Intifada. Bassem remembered it once taking twelve hours to bring Waed, then a toddler, to see a doctor in Ramallah, usually a twenty-five-minute drive away.

The first suicide bombing of the Intifada came in December, three months in. Hamas took credit. The next year brought two dozen more. In the beginning it was just the Islamist factions: Hamas and Islamic Jihad, whose members had been killing several dozen Israelis a year between 1994 and 1997 by blowing themselves up on buses and in crowded streets. By 2002, Fatah's Al-Aqsa Martyrs Brigade and the leftist Popular Front for the Liberation of Palestine had also embraced the tactic. More than half of the nearly 700 Israeli civilians killed during the Second Intifada would die in suicide attacks. In one early bombing in August 2001, a woman named Ahlam Tamimi, a twenty-year-old journalism student from Nabi Saleh, escorted a young man named Izz al-Din al-Masri to a crowded Sbarro pizzeria in downtown Jerusalem. Shortly after she left him there, he detonated an explosive, wounding 130 people and killing himself and 15 others. Eight of the dead were children. Ahlam was sentenced to sixteen consecutive life sentences and released in 2011, when Israel traded 1,027 Palestinian prisoners for the Israeli soldier Gilad Shalit, who had been captured by Hamas five years earlier. Ahlam was exiled to Jordan, where she now works as a journalist on a Hamas-run television station. Her relatives in Nabi Saleh still speak of her with great affection.

Israel responded not just with curfews and arrests, but with tanks and F-16s. The major cities of the West Bank were besieged, reoccupied, assaulted from above with fighter planes and helicopter gunships. Sharon, who was soon elected prime minister, told the chiefs of the IDF and the Shin Bet that Palestinians "need to pay the price. . . . They should wake up every morning and discover that they have ten or twelve people killed."* Hundreds of roadblocks and checkpoints went up around the West Bank. A barrier composed of eight-meter-high concrete walls and chain link "smart fences" equipped with cameras and electronic motion sensors began snaking along the Palestinian side of the Green Line—the border established in 1967 between Israel and the West Bank—often dipping miles deep within it, separating Palestinian communities not only from Israelis, but from their own land and from one another.

In 2002, residents of the village of Jayyous, near the northwestern West Bank city of Qalqilya, received notice that three fourths of the village's most fertile land and all of its wells and irrigated fields would be confiscated to make way for the wall. The notices were left pinned to trees, and gave residents one week to appeal. The route of the wall had little to do with security and everything to do with taking land—in this case, to make room for the expansion of the Israeli settlement of Zufin. The barrier, the Israeli scholar Idith Zertal and journalist Akiva Eldar wrote, was "constructed with no reckoning and no logic other than the purpose of enclosing as many settlements as possible on the Western, Israeli side and dividing up and seizing Palestinian land. The point was to implement the Bantustan idea." The people of Jayyous chose to resist. They stood in the way of the bulldozers, refusing to leave their fields and orchards. Soldiers forced them away at gunpoint. They came back again accompanied by sympathetic

---

*If we consider the Second Intifada to have ended with the Sharm al-Sheikh Summit in February 2005, Sharon's forces killed about two people a day.

activists from Israel and abroad. The soldiers chased them off with gunfire and gas. The young men threw rocks. They kept coming back, but in the end, they lost. The wall went up. The strategy, though, caught on.

In the rest of the West Bank, Palestinians were fighting with Kalashnikovs and explosives, but all along the proposed path of the wall, villagers forswore armed violence and returned to the methods of the First Intifada. They marched to their land and refused to leave. When the bulldozers came, they tried to block them. When the fence went up, they tore it down. They invited Israelis and foreigners to join them. The costs were high. In Biddu, just west of Ramallah, five Palestinians were killed, three of them in one day. The wall went up and the protests stopped. In Beit Liqya, soldiers shot and killed two cousins, ages fourteen and fifteen, on a single day. Another fifteen-year-old was killed two months later. The wall went up. They lost in Beit Ijza too. The wall went up. The protests stopped. In Budrus, though, about twenty minutes northwest of Nabi Saleh, the villagers won. After fifty-five demonstrations and many injuries and arrests, the army agreed to move the route of the wall back to the Green Line. The strategy spread to nearby villages—to Bil'in and Ni'lin—and to other villages where the wall was not the issue: in 2006 to al-Ma'sara, near Bethlehem, and in 2009 to Nabi Saleh.

It wasn't that they were opposed to taking up arms, Bassem explained. The popular resistance, he insisted, was "born from the military resistance." But Palestinians had gone down that path and been defeated. The Second Intifada had been catastrophic. Thousands had been killed and nothing gained but the wall and the checkpoint regime, more land lost, more settlements, more prisoners, the complete isolation of Gaza from the West Bank. The leadership had been decimated, the economy wrecked, the people exhausted. "Politically," Bassem said, "we went backward." The solidarity that had characterized the First Intifada was long gone, giving way in late 2006 to open combat between Fatah and Hamas. The scars were still fresh. They weren't even scars; they were open wounds. In terms of international support too, the uprising had been a profound defeat. The First Intifada had changed the world's image of the Palestinian struggle, replacing the hijackers of the *Achille Lauro* with unarmed children standing up to one of the most powerful militaries in the world. Suicide bombings—"the big mistake," Bassem called them—had reversed all that. It didn't help that one year into the Second Intifada, George W. Bush had declared an unending war on something called "terror." Whatever that meant—and its meaning seemed to shift depending on the ethnicity of the perpetrator—suicide bombings seemed to fit the description. "Palestinian," in much of the Western media, became a convenient synonym for "terrorist."

That, Bassem hoped, could be reversed. Taking up arms again would be foolish, he said. "Israel has nuclear weapons. We haven't the smallest power in front of it. But by popular resistance we can push its power aside." When the cameras were on—and only when they were on—even small-scale civil disobedience could turn Israel's greatest strength into a liability. In 2011, Wikileaks released a confidential cable sent one year earlier from the U.S. ambassador in Tel Aviv to the State Department in Washington, in which the ambassador reported on a conversation he'd had with Israeli major general Avi Mizrahi about protests in the West Bank. The general had "visited" two such demonstrations, and seems to have been confused: "he said he did not know what they were about: the villages were not near the barrier and they had no problems with movement or settlers."* He was not apparently curious enough to inquire about the nature of the villagers' grievances: Mizrahi warned the American ambassador that the army would be "more assertive in how it deals with these demonstrations, even demonstrations that appear peaceful." You can almost hear the sigh: "Less violent demonstrations," the ambassador concluded, "are likely to stymie the IDF." He cited a recent confession to U.S. officials by Israeli Defense Ministry policy chief Amos Gilad: "We don't do Gandhi very well."

Of course the British didn't "do Gandhi" very well either. Which was the point. Even on good days, Bassem had no illusions that Nabi Saleh could topple the occupation on its own, but it could provide a model, he

---

*Mizrahi had presumably visited Nabi Saleh and al-Ma'sara, just outside Bethlehem.

hoped, some path forward out of the morass in which the West Bank was sunk. "To be silent is to accept the situation and we don't accept the situation," he said. If the movement there was smart enough and strong enough, other villages might follow its example. Popular resistance would spread and, when the time came, provide a foundation for a broader insurrection, one that might convince the world of the justice of its cause. The revolution to which Bassem had given his youth might finally be won.

That, at least, was the idea. It was not yet clear to me that those two goals—spreading resistance within the West Bank, and spreading the word to the outside world—might not always be compatible, and that their incompatibility might be the movement's downfall. If it had occurred to Bassem, he didn't let on. "If there is a third intifada," he told me one afternoon, "we want to be the ones who started it." He was feeling good that day, and added, "I don't think it's far away."

EXCEPT WHEN THEY were long and furious, the days in Nabi Saleh were uneventful. Most of the men worked in Ramallah, and the village emptied out until the evenings. If you didn't notice the watchtower or the military base just outside the settlement, or the settlement itself, life might have seemed idyllic. Everyone knew everyone, and everyone was related by some link of blood or marriage. Children were free to run in screaming swarms from house to house, knowing that someone would feed them in whichever kitchen they ended up. Often, when the kids weren't around and I asked Nariman where they were—usually it was Abu Yazan who was unaccounted for—she would shrug and reply, "In the village." They might be playing soccer in the pitted field behind the mosque or chasing one another through the olive groves or picking figs or playing video games in someone else's living room. Only if she heard shots was there any reason to worry.

In the evenings, neighbors visited neighbors. It was summer, so they sat outside in white plastic patio chairs, enjoying the cool air, talking and smoking, watching the sky for shooting stars and the valley for the brake lights of cars if the soldiers were stopping cars. Bats swooped and dove in the darkness. Bassem would lay pillows in the doorway and carry his mother out from the back of the house so that she could sit and feel the breeze and see the children and the guests even if her voice was too weak to let her join the conversation. She looked like a frail, brittle child in his arms, her legs hanging uselessly over his elbow. One or another of Bassem's old prison friends—he seemed to know half the men over forty in the West Bank—might drop in to pay respects. Nariman's older brothers—quiet, sad-eyed chain smokers—would come by for a coffee. Little six-year-old Hamoudi, whose father Naji was still in jail, was almost always around. One night Salam touched a piece of paper to the coals of his mother's *arghile* until it lit aflame. He swung the smoking scrap over his head, yelling, "Gas bomb!" No one noticed, so he curled up in Nariman's lap, dozing as she bubbled away. The kids fought often. The same boys and girls who in the daytime stared down Israeli soldiers would at night make one another cry and wail and break into laughter mid-howl and seek solace in their parents' arms. Usually it was Waed tormenting Ahed, or Abu Yazan twisting Salam's arm, or Abu Yazan melting down for one reason or another until Bassem barked, "Enough!"

PEOPLE DID A LOT of speculating. They didn't have much control over anything, so they guessed as best they could and searched for signs. One afternoon Waed predicted there would be a raid that night because some of the boys had been throwing stones at the soldiers, the soldiers had responded with tear gas, and one of them had shot another in the foot with a grenade. Surely there was some logic to the world and the soldiers would raid to seek revenge. (They didn't.) Another evening I sat outside Bassem's house with Mohammad Ataallah Tamimi. He was twenty-two, high-strung, and always sharply dressed. In the first year of the demonstrations, Mohammad had begun posting news to a Facebook page under the name Tamimi Press, which soon morphed into a media team composed of Bilal with his video camera, Helme and Mahmoud* shooting stills; and Mohammad, who maintained the Facebook page (16,779 followers at last count) and each Friday wrote a press release that he e-mailed to five-hundred-odd reporters. Bilal's wife Manal supplemented their efforts with a steady outpouring of tweets. That night Mohammad pointed into the darkness and predicted there would be a raid because the lights on the watchtower were out. The soldiers didn't come that night either, but they raided Bassem's house two nights after I left, and raided the village five days in a row the following week.

FOREIGN VISITORS to Nabi Saleh—and there were many—tended to ask some version of the same questions again and again. They wanted to know, for instance, how the villagers could bear to put their children at risk, and if it wasn't irresponsible to let them take part in the demonstrations. The villagers had a standard answer: Experience had proven that there was no safe place to hide the children, and by participating in the demos, the kids would learn to overcome their fear and to see themselves as something other than passive victims. In private, though, as parents, they were keenly aware of the costs: the nightmares and the bed-wetting, the tantrums and defiance. What child who has learned not to fear gunfire will go to bed when told? The boys especially had a hard time focusing in school. What was the point of studying? They knew what future awaited them. "They are not interested in normal things," Bassem complained. Even on Facebook, they didn't post about pop stars and sports, only clashes, prisoners, the latest martyr. Still, the public answer was an honest one. What choice did they have? Would it be more responsible to send all the children away on Fridays, to teach them to hide, to raise a generation too afraid to stand

---

*Mahmoud was Bassem's nephew, the boy Bassem's sister was visiting in jail on the last day of her life. I knew him as a large man in his thirties with a heavy brow, usually unshaven. He was married, with a family of his own.

up? The day the marchers made it to the spring and the soldiers chased her from the road, Ahed was her usual stoic self. That night, though, she had nightmares—she talked in her sleep until morning, waking again and again in panic and fear. "I don't know what to do," Nariman said, "but raise my children to be strong."

And the visitors asked about stone throwing. Almost always. Especially the Americans.* "Wasn't it violence?" they wanted to know. Didn't it hurt the Palestinian cause? Wouldn't they do better to emulate Gandhi and Dr. King, to march or sit and accept whatever blows were hurled against them?

Bassem had a hard time concealing his frustration. In private, he would scoff and tsk and rant. Why didn't they ask the Israelis about violence? The IDF shed Palestinian blood on an almost daily basis, yet no one asked Netanyahu to clarify his attitude toward violence, or suggested that he renounce it and disarm if he wanted the support of the international community.† And that wasn't even acknowledging the less visible but equally deadly forms of systemic violence—the land theft, the permit system, the military courts, the economic hard squeeze in its multitude of forms—that every Palestinian was born into and endured every day of their lives. And in the face of all this, Bassem exclaimed, they wanted to talk about *stones*, stones thrown at soldiers wearing helmets and body armor, soldiers who routinely fired far more sophisticated and lethal projectiles?‡ Was there no

---

*Americans have always had a hard time with the stones. While visiting Palestine in 1857, Herman Melville wrote in his journals that the region "is one accumulation of stones—Stony mountains & stony plains; stony torrents & stony roads; stony walls & stony fields, stony houses & stony tombs; stony eyes & stony hearts. Before you & behind you are stones. Stones to right & stones to left. You see heaps of stones here & there; and stone walls of immense thickness are thrown together, less for boundaries than to get them out of the way. But in vain; the removal of one stone only serves to reveal there stones still larger, below it."

†On the contrary, the United States has supplied Israel with $3 billion of military aid a year, making Israel the single largest recipient of U.S. military assistance. The tear gas used in Nabi Saleh, I was frequently reminded, is manufactured in Pennsylvania.

‡In the many demonstrations I went to in Nabi Saleh—I lost count, but it was probably around twenty—I only once saw a soldier hit with a stone. The guys cheered. The soldier fell to his knees, paused, and stood up again.

form of Palestinian resistance so innocuous that it would not win condemnation?

In public, Bassem labored to be polite, but he refused to engage with the question of whether stone throwing counted as violence or not. He didn't bother with the term "nonviolent." Nabi Saleh's resistance was *unarmed*. Boys throwing stones were not armed. Soldiers were. That was the distinction that mattered. The larger issue was tactical, not moral. Palestinians had a right to armed resistance, Bassem insisted, like any people under occupation, whether it be the Czechs under the Germans or the Algerians under the French. Nabi Saleh had rejected that path because it hadn't worked, not because it lacked legitimacy. No one hoped to defeat the IDF by force of stones alone. For all the millions of stones Palestinians had hurled at Israeli troops over the years, not one had killed a single soldier.* If they were a weapon, they were a symbolic one. The demonstrations were theater, a ritual performance repeated week after week. "We see our stones as a message," Bassem said. The message they bore was simple: "We do not accept you."

I talked to some of the guys about it. I asked them why they bothered playing such an elaborate and dangerous game, knowing that they couldn't hope to do more than annoy the soldiers. They had no illusions. "I want to help my country and my village," one of the guys said, "and I can't. I can just throw stones."

AFTER DINNER ONE EVENING, Nariman put on a DVD of outtakes from Bilal's footage, a sort-of *Worst of Nabi Saleh* compilation. We watched a night raid at Bilal's house shot early in 2011, when soldiers were entering every house, waking all the male children and photographing them. "They

---

*The IDF spokesperson's office confirmed this to me in an e-mail. There had been severe injuries, the spokesperson wrote, but "we have no record that soldiers have been killed as a result of rock-throwing."

were mapping the village," Bassem explained. On the television, Bilal's son Osama, then fifteen, sat up and rubbed his eyes, perplexed at the sight of four armed and helmeted soldiers at the foot of his bed. We watched another clip shot in the room in which we sat. Nariman had filmed this one just a few months earlier, while Bassem was in prison. Soldiers rifled through the boys' bedroom while Salam and Abu Yazan hid beneath the covers. They took two computers, various books and official documents, Waed's camera, his schoolbooks—not all of them, just geography and Palestinian history— even his old report cards. Nariman yelled while they ransacked the children's rooms: "What manliness this is! What a proud army you're part of!" We watched footage of her and Bilal's wife Manal being arrested during one of the early demonstrations. Soldiers had fired tear gas into Manal's house, Nariman explained. Manal ran in to fetch the children. When she came out, a soldier ordered her back in. She refused, so they arrested her. Nariman tried to intervene. They arrested her too. We watched another clip of crying children being passed one by one from a gas-filled room out a second-story window, down a human ladder to the street. We watched footage of a soldier dragging a nine-year-old boy in the street, of another soldier striking Manal's seventy-year-old mother, of the skunk truck spraying the water tanks on Bilal's roof and on the roof of the house across the street. Finally, Nariman shook her head and turned off the disc player. *Glee* was on, so we watched that instead.

IN RETROSPECT, those were hopeful times, but the fault lines were already evident, even if I couldn't see them yet. The death of Mustafa Tamimi the previous December had been an enormous loss. Nabi Saleh was small. Everyone had known Mustafa and everyone I spoke with appeared to grieve him deeply. He had been part of the demonstrations from the very beginning. Most of the guys had been there when a soldier opened the rear door of the jeep he was riding in and fired a steel tear gas canister directly into Mustafa's face. When I visited his family, his father, Abd al-Razzaq, didn't say much. He was ill and had been for years. He owned a taxi, a yellow minibus that he drove on a fixed route from Ramallah through Nabi Saleh to the neighboring village of Beit Rima and back again. One of Mustafa's brothers was there too. I'm pretty sure it was Odai, only because his twin, Loai, was in prison then. They were nearly impossible to distinguish except that Odai's brow was scarred, and Loai was the shy one, but those subtleties were apparently too much for the IDF. They had come looking for Odai and arrested Loai by mistake. If Odai gave himself up, there was no guarantee that they would release his brother, so Loai was serving out the sentence—nine months—in silence, and Odai knew that when Loai was released, it would almost certainly be his turn soon.

Mainly their mother, Ekhlas, talked. She was about forty-five with an oval face and wide brown eyes. The walls were covered with framed photos of her eldest son: a giant close-up of Mustafa, another shot of Mustafa in profile wearing a red Spider-Man mask as he slung a stone at soldiers outside the frame. Even her mourning contained a sort of hope. Her son's death had confirmed not just the stakes but the validity of the path the village had chosen. The Israelis were willing to kill to stop them. Which meant they were afraid. Ekhlas told me about the day her son died, how twice in the weeks before his death soldiers had come looking for him and twice he had escaped them, and that Friday morning he had woken earlier than usual and asked her to iron a white shirt for him. "He polished his shoes like he was going out," she said, "not to a demonstration." When her phone rang that afternoon and a soldier told her to bring Mustafa's ID to the watchtower, she thought they had arrested him, "like all the other times." By the time she got there, an ambulance had already taken him away. "It's fine, it's a simple injury," she remembered the soldiers telling her. But Mustafa was already dead.

She told me about a dream she'd had. Mustafa was standing on the roof, wearing his red mask. There were soldiers in the distance. She called to him, "Mustafa! Mustafa, come down! Everyone thinks you are dead—it's better that they don't see you."

In the dream he turned to her, she said, and he told her: "No. I'm standing here so that they will see me."

WHILE EKHLAS WAS TALKING, an extremely tall young man took a seat beside me on the couch. His name was Bahaa Tamimi. Mustafa had been his best friend. He had a small and narrow face that, above his long arms, long torso, and longer legs, looked like it had been borrowed from a shorter man's body. I had seen him before in the hills with the guys, his face rarely masked—why bother, when his stature made him so easy to pick out? Usually Bahaa was laughing and it was usually he who led the chants when the marchers left the square. That day he was scrolling through photos on a laptop. Most of them depicted Mustafa in one pose or another. Bahaa kept returning to the same two shots, clicking back and forth between one of his best friend in a crisp white shirt, falling to the ground a few feet behind an IDF jeep, and another, taken moments later, of Mustafa's crushed and bloody face. Bahaa had been behind him as they ran after the jeep, just a few paces behind the photographer who took the photos that he now, as he wept, was clicking so compulsively between, as if he were trying to recreate Mustafa's steps that day, and his own, to see his best friend in his last moment one last time, and then to do it again, and again.

IT WASN'T ALL SADNESS. People laughed a lot. Or perhaps I should say that sadness has many faces, and laughter is one of them, though that's not quite right either. It's just that grief was not something special. There were greater and lesser sorrows, but sorrow was a given. So was the pain of humiliation, the hard pride of refusal, a certain saving rage. They spilled over everything. What mattered was that these emotions were not suffered individually. They were shared, and in that sharing it was possible to laugh.

After the demo one Friday night, I came across Bassem sitting with

Mohammad. They were laughing. "He's saying bad things!" Mohammad said, barely able to get the words out. That afternoon, one of the village's more dignified elders had been detained. I will call him Abu Issa, though that was not his name.* A Border Police officer told him to move. I was there when it happened. Abu Issa answered that he was on his land, in his village, and wasn't going anywhere. The officer took him by the arm and led him off to the tower. The soldiers released him an hour later, but that's not why Mohammad and Bassem were laughing. Bassem caught his breath, wiped his eyes, and explained: He had joked to Mohammad that the soldiers had filled the skunk truck with water but had run out of the chemical that makes it stink, "so they arrested Abu Issa." Mohammad just managed to finish the joke—"and they put *him* in the water!"—before the giggles overtook them again.

BILAL HAD A NIECE named Janna. She was about six years old and had bright green eyes and light brown hair, which she wore parted into two braids long enough to reach the small of her back. She was probably the most beautiful child in Nabi Saleh, which is saying something. Her mother, Nawal, was Bilal's sister, and her father had emigrated to the United States. He lived in West Palm Beach, where he ran a grocery store. Shortly after the demonstrations began, Nawal became concerned for Janna's safety, and flew her to Florida. They stayed long enough for Janna to enroll in school and begin to learn English, but Nawal couldn't stand the isolation of American life, she said, so they returned to Palestine.

Janna had always been easily frightened, Nawal said. She would wake every time the soldiers entered the village and would hide beneath a table.

---

*In the more than three years that I knew Bassem, he asked me to censor only one thing: the identity of Abu Issa, who was his friend, and who, it should be said, was always impeccably groomed, and smelled faintly and sweetly of aftershave.

Once, in the very beginning, the adults had gathered all the children into one second-story room, thinking they would be safe there. Soldiers fired gas grenades into the house. The room filled with tear gas. I had seen the video: this was the day they had to pass the children through the window to the street below. Janna had cried and begged her mother not to throw her out the window.

"She didn't understand," Nawal said. "That was very difficult." It was after that incident that the villagers decided it would be safer to let the children march with the adults.

Two weeks before my arrival in Nabi Saleh, something strange had happened. It was a Friday and the soldiers' jeeps were parked just outside the house. Instead of hiding as she usually did, Janna raced outside. Bilal caught it on video. Nawal showed me the clip. Janna, in a black dress and with a headband printed in the colors of the Palestinian flag tied over her braids, ran up to the soldiers. "Stop," she yelled in English. "Stop! Why did you make Mustafa dead? He's my best friend. I loved him!"

Five soldiers and a Border Police commander turned their backs on the little girl. Janna kept shouting. Photographers gathered. Janna recited a poem: "All your armies, all your fighters, all your tanks and all your soldiers against a boy holding a stone . . . I wonder . . . who is weak and who is strong?"* The soldiers huddled around the hood of their jeep. "Why are you laughing?" Janna yelled. "Why are you laughing, huh? Go into your house. Not in Nabi Saleh. I love Nabi Saleh. Why did you kill Mustafa? He's my best, best friend. Why do you come in the night? I can't sleep in the night. But you are coming and coming and coming."

After that, almost every Friday, Janna joined the demonstrations. Nawal, who had always been too scared, began marching as well.

---

*No one in Nabi Saleh, Janna included, seemed to know the verses' origin. I later learned that it was not a poem but the lyrics to a song called "My Only Wish" by the British-Azerbaijani singer Sami Yusuf.

————

I SPENT A fair amount of time with the children in the village. Generally, I like kids better than adults. Not because they're cute, but because they're honest. One night, for instance, Salam stomped about in front of the house, pumping his fists and raising his knees almost to his ribs. "I am Salam," he shouted, "and life is beautiful!" This declaration had no place in the usual narratives of sacrifice and suffering, but it was honest, and it was true. Not that I felt that anyone was deceiving me. I spent enough time in Nabi Saleh to be able to confirm the truth of most of the stories I was told—those, at least, that could be confirmed. That I know of, no one lied to me about anything of consequence. (I am not counting lies of politeness: "This is your home," or "I will be there in fifteen minutes.") As they always are, details were omitted. Sometimes people exaggerated, or repeated rumors that turned out to be false—I once spent most of a day driving and walking around the periphery of Halamish, searching for signs of new construction. Ma'an, the official Palestinian news agency, had reported that bulldozers had begun digging and soldiers and settlers had trucked in fifty new mobile homes. Everyone I asked in the village agreed that the story was true. They hadn't seen the caravans themselves, but they were sure they were there, right over there on the other side of those trees. I looked everywhere. They weren't there. There were no tracks indicating that bulldozers had been there. The people I asked weren't lying. Everything they had witnessed testified to one enormous truth: it is in the nature of settlements to expand. How else had so much of Palestine been lost? But whether there were fifty caravans or five, whether they were there already or would arrive within the year: these were minor details.

Similarly, certain stories were told again and again, polished through repeated telling and handed to visitors like shiny coins to carry home. The stories weren't false—many had been documented on video, others could be verified by multiple witnesses—but their use nonetheless felt propagandistic. "The media is the most important thing in the popular resistance,"

Bilal had told me the first time we spoke. I know because I wrote it down so that I could quote him later. The people of Nabi Saleh were crafting a narrative of their own struggle, their own courage, their sacrifice, steadfastness, heroism. It wasn't false, no more so than any other narrative. Which is to say it wasn't complete. I don't mean because they didn't include perspectives other than their own, or because they didn't take into account the emotions of their enemies. I mean because they left things out. Simple things, big and small. Everyone does. They had to. Who can notice everything, much less remember it all? "Memory," wrote the Lebanese novelist Elias Khoury, "is a process of organizing what to forget." We settle on stories like paths worn through tall grass. They take us where we need to go. Or where we think we need to. And the people of Nabi Saleh, like any people, needed to be seen a certain way, and to see themselves a certain way, and they told the stories that would allow for that specific sort of seeing. I had different needs. I asked a lot of questions, and noticed different things, so this story, these stories, will take us down a different path.

INTERLUDE

OCCUPATION CABINET
OF CURIOSITIES

Mas'ha

T he wall was concrete and eight meters high. It was May and hazy, the
sky a whitish blue. Just before the cement of the wall gave way to a
chain link fence studded with motion sensors and topped with nine
strands of barbed wire, someone had painted a Palestinian flag on the concrete and the words, in Arabic, "WELCOME TO THE NATION OF HANI
AMER." A padlock locked the high and rusted metal gate connecting the
fence and the wall. I stood waiting outside it with Irene Nasser, a journalist
and producer who seemed to know people everywhere. She had been here
once before and laughed as I stood marveling at the wall and the yellow-
painted gate, trying to make sense of it. Then she made a phone call, and
after a minute a little boy ran out from Hani Mohammad Abdullah Amer's
house. He struggled on tiptoes to reach the lock and, managing at last to
turn the key, removed the lock and let us in.

Amer sat waiting on a long metal swing beneath a pomegranate tree
outside his home, perhaps forty feet from the wall. The pomegranates
were just beginning to redden. The skin around Amer's eyes was wrinkled

deeply but his mustache and eyebrows were still bushy and black, his hair cut short and hidden beneath a white, woven cap. He was fifty-seven, he said, "maybe a little more, maybe a little less." The boy crawled up on the swing beside him.

"I'm tired of telling this story," Amer told Irene. I asked him to tell it anyway, because I couldn't understand what I was seeing. There was the wall and the gate beside it, and, on the other side of Amer's home, perhaps twelve feet from its rear windows, another fence, a line of coiled razor wire behind it, and just beyond that, the red-roofed houses of a settlement. It was as if the earth had been folded, the folds marked with concrete and barbed wire, and Amer trapped between them, in the crease.

Grudgingly, Amer began at the beginning. His father was born in the village of Kafr Qassem, just to the north and west in what is now Israel. In 1948, Amer said, soldiers killed his grandfather and pushed his family from their home. His dating was likely more symbolic than precise: the *Nakba* began in 1948, but the infamous massacre of Kafr Qassem, in which forty-nine Palestinians were killed by Israeli Border Police, did not occur until 1956. Yshishkar Shadmi, the officer who ordered the massacre, was famously punished by the Israeli courts with a fine of one piaster. The survivors fled here, to Mas'ha, six or seven kilometers east of the Green Line, leaving their land and property behind. In 1977, the settlers arrived: Gush Emunim, the same group of religious nationalists who built Halamish. Among them was a young officer named Shaul Mofaz who would later become the IDF's chief of staff, and after that the minister of defense. He was the security liaison for the settlement, which would be called Elkana. The settlers, Amer said, caused endless trouble. "They've shot at us, thrown stones, come into our homes." One of his sons was hit with a rock just above his eye. "They broke all the windows on the other side of the house," Amer said, tying his grandson's shoelace on his knee. His own shoes were caked red with dirt. "The last problem that we have," he said, "is the wall, which you see."

They came, he said, sometime between 2000 and 2002—he didn't remember exactly. The police came, and the army, and the Civil Administration, the Israeli military bureaucracy charged with governing much of the West Bank. "They said, 'We're going to build a wall and your house is on the route of the wall.' They said, 'You have two choices, either we can demolish your house and you can live on the other side, or you can stay in your house and we will build the wall around you'" Mas'ha is several kilometers from the Green Line, but the wall here dives far from Israel's internationally recognized boundaries, carving out a finger that juts deep inside the West Bank to enclose the settlement city of Ariel, the settlement industrial zones and smaller settlements to its west, and all the Palestinian land that falls in between.

Two more little boys joined Amer on the swing. They were his grandchildren. "I don't like adults," Amer said. "I like kids." He told the Israelis that there was a third option: they could build their wall in the space between his house and the settlement so that he would not be caged in and cut off from the rest of the village. They said they would think about it. A few days later they came back. An electric line would have to be moved, but they had talked to the engineer and it wouldn't be a problem. "We can move the pole and build the wall between you and the settlement," they said. "Congratulations." But when they returned a month or so later, the deal was off. "The bulldozers came and they bulldozed everything around the house, the greenhouses, the garden, everything." Amer lost two thirds of the land around his house, plus another twenty dunams (about five acres) on the other side of the wall, which he could no longer reach.

Amer's home was soon surrounded: the wall on one side, the fence on the other. They built a gate and told him to choose a time and they would come and open it for fifteen minutes every twenty-four hours. He demanded a gate of his own with a key of his own, so that he could let himself in and out when he wished, so that his home would not become for him a prison. They refused. He told them he would destroy their wall. They said they'd shoot him. "I said, 'So shoot me. If you're going to sentence me to death, do it quickly.'" He brought in activists, human rights groups, the United Nations, the press. Soldiers raided the house at night and several times arrested Amer. In the end they relented. They gave him his own gate, his own lock, his own key.

At first the soldiers told him that only his immediate family could pass through the gate. Amer ignored them and invited whomever he wished. They locked the gate to punish him. The longest confinement lasted two weeks, Amer said. "Eventually we learned to be in touch with the Red Cross and the Red Crescent and they wouldn't close it for so long, just a day. But if they locked us up for six months, we would be fine." The shelves in his kitchen were lined with jars of pickled vegetables. "We have every-thing," Amer said. "The basics: oil, *za'atar*, preserved tomatoes, flour, bul-gur, beans." Again the army relented. Anyone could come, they said, just no press, no cameras. Amer smiled and nodded at me, the proof of his defiance.

Eventually, he said, "We started creating a life here." He began fixing up the house, building a garden with raised beds just beside it. "There are different types of victories," he said. "There are military victories, where people destroy and conquer, but there is also the sweeter victory, where people try to create death and you create life out of that." We walked through the garden. He listed the trees he had planted: olive, fig, pome-granate, clementine, lemon, apple, peach, almond, cherry, mulberry, apri-cot, carob, grapefruit, plum. Most were still too young to bear fruit. He named the vegetables he had planted between them, pausing as he walked to tear off a dead leaf or uproot a weed, to sit and pull his youngest grand-son onto his knee. There were tomatoes. There was corn, peppers, onions, cucumbers, okra, herbs, watermelon, and squash.

Just across from Amer's door, someone had painted an enormous bird on the concrete canvas of the wall. It wasn't a dove. Its tail was long, its wings spread, its plumage fiery and wild. I asked Amer what he thought each morning when he woke up, left his house, and saw the wall. He chuckled. Maybe the wall looked like something to people who hadn't suffered everything that he had, he said, but to him the wall was nothing. That's what he said at least. "Instead of seeing the wall," he said, "I try to see the garden."

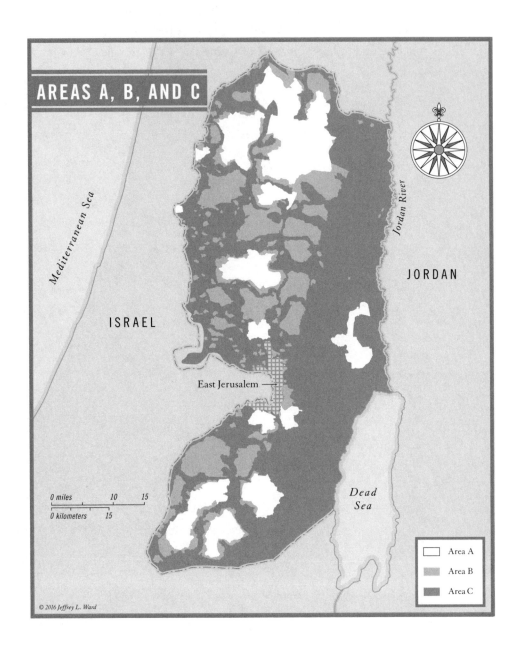

AREAS A, B, AND C

Mediterranean Sea

ISRAEL

East Jerusalem

Jordan River

JORDAN

Dead
Sea

0 miles   10   15
0 kilometers   15

Area A
Area B
Area C

© 2016 Jeffrey L. Ward

2.

THE PEACE OF THE BRAVE

Nabi Saleh, Ramallah

Here you may witness the blessings of the revolution caught in
a single tear.

—Mariano Azuela

t was Friday and Bassem and Nariman's daughter Ahed and her cousin
Marah were right out front again, undeterred by their previous week's
adventure. Little Janna, wearing a black "I ♥ Palestine" T-shirt, marched
beside them. They went straight down the road past Bassem's house and
over the hill behind it toward the spring. Eight soldiers stood at the base of
the slope, the riot shields on their helmets gleaming. More jeeps arrived,
and more soldiers. The marchers spread across the hillside, slowly picking
their way down through the rocks. A voice called up to them in Hebrew,
amplified through a megaphone: "This demonstration is not allowed. This
is a closed military zone." And then, thirteen minutes after the protest left
the square, before a single stone had been thrown, the soldiers began firing
gas grenades, at least a dozen in less than a minute. We raced, gasping,
back up the hill. The guys in their masks and keffiyehs appeared above us,
swinging their slings in the air. Gas grenades tore through the sky, the blasts
echoing across the valley.

Later, the guys barricaded the road with boulders, an overturned Dumpster, burning tires. Children gathered dry brush to feed the flames. About
twenty of us marched on past the barricades. Someone yelled, "Skunk!" A

white truck sped around the bend, a jet of fluid arcing ahead of it. Everyone ran. Behind me a blast of skunk water hit Nariman and one of the activists from Ramallah, a woman I will call Shireen. It knocked them both off their feet and Shireen off the road entirely. I ran through a cloud of tear gas and jumped over the burning tires, glancing behind me long enough to see Nariman, standing drenched and defiant, waving a Palestinian flag, letting the cannon soak her. When I could open my eyes again she was still there, waving the flag at the truck's grated window, doing a strange little dance, skipping and dodging to avoid its blasts. The truck was reversing. Nariman was chasing it away. Then three soldiers jumped onto the road from the hillside, and she finally fled.

About ten minutes later, I ran into Bassem at the cash register of the gas station convenience store. He was paying for a bottle of Head & Shoulders. I saw him again back at the house after an hour or so. A dozen activists had gathered in the living room. Nariman, her face flushed with scrubbing, was in the kitchen, making tea.

I don't know if it was that day or the next that Waed composed a song. He sang it for us all outside the house one night. For a little while, half the kids in the village were singing it. The rhythm gets lost in translation, but it began like a blues number: "I was walking down the road."

Then it took a turn: "They sprayed Shireen and my mom with shit."

Nariman grinned. Bassem too. Waed kept singing: "She went home and my father said/ Oh my, oh my, what am I going to do with this woman?"

Laughter. Finally, the refrain: "My mom smells like shit, my mom smells like shit. . . ."

Everyone had heard it before, but they laughed anyway. Nariman especially.

NARIMAN WAS BORN in Saudi Arabia and grew up there and in Jordan. The wars of 1948 and 1967 had sent hundreds of thousands of Palestinians scrambling to refugee camps in Jordan, Lebanon, and Syria, to the Fatah bases on the eastern banks of the Jordan River, to search out work in the oil-rich Gulf. King Hussein's massacres in 1970 and 1971 and Israel's invasion of Lebanon in 1982 pushed them farther afield, to Yemen, Tunisia, wherever they could find refuge. Oslo allowed some to return. Most Palestinians are exiles, refugees, immigrants. For most of Bassem's youth, his father lived in Brazil. Bilal spent his childhood in Amman. Bassem's cousin Naji's brother was killed by Israeli airstrikes in Lebanon. Manal's father died there too. Nariman's father, born in Nabi Saleh, didn't live long enough to see Palestine again. She arrived in 1994 without him. She married Bassem. She was seventeen at the time. Bassem had been released from prison nine months earlier, having emerged from a coma and emergency brain surgery. Nariman gave birth to Waed two years later, Ahed four years after that. The Second Intifada started. Less than two months after Abu Yazan's birth, Bassem was arrested again.

With a pair of small metal tongs, Nariman placed a fresh coal on the *arghile* and sighed. Dogs were barking somewhere in the dark. When the demonstrations began in the village, Nariman said, she was grateful for the release. "It was the first time I could express myself. The anger that I felt for so many years—I could share it." She was arrested twice in the early months of the protest movement. The first time was at the second demo. The soldiers kicked and beat her, she said. "There was no media, no witnesses." They let her go after six hours. The second arrest was worse. More than two years later, she could tell the story moment by moment, hour by hour. I had seen the arrest on video. The soldiers took her, Manal, and one other woman. "They beat us in the jeep," Nariman said, and again at the IDF base beside the Halamish settlement. From there, they took her to the police station in the settlement shopping center in Sha'ar Binyamin, about twenty minutes away. They beat her there too, she said. From Binyamin they took the women to the IDF base at Beit El, outside Ramallah, and in the morning, shackled in the back of a jeep, to a prison inside Israel. But the women's section was full, so they drove on to another prison. "They put us in a sort of cage full of Israeli criminals. All of them were men. We were separated by bars, but they were shouting at us." There was no room there either, so the soldiers carted them to another prison, this one in HaSharon. Two full days had passed. They were cold, had barely eaten and hadn't slept at all, but, Nariman said, her main source of suffering was Manal's sweater. Manal had been so badly tear gassed that "every time they beat her, the gas came out of her sweater."

Ahed came outside and sat beside her mother. She lay her head in her arms, listening. A full moon rose behind the house.

Manal and the other woman, Nariman said, kept weeping over how much they missed their children. "I thought if everybody kept crying we would die. I tried to think of beautiful things so I wouldn't think of my children too. I started dancing and singing to make them forget for a while, so we could laugh."

They released Manal first. Abu Yazan fell from the branches of the tree he was climbing when he saw Manal return to the village without his mother. That night, the guards took Nariman from her cell. They put her in a jeep. She couldn't see where they were taking her. After a while they stopped, unshackled her, and left her on the side of the road. She had no money, no credit on her cell. She found some men speaking Arabic, borrowed a phone to call Bassem, and eventually found her way home.

The experience had clearly traumatized Nariman, but it also encouraged her. "They beat me and they arrested me—that meant they wanted to silence me, which meant that what I was doing was important."

She was sentenced to a month's house arrest. After that, some of the men in the village wanted to forbid women from taking part in the demonstrations because, Nariman said, "no one would be able to take care of the children." It didn't work out that way. She stayed home until her sentence was over and then returned to the demonstrations. She took first aid classes so that she could help treat injured protesters. She forced herself to become more comfortable talking to the press. When Bassem and his cousin Naji were arrested, she, Manal, and Naji's wife Boshra stepped into the roles the men had left vacant. "All the relationships that Bassem had with foreigners and with Palestinians," she said, "we kept those up and built on them." She was no longer just cooking and making coffee for the activists and journalists who visited Nabi Saleh. She was the one they called, the one they interviewed.

Nariman grinned. Prison's sole virtue, she said, was the water pressure. "You could take a good shower."

The Oslo Accords had given Israel full control of the West Bank's water supply.* Nabi Saleh, like most Palestinian villages connected to the Israeli water grid, got a few hours of running water a week, long enough to fill, or partially fill, the black plastic storage tanks that sit on the roofs of the houses. By the end of each week in Nabi Saleh, turning the tap produced barely a trickle. The dishes sat unwashed, the toilets went unflushed. Showers were out of the question.†

When he was little, Nariman told me, Abu Yazan once asked her what the sea was. Before the Second Intifada, the Mediterranean was less than an hour's drive away, but now, with the checkpoints, it might as well have been on another planet. Nariman decided to walk him to the spring so that she could explain, she said, that "the spring is like the sea, but the sea is much bigger." The soldiers wouldn't let them pass, so she settled on filling the sink with water. "It's like this," she planned to tell him, "only bigger." She turned the tap. Nothing came out.

"This," she said, laughing, "is the problem."

---

*Palestinians were allotted just 20 percent of the water pulled from the Mountain Aquifer, most of which lies within the West Bank. During the talks leading up to the agreement, Palestinian negotiator Ahmed Qurei made a habit of gently mocking his Israeli counterpart, Noah Kinarti, by asking permission each time he took a sip of water. "Just a few drops," Kinarti reportedly replied.

†In areas connected to the water grid, the average water consumption for West Bank Palestinians is about 73 liters per capita/per day (l/c/d), significantly below the 100 l/c/d recommended by the World Health Organization to meet basic sanitary needs. Some West Bank settlements use nearly ten times as much as their Palestinian neighbors.

THE DAY I ARRIVED in Nabi Saleh, Bassem had hinted that all was not well. It's easy to get things started, he had said, and hard to keep them going. In the very beginning, almost the entire village had participated in the demonstrations, but by the time I arrived the people of Nabi Saleh had split into two factions. They had names even: the Resistance and the Opposition. Bassem's, Bilal's, Naji's, Bashir's, and a few other families made up the Resistance. By choice or by attrition, everyone else fell into the Opposition. I interviewed some of them. There was no obvious ideological or factional difference between the two sides. Everyone in the village was with Fatah. Everyone opposed the occupation. The people who no longer took part in the protests resented the leadership and dominance of those who still did. They complained of a lack of transparency and democracy. Certain leaders of the Resistance, one member of the Opposition told me, wanted "to be movie stars." He didn't name names, but it was clear he was talking about Bassem, and that his annoyance was compounded by the presence of the journalist in front of him.

The division widened as the months passed. No one feuded openly, but certain families no longer visited other families. People who had once been close no longer were. In a village the size of Nabi Saleh, this was no small thing, but at the time I found it easy to dismiss the schism as an occupation-induced calcification of the usual resentments of small-town life. What family does not have its factions? This was the narrative that Bassem favored too. People were exhausted by their losses and afraid of losing more, so they withdrew from the protests and fell back on personal grievances. "You can't tell your children that you are scared," he said with a shrug, so you found someone else to blame. For a while, that explanation made sense to me.

ONE EVENING, Bassem and Nariman arrived at the house after spending the day in Ramallah. They seemed depressed. Bassem sat in front of the TV, fidgeting with his cell phone. Nariman disappeared into the bedroom. The news was on. The Muslim Brotherhood candidate, Mohammad Morsi, had won the Egyptian presidential election and had been sworn in the day before. Bassem, who had little love for Islamist politics, wasn't pleased, but it was a more local development that had ruined his mood. A few days earlier word had spread that Shaul Mofaz had been invited to Ramallah to meet with PA president Mahmoud Abbas in the *muqata'a*, the presidential compound. This was the same Mofaz who as a young IDF officer was the security liaison for the Elkana settlement. He was now a prominent Knesset member and the head of Israel's Kadima Party. In March 2002, forces under his command had laid siege to nearly all the major cities in the West Bank. Israeli tanks rolled into the center of Ramallah. They destroyed all but one building in the *muqata'a*. Yasser Arafat would effectively remain a prisoner in what remained of his headquarters until just before his death in 2004. Now Abbas, his less-than-beloved successor, was inviting Arafat's jailer in for a chat.* A small group of young activists, some of them veterans of the March 15 group, marched from al-Manara toward the *muqata'a*, a distance of less than half a mile. They didn't make it. PA police and *mukhabarat* attacked them a few blocks from the square. The next day, a slightly larger group marched. Again they were beaten, this time more severely. "Oh, the shame of it!" the protesters had chanted. Several were hospitalized. Everyone I spoke with was disgusted. Such assaults had not yet become routine. That evening, I asked Bassem what the infighting would mean for the popular resistance.

He didn't look up. "It will kill it," he said.

Oslo: those two syllables fell off people's tongues like a curse. Not the many-headed monster of the occupation, but a plague that Palestinians

---

*Later that year, Mofaz was forced to hurriedly abandon a fund-raising tour of England when he learned that British authorities were investigating him for war crimes. No charges were ultimately pressed.

themselves had willed into the world. In September 1993, after months of secret negotiations by their aides in Paris and in the Norwegian capital, Yasser Arafat and Yitzhak Rabin clasped hands on the White House lawn. Peace was upon us, or something like it. Arafat had agreed to give up armed resistance and formally recognize the state of Israel. Rabin, in exchange, recognized the PLO as "the representative of the Palestinian people," i.e., not quite a state. Not really a state at all. But that would come, perhaps. One day it might. Bill Clinton, standing behind the two leaders, smiled with somber satisfaction. "A peace of the brave is within our reach," he said.

But where were the brave? Where are they now? Not at the White House. Not in the Knesset. Not in the *muqata'a*. The deal was meant to be temporary, an interim arrangement leading up to Permanent Status Negotiations, which were to conclude within five years and would resolve all the stickiest issues: borders, natural resources, the status of Jerusalem, the fate of the settlements, of Palestinian refugees, of political prisoners. That didn't happen. More than twenty years later it still hasn't happened, but more agreements did: the Paris Protocol, signed in 1994; what is known as Oslo II, signed in the Sinai resort town of Taba in 1995; and a supplementary agreement on the city of Hebron signed in 1997. Those agreements, and two smaller ones, would collectively be known as the Oslo Accords or, metonymically, just "Oslo." Together, they would compound what Edward Said already recognized in late 1993 as "the truly astonishing proportions of the Palestinian capitulation."

If the First Intifada was the revolution Palestinians had been waiting for since 1967, if not 1948, Oslo was the Thermidor. It created the Palestinian Authority as a temporary body charged with governing its people— most of them at least—until a final agreement could be reached. From the beginning, that authority was highly limited. Oslo carved the West Bank into three distinct geographic zones: Area A, where the PA was in charge of both security and governance, and which, in its earliest incarnation, comprised only 3 percent of the West Bank, on which about 20 percent of the Palestinian population resided; Area B, where the IDF and the PA would share responsibility for security and the PA would otherwise govern, and which included 24 percent of land on which 70 percent of the population lived; and Area C, which covered nearly 70 percent of the West Bank, and where the Israeli military would be the sole potentate over the remaining 10 percent of the Palestinian populace.* The idea was to give Israel control over as much of the land as possible and at the same time, in the words of scholar Adam Hanieh, "to transfer frontline responsibility for Israeli security to a Palestinian face, in this case the PA, while all strategic levers remained in Israeli hands." In Area C, nothing could happen without Israeli approval. A well could not be dug, a pipe laid, a road paved, a home or an outhouse built without a permit issued by the Civil Administration, Israel's governing body in the West Bank, which despite its name is a subunit of the Ministry of Defense and forms part of the IDF General Staff. Such permits are almost never granted, and structures built without them are subject to demolition by Israeli troops. Between 2000 and 2012, less than 6 percent of all requests submitted by Palestinians for building permits in Area C were approved by the Israeli Civil Administration. From 2006 to 2013, the IDF demolished more than 1,600 unpermitted structures in Area C, displacing nearly 3,000 Palestinians. The military has subtler weapons at its disposal than firearms and tanks.

"The fact is," Said wrote, "that Israel has conceded nothing." After Oslo, Israel still controlled almost all of the land, access to the vast reservoirs of water beneath it, the airspace above it, the borders that defined it. Arafat won no real sovereignty, only the responsibility for administering to his own population's needs. The PA would, in other words, assume the obligations international law assigns to occupying powers: providing for the safety,

---

*The boundaries have since shifted. Some parts of Area C were transferred to Areas A and B under the terms of the Wye River and Sharm al-Sheikh negotiations in 1998 and 1999. Area A now includes nearly 18 percent of the West Bank's land, while Area C includes 61 percent of the land and approximately 12 percent of the Palestinian population.

health and hygiene, education, and religious freedom of the occupied. Israel was, to use Israeli political scientist Neve Gordon's phrase, "outsourcing the occupation," subcontracting out the unpleasant—and expensive—duties of the occupier. Outsourcing, Gordon writes, "should be considered a technique employed by power to conceal its own mechanisms. It is not motivated by power's decision to retreat, but, on the contrary, by its unwavering effort to endure and remain in control." For Israel, Oslo represented neither compromise nor sacrifice, just a change of clothes.

Arafat would be allowed to return to Palestine, but he effectively gave up nearly all of the West Bank in exchange for a phantom state, the trappings of sovereignty without the thing itself. The Palestinians in his charge—those living in Areas A and B—would be confined to what scholars of the occupation variously refer to as enclaves, Bantustans, or cantons: shrinking atolls of self-rule, or something almost like it, in a rising sea of settlements. "It's like when you give a dog a bone," Manal once told me. "This is the bone they gave us. They want us to be busy with the bone until they're finished with what they're doing."

The losses were not merely geographic. The Paris Protocol allowed Israel to retain almost complete control over the Palestinian economy. Israel reserved for itself the right to collect customs duties on goods destined for Palestinian markets and to deliver those funds to the PA each month. The newly created PA would depend on Israeli goodwill for about two thirds of its revenues, which Israel could, and did, withhold in order to enforce its will politically. All currency controls were also left to Israel, as was the power to determine what the PA was permitted to import (mainly Israeli goods) and what it was allowed to export (not very much), turning the West Bank into a captive market for its own products. Much of the international aid that poured into PA coffers—and there was a lot of it: one third of the PA's budget was supplied by foreign donors—thus flowed smoothly back across the Green Line into Israeli bank accounts.

At the same time, seeking to protect itself from future iterations of the strikes and boycotts of the First Intifada, Israel had been reducing its reliance on Palestinian labor, importing foreign workers from eastern Europe and from south and southeast Asia. Before the Intifada began, more than a third—and possibly as much as half—of the Palestinian workforce in Gaza and the West Bank was employed inside of Israel or in the settlements. By 1996, that figure had dropped below 15 percent. Palestinian unemployment had skyrocketed. Some 150,000 Palestinians found jobs in the security forces and the fledgling bureaucracy of the PA. Public sector salaries became one of the few forms of welfare the PA could offer in the artificial economy of the post-Oslo years. But there too, Israel kept the PA on a short leash. If it held back customs receipts for long enough, the Authority would be unable to pay its workers and would lose the most material form of legitimacy it had to offer: paychecks.

The economic transformations—and perverse dependencies—didn't end there. Another large slice of the Palestinian population found work in the estimated 2,100 NGOs that sprang up in the years after Oslo. Nearly all of those organizations survived on funding from international donors, mainly North American and European. (On the bookshelf of a Nablus community center, I once found a directory of all the NGOs in the West Bank: it was as thick as an old Manhattan phone book.) Their work inevitably reflected the priorities of the donor nations more than the needs of Palestinians. The donors, after all, despite occasional protests about human rights and international law, were allies of the occupier. Add to this the birth of a new economic elite born of exclusive contracts and PA-approved monopolies, one whose fortunes depended on a privileged relationship with higher-ups in the ministries. The result was that a significant number of Palestinians found their destinies tied either to the PA—and hence to the various forces capable of bullying or cajoling Abbas, of which the United States and Israel ranked highest—or to the happiness of the donor states, which, however much they at times complained, nonetheless tended to obey Israel's dictates at a slight remove.

"It is most dangerous," wrote the poet Mahmoud Darwish, "for the homeland under occupation to turn into a loaf of bread."* No one liked to say it, but it was obvious enough that prospering in post-Oslo Palestine—and sometimes just surviving—meant investing in the status quo. Which is to say: in the occupation. Resistance still had great rhetorical value. But it didn't pay.

"I DON'T KNOW how they fell for this trick," Bassem said, emptying his coffee cup one evening. "We stopped our revolution and we took nothing."

Bassem's indignation felt painfully familiar. It was the almost universal cry of the late-twentieth- and early-twenty-first-century left, the same one Victor Serge had raised in exile from the Soviet Union in 1946: "How did we—insurgent, united, uplifted, and victorious—bring about the opposite of what we wanted to do?" There is a Palestinian answer to Serge's Russian question: Arafat was weaker than he had ever been. His revolution, which was never identical with the one fought on Palestinian soil, was withering in exile, and almost friendless. He had lost the backing of the Gulf states for throwing his support behind Iraq after Saddam Hussein's invasion of Kuwait. The networks of solidarity that had once united anticolonial movements across the planet crumbled well before the Berlin Wall did. And the growth during the Intifada of an indigenous Palestinian leadership unmoored from the exiled PLO hierarchy had seemed a sure sign that Arafat's relevance was on the verge of expiring. Oslo was his only chance. He took it. If it was a bad deal, it was a start. It was, after all, an "interim agreement." The real issues would be negotiated later.

But they weren't. Talks collapsed in early 2001. The Second Intifada came and went. If that uprising began, in part, as a revolt against the humiliating concessions of Oslo, it ended in a deeper, tenser torpor, with Palestin-

---

*But on the same page, he wrote, "When the guns are silent, don't I have the right to feel hungry?"

ian society broken not only by Israeli guns, but by factionalism, fragmentation, and despair. When he was jailed in the past, Bassem told me, the struggle hadn't stopped at the prison gates. Prisoners organized themselves to demand better conditions from the guards. With the universities shuttered, a generation of Palestinians was educated inside Israeli jails. Inmates read poetry and political theory and studied English and Hebrew. Now prisoners mainly watched TV. Fatah and Hamas members were confined in separate wings. No one mentioned solidarity. This last time, Bassem said, his old friends couldn't understand why he was still fighting instead of leaning back and cashing in, using his connections to get rich, as so many others had, off the spoils of the occupation. "You're smart," they told him. "Why are you doing this? Don't you learn?"

Outside it was no better. When Mahmoud Abbas, or Abu Mazen, as he was more informally known, addressed the United Nations in September 2011, he nodded to the movement that had begun in villages like Nabi Saleh. "Our people will continue their popular peaceful resistance to the Israeli occupation," Abbas swore. It was an easy promise to make. "On the ground," Bassem said, "they don't do anything." Shortly after the demonstrations began in Nabi Saleh, Palestinian officials from the District Coordination Office, or DCO—the bureaucratic interface between the Israeli military and PA—contacted the village. What you're doing is fine, they said, so long as you stay out of Area A, where the PA, technically, was the sole authority.* In other words, don't do anything that would force us to take a side, either to challenge the Israelis or to join them—don't make this our problem. The PA, Bassem sighed, "is the class of the occupation."

But Bassem also worked for the PA. "I am part of this system," he admitted. He had a job with the Interior Ministry in a department charged with approving entrance visas for Palestinians living abroad. In practice, he said, "They have no authority": the real decisions were made in Israel and

---

*General Adnan Damiri, a spokesman for the PA's security forces, denied this conversation took place. Bassem and Manal maintained that it did.

passed to his department for rubber-stamping. I never saw Bassem go to work, or heard him complain about a day at the office. He regarded his salary as his right, as a veteran regards his pension, and not without some bitterness: "We didn't build a revolution and give the lives of our cousins and brothers and sisters and fathers and sons and husbands and wives to get a salary," Bassem said. "We don't want wide streets under occupation or a stable life under occupation." The point, once upon a time, had been to *end* the occupation. "It doesn't matter if it's a gold cage or an iron cage," Bassem said. "It's a cage."

I once asked Bassem and Bilal how many people in Nabi Saleh depended on PA salaries. Bilal worked for the PA too, as a graphic designer for the Ministry of Public Health—he did have to go to work each day. The two men conferred, counting on their hands. It took them a few minutes to add up the names. "More than eighty," Bilal concluded. "Let's say two thirds of the village."

THIS IS WHY Bassem looked so depressed after the Shaul Mofaz protest in Ramallah. Abbas's security forces had turned on their own people, twice. "They have the power," Bassem said, "more than the Israelis, to stop us." And it wouldn't take overt violence to stop the village demonstrations. PA officials could instruct every government employee to stop participating. They could order Palestinian media to stay away on Fridays. They could make Bassem sit at a desk all day every day.

I was in Ramallah the day of the third anti-Mofaz protest. By all accounts it was bigger than the first two. Still, it wasn't large, a few hundred people marching to the *muqata'a*, shouting along to a chant popularized in Tahrir Square, but changing the Egyptians' "Down with the regime!" to the more oblique "Down with Oslo!" Shoppers looked on from the sidewalks and drivers, trapped resentfully in traffic, from their cars. A few of the marchers had bandaged limbs from the last protest, but this time the security forces kept a careful distance. I recognized Bahaa, Mustafa Tamimi's very tall friend, and a few of the other guys from Nabi Saleh. At the front of the march, to my surprise, I found Bassem in a black shirt, marching behind a giant Palestinian flag. He took me by the arm and grinned. "We are making a revolution," he joked, "against our parents' authority."

The Mofaz visit, in the end, was canceled.

THE FOLLOWING FRIDAY was supposed to be my last. I had a flight out of Tel Aviv the next night. The demonstration would be a short one, Bassem promised over breakfast. One of the guys from Nabi Saleh was getting married to a girl from Deir Nidham, the village down the road, and the engagement ceremony was scheduled for that afternoon. In the living room, the TV was blasting a fantasy film. Waed and Ahed sat transfixed as demon soldiers with spiky, black exoskeletons raided a humble village, swinging giant, rusty swords. Ray Liotta played the lord of the demon army, Burt Reynolds the king of the humans. "We are men!" he yelled, rousing his troops. "They are beasts and bloodless!" The call to prayer was sounding. Waed yawned, stretched, and stood.

The march began as they always do. Salam was out in front. Little Janna hung back in the shade of a tree opposite the gas station. "You see?" said Nawal. "She's scared!"

Four armored cars waited at the bend in the road, the skunk truck idling behind them. Manal pointed to a few civilian policemen accompanying the soldiers. It was the first time she had seen them in the village. "There is a new law," she said by way of explanation, "that they can arrest internationals."* About half the marchers headed down the hillside. Soldiers were waiting beneath. They arrested Jonathan Pollak again, and with him four more Israelis and old Bashir, the owner of the land around the spring. Mohammad

---

*It wasn't a law exactly: earlier that week, defying the rulings of the Israeli High Court, the IDF had issued an order authorizing Israeli immigration police to arrest foreigners in the West Bank.

raced uphill, outrunning the soldiers behind him. Everyone cheered. I heard a bang somewhere over the ridge, and then another.

And so it went: beside the gas station, one of the guys hid behind a Dumpster, ducking out every few seconds to fling a stone. Rubber-coated bullets ricocheted off the asphalt. The guys took refuge in an olive grove. The soldiers fired so much tear gas that I couldn't see the trees. The skunk truck sped past, but everyone had already fled. It soaked Bilal's house anyway. I could see him on the roof with his camera in one hand, crouching to avoid the spray. The truck blasted Mohammad's house next, the jet of fluid smashing the first-floor windows and knocking him from his feet. He had just come home, triumphant from his close escape. Shattered glass cut his face and chest. Skunk water saturated the carpets and couches.

At the corner of the road to Bassem's house, I watched as soldiers tossed grenade after grenade over a fence into an empty garden. Three jeeps roared around the bend. Everyone scattered. I ran through a gate and into the house beside Bahaa's and, after a few minutes, ventured out to peer at the soldiers on the other side of the garden wall. Two girls joined me. Suddenly, I noticed, they were no longer standing beside me. Twenty yards away a soldier was aiming a grenade launcher at my head. I followed the girls inside.

When I came out again, Nariman was standing in the road with a Scottish activist. I walked over and said hello. Four soldiers approached. Two of them grabbed the Scottish woman. The others took me by the arms, pulled me to a jeep, and shoved me in. I showed my press card to the driver. His expression didn't change. Two very frightened young British women were already locked inside. One of them was hyperventilating. An hour passed. The jeep stayed put. The soldiers brought two more captives, a Swede and an Italian who had been hiding in the convenience store bathroom. Through the grated rear window I could see Bilal filming, and a soldier covering the lens with his hand. More soldiers piled in. I again showed one of them my press card and asked if he understood that I was a journalist. He nodded. The driver pulled onto the road. As we passed the gas station, the guys ran after us. Stones clanged against the jeep's steel walls.

"They were so beautiful a few minutes ago, right?" the soldier beside me said. "They were so cute."

The jeep drove past the tower, up the hill and through the gates of the army base beside Halamish. The soldiers herded us into the old British fort. They took our passports and parked us on a bench in the hallway. More soldiers milled about, ignoring us, their rifles strapped to their backs. I asked one if his officers knew they had arrested a journalist. He nodded. My cell phone rang. It was Captain Eytan Buchman, the chief IDF spokesperson for North American media. We had been in touch earlier in the week to arrange some interviews, but I hadn't told him I would be in Nabi Saleh. Someone apparently had. (Before I stepped out of the jeep, I later learned, the news of my arrest was circulating on Twitter.) Buchman was calling to inform me that no credentialed journalists had been detained in Nabi Saleh. I disagreed. Half an hour later, an officer escorted me to the gate. He returned my passport and press card. "Have a nice trip," he said. The other five foreigners stayed behind. All would be deported the following week.

The road to the village was empty, but the air was still peppery with tear gas, and the breeze smelled of shit and decay. A cloud of gas drifted over the olive groves. Grenades arced through the sky. It was nearly six, but I made it in time to join the slow, raucous caravan of cars and vans that cruised out of the village, music blasting, the guys dancing in their seats. A soldier flipped us the finger as we drove past the tower. The guys laughed and kept on dancing. They were dancing later too, back in the village after the ceremony. Someone had set up speakers and flashing lights a few houses down from Bassem's. The women watched from plastic chairs. Osama crouched beside them on the sidelines, but Waed was dancing, and so were Bahaa and Mohammad. They danced hand in hand with the rest of the guys, all of them kicking in unison, shouting and clapping, laughing still, the light bouncing in their eyes.

INTERLUDE

SEPARATION BARRIER

Mediterranean Sea

ISRAEL

Jordan River

JORDAN

Dead
Sea

0 miles   10   15
0 kilometers   15

Green Line
Existing Wall
Wall to Be Built
International
Borders

© 2016 Jeffrey L. Ward

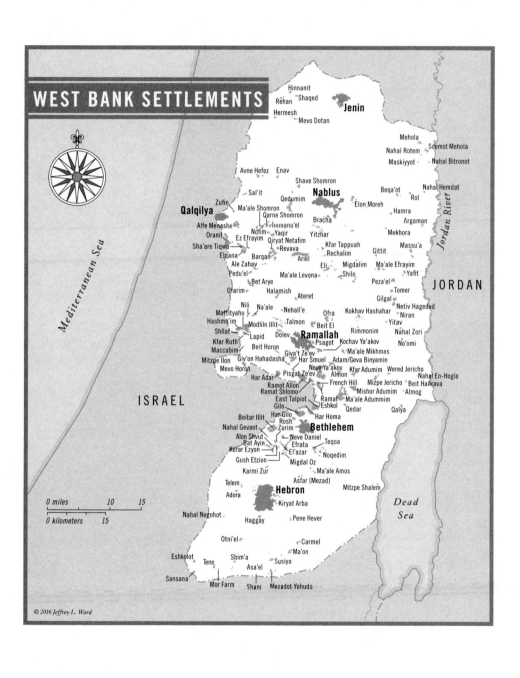

WEST BANK SETTLEMENTS

Mediterranean Sea

Jordan River

JORDAN

ISRAEL

Dead Sea

0 miles 10 15
0 kilometers 15

© 2016 Jeffrey L. Ward

Hinnanit
Rehan · Shaqed
Hermesh
Jenin
Mevo Dotan

Mehola
Nahal Rotem · Sdemot Mehola
Maskiyyot · Nahal Bitronot

Avne Hefez Enav
Shave Shomron
Beqa'ot Nahal Hemdat
Sal'it Qedumim **Nablus** Rol
Zufin Elon Moreh
Qalqilya Ma'ale Shomron Hamra
Qarne Shomron Bracha Argaman
Alfe Menashe Immanu'el
Oranit Nofim Yaqir Yitzhar Mekhora
Ez Efrayim Qiryat Netafim
Sha'are Tiqwa Revava Kfar Tappuah Massu'a
Elqana Rechalim Gittit
Ale Zahav Barqan Ariel Eli Migdalim Ma'ale Efrayim
Pedu'el Ma'ale Levona Shilo Yafit
Bet Arye Peza'el
Otarim Halamish Ateret Tomer
Gilgal
Nili Na'ale Nehall'e Netiv Hagedud
Mattityahu Ofra Kokhav Hashahar Niran
Hashmo'im Modliln Illit Talmon Yitav
Shllat Dolev Beit El Rimmonim Nahal Zori
Lapid **Ramallah** Kochav Ya'akov No'omi
Kfar Ruth Beit Horon Psagot
Maccabim Giva't Ze'ev Ma'ale Mikhmas
Mitzpe Ilon Giv'on Hahadasha Har Smuel Adam/Geva Binyamin
Mevo Horon Neve Ya'akov Kfar Adumim Wered Jericho
Har Adar Pisgat Ze'ev Almon Nahal En-Hogla
Ramot Allon French Hill Mizpe Jericho Beit HaArava
Ramat Shlomo Mishor Adumim Almog
East Talpiot Ramat Ma'ale Adummim
Gilo Eshkol Qedar Qalya
Beitar Illit Har Gilo
Nahal Gevaot Rosh Har Homa
Alon Shvut Zurim **Bethlehem**
Bat Ayin Neve Daniel
Kefar Ezyon Efrata Teqoa
Gush Etzion El'azar
Migdal Oz Noqedim
Karmi Zur
Asfar (Mezad) Ma'ale Amos
Telem Mitzpe Shalem
Adora
Hebron
Nahal Negohot Kiryat Arba
Haggay Pene Hever
Otni'el
Carmel
Eshkolot Shim'a Ma'on
Tene Susiya
Sansana Asa'el
Mor Farm Shani Mezadot Yehuda

OCCUPATION CABINET
OF CURIOSITIES

EXHIBIT TWO: EVERY BEGINNING IS DIFFERENT

Beit Ijza

Bassem had told me about Beit Ijza. He had a friend there, he said, who had told him about another surrounded house. That was all he said, but even if he had described it in detail, he couldn't have done much to spoil the surprise. In August 2013, he and Irene Nasser and I drove out through al-Masyoun, an affluent neighborhood of new and ugly apartment towers and sleek cafés constructed since the beginning of Ramallah's post-Oslo boom. We passed the Mövenpick and the Grand Park hotels, where foreign dignitaries and wealthy Palestinians from the diaspora stayed for hundreds of dollars a night, and the buildings grew squatter and the landscape more broken and industrial as we drove east through Beitunia until finally, of course, we hit the wall.

The wall rode the hills in front of us and to our left like a ridge of spines on a reptile's back. Then it did something odd. It branched off in a Y. Why the fork? If its purpose was security, to protect Israelis from Palestinians, what could the two branches possibly be enclosing? The Israeli architect and theorist Eyal Weizman observed in 2007 that the wall had by then become "a discontinuous and fragmented series of self-enclosed barriers that can be better understood as a prevalent 'condition' of segregation—a shifting frontier—rather than one continuous line neatly cutting the territory in two." We were close enough to Jerusalem and its myriad suburban settlements that the wall formed neither a line nor a simple zigzag. The intricacies of separation and control fractured its path into a jagged cuneiform script scrawled in concrete across the earth. We passed beneath it through a tunnel, from Palestine to Palestine, and drove on past supermarkets and olive groves before we hit the wall again and dropped into another tunnel, this one almost impossibly long—Irene measured it on the odometer at a kilometer and a half. We entered it in al-Jib and emerged one village over, in Biddu. Again: from Palestine to Palestine. We had crossed beneath no river and through no mountain, through no natural impediment at all. The obstacles we had passed beneath were ethnic and political: the land above and around the tunnel had been seized from the neighboring villages to create the settlements of Giv'on Hahadasha and Har Smuel, and to build the smooth settlers' highway—Road 443—that connects the central West Bank settlements to one another and to Jerusalem and Tel Aviv, a road that the journalist Gershom Gorenberg has described as a "long, narrow settlement" in its own right.

Irene recalled that there had been demonstrations here in the early days of the popular resistance fight against the wall. Five men had been killed in Biddu, three of them when the army opened fire on the village's third demonstration in February 2004. They had lost, and stopped the protests. Biddu and the seven villages around it—Beit Ijza being one of them—had been turned into a canton, an enclave walled off from the surrounding Palestinian populations of both Jerusalem and the West Bank, accessible from Ramallah only through that tunnel, which could be closed at any time by a few soldiers in a single jeep.

We turned off the main road and onto a smaller one, potholed and dusty. It came to an abrupt end at a fence edged with coiled razor wire. We parked the car. On the other side of the fence we could see the red-roofed stucco homes of Giv'on Hahadasha, quiet and clean as any Florida subdivision. Just past what appeared to be the last house in Beit Ijza stood a short section of concrete wall. It was about twelve feet high and rimmed with another six feet of chain link. A gate opened in the wall: a heavy metal door, painted yellow, that led onto a narrow driveway perhaps sixty feet long. Low cement walls topped with twelve or fifteen feet of heavy mesh fencing rose on both sides of the driveway. At the end of this concrete and steel tunnel stood a single house, a pretty, one-story stone building with a lush arbor growing over its front patio and fruit trees in the yard. The house too was encircled by a high barrier of thick steel mesh.

Bassem was laughing as he opened the gate. I suppose it was the look on my face. I don't know if in the minutiae of this description I have managed to be clear: the house had its own wall, not one that happened to snake across its yard, as with Hani Amer's home in Mas'ha, but a wall that had been purposefully and with considerable care wrapped around it, sealing it off equally from the settlement and from the village of which it had been part. The house was entirely encaged.

WE WERE GREETED by a man named Sa'adat Sabri. He had a soft voice, a delicate, almost feminine face, and a construction worker's rough and callused hands. Inside, the house was spotless. The sitting room was airy and bright. Its white tile floors had been scrubbed to a shine. Nowhere could I spot a stray hair or mote of dust. Sabri was thirty-two years old, which made him two years younger than Giv'on Hahadasha. The settlers—they too were from Gush Emunim—arrived before he was born, but his father, who had died in this house in 2012, had told him stories. The settlers first came, as they usually did, in caravans—glorified shipping containers that could be dropped in overnight as temporary lodgings. The leader of the settlers' council, a woman named Rachel, approached Sabri's father and asked to buy his land. She brought a suitcase filled with money, Sabri said.

At first she asked for one dunam—about a quarter of an acre—but when he refused and continued to refuse she said she would settle for less, "even if it's just a meter," so long as he delivered his signature on a document ceding his rights to the land. His answer, he said, would always be the same.

Sabri laughed. "After that," he said, "our problems started."

The settlers, Sabri said, seized 40 of the family's 110 dunams. In the daytime, they put up fences and electric lines. At night, Sabri's father and brothers tore them down. The soldiers came and arrested them. The settlers took their own retaliation, targeting the house with rocks and Molotovs. This went on for fifteen years: "From 1979 to 1994, not one stone was laid on this land. There wasn't a year when one of us wasn't in prison." When the settlers brought in workers—it is a little-mentioned truth that Israeli settlements are built by Palestinian laborers—the Sabris would figure out where they were from. They would visit their families and dissuade them from returning to work. Sabri didn't specify how. His father had deeds to the land going back to the Ottoman Empire, so they tried the courts. It didn't help: sometimes the High Court would issue a stop-work order, but the settlers would ignore it and the soldiers would defend them. When Arafat returned from exile in 1994, Sabri's father sought an audience with him. "There's nothing I can do," Arafat told him. "Just keep resisting."

Resist they did. Their tenacity would not go unpunished. About a year after Oslo, the settlers brought in so many workers that the Sabris could not hope to persuade or scare them all away. The settlement grew. The Intifada broke out. By 2005, the wall around the village had gone up. Sabri, his father, and one of his brothers were all arrested. When he got out, the fence around the house had already been built. His home had been transformed into a single-family jail. One morning not long thereafter, Sabri woke up to find the gate locked. There was no soldier to complain to—just the intercom and a camera wired to communicate with a Border Police station several miles distant. Sabri went out to the gate at seven a.m. and rang the intercom. He waited beside the gate, he said, for eight hours. Finally, an officer arrived. He had orders. No one would be allowed in the house, he said, other than those family members who already lived there. The gate would be opened at certain times each day. Whoever wished to enter would have to hold their documents up to the camera so that their identification could be verified.

Sabri smiled. "I'm just taking this as a conversation," he told the officer. "I'm not taking what you say seriously." Hypothetically, he wanted to know: what about his sisters who had married and moved out of the house? What if they wanted to drop by to see their parents?

They would have to submit a request for a permit a week in advance, the officer answered.

"I told him no way," Sabri said. "We refuse completely."

The gate stayed locked for the next three months. The Sabris appealed again to the Israeli courts. When they needed to leave the house—which they often did, as Sabri's father was by this time quite ill—they would contact the Red Crescent, the UN, and the DCO, and wait for others to intercede on their behalf. Sometimes it would take five minutes, Sabri said, but sometimes it took hours. Either way, you had to stand outside and wait for the gate to click open. If you missed it, the whole process started over.* Finally, at the end of 2006, the courts decided in the Sabris' favor. The gate stayed open.

"Man is a creature that can get used to anything," wrote Dostoevsky after four years in a Siberian prison camp. "That is the best definition of him." Life went on. It has to. Sabri's father died. His battles continued: The family was still in court over the fate of the seventy dunams that remained to them which, like all of Beit Ijza's agricultural land, were cut off from the village by the wall. In the meantime, they planned to stay put. Sabri's grandmother remained in the house, along with two of his brothers, their families, and his own. His wife had given birth to a son. She was pregnant again. As we spoke, Sabri's son and his nephews toddled into the

---

*"In the occupied territories," observed the French writer Christian Salmon, "Israel is occupying time as well as space. . . . "

room, climbed over his lap, fingered his cigarette lighter, his coffee cup and saucer, fell, cried, recovered, and scurried off again.

"Every beginning is different," Sabri said. When the wall first went up, "we saw it as the end." Now the house was full of children. They saw the fence and the barbed wire every time they glanced through a window or stepped outdoors. It was the same with the gate, Sabri said. In the beginning it seemed unbearable, but he knew now that they would have been okay even if the worst had happened and the gate had remained locked. Eventually, he said, smiling at this strange and painful knowledge, they would all have gotten used to it.

3.

ABOVE THE CAROB TREE

Burin, Nabi Saleh

And if the dead by displacement and the dead by weapons and
the dead by longing and the dead by simple death are martyrs,
and if poems are true and each martyr is a rose, we can claim
to have made a garden of the world.

—MOURID BARGHOUTI

The hills were a glorious green, the grasses scattered with red poppies, yellow buttercups, and delicate purple lilies. It was early in February 2013, a Saturday. Four months of winter rain had fallen since I left Nabi Saleh. A lot had happened in the meantime. Everyone was reeling. That morning, I was climbing a rocky slope above the village of Burin, just south of the city of Nablus. An hour or so earlier a tractor had arrived in the center of the village towing a stack of nine prefabricated, semicylindrical huts constructed of gleaming aluminum welded over steel frames. A dozen men were carrying the first hut up the hill. It was hard work—their burden was heavy and the hills were worse than steep—but the men were cheerful, chanting and singing as they climbed. Behind them was another group with another hut, and there was another group behind that one. They had reason to rush: they had to reach the top before the soldiers arrived, or worse, before the settlers did.

For months, popular resistance activists had been struggling to build momentum, to shake their movement out of the dull routine of Friday demonstrations. Who could have guessed that getting skunked and shot at once a week could become so comfortable a rut? In mid-October they blocked a settler road outside Ramallah. Twelve days later, they staged a protest in a settlement grocery store. They blocked more roads, trying hard to push the resistance outside of the small handful of villages in which it had for so long been stalled. In January, a week before I landed, activists built a "village" on a hilly plot of West Bank land outside Jerusalem that Netanyahu had recently claimed for settlement expansion. A month and a half earlier, the United Nations had voted to recognize Palestine as a "non-member observer," granting not-quite status to the not-quite state. The Israeli prime minister retaliated by announcing plans to construct three thousand new units of settlement housing and to begin developing a parcel known as E1, located strategically between Jerusalem and the settlement of Ma'ale Adumim. The activists got there first. They erected tents, hooked up electric power, established a clinic and a media center, and invited Palestinians to join them. "We the people," the press release read, "without permits from the occupation, without permission from anyone, sit here today because this is our land and it is our right to inhabit it."

They called the village Bab al-Shams ("The Gate of the Sun"), after the novel of the same name by Elias Khoury, or, more specifically, after the cave in the Galilee that Khoury invented in that novel, the hideaway to which an exiled Palestinian resistance fighter again and again risked his life to secretly visit and make love to the wife he left behind. Bab al-Shams was meant as more than a clever rebuke to Netanyahu. The name evoked the beloved Palestine of the sentimental imagination, a place more intimate than any actual territory lost in 1948. It was, in Khoury's words, "the only liberated plot of Palestinian land," the part that remained unseen and unspoiled, and that people had for generations defended not with guns but with laughter, tears, and caresses, with infinite, often invisible strategies of preservation and resistance.

The press came flocking—not just the usual handful of local crews and freelancers but reporters from the big international dailies and the major TV networks. For the first time in a long time, Palestinians were making the news for something other than their losses. The nights were freezing. There weren't enough blankets and there wasn't enough food. Almost everyone got sick. But everyone I spoke with who was there seemed transformed by the experience. The community that was briefly born at Bab al-Shams managed to reawaken the tenderness and love without which not a centimeter of earth is worth fighting for. It lasted forty-eight hours. Netanyahu personally gave the order, violating an injunction issued by Israel's High Court. The soldiers came in the night, dressed all in black. They arrested everyone, beating many in the process, packing them onto buses and dumping them at Qalandia checkpoint, just outside Ramallah.

Bassem had been arrested two and a half months earlier, at the settlement grocery store protest. The Border Police had grabbed at Nariman and when Bassem stepped between them, the police took him instead. He was still in jail. He missed Bab al-Shams. Later, he told me that he watched the news reports on TV from his cell. I asked if he wished he could have gone. He smiled a rare, wistful smile. "Without further comment," he said. "Yes." But Nariman was there. So were Manal and the kids, and a few of the guys from the village. Within days, without prior coordination, two copycat protest villages sprang up—one in the north, outside Jenin, and another near Jerusalem called Bab al-Karameh, the Gate of Dignity. That one lasted three days before the army bulldozed the site.

The action I was witnessing in Burin was the next step. The stakes were higher this time. There had been no settlements in the immediate vicinity of Bab al-Shams, but Burin was surrounded by some of the most aggressive settlers in the West Bank. In 2011, when the UN's Office for the Coordination of Humanitarian Affairs surveyed settler violence in the West Bank, it found that Yitzhar, Burin's neighbor to the south, was responsible for more attacks on Palestinians than any other settlement. The previous year, nearly two thousand of Burin's olive and almond trees had been damaged, and thirty-six of its residents injured in assaults. Another UN agency found that in the first ten months of 2013, settlers in the area burned, poisoned, or uprooted nine hundred olive trees and scorched another one hundred acres of agricultural land. Halamish, by contrast, was a sedate commuter suburb. Erecting a protest village in Burin—this one would be called al-Manatir, after the traditional stone shelters from which farmers watched over their fields—meant directly challenging the settlement enterprise in its most messianic and violent manifestation. If that was scary, that was the idea: to push Palestinians past whatever fear still held them back. The goal was to stay longer than activists had been able to in Bab al-Shams, to establish al-Manatir as a semipermanent node of resistance. Theoretically, the army would need a court order to demolish any structure more permanent than a tent. (Settlers had for years taken advantage of this technicality by towing in caravans to establish outpost after outpost in flagrant violation of Israeli law, usually with the full cooperation of the authorities.) Hence the aluminum huts. And the site was in Area B, which meant that theoretically, under the terms of the Oslo Accords, so long as the protesters had the PA's permission to be there—which they did—the IDF could not legally chase them off.

But before the first hut had arrived at the top of the hill, the man beside me began shouting. "Settlers!" he yelled, pointing up at a dozen figures racing toward us from the outpost on the next hilltop over. They wore long beards and forelocks and large white skullcaps. White robes trailed behind them as they ran. Some of them had covered their faces with ski masks and scarves. The soldiers were coming too, but the settlers dashed past them like lost extras from some Hollywood Old Testament epic, hurling stones in our direction as they ran. The soldiers caught up and pushed them back. It took three of them to restrain a single, black-clad settler. His dog bolted ahead of him, barking as its owner cursed.

The second hut arrived, and the third. More soldiers sprinted over to block the activists hauling up the fourth hut. The activists pushed past them, whistling and cheering. A fifth hut made it up, and a sixth. Soon the soldiers had formed a line and there were stun grenades exploding everywhere and the hillside was blanketed in tear gas. The gas drifted off and the activists—maybe 150 now, plus the journalists—reassembled around the huts, coughing and spitting and cheering once more. The soldiers repeated the same process again and again, each time pushing the crowd a few meters farther back, here and there pepper-spraying someone or arresting someone, or both. I watched one soldier stand on the chest of a man named Wahib Qaddous as more soldiers punched and kicked him and pepper-sprayed him in the face.

The day dragged on. The soldiers shoved and gassed everyone back. The settlers ran in behind them and overturned the huts and began to drag them off. I didn't see what they did with them—the soldiers were pushing us to the edge of a steep escarpment. A cliff, really. We scrambled down, blasts still sounding above us, and learned at the bottom that settlers had entered the village and shot sixteen-year-old Zakaria Najjar in the thigh. The army came in after them and began firing tear gas and rubber-coated bullets. Not at the settlers of course. That evening, when all the journalists had left, soldiers raided the village again.

In the end four protesters were injured and eight or nine arrested. Three were prosecuted. I went to their hearings five days later in the military court attached to Salem prison, near the ancient city of Megiddo, also known as Har Megiddo, or Armageddon, where Satan and the armies of Gog and Magog will face off against the righteous at the end of times. For now it's just another prison. The prosecutor requested that the activists' detention be extended by five more days, though they had not yet been charged with a crime. Neither the defendants nor their attorneys were allowed to see the evidence against them. The judge agreed to extend their detention and, five days later, extended it again. No settlers were arrested. It came out in court that, despite the shooting of Zakaria Najjar and the settlers' having thrown stones in full view of dozens of soldiers, not a single settler had been questioned about the day's events.

All told, al-Manatir had survived for approximately three and one quarter hours.

I CAUGHT A RIDE from Burin straight to Nabi Saleh. The kids and the soldiers were clashing by the tower when I arrived. The guys weren't around. It was just the little boys. They were throwing stones and the soldiers were firing rubber-coated bullets from behind concrete blast walls. Abu Yazan crouched beneath a boulder.* It started raining and the kids retreated and I walked with them back up to the center of town. They were in high spirits. A young Belgian filmmaker had shot a documentary partly in Nabi Saleh and partly in Halamish. *Thank God It's Friday*, it was called. He wanted to screen the rough cut in the village, film the screening, and incorporate the villagers' reactions into his final edit. Bilal was already in the *diwan,* a plain, rectangular building that functioned as a sort of meeting hall. He was setting up his camera on a tripod, preparing to film the filming of the film. And I was there with my notebook, one last mirror in the hall.

By eight o'clock, every chair was full. The room was cold and brightly lit. Posters were taped to the walls, photos of a thin-faced man in a white shirt with black buttons. He looked startled. "MARTYR AND HERO," the posters read, and then his name: Rushdie Mahmoud Tamimi. He was Nariman's youngest brother. She claimed I had met him at the house once over the summer, but if I had I couldn't remember. He had worked nights as a policeman in Birzeit, and wasn't around much. On November 19, 2012, a soldier shot him with live ammunition just down the hill from Bassem and Nariman's house. He died in the hospital two days later.

Nariman sat a couple of rows from the front, Salam squirming in her lap and her brother's image all around her. Later, she told me that she had seen him staring back at her. He wasn't the only one missing. Bassem was still in prison. His mother had passed away over the summer, a couple of months

---

*IDF regulations forbid soldiers from firing the "less-lethal" projectiles at women and children. Since 2000, at least eighteen Palestinians, two thirds of them children, have been killed by rubber-coated bullets.

before his arrest. Abd al-Razzaq, Mustafa Tamimi's father, had died in October. He had been ill for years, but everyone agreed it was grief that killed him. His widow, Ekhlas, sat in the front row beside Naji's wife Boshra. Naji, who had been in prison all summer and for most of the previous year, saved me a seat. Waed had been arrested for the first time, but he was out now. Young Mohammad Ataallah, founder of the village's media team, wasn't around. He had spent most of the fall in jail. He had been released in December and had just flown to Italy, where he would be working for a few months and, he promised, spreading the word about Nabi Saleh's struggle. "Tamimi Press, Rome bureau," he joked before he left.

The lights went out. The movie started. People found a lot to laugh about. Like when one of the settlers said, "There is no such thing as Palestinians." And when another claimed that there had been no birds in the area until after the settlement was founded. And when Abu Yazan cried after the tire he had lit aflame and kicked down the hill toward the road to Halamish tumbled over and shuddered to a stop a few hundred yards short of its target. The room went silent as images of the settlement's streets and gardens flashed on the screen, the trees and flowers, the playgrounds, the swimming pool. ("It's beautiful," Nariman told me later.) There was one brief shot of Mustafa, still alive, sitting quietly. Everyone applauded. Ekhlas sat bent in her chair, covering her face.

When it was over everyone stood and cleared the chairs from the floor. It was time for *dabke*, a traditional dance. The girls came in first, six of them, clapping twice on the left, twice on the right, hopping and stepping with one leg crossed over the other. Six boys—Bahaa, Odai and Loai, and three others—danced in, skipping past the girls, their hands behind their backs. The troupe had formed shortly after Rushdie's death. It was called Palestinian Revolution. This was their first performance. The music was blasting—oud, synth, cymbals, thunderous drums. Bahaa stood in front, his long arms raised, leading the others, towering over them, skipping and stepping like a giant, almost-graceful spider. They paired off and danced in couples, then lined up and clasped one another's hands. The girls took a turn, kicking and clapping in unison, and then the boys, Mustafa's brothers out in front with their hard jaws and shining eyes, their spines tight despite their smiles.

THE MULBERRY TREE in front of Bassem and Nariman's house was bare. One of the windows was broken and the yard was even more of a shambles than it had been over the summer. The grass was high and green, and in addition to the usual debris there were two rusting bicycle frames I hadn't seen before and a cracked white plastic table, the latter a casualty, Nariman said, of a recent game of *jeish ou shebab*, or army-versus-guys, the local equivalent of cowboys and Indians. The old "FREE BASSEM TAMIMI" poster above the television had been joined by posters honoring Rushdie and Mustafa, and one for Mustafa's father Abd al-Razzaq who, though he had not been killed by an Israeli bullet, was considered a martyr of the occupation. The embroidered image of the al-Aqsa mosque was still there, now with a snapshot of Bassem's mother taped to the frame.

Nariman seemed giddy. She was laughing more than I'd ever seen, but it rarely took more than a question or two to push her to tears. She was limping. She had fractured her foot during a demonstration two weeks earlier. She was running from the skunk truck and had dropped the poster she was carrying—a photo of another martyr, sixteen-year-old Samir 'Awad, shot in the leg, back, and head in the village of Budrus that January 15. When she bent to pick it up, a blast of skunk had knocked her from her feet. She wore a bandage but no cast, and she shrugged off all suggestions that she should return to the hospital to get the bone set, or at least try not to walk on it.

We started with Bassem's arrest. The protest had already left the grocery store, Nariman recalled. It was in the settlement shopping center of Sha'ar Binyamin, next to the police station where Nariman had been held and beaten nearly three years earlier. As they marched down the driveway toward the street, a police commander stopped Nariman. Bassem stepped between them to put his arms around his wife. They beat him pretty badly

as they dragged him off. I asked if Bassem hadn't been worried before-
hand, given the terms of his previous release, which more or less guaran-
teed a prison term if he was caught at a demonstration.

If he felt any fear, Nariman said, he didn't mention it. He just asked her
not to be in the front line.

But she hadn't been, I said. I had seen video of the protest.

She smiled. "Yes. That's how it is."

Having Bassem in prison was almost normal. Nariman had been through
it enough times before. But her eldest son's arrest, she said, "was something I
couldn't take." It happened on a Friday. The guys were on the hillside. Waed
had stuck his head through the door of an abandoned house and been surprised to find soldiers waiting within. They grabbed him before he could
run. Nariman had to watch the soldiers beating him and, later, to see him
appear in court covered in bruises and scabs. "I felt like there was a fire
exploding inside me," she said, "like my heart was burning." She twisted a
shred of paper between her fingers as she spoke. "For the first time, I asked
myself, 'Where am I leading my children?'" She thought a lot about Mustafa,
she said, and his mother's wish that the protests continue despite her loss and
the risk to her surviving sons. In the end, Waed was released after just a few
days. The judge saw his bruises and threw out the charges.

It's an odd world. Waed's arrest made his sister famous. In a single moment, the strange theater of the village demonstrations had at once inflicted
a painful wound and delivered a victory on a scale that no one had expected.
This is how it seemed to go: no triumph without commensurate loss. A
camera had caught Ahed shaking her fist in an Israeli soldier's face, demanding that her brother be released. The images went viral. Suddenly Ahed was
showing up on Facebook feeds and in tweets that crossed the planet. The
full video was excruciating—Ahed curses and howls, helpless as the soldiers laugh. The stills, though, were easy to feel good about: the tiny blond
girl unafraid, her fist in the face of a soldier two feet taller than she is, his
rifle hanging between them. She and Nariman were invited to Istanbul. To
a conference, they thought. They were greeted at the airport, Nariman said,

by dozens of reporters and 150 children wearing T-shirts printed with Ahed's photo. She was a star, the living image of Palestinian courage and defiance. They drove past billboards with Ahed's face on them. Crowds gathered when they walked in the streets. Recep Erdogan, the president of Turkey, met them in the eastern city of Urfa, flew back with them to Istanbul on his private plane, and gave Ahed an iPhone. She did one interview after another. One of them stuck in Nariman's mind. The journalist had asked her, "Why does this child not smile?"

For her part, Ahed seemed unaltered by her celebrity. She was as quiet as ever and had the same uncanny poise. She wore a pendant in the shape of Palestine on a thin silver chain. She fiddled with it, pulling the chain up over her nose, back down over her chin, up into her mouth. I asked her what she had liked best in Turkey. "The sea," she said, though it had been too cold to swim. The attention had been a bit much, but she hadn't been ready to leave—she wanted to stay at the sea a little longer. For now, she missed her father, she said, and she was mad at her mother. Her birthday was coming up. She was turning twelve and wanted to have a party, but Nariman, who was still in mourning, wouldn't allow it.

Rushdie had been Nariman's youngest brother. He was thirty-one when he died, six years younger than she was. Because he worked Fridays, he had never taken part in the demonstrations. On November 14, Israel had launched a weeklong air war on the Gaza Strip. Six Israelis and 167 Palestinians, most of them civilians, were killed. Protests spread across the West Bank. In Nabi Saleh, there were clashes nearly every day. "It felt like the third intifada," Manal told me excitedly over the phone soon after. Rushdie happened to be in the village that Saturday. He and Nariman's mother were visiting her at home. Nariman rolled the scrap of paper between her fingers into a tight cylinder as she told the story. One of the guys had come to the door saying that someone had been hit with a rubber bullet. Rushdie jogged out to the hill to see if he could help.

A few minutes later, Nariman heard gunshots—not the usual bang of gas grenades or the louder boom of rubber-coated bullets, but the distinctive popping crack of live ammunition. She ran outside. Everyone else was running in the opposite direction. People were shouting for an ambulance. Waed threw his arms around her. "Don't go," he pleaded. "They're shooting."

Nariman kept running. The guys were scattering and crawling on the ground for cover. She grabbed a video camera out of Helme's hands. "I felt like the camera could protect me," she said. She hit Record. Naji was there. The soldiers screamed at them to go. "From then on I can't remember exactly what happened," Nariman said. She still hadn't been able to watch the footage. Before she arrived, Waed and Bahaa had been right next to Rushdie on the hillside, just above the carob tree. He was hit first in the lower back, they told me, with a rubber-coated bullet. He fell and couldn't get up. The guys shouted to him, telling him to run. Rushdie was trying to stand when a soldier approaching from below shot him from a distance of three or four meters, this time with a bullet from his M16. It hit Rushdie in the buttock and exited through his gut. When Nariman reached him, he was lying on the ground.

"I said, 'What's the matter, brother?' He said, 'I can't move.'"

She shouted to the nearest soldier—the one who had shot him—that Rushdie needed help. "He can die," the soldier said.

Irene was with me. Nariman limped to the kitchen to pour us coffee. She wouldn't let us stop her. Two weeks earlier, an IDF inquiry into her brother's shooting found that the soldiers had opened fire "without justification," firing eighty rounds—Bahaa was certain it was more—and preventing anyone from coming to Rushdie's aid. The unit commander, who had not bothered to report the shooting to his superiors, was reportedly relieved of his command. That was it. No one would be charged with Rushdie's murder.

Nariman sat. At the time, she said, she wanted to attack the soldier who had shot him and who was preventing her and Naji from carrying him away so they could get him to a hospital. "I wanted to kill him and die with Rushdie right there," she said. "But I knew that I had to be stronger than that. I had to be stronger than them. Why? Why is it required of me to be more humane than they are?"

———

EVENTUALLY I CAUGHT UP with Waed. He was still small for his age, but he carried himself differently than he had over the summer, as if something in his thin frame had tilted from boy to man. He spent less time tormenting Ahed and his brothers and more time hugging them, as if he understood that they were children and he was something else. We talked about his arrest and his interrogation later that night at the Binyamin police station. He beamed as he recounted that the interrogator told him that he was just like his father: he didn't talk. They brought him to Ofer early the next morning and to the military court within the prison complex the next afternoon. He was ordered released on two thousand shekels' bail, but it was too late in the day to pay it. He would have to stay another night. The guards escorted him back to the prisoners' waiting area. He found his father waiting there. Bassem's lawyer had arranged a court appearance for him so that he would have a chance to see his son.

"When he saw me he had tears in his eyes," Waed said. They were both handcuffed and shackled. "He wanted to know how I was doing, if I needed anything," Waed said. A bus arrived to cart them back to their respective wings. "At some point he had to go left," Waed said, "and I had to go right. We said good-bye." But the next day, they got lucky. "Every two months they allow prisoners who are close relations to see each other," Waed explained. It was that day. They were able to spend two hours together. Waed told his father all the news, everything that had happened in the village since the day of Bassem's arrest. Bassem teared up again when they said good-bye. Waed didn't. "I was stronger than him!" he told me.

Rushdie's death came less than two weeks later. Mohammad Ataallah was in prison with Bassem at the time. I saw him just before he left for Rome. He too had changed. Over the summer, even at his most serious he had always seemed on the verge of laughter. Now even when he was laughing he looked like he was about to cry. He had been arrested on the night of October 10. He was at home, in bed. He had posted a song on Facebook,

he said, "a sad song," and gone to sleep. Two hours later his mother opened
the door to his room and told him the soldiers had come for him. He was
at Ofer, lying on his bunk, when he heard about Rushdie on the TV news.
Bassem was in the next cell over. They saw each other the following day
when they were let out for recreation. "He hugged me," Mohammad said,
"and we both started crying." From inside Ofer, cut off from everything,
the news felt unreal, like a terrible dream.

IT RAINED ON AHED'S BIRTHDAY. All the way from Ramallah, the fog was
thick. The house was cold despite the fire in the woodstove, and everyone
kept on their coats indoors. Salam with his big mop of hair was wearing a
thick black scarf, and little Hamoudi, Naji's youngest son, had his gloves
on. Nariman had relented. Ahed's cake was drizzled with chocolate and
frosted with a sugary yellow-haired Cinderella in headphones. Paper plates
of marshmallows, chips, and cookies did the rounds, and bottles of soda to
wash it all down. The birthday girl wore a giant, radiant smile. Nariman
filmed the festivities with the same camera she had used to record her
brother's shooting. Irene, who had come from Jerusalem, blew bubbles at
the kids, her laughter filling every corner of the room. The activist Abir
Kopty had come from Nazareth and brought a bag of Israeli chips. None
of the kids would touch them until Waed began tossing them in the air
and catching them in his mouth like a seal and the younger kids did their
best to imitate him and Salam was laughing madly and one smile after
another stole across Ahed's face. Salam covered his eyes and began counting aloud and the other kids understood the cue and began scrambling for
hiding places—between the sofas, under the coffee table, beneath the
kitchen counter. Irene, who was taller than any of the men in the room,
slipped behind the curtains. Abir, who is short, hid in plain sight. Nariman
stood on one arm of the couch in her slippers, her ankle still bandaged,
filming the chaos as Salam charged around the room and the children,
shrieking, scattered.

———

THE ROOM WAS LIT by a single fluorescent bulb hanging from the ceiling. Sitting on the low couch, his knees nearly to his ribs, Bahaa smoked cigarette after cigarette. He had been there too that day, above the carob tree. He filled in some of the gaps in Nariman's memory and confirmed what Waed had told me. After a few minutes he was squeezing his eyes shut to keep the tears from falling. He spoke slowly, one shaky phrase at a time. Grief spills into grief—it is one country, with no borders—and before I noticed the shift, he was not talking about Rushdie anymore but about Mustafa, about how the first time Mustafa was released from prison, he and Bahaa stayed up talking until three in the morning, sitting outside, just next to the door. "Until today," Bahaa said, "whenever I leave the house I can't look to that side."

"Even if my brother died," he said, "I wouldn't be as heartbroken as I was over Mustafa's death." His voice was breaking. "When I walk around the village, every corner, every house, every street, every little nook is a story or a joke that we shared. When I go to Ramallah, I remember every street we walked down, every store we went into, every coffee we drank." He wadded at his eyes with a tissue and lit another a cigarette. Before Mustafa's funeral, Bahaa went on, an attendant at the mosque had let him inside so he could be alone with Mustafa's body. His tears were rolling freely now. "Take me with you," he had said to his friend. "Why are you leaving me behind?"

When they started the demonstrations, Bahaa said, "we knew we would face losses." He couldn't have guessed that it would hurt so much. But Fridays had gained in importance for him. "If you stop in the middle," he said, "you become ridiculous. You're just trading in their blood."

SOME OF THE ACTIVISTS who organized the March 15 protests ended up in Nabi Saleh. Not living there, but driving from Ramallah every Friday and coming back for weddings, funerals, and holidays, showing up in court when people from the village were arrested and in the hospital when they were hurt, often getting arrested and injured themselves. Nabi Saleh became their second home, the Tamimis their extended family. Several of them became my friends. One was a woman who I know would not want me to use her real name, whom I have been calling Shireen. She was born into Jerusalem's elite, went to university abroad, had a good job in Ramallah that afforded her a level of independence—a car, an apartment of her own—still rare among Palestinian women. Her nails were always manicured. Their color usually matched her clothes. For the first year that I knew her she was always in and out of surgery: her neck had been broken at one protest, her foot at another. Her doctors told her that if she continued to put herself at risk she would almost certainly end up paralyzed. She ignored them and kept going to Nabi Saleh Friday after Friday, often in her neck brace, spitting curses at the soldiers, never hanging back, always in the front lines. Other activists were careful tacticians, intellectuals, theoreticians of revolt. Shireen could be extremely eloquent, but she was none of those things. As far as politics went, she seemed never to suffer a moment's doubt. She was impatient, furious, ebullient in her commitment.

Only once did I make Shireen sit down with me for a formal interview. She talked about the need to rebuild what she called the "culture of resistance" that she remembered experiencing during the Second Intifada, but which had since evaporated, replaced by a dull consumerist individualism, by "this illusion that if I forget about Palestine, build a career, take a loan, buy a car, build a house, watch *Arab Idol* on TV, it'll all be okay; that if they're not raiding *your* house, you're okay." In a culture constructed around a shared goal of liberation, she said, "my house is your house and your son is my son and if they kill me today they will kill you tomorrow." That, she said, is what kept her going back to Nabi Saleh.

Shireen said one other thing that I couldn't get out of my head for a while. "All people," she said, "are born free, and all people squirm for freedom." I thought of her a few days later, when some friends and I walked into a pet shop in Ramallah. Dogs were chained outside in the sun. They lay on the concrete, their fur matted, too thirsty even to pant. Inside were the usual sad bunnies in squalid cages. There were a few rare animals too. I heard they once had a baby kangaroo. That day there was something called a coati, a fluffy, ring-tailed creature caught somewhere between the kingdoms of bears and raccoons. Its cage was only an inch or two wider than the animal was long, just large enough for it to turn around in place, which it did, desperately and endlessly spinning in the same constricted orbit. There it was, squirming to be free, struggling to move in the only path available to it. Which happened, for the time being, to be a circle.

THE NEXT FRIDAY the wind was against us. I was laughing, congratulating myself for having outrun the skunk truck and dodged its spray when a foul and misty gust blew hard against my back. The smell would eventually wash out. The gas, though, was a problem. The soldiers could lob their grenades almost anywhere and the wind did the rest, pushing it straight uphill in our direction. I ducked into the gas station and found Abu Yazan bent coughing beside the ice cream freezer. Outside, Nariman leaned against a wall with her eyes squeezed shut. I spent a few minutes talking with a young Israeli named Renen Raz. He wore an "ANARCHY IS FOR LOVERS" T-shirt, a black hoodie, and a keffiyeh. He had been arrested in Nabi Saleh five times, he told me proudly, and the Shabak had just called to invite him in for a chat. Later, a soldier tossed a stun grenade at us and we ran behind Nariman's house to hide. Crouching there, waiting for the soldiers to move on, Renen told me about his childhood in a kibbutz barely a mile from the Gaza border. His parents, he said, were "right-wing Zionists, hard-core." They didn't talk to him anymore.

"That must be hard," I said.

"There are things that are harder," he answered. When they were still speaking to him, he said, his father once told him he hoped the Border Police would shoot him in the head.

It was a short day, and strangely calm despite it all. I remembered something Mohammad had said before he flew to Rome: "We are all still living the shock of Rushdie's death." The quiver in his voice wasn't the only proof. I sat on the hillside with Naji, his wife Boshra, a few others. The guys were throwing stones at the soldiers a couple of hundred feet beneath us. Someone had lit a fire for warmth. Naji had brought a cushion to sit on. Boshra talked about France. She, Manal, and Nariman had been invited for a lecture tour early in the fall. They had been in a different city every day for nearly a month. The schedule had been grueling, but their eyes all went a little gauzy when they talked about it. They found the country beautiful, the people warm and welcoming, but it was the food they kept coming back to. Nariman and Manal had enthused about the seafood, Boshra the meat—lamb and beef at almost every meal. Bilal, who had recently gone to Sweden, joined us for a bit, sitting on a boulder, his camera resting on his thigh. Mahmoud picked his way between the rocks carrying a thermos full of coffee and a stack of plastic cups. Beneath us, the soldiers were shooting at the guys. Poppies shivered in the wind. The guys were slinging stones. We sat, sipping coffee, until three salvos of grenades landed on the hill a few meters down and the gas crept up and sent us running.

IT WAS FOGGY AGAIN. On the drive from Ramallah I couldn't see much more than the occasional tree silhouetted against the gray. The wall outside Bassem and Nariman's yard was strung with flags: yellow Fatah banners and red, green, white, and black Palestinian ones. Twelve more hung from the house and there was another on the pigeon coop. The kids were dressed up: Waed in new shoes, Ahed with her hair in a black bow. Salam had a fresh bowl cut. Naji and Boshra arrived and soon Jonathan Pollak was spinning a giggling Abu Yazan on his shoulders.

By six p.m., the fog had swallowed Halamish. Nariman's older brothers had arrived and so had Manal's brother, and Janna and Nawal, and Bilal's two younger sons. Nariman was crouching in a side room, laughing at the two photographers—one Israeli, one American—competing for shots in the doorway as she spread oil, sautéed onions, and sumac over flatbreads. A few more Israelis appeared and some of the activists from Ramallah. Bilal came with his daughter Rand and his son Osama, and Bahaa showed up with Mustafa's eldest brother. Hamoudi darted around the house, snapping rubber bands against people's hands and thighs. Waed bit Ahed on the ear. Through the fog I could make out the green light on the minaret and a yellow one beneath it on the watchtower but I couldn't see much else. Every time a car pulled into the yard, Salam went running for the door.

At a little after seven, we all piled into cars—twenty-five of us crammed into three little compacts—and headed for the center of the village. We waited in the fog, pacing, talking, smoking. The light above the *diwan* reflected off the mist. Waed was dancing in place, shadowboxing whoever came near him. Finally, a car pulled up, a dark Ford sedan with one working headlamp. Waed ran to open the door. Bassem stepped out. Everyone fell silent. He hugged his son, kissed each of his cheeks in turn and then his forehead. Ahed was next. Then Naji. The silence billowed, too large for the square to hold. Everyone waited their turn, stepping forward one by one for a brief embrace and a kiss until Bassem, his eyes gleaming in the ghostly light, had greeted all of them. He walked around behind the mulberry tree to the cemetery until he reached the one fresh grave. Rushdie's. Bassem looked thinner than he had the last time I had seen him. Perhaps a little grayer. He closed his eyes, held his hands open at his sides, and muttered a quick, quiet prayer. He did the same at his sister's grave, then Mustafa's, then his mother's. Salam stood beside him, his fists filled with potato chips.

Back at the house, Bassem looked dazed. Joy, sorrow, and exhaustion were fighting in his eyes, and whenever I glanced over a different one was winning. He kissed all the children and everyone he hadn't already embraced in the square. He gave Nariman a long hug and held her face between his palms. Only Abu Yazan was missing. He had fallen asleep in the back bedroom. Bassem tried to wake him, but he couldn't be roused. Nariman broke down in Bassem's arms and rushed outside to hide her tears. Everyone ate.

Waed looked so happy I thought he might float off. He stuck close to his father's side, his arm on his shoulder, reminding him that when they had seen each other last, it was Bassem who had cried. "I was *strong*," he said, and laughed.

Outside, the young men couldn't keep up the solemnity for long. They started with little Hamoudi, tossing him back and forth between them and then high in the air above the yard. Soon Hamoudi's giggles turned to howls and they took pity and set him down and grabbed another slightly older boy named Ahmad and threw him back and forth and up like a kicking and wriggling ball. Shireen and Irene stood behind them, laughing while the guys put Ahmad down and worked their way up to a full-grown and bearded American photographer, throwing him and catching him then setting him down too and taking turns tossing one another into the night sky as high as they could, hooting and shouting in the small circle carved out of the fog by the harsh fluorescent light above the door.

INTERLUDE

OCCUPATION CABINET
OF CURIOSITIES

EXHIBIT THREE: STAGECRAFT

The Muqata'a

Later, in Ramallah, I would walk or drive past the *muqata'a* almost every day. From the sidewalk and the street I would see as much of the place as any ordinary person can. Which was not much. The *muqata'a* was a forbidding presence. Mainly I saw the high stone wall that surrounded the compound and Abbas's official residence. Above it I could make out the top floors of the drab, modern buildings within, which, like the guard towers along the wall and the wall itself, were faced with smooth white stone. In the driveway and all around the periphery of the compound, members of Abbas's Presidential Guard stood watch in red berets, Kalashnikovs slung over their shoulders. They were taller and fitter and looked better fed than any other members of the Palestinian security forces. As well they should. They were equipped and specially trained by the United States, which had poured an average of $100 million a year into the Palestinian security services since 2007. Hamas had won the Palestinian legislative elections in 2006, and the U.S., with the approval of Israel's internal intelligence service, began to support the creation of an elite gendarmerie answerable only to Abbas.* "One authority, one gun," as U.S. lieutenant general Keith Dayton would later put it.

A decade ago, most of the *muqata'a* was rubble, laid waste by Israeli tanks during the Second Intifada and the IDF's long siege. Only a small segment of the concrete structure in which Arafat spent his final years still stands, hidden in the interior of the compound. But however hard the new buildings and high walls may work to replace that past with a slick and seemingly impregnable modernity, the *muqata'a* survives as a sort of stone palimpsest of eighty years of colonial and now neocolonial rule. Its core—the concrete structure in which Arafat was confined—was originally erected by the British, specifically by an Irish Protestant policeman named Charles Tegart. England's colonial adventures began closer to home, and, between stints in Calcutta, Tegart had worked as an intelligence officer for the British crown during the Irish war for independence. He later proved so talented at crushing anticolonial insurgencies in India that he was granted a knighthood. His efforts there were not universally appreciated—Tegart survived no fewer than six assassination attempts and developed a reputation for rough methods ("torture" would be the contemporary appellation) that would follow him to Palestine, where he arrived in 1937, one year into the Arab Revolt. In Palestine, Tegart sketched out an early draft of what would become the basic infrastructure of Israel's occupation: he militarized the colonial constabulary, constructed the region's first border wall along what is now the Israeli-Lebanese frontier, erected pillbox guard towers along the roads, and built sixty-two reinforced-concrete forts, each designed to withstand a month-long siege.

This was the architecture of domination: unapologetically practical structures designed to protect and sustain an occupying army stationed amid a populace that did not want it there. After 1948, many of the Tegart forts that fell inside Israel remained police stations for the new Jewish state.

---

*The other branches of the PA security forces fall under the authority of the Ministry of the Interior.

Some became museums. Others were abandoned. One became a secret IDF prison and interrogation site known only as Facility 1391.* Tegart, who had imported waterboarding to Palestine and in addition to his forts constructed a series of so-called Arab Investigation Centres, would have approved. The forts that fell in the West Bank turned into military bases and bureaucratic centers for the Jordanian authorities. Israel took them over after the 1967 war. The old British police station into which the settlers who founded Halamish first moved, which is now the nucleus of the IDF base outside Nabi Saleh, where I was briefly detained, was originally a Tegart fort.

So was Ramallah's *muqata'a*—the word just means "district" or "division," a node of administrative power—which soon became the regional headquarters for the occupation authorities, who added a jail and military court. It was there that Bassem's sister died, and there that he was repeatedly imprisoned during and after the First Intifada. These transitions are shockingly smooth: when Israeli troops pulled out of Palestinian cities as part of the Oslo agreement, control of the compound passed to the Palestinian Authority. Briefly in 1995, the *muqata'a* was opened to the public. "There was such euphoria then, and a sense of pride that the prison and torture chambers where so many had suffered had been liberated," recalled the writer Raja Shehadeh. "I remember looking forward to the day when former detainees would accompany young Palestinians and describe to them the bitter history of our embattled nation."

But that day would not arrive. On a later visit to the *muqata'a*, Shehadeh was distressed to find that the PA had left the military court and the prison intact, adding "an annex to accommodate the activities of the new regime." None of those structures would survive the Intifada. After Arafat's death in 2004, the PA announced plans to construct, from the wreckage of the *muqata'a*—in the words of Abbas's then chief of staff—"a new headquarters

---

*Prisoners held at the site, the existence of which Israel denies, report being kept blindfolded in blackened cells. One former prisoner there was told he was on a submarine, another that he was "on the moon." Others have alleged less whimsical varieties of torture, including rape.

for the President where he can meet world leaders and deal with them in a modern and civilized manner." There would be no room for "bitter history," or for any suggestion that past humiliations had leaked into the present. The new *muqata'a* would be a heavily fortified stage on which the rituals of statehood might be convincingly performed. Like the legislature that hadn't sat for years and the government ministries that depended on Israeli permission for even the most trivial official acts, it was part of the show. The idea, said one official quoted by the scholar Linda Tabar, was to build something grand enough that it "creates the impression that we have a state." Appropriately, the refurbished *muqata'a* was built with funds provided by foreign donors. "These civilized spaces," Tabar wrote, "are the antithesis of what the Palestinian liberation movement has struggled for; they amount to sites of defeat where being modern is collapsed into accepting the very modes of domination Palestinians have struggled against."*

---

*I might have quoted Elias Khoury here instead: "The end of a revolution's the ugliest thing there is. A revolution is like a person. It gets senile and rambles and wets itself."

4.

THE ANT AND THE SWEET

Ramallah, Nabi Saleh, Haifa, Acre

There is a point at which methods devour themselves.

—FRANTZ FANON

On my first evening back in Ramallah, I walked down to al-Manara, the central square. Four months had passed. It was early June and the nights were cool and one lane of the Jerusalem road had been closed to traffic and lined with neat rows of white plastic chairs. *Arab Idol* was on, and the show was being screened from the giant digital billboard on the roof of a four-story building across from the main produce market. A Palestinian was competing, a handsome young Gazan named Mohammad Assaf. The story went that it had taken Assaf two days to cross the border into Egypt and when he arrived in Cairo the doors to the hotel where auditions were being held had already been shut. No stranger to closed doors, he leapt a wall, snuck in, and since then had been steadily advancing round by round. There were only two rounds left before the final. The seats slowly began to fill. Assaf was singing, a keffiyeh draped over his blazer. The old woman to my left began to weep. "No one has had to be as patient as we have," she said. "Our hearts are always bleeding."

Two weeks later, on the night of the finals, the square was packed to bursting. They were broadcasting the show outside the *muqata'a* too, and Irsal Street was crammed all the way there. I didn't even try to push my way through. There were thousands if not tens of thousands—as if every young man from every village and refugee camp within an hour's drive of Ramallah had come in for the show. There were guys on the stone lions around the fountain in the middle of al-Manara, guys climbing flagpoles and lampposts and trees. Every rooftop was full, and every window ledge. The awnings of the shops were sagging with the weight of the young men balanced precariously atop them. The moment arrived. The winner was about to be announced. The crowd went silent. Then Mohammad Assaf fell prostrate to the stage and all of al-Manara roared. Everyone was in tears, shouting, clapping, chanting, embracing one another. It was as if the occupation had ended, as if the checkpoints and prisons had suddenly evaporated, as if all the beloved dead had risen and returned. For hours, until two the next morning, fireworks lit the skies and the streets echoed with car horns, whistles, shouts. A Palestinian, for once, had won.

TEN DAYS BEFORE Mohammad Assaf's victory, I went back to Nabi Saleh. There was a new, bright pink Bank of Palestine ATM outside the gas station, and somebody had stenciled the word MUQAWAMEH ("resistance") in red paint on the sign at the entrance to the village. Bassem's house had been transformed. The beginnings of a porch had been laid outside the room in which I had stayed the previous summer. In the front of the house more elaborate plans were under way: low stone walls had been partially constructed outside the kitchen, and another area just beyond it had been graded for a patio. The pigeon coop lay in rubble. Bassem seemed a different man from the one I had last seen. We had said good-bye the day after his release from prison. In the wake of Rushdie's killing and Waed's brief imprisonment, he had appeared equally weighed down by sorrow and eager to begin again, his optimism cut by a more intimate awareness of how much there was to lose. In the months since, the momentum that had then appeared to be building had collapsed. Bab al-Shams, it turned out, was not the beginning of a new stage of resistance, but the climax of an old one. Everything goes in cycles. I was learning this: events would gather speed before they crashed or ran out of fuel and stuttered to a halt. From a distance, it was easy to mistake velocity for hope. Even in the thick of things it was. But the wheel kept turning and now all of Palestine was in a trough, the popular resistance back in its old rut. Except for Mohammad Assaf, nothing new had been happening for months.

Bassem was cheerful, though, almost lighthearted, as if a burden had been lifted from him. He had just returned from a lecture tour of France, his first trip outside of Palestine. He had been impressed by how structured European life was. You could make a plan a whole week in advance, a month even. At home, it was hard to plan for the next afternoon. But Bassem was disturbed, too, by the racism and inequality he had witnessed, and by the shapes of people's lives, their haste and busyness, the rigidity of life under a more totalizing form of capitalism. "There is no time to be human," he said.

We walked with young Mohammad Ataallah over to Naji's and from there to the house where Mohammad lived with his father, Abu Hussam. Bashir came by. We sat outside and drank coffee and then tea. Everyone was feeling good. Mohammad told me a story: A man puts out a sweet, a piece of candy. An ant comes to investigate. The sweet is too heavy for the ant to carry alone, so it leaves and returns with more ants. While it's gone, the man takes the sweet away. The ants look around for a few moments, then, finding nothing, file off back to their homes. The man replaces the sweet and the same ant comes out again. It races home to get the other ants, but once again, before the ants return, the man hides the sweet. Deceived a second time, the ants turn on the first ant and kill it.

Mohammad gripped my wrist. "Is it true?" he asked.

I asked who the ant was. Everyone laughed.

Bassem explained: Mohammad had told him this story when they were in prison and claimed he had actually seen the experiment performed. Later he said he had seen it on YouTube, but now, no matter how much he searched, he couldn't find the video.

Again they all laughed: the story about the ant and the sweet had itself become the sweet, and Mohammad had become the ant. The mockery hadn't killed him yet. But this meta-level, funny as it was, was not the point Mohammad had been trying to make. The point was not so funny.

The sun began to sink. Bassem walked me to the gas station and waited with me there for a taxi. "We are in a corner," he confessed.

THE NEXT FRIDAY, the soldiers used a drone. Every now and again I could make out a distant white dot in the sky, but mainly I heard the thrum of it, a throbbing whine that seemed to be coming from inside my own head. There couldn't have been too much to see from up there. Only five or six of the guys turned out. The demo was small and ended early. On the hillside, Renen, the Israeli activist, told me about his cat. "She is very aggressive," he said, grinning. He showed me his arms, a mess of scratches. A loud bang echoed beneath us. The soldiers were firing rubber-coated bullets. Renen said he wanted to study veterinary medicine. A Border Police officer kicked Bilal, bloodying his shin. There were soldiers above us too, firing gas from the top of the hill. We scrambled over the rocks as gas canisters rained down around us. "If it has no fur or hair you know it's not a mammal," Renen explained. He preferred reptiles. We rested. No one was even bothering to try to reach the spring. More gas fell. We ran again. The dry brush was catching fire all around us. A giant lizard scampered across a boulder, stopping Renen short. "Yay!" he shouted, but the lizard darted off and the gas caught up to us and soon we were bent, coughing and spitting, staring down through bleary eyes at the sheep dung and the last of the spring flowers.

Bassem and I met in Ramallah a few days later at the usual café. He was about to leave for Amman, he said, to see Nizar Tamimi, who had been arrested with him for Chaim Mizrahi's murder and released from prison in the Gilad Shalit deal. I asked him about the protests shrinking. "It's good," he said. He seemed to mean it. There was less risk, he said. "The bad thing is that we did not do this as a decision." The guys simply weren't coming anymore, and when they did they went home early. "We had no single goal," Bassem said—no wall to stop, or road to open. Just a message to spread, symbols to disseminate. I had heard Bassem say it again and again: the spring is only the face of the occupation. But avoiding concrete goals meant that they had no clear accomplishments, nothing anyone could point to that made it all worthwhile. Too many losses had piled up—not just Rushdie and Mustafa but injuries, arrests, paychecks lost to prison, bail to pay. And rumors had been spreading, Bassem said, about money and women, the usual sort of petty talk that tears both families and movements apart: that behind closed doors visiting foreigners handed out money, that unseemly things occurred when foreigners stayed in people's homes, or when people from the village traveled abroad. He swatted the thought away.

"It's okay," he said. "Sometimes I can't believe we have made it this far." What mattered, he said, as if he were trying to convince himself, was that the message still got out.

THE NEXT FRIDAY, Nariman was arrested. It was a sad show from beginning to end. Bassem had left for Jordan. The guys had all gone to a soccer game in a neighboring village. As everyone gathered beneath the mulberry tree and waited for prayer to let out, Nariman slipped off to the cemetery and kneeled before her brother's grave. A few minutes later, the marchers cut down the hill toward the spring. The few foreign solidarity activists who had shown up all hung back at the gas station. Nariman yelled, exasperated: "Internationals!" No one followed. The soldiers started shooting gas. Not one stone had yet been thrown. I was a few yards in front of Nariman when she got caught in a cloud of gas, blinded as the canisters fell around her. Naji and his brother-in-law Iyad shouted directions at her ("Straight!" "Right!" "Shells!") until she emerged, her eyes squeezed shut, in the open air again.

Eight soldiers were spread out at the bottom of the hill. Nariman kept walking. Only two activists, both of them from outside the village, joined her. The soldiers stopped her and told her to leave. She refused. The rest of us waited from a safe distance, watching. I sat on a rock with Mohammad, Naji, and Jonathan. More soldiers appeared a few meters above us. They were coming up from below as well, running toward us. Soon we were sprinting over the flank of the hill. Only later, sitting in the shade beneath Naji's house, did Jonathan get a phone call and learn that Nariman and two others had been arrested for the sole apparent crime of refusing to run.

For hours, we sat around at Naji and Boshra's. Everyone stared at their phones, talking idly about Egypt—the anniversary of Mohammad Morsi's inauguration as president was two days away, and mass protests had been called to demand his resignation. In Egypt too, things moved in cycles. Or perhaps it was a spiral. Iyad stared out the window.

"No *jeish*," he said, using the Arabic word for "army." "It's boring."

A French student who had been staying in Nabi Saleh asked him what Palestinians would do when the occupation ends.

"We will fight each other," Iyad answered. "For a little while. Then we'll have to find something new."

I suggested football. Out the window I could see tear gas floating in low drifts by the tower. The guys had come back from their game. Boshra served dinner. We could hear a truck engine roaring on the road. "Skunk," someone said, but everyone was eating, and no one got up to look.

ON JULY 1, Mohammad Assaf played a free concert in Ramallah. As a gesture of gratitude to his fans, he had promised to play in Bethlehem, Nablus, and Hebron too. The streets in the center of town were packed, but I missed the show. After three days in prison, Nariman was being released from Ofer, in Beitunia, on the western outskirts of the city. Traffic was bad and by the time I arrived she was already out, standing in the dirt parking lot surrounded by a small group of friends. It was a surreal scene: the razor wire coiled in the dark on the edge of the lot, the long shadows cast by the harsh spotlights around the prison. Nariman was giddy with a strange, manic joy.

"I am very, very strong!" she said.

The concert was a bust. There were no seats and no order to the throng and the sound system could barely be heard above the crowd. Assaf—the Dream of Palestine, they called him—played three songs and left the stage after less than half an hour. The rumor was that PA security forces, fearing a riot, cut the show short. That victory too had turned to defeat. Or at least gone slightly sour. The free concerts in Nablus and Hebron were canceled. A week later, Assaf played in Ramallah again, at the Grand Park Hotel. Tickets went for 450 shekels, or about $125, about a third of the average Palestinian monthly wage.

SITTING ON the sofa with his hands on his knees and his long legs crossed beneath him, tall Bahaa looked like a king crab, or like a cartoon of one with pale blue and very human eyes in an almost painfully sensitive face. He was chain-smoking again. Irene and I had arrived at his house in the middle of a crisis. Bahaa's brother had been having seizures and had just lost feeling in his left arm and leg. His little niece also suffered seizures, and the family didn't have money for a doctor. There was good news too. Bahaa was engaged, or almost engaged. It was a very Palestinian love story.

He had met a girl while out with some friends in Ramallah and had begun courting her over the phone. They fell in love. Her parents were dead and two of her three brothers were in prison. All three had been arrested together, Bahaa said, and each had told the Israelis he was the guilty one so that his brothers could go free. They released one brother, sentenced one to fourteen years and the other to life. Bahaa called the first brother to ask for his beloved's hand. He said he would have to consult with the others. A few days later, Bahaa's phone rang. It was the second brother, the one doing fourteen years. He was calling from prison in the Negev. He asked what Bahaa wanted with his sister. Bahaa said he wanted to marry her. "He said, 'You know that she's graduating from Birzeit University and you haven't even graduated from high school.'" (Bahaa worked in a warehouse in Ramallah at the time. He didn't want to talk about his job.) "I said, 'Yes, but this is love.'" In the end, the second brother told him that he couldn't make a decision without talking to the third brother, but the third brother was in solitary confinement, so Bahaa would have to wait.

"I'm still waiting," Bahaa said, smiling. "It's been four or five months."

I asked why I hadn't seen him at the demos. Bahaa let out a long, theatrical sigh. He wanted to start at the beginning. In what was now remembered as the first demonstration, a few of the guys and some friends of theirs, students from Birzeit, decided to walk together to the spring. "It was all very spontaneous," he said. The settlers blocked them. Soldiers arrived. When the clash had ended, they decided to come back the next week, and to keep coming back. His point was that it started with the guys, not with any of the people now in the leadership. Then came the arrests. First Mustafa and his brothers, then Bahaa, and then in 2011, Naji, Bassem, and many others. The problems started then, he said—of all the people sent to prison, only a few were lauded in the media and "called defenders of human rights and all kinds of ludicrous things." He didn't mention names, but he could only have been talking about Bassem. Funds were raised to cover some people's bail, while others had to scramble and borrow. Resentments were born.

The villagers had begun meeting, forming committees, dividing roles, "but what ended up happening was that they took control of everything." *They* meaning the elders. The guys were taking the biggest risks, Bahaa complained, but it was the older generation who stood in front of the cameras and accepted awards from NGOs. "Then travel became an issue," Bahaa said. A few members of a few families were invited on speaking tours to the United States and Europe. For Palestinians hemmed in by the occupation, these were almost unimaginable opportunities. But the elders didn't consult anyone about who got to go and who stayed home. They just went. Delegations started arriving—sometimes students, foreign activists, or political tourists, but also diplomats and representatives of major NGOs. "We didn't know what kind of support they got," Bahaa said, "if it was financial support or something less material." It might have all been innocent, he said. The point was that no one knew: it all took place behind closed doors.

And no matter what else happened, the routine remained the same, Friday after Friday, the same ritualized march to the spring. "Routine can be murderous," Bahaa said. He had seen a BBC documentary in which the reporters spent time with the soldiers in the base at Halamish. "I realized there were people sitting at desks and all they're doing is thinking about how to kill the demonstrations." The villagers had to be just as smart, but even after Rushdie's death, he said, "it's still the same story, the same thing over and over again."

No formal decision was made. The guys just stopped turning out. A little less than three months earlier, Bahaa had decided to withdraw. Most of the elders stopped speaking to him. "Only Nariman still talks to me," he said. "She has a pure heart." More recently, the guys had begun meeting with the elders to see if the situation could be mended. "It's like digging into a mountain with a needle," Bahaa said. For now, he said, "I'd rather just sit at home."

It must, I knew, have been a painful decision to make. I told him so. He shrugged. There were other ways to resist, he said. He had written two songs and a play, he told me, about Rushdie and Mustafa. He was very proud of them. The village's children performed the play on the fortieth day after Rushdie's death. He wanted it to be filmed so that it could be screened abroad when people from the village traveled, "so that the world understands," he said. Bilal recorded it, but it rained that day and almost no one showed up to the performance.

BEFORE LEAVING THE VILLAGE, we dropped in on Nariman and found her struggling to change the lightbulb above the door. I stood on a chair and did it for her. The ecstasy of her release appeared to have worn off. She had been in court at Ofer since early that morning and had just made it home. Bassem was still in Jordan. She had to go back to Ofer tomorrow for another long day of waiting. She seemed tired, depleted. Boshra came by. Irene's car wasn't in the driveway and Boshra, surprised to see us, asked if we had driven. The car was at Bahaa's house, Irene explained.

Boshra turned to me. "Why did you interview Bahaa?" she asked, and before I could answer, added, "He turned against the Resistance."

THE WHEEL KEPT TURNING. Bassem came home. It was late June 2013. More than ten million people marched in Cairo to demand that Mohammad Morsi step down from the presidency. The Egyptian revolution appeared to have reawoken. Bassem was in awe at the scope of the protests. If it could happen there, why not here? A good question. It didn't last. A popular uprising became cover for an old-fashioned coup: the Egyptian military deposed Morsi and suspended the constitution. Five days later, soldiers mowed down 51 Muslim Brotherhood members as they knelt in prayer in Cairo. At the end of the month, they slaughtered another 120 Morsi supporters, and two weeks later killed more than 800 in a single day. With its revolutionary energies exhausted, Egypt was stuck with a more brutal regime than the one it had originally risen against. Meanwhile the death toll in Syria had climbed over 100,000. But U.S. secretary of state John Kerry had for weeks been caught in a loop between Jerusalem and Ramallah, trying to persuade Netanyahu and Abbas to commit to a fresh round of talks. Even the attempt was mildly embarrassing. *The Washington Post*'s editorial board posed the question: "What . . . could possibly possess Mr. Kerry to so intently pursue such an unpromising initiative, even as the United States refuses to exert leadership on crises of paramount importance to the region?" Netanyahu's deputy defense minister Danny Danon told *The Times of Israel* that the governing coalition was "staunchly opposed to a two-state solution and would block the creation of a Palestinian state if such a proposal ever came to a vote." Netanyahu, he said, was playing along only because he knew no actual agreement was in reach. Kerry, with a stubborn optimism that could be mistaken for arrogance, or for blindness, did not heed the warning.

I went to Nabi Saleh on a Thursday. Three soldiers stood outside the base in Halamish with a 50 mm machine gun on a tripod. The village, though, was calm. I got out of the taxi at the gas station and found Salam and Abu Yazan sitting beneath a fig tree, their faces and hands sticky and almost black. Salam called my name and handed me a plump, soft fig. The last time I had seen Abu Yazan was in the hospital. He had been hit in the thigh with a rubber-coated bullet. I asked him how his leg was. "Good," he said, and almost smiled.

Ramadan had begun. We ate dinner outside on the half-built new patio as soon as the sun sank and the call sounded from the mosque. "God is great," giggled Salam, and lifted a glass of water to his lips. I asked Bassem if he had heard the news—Abu Mazen, as Abbas was known, had rejected Kerry's proposal for talks because Netanyahu was categorically refusing to freeze settlement construction. The negotiations were off. "Good," Bassem said. I asked him about the guys' withdrawal from the demonstrations. He was at times dismissive, at times defensive, at times contrite. The guys wanted a larger role, he said, but they weren't willing to put the work in. "They are like children," he said. "They have no strategic way of thinking." They complained about people traveling abroad, he said, but the invitations came for specific people—for him or Nariman or Manal—and they couldn't just send anyone. Still, he knew he had made mistakes. "The responsibility is on our shoulders," he conceded. "We've become careless. But we are human beings too, and we are tired."

The next day's demonstration lasted less than an hour. Only four of the guys showed up. Sarit Michaeli, a researcher for the Israeli human rights group B'Tselem who a few months earlier had authored a lengthy report on the IDF's improper use of crowd-control munitions, was shot with a rubber-coated bullet at sufficiently close range that it lodged deep in the flesh of her thigh. I helped carry her up to Bilal's house, blood and pink muscle tissue clotting on the torn leg of her jeans. She kept filming the whole time, insisting she was fine. When the soldiers finally retreated, two of the guys walked down the road after them, swinging their slings.

"Enough," Bassem yelled.

They ignored him and kept walking, but only to clear what remained of the barricades from the road.

An hour or two later I checked the news on my phone. Netanyahu had agreed to the release of 104 Palestinian prisoners. Kerry had successfully lured Abbas back to the table. The talks were on again.

BAHAA HAD SAID one thing that stuck with me. The most important work, he said, had to happen inside the village. It had nothing to do with receiving diplomats or NGO officials or flying abroad to give talks and interviews. "It's like you," he said. "You come and you participate in the demonstrations and you take notes. You'll write about it in an article or a book, but this isn't your life. One day you're going to leave." He was right of course. Bahaa wasn't trying to call me out. He just meant that something had gotten lost, something important, and that the village's strategy, as Bassem and "the elders" had formulated it, had become a trap.

It was puzzling. Several times, I had heard Bassem and Irene talk after one dinner or another in Nabi Saleh about the years of organizing that had preceded the First Intifada, the volunteer work and the committees that had provided a loose, popular infrastructure for the uprising, that had given it its democratic character and made mass participation possible. He had talked about the importance of building strong connections between and within villages, about the kind of thankless grassroots organizing that slowly, almost invisibly pulls communities together and gives them the strength and motivation to resist an opponent that is in every calculable way far stronger. The PA made that harder now—it had replaced the old personal networks with bureaucratic hierarchies, and salaries to protect— but Bassem hadn't forgotten any of it. Nabi Saleh had been trying something different, using the shiny new tools the fates had provided: the Internet, the media, the ease of communications with the world outside that could instantly spread a message across continents that would have otherwise never made it past the checkpoints. Nabi Saleh's local dramas could—and did—become global affairs.

But tools are never innocent. They have agendas of their own. They move things in one direction or another and determine the shapes available to them. This time, perhaps without Bassem's noticing, they took over. Media insists on visibility, and on celebrity. Stories need protagonists. This one too. Unless people take pains to avoid it, campaigns that rely solely on media are almost inevitably antidemocratic. Their logic runs counter to the kind of slow and subterranean organizing that Bassem himself argued was needed in the West Bank. And of course I was complicit.

Nearly every time we spoke, Bassem said the same thing: it was okay that the demonstrations were shrinking. What mattered was the message. But the message, and his role as messenger, had eclipsed almost everything else. Bassem spent more time talking to me than to many of his neighbors. I don't know that he was wrong to do so. He had choices to make. None of them were easy. I had helped put Nabi Saleh, and his face—and Nariman's and Ahed's and Naji's and Boshra's and Bahaa's—on the cover of *The New York Times Magazine*. I don't say this boastfully, but it happened, and Bassem knew that by talking to me he could potentially, if all went well, be talking to thousands of people around the world. That was the gamble. It had its costs. Wrong or right, Bassem had become Mohammad's ant, promising sweets that no one could deliver. Nabi Saleh's resistance had always been in part a ritual performed for the world outside. The audience adored it, but the audience had a short attention span, and other commitments, and lived far, far away. And Bassem's neighbors three doors down were receiving a different message, one he had never intended to send.

THERE WAS ONE piece of news that summer that made almost everyone in Nabi Saleh happy. Among the names on the list of the 104 prisoners whom Netanyahu had been persuaded to release was that of Said Tamimi. Said was the only one of the three men from Nabi Saleh convicted for the killing of Chaim Mizrahi who, twenty years later, remained in jail. His freedom, Bilal told me one balmy Thursday evening, "is the only good thing we expect from the talks." They had been close, Bilal said, before Said's arrest. During the First Intifada, they had spent many nights distributing communiqués from the national leadership, pushing them through windows and leaving them at people's doors. They would paint slogans on walls and raise Palestinian flags from trees and electric poles, all under cover of darkness. In those days, Bilal said, "everyone was united," and not just politically. "During the olive harvest, when you finished your fields, you would help your neighbors with their trees. If you were building a house, the whole village would come out to build it with you." He missed it, he said. A lot.

But no one knew when Said would be allowed to return to the village: the prisoners were to be let out in batches spaced over the nine months during which Israel and the PA had agreed to parley their way toward a long-dreamed-of "final status agreement." On July 30, Saeb Erekat and Tzipi Livni, the chief Palestinian and Israeli negotiators, formally launched the new round of talks over an *iftar* meal at the State Department with Kerry and Martin Indyk, the former ambassador to Israel and onetime AIPAC functionary whom Kerry had appointed his special envoy for Middle East peace. Together, they broke the Ramadan fast with grouper, spelt risotto, and an apricot upside-down cake. It was, Kerry said, a "very, very special" moment.*

ALL WEEK, NARIMAN SAID, Abu Yazan had been talking about nothing but the coastal city of Acre, and the sea. He had never seen the open water, never swam in it, never heard the rhythm of the waves rolling in. In school

---

*Two nights earlier, the leftist Popular Front for the Liberation of Palestine, which since its foundation in the late 1960s had opposed the division of Palestine into two ethnically determined states, had staged a march to the *muqata'a* to protest the return to negotiations. PA riot police broke it up with clubs and arrested five protesters, three of them at the hospital, where they had gone to seek treatment for injuries sustained in the street.

his class had studied Acre with its ancient citadel and old Crusader walls rising from the blue Mediterranean—Abu Yazan wanted to dive from their heights into the water below. He had seen photos, had heard his mother sing Acre's praises. "You haven't lived," she told me once, "until you've seen Acre." It was barely a couple of hours' drive away, but it had been fifteen years since she and Bassem had been able to cross into Israel to make the trip. Before that, they had only been there once, in the first year of their marriage, with Boshra and Naji. "We all just cried," Nariman said, at the beauty of the places that had been lost to them.

But it was Ramadan, and every Friday the Israeli authorities were allowing some West Bank Palestinians—women and girls, plus men over forty and boys under seventeen—to cross through Qalandia checkpoint into Jerusalem to pray at the al-Aqsa. I met the Tamimis near the East Jerusalem bus station with three Israeli friends. The kids were almost frantic with excitement. They had skipped the mosque, and that week's demonstration in the village. We were going to the beach.

Ahed withdrew into her iPhone as soon as we got in the car, but her little brother's eyes took in every vehicle we passed and every detail of the landscape, much tamer here than in the rocky hills of the West Bank. I could almost hear Abu Yazan's brain buzzing from the backseat. He asked his mother if it was true that Napoleon couldn't conquer Acre because the city's fortifications were so strong. She told him that it was.

"Then how did the Jews take it?"

"They didn't," Nariman said. "I don't understand how we just gave it away."*

The highway widened to six lanes. "Hey!" Abu Yazan yelled. "I see the sea!" He didn't really. We were still miles from the coast.

---

*In 1946, only 50 of Acre's 13,560 inhabitants were Jewish. In May 1948, after an outbreak of typhus, days of shelling and siege, and the complete destruction of several nearby villages by the Haganah (the pre-state militia that later formed the core of the IDF), nearly 80 percent of Acre's Arab population fled, surrendering the city.

Abu Yazan spotted a sign for the turnoff to Nazareth. "Is there a sea in Nazareth?" he asked.

We passed the domed concrete silos of a power plant and then Haifa was in front of us, not the sea yet, but the shipyards and the trainyards and the rear slope of Mount Carmel. Then there it was, the sea, big and blue between the buildings of the port. Everyone was quiet.

"How beautiful our country is," said Nariman.

"This isn't our country," Abu Yazan said.

"Then whose is it?"

"It's the army's country."

But the kids would have to wait. We went first to the Bahá'í Gardens with their palm trees and groomed hedges and flowers spilling in terraced cascades down the western slope of Mount Carmel. Waed took photos of the flowers. Abu Yazan climbed everything that could be climbed. The sea gleamed beneath us in the distance. We headed for the cars. Bassem wanted to drop in on a friend. It was too much for Abu Yazan. He couldn't wait another moment. He howled and made a break for it, running into traffic. I darted after him and carried him squirming to the car.

Eventually we drove north to Acre. Abu Yazan raced up the stone steps of the seawall, scrambled over the rocks beyond the guardrail, and leaned out over the edge to watch the surf crash in below. I had to catch him by his shirt. We walked beneath the ancient arches of the old city and through its narrow alleys. It was 95 degrees and humid. The children ran screaming through the streets, splashing one another with bottled water, their shouts echoing off the thick stone walls. We watched the local kids jump from the seawall into the water thirty feet below. Waed and Abu Yazan peeled off their T-shirts and dared each other to make the leap, but in the end they didn't do it. Which was just as well, because neither of them could swim.

It was nearly six by the time we made it to the beach. The sun was still hot. It wasn't much of a beach, just a narrow strip of shore wedged between a row of four-story, Soviet-style apartment blocks and the sea. The sand was flecked with colorful shreds and shards of plastic, surf-degraded shopping bags and random junk in blue and green and pink. Before I stepped out of the car, the kids had bolted for the water. Bassem sat in the shallows and let the waves tickle his bare feet. Nariman lay on a blanket with the others. Abu Yazan, who had waded to the far end of the beach, was screaming.

"A fish!" he yelled. "A fish!"

I swam over, expecting whatever it was to be gone by the time I reached him. But the fish was still there, about six inches long and very dead, lolling with the current. Abu Yazan reached to grab it, got scared and pulled his hand back. I told him not to touch it, but Salam waded over, picked it up with a drifting shred of plastic bag and ran off to show his mother, swinging the fish by its tail.

The sun sank and the water turned white and then gold and then gray and flat as the sun disappeared behind the clouds. Bassem and Nariman walked alone down the shore. I had never seen them hold hands before. The sun was gone. Everyone else on the beach had left. The kids were in the water, shrieking and splashing and paddling about. It was dark by the time they slumped back to the cars, wet towels on their pale skinny shoulders, shivering a little and smiling still.

PART TWO

HEBRON

PROLOGUE

Ramallah, Wadi Naar, Hebron

And on the whole, nothing was clear.

—Viktor Shklovsky

L ate in July I got word that the army had raided a Hebron community center run by a group called Youth Against Settlements. I was in Ramallah at the time. I hurried to the bus station to meet Abir Kopty. Together, we caught a shared taxi south to Hebron, the largest city in the West Bank, and by far the strangest town I have ever visited. In kilometers or miles, the distance between Ramallah and Hebron is quite short, but Jerusalem lies between the two cities and the landscape of Palestine contains furrows and folds that cannot be seen on a map. Vehicles with green and white West Bank plates,* for instance, cannot cross into Israel—neither, generally speaking, can the human beings they transport—so Palestinian taxis, and all Palestinian vehicles wishing to travel from the center of the West Bank to the south, must take a long, roundabout, and treacherous route through Wadi Naar ("the Valley of Fire") in order to circumvent Jerusalem and the massive settlement bloc of Ma'ale Adumim.

---

*The occupation is color coded: Israeli vehicles, even when their owners live in West Bank settlements, are issued yellow tags. For easy differentiation, Israeli identity cards must also be carried in colored plastic sleeves: blue for Jerusalem residents and Israeli citizens, green for West Bankers, orange for Gazans.

Ramadan had not yet ended. It was late on a Thursday and two or three hours before the fast could be broken, so the streets were crowded, the drivers hungry and ill tempered. We idled for half an hour in the heat, the sky white with dust as we inched forward outside the Qalandia refugee camp, staring through the windows at the guard tower, which was blackened from Molotovs and burning tires, and at the iconic stretch of wall leading up to the checkpoint, the concrete painted with portraits of a young Yasser Arafat and of Marwan Barghouti clasping his shackled hands. Between the two beloved Fatah leaders—one dead, the other imprisoned—was a mural of a keffiyeh-masked figure launching a bright red heart from a slingshot. "FROM PALESTINE WITH LOVE," it said.

We couldn't cross into the smooth and dustless world on the other side of the checkpoint, so we turned and drove alongside the blast walls stenciled with the names and faces of prisoners and with ads for medical clinics and computer repairs. The traffic lightened, and the driver sped past the gated driveway to the settlement named simply "Adam" and the tarp-roofed shacks of the Bedouin encampment trapped between the settlement fence and the highway. We skirted the wall that separated the town of Hizme from the settlement high-rises of East Jerusalem and made a hard left to the east, though our destination was straight south. Ma'ale Adumim and its satellite settlements were in the way, garlanding the hilltops, and the wide circle that we drew around them took us nearly to Jericho. The hills became rocky and barren, no olive trees, just dusty brush. We passed another Bedouin village at the floor of a dry valley—a few shacks of patched aluminum siding, goat pens fenced off with wooden pallets. A truck had flipped over, its wheels in the air. The driver was standing beside his vehicle, anxious but intact. Two Israeli policemen stood warily by with M16s.

The taxi flew through Abu Dis, a chaos of open-air mechanics' shops, lighting shops, furniture shops. Beyond it was the checkpoint called Container, where a young man named Anas al-Atrash would be killed a few months later. Two green-bereted soldiers with machine guns stood beside the lonely tollboothlike structures, waving some cars on and stopping others. As we approached the checkpoint, the temperature in the minibus rose. It dropped again when the soldier waved us through. The driver sped down into Wadi Naar, the brakes squealing around steep and gut-wrenching curves. We drove through villages of blocky white stone buildings, a black water tank on each roof like a bellboy's cap, past quarries and stonecutters' yards and vineyards and fields of green cabbages and more red-roofed settlements behind barbed wire. How green they looked, how tall their trees!

At last we again hit Route 60, which, had we been free to drive straight through Jerusalem, would have had us in Hebron in forty-five minutes. (It had been twice that long since we had left Ramallah.) We passed the Gush Etzion roundabout, from which three Israeli teens would be kidnapped one year later, and the settlement car dealership and the settlement shopping center and the concrete watchtower outside it. We drove through orchards of dusty plum trees heavy with purple fruit. We passed the al-Aroub camp and the driveway to the agricultural college on the other side of the road where seven months earlier a twenty-one-year-old woman named Lubna Hanash had been shot in the head by Israeli soldiers as she waited for a taxi after class. The sunlight was slanted now and almost golden.

We passed through Halhul, where the bodies of the teenagers kidnapped from the roundabout would be found three weeks after they disappeared. There were more fig trees and more vineyards, a junkyard, a bright *arghile* store, crumbling homes of ancient stone, a man sitting in the shade behind a table piled with colorful stuffed animals, a father walking hand in hand with his son. "Oh my God," said Abir, and I looked up to see a sheep lying on its side on the asphalt beside a corner butcher shop, the butcher's rubber boot holding down the animal's head as blood gushed from its throat. We passed more shops selling watermelons and mattresses and birdcages both empty and full and car bumpers and floor tiles and bright yellow ladders and blue tanks of propane. The streets were clogged with Thursday evening traffic. We passed kebab shops and pizza and fried chicken joints, a book shop, banks and bakeries and jewelers and endless cell phone shops, furniture stores selling enormous, puffy, white and scarlet sofas, bridal shops selling enormous, puffy, white and lilac gowns. We had arrived. We were in Hebron.

WE MADE OUR WAY to Bab al-Zawiya, the neighborhood at the edge of the old city, and passed through the dingy beige shipping container that serves as a checkpoint at the blockaded end of Shuhada Street, taking off our belts and removing our keys and phones from our pockets, walking under the metal detector and handing our IDs to the soldiers on the other side. Hebron is nothing but other sides, like a single page you can keep flipping and flipping without ever finding the same text. If all of Palestine is marked by furrows and folds, realities that overlap but almost never intermingle, Hebron is a cartographic collapse, a mapmaker's breakdown. It is the only city in the West Bank in which Israeli settlers have established a permanent presence—hence the checkpoints, and the hundreds of soldiers stationed within the city. Hence the near-kaleidoscopic fragmentation, the cities inside the city and the cities inside them, and, above and beneath and between them all, in the cracks that separate each side from its other, the imagined cities of Hebron's inhabitants.

We found Issa Amro, the head and cofounder of Youth Against Settlements, waiting for us at the group's center, an old two-story stone house just below the peak of the hill known as Tel Rumeida, the oldest neighborhood in one of the oldest cities on the planet. The first human settlements in Tel Rumeida date back more than four thousand years, which makes the YAS house quite new, perhaps half a century old. It had been abandoned, taken over by the army and thoroughly trashed, abandoned again and briefly seized by settlers before Issa was able to procure a lease from its Palestinian owners, renovate the building, and turn it into a headquarters and gathering place for local antioccupation activists. Since then, his presence had been a constant source of irritation for his settler neighbors up the hill. They were not a timid bunch. An Israeli soldier was stationed at all hours just behind the house. Issa, an intense and dark-eyed man in his early thirties, had been arrested more times than he could count, most recently two and a half weeks earlier. Border Police officers had taken him to the police station outside the Ibrahimi mosque, also known as the Cave of the Patriarchs, where Abraham, Isaac, and Jacob and their wives Sarah, Rebecca, and Leah are said to be buried. They beat him so severely on his back that he had to be hospitalized.

His gait was a little stiff still and he couldn't sit for long, but Issa was in a strangely good mood. He told the story of the previous night's raids with a certain buzzing, bitter cheer that I would later recognize as his fallback disposition when anger or exhaustion didn't get the better of him. They came for the first time at around nine-fifteen, he said. He had been lying down and his brother Ahmad and a few of the other regulars were sitting on plastic chairs on the patio, smoking *arghile* and drinking tea. "Suddenly there were five soldiers here"—Issa pointed right—"and five soldiers there"—he pointed left—"and five soldiers from up there and another five from up over there, all pointing their guns at us. Oh my God!" He laughed. He noticed something strange: there were no magazines in their rifles. "It was a training, an exercise."

But training for what? The sole point was intimidation, Issa said, "to scare us." They broke an *arghile*, and left a mess. "Ahmad was very angry," Issa laughed again, "but only about the *arghile*." The soldiers returned to repeat the exercise about twenty minutes later, and then once more at around midnight. "It is hard," Issa said, "to be a training *object*." He bit off the last word and spat it out.

The sun had fallen. The call to prayer rang out, starting in one mosque and then another, and then, staggered by fractions of a second, in another mosque and another, so that the muezzins' cries seemed to bounce and ring out from all directions at once, near-cacophonous praise of the creator echoing stereophonically from one side of town to the other. We ate dinner on the concrete patio overlooking the white stone buildings of the old city and the patriarchs' tomb. I could spot one military base on the top of the next hill over to the south—a giant menorah lighting up the blast wall and guard tower beside it—and two more bases on the hills to the east and northeast.

The fireworks started about halfway through the meal. Results for the *tawjihi*, the matriculation exams that Palestinians take in their last year of high school, had just been released, and the families of every kid with a passing score had something to celebrate. Loud bangs were sounding from every direction at once. The sky was bright with bursts of pink and green and gold. Someone joked that it sounded like the Intifada all over again.

We were sitting in a wide circle on the patio. There were eight or ten of us—Abir and Irene, who had driven down from Jerusalem, myself, Issa, his brother, and four or five others. One man in particular left an impression, a proud and handsome fellow with a gray mustache. He wore a long and spotless white *galabiya*. His hair was perfect. He carried a cane, sat with his legs crossed, and seemed to exhale elegance with each drag on his cigarette. I was a few chairs away, beneath the window with my back to the wall. We were balancing plastic plates on our knees and eating *qatayef*—a Ramadan treat of pancakes stuffed with cheese or nuts and drenched in a sugary syrup—when something clanged hard into the steel shutter a foot or two above my head. The guys scattered, racing into the olive groves that surround the center, assuming that someone—a settler—had thrown a rock and that they might be able to catch him if they were fast enough. I followed Ahmad and another guy named Tamer. We ran between the trees in the darkness, but found no one. Back at the center, the guys were searching the floor for the rock. But there was no rock. Just a bullet.

Two soldiers on patrol passed by the center. Irene told them we thought someone had just shot at us. She had a way of rendering soldiers docile. They were, after all, nineteen-year-old boys, and she was a tall and imposingly beautiful woman of thirty-one whose intelligence and stubborn, defiant charm could evaporate almost any barrier. Once, at the checkpoint at Bab al-Zawiya, I saw her refuse to hand a sullen soldier her ID until he said "please." His friends mocked him, but he said it. Her magic didn't work this time. The soldiers grunted that they hadn't seen anything and walked away. Issa called the police. The guys were inspecting the shutters for a bullet hole. They didn't find one. They found a dent.

Tamer speculated that someone might have flung the bullet from a slingshot, but it seemed more likely that some careless celebrant had fired a gun in the air somewhere across the city, giving the bullet plenty of time to lose momentum before it collided with the shutter above my head. Still, it was hard not to see things in the darkness.

The police came after five phone calls and more than forty minutes, two Israelis in blue uniforms carrying M16s followed by nine soldiers in full battle gear. Two of the soldiers photographed us with iPhones. Issa complained to one of them that the soldiers on patrol had ignored him.

"We were afraid," Issa said. "Who will protect us?"

"We'll be here all night," the soldier answered, reassuring no one.

In the end, nothing happened. Issa went to the police station to make a statement. The policemen tried to walk him through the settlement behind the house, but a settler leader named Baruch Marzel yelled that he didn't want him anywhere near the settlers' homes. The policemen obeyed and took the long way around. In retrospect, I am almost certain that no one shot at us, but the vulnerability that we all felt, the sense of absolute exposure and the knowledge that anything could, suddenly and without warning, go violently bad, and the further certainty that there would be no one at all to turn to, all of this proved an excellent introduction to Hebron.

I went back a few weeks later and made arrangements with Issa to return and stay for a few weeks.

"You are welcome," he said, and grinned.

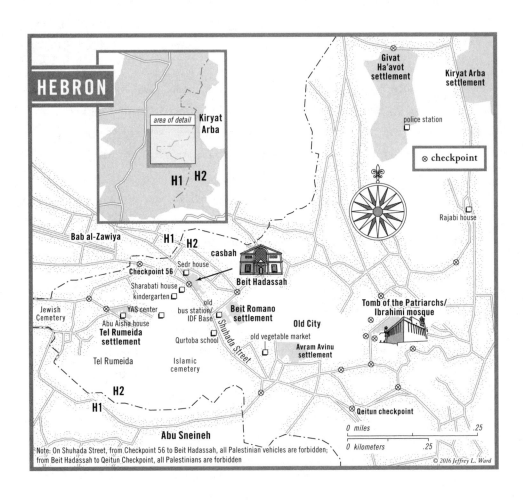

HEBRON

area of detail

Kiryat Arba

H1 H2

⊗ checkpoint

Givat Ha'avot settlement

Kiryat Arba settlement

police station

Rajabi house

Bab al-Zawiya

H1 H2

casbah

Sedr house

Checkpoint 56

Beit Hadassah

Sharabati house

kindergarten

old bus station/ IDF Base

Beit Romano settlement

Tomb of the Patriarchs/ Ibrahimi mosque

Jewish Cemetery

YAS center

Old City

Abu Aisha house

Tel Rumeida settlement

Qurtoba school

old vegetable market

Avram Avinu settlement

Tel Rumeida

Islamic cemetery

Shuhada Street

H2

H1

Qeitun checkpoint

Abu Sneineh

0 miles .25

0 kilometers .25

Note: On Shuhada Street, from Checkpoint 56 to Beit Hadassah, all Palestinian vehicles are forbidden; from Beit Hadassah to Qeitun Checkpoint, all Palestinians are forbidden

© 2016 Jeffrey L. Ward

5.

A MATTER OF HOPE

Hebron, Beitunia, Ramallah

Normality is the essence. It's our secret weapon.

—YIGAL KUTAI, DIRECTOR, HEBRON HERITAGE CENTER

Planet Hebron is far, far away. The fact that you can drive there, or take a bus, only makes things more confusing. If Hebron were hidden away on a mountaintop or deep in a canyon at the bottom of the sea, if getting there meant descending through dim, crumbling shafts to the center of the earth, or undergoing cryogenic treatment in preparation for a multi-light-year journey, it wouldn't feel so odd. But it's right there on the crust of this same globe, just like Tel Aviv or Amman or any other terrestrial metropolis. Maybe it's more useful to think interdimensionally and to understand Hebron as a warp in the mold, a weird crease in the weave of things that through its distortions and deformations and awful echoing feedback somehow manages to tell us exactly who we are.

Let's start with a list. People in Hebron used the word "normal" a lot. Here are a few of the things that people there told me were "normal":

Screaming. "If you hear someone screaming because soldiers are beating him, or settlers are beating him, it's normal." Mufid Sharabati said that. He was my upstairs neighbor in the weeks I spent in Hebron. We were sitting on his rooftop and heard screams from Shuhada Street below.

Mufid didn't seem concerned. He couldn't get up to check anyway—he had been beaten by soldiers so badly that he couldn't stand without assistance.

Being shot at and having rocks and Molotov cocktails thrown at your house. Jamal Abu Seifan lived on the edge of Hebron just downhill from the settlement of Kiryat Arba. His neighbors weren't always very neighborly. The Molotovs took some getting used to. "Now it's normal," he said.

Soldiers firing tear gas at schoolchildren to mark the beginning and end of each day of classes. This is in fact perfectly normal. You could set your watch by the blasts. "It's like this every day," said a shopkeeper across the street from the UN boys' school, a block or so past Checkpoint 29. Soldiers had taken positions on the roof of the apartment building next door. In the street just down from the school they were shooting tear gas grenades at children. Usually the kids threw stones, but if they had that day I didn't see them. The shopkeeper didn't bother to close up. He stood outside his shop, watching as the teachers linked arms outside the gate to the school and formed a chain to shepherd the smaller children away from the clash.

Being arrested, questioned for hours, and released without charges or apology. "That's a normal thing," said Zleikha Muhtaseb, a woman in her fifties whose door was welded shut by the army and whose balcony is caged with heavy, steel mesh to protect her from objects thrown by her neighbors. Soldiers had come for her the previous spring after settlers complained that she had somehow thrown stones at them from inside her cage. The arrest was just a warning, she said, issued because she talked to too many activists, and to foreigners like me.

Having your ID taken at a checkpoint by a soldier who slips it in his pocket and keeps it there until the whim strikes him that you've waited long enough. This happened to me too. "Don't fuck around," the soldier told me as he handed my passport back. He had earlier snarled a few commands in Hebrew, and I had just finished suggesting that perhaps he had slept in on media-sensitivity training day. It turned out that his English was better than his sense of humor. But it was Jawad Abu Aisha, one of the Youth Against Settlements volunteers, who assured me that this was normal. We were walking not far from the Ibrahimi mosque and a Border Police officer had just taken his ID. Sometimes this happened two or three times a day, Jawad told me, sometimes not for a week. "It's okay," he said. "This is our lives."

Having a soldier with an automatic rifle stationed at all times just behind or in front of your house. I'm thinking of the Youth Against Settlements house, but it's far from the only one. Everywhere that a Palestinian home abutted a property inhabited by settlers, a soldier guarded the boundary between them. Boundaries are everything in Hebron. Would the city collapse without them? There was always a soldier outside the Sharabati house too, close enough that I could hear him chatting on the phone when I lay awake inside at night. One day Imad and Zidan disagreed over the Hebrew word for cigarette lighter. We were sitting on the patio of the YAS center. Imad winked at me and yelled behind the house to ask the soldier stationed there to resolve their dispute. The soldier played along and shouted an answer back. Zidan frowned. He was sure it was another word, so Imad, with another wink, asked again. "That too," the soldier yelled.

Everything. "It's very normal," said David Wilder, the spokesman for Hebron's settlers. "There's nothing here in terms of everyday life that's different from anywhere else." He was suffering a bad case of shingles and was stuck in his small apartment in Beit Hadassah, just across from the Sharabati house. He got up only to show me the bullet hole in his children's closet, and the one in the thick book of Jewish law that he pulled from the shelf in his living room. That was normal too. Everyone seemed to have a few bullet holes somewhere, and whether it was Jews or

Arabs that I was visiting, there came a point in almost every interview when they wanted to show them off. In Hebron, nothing was more normal than holes.

OVERALL I SPENT about a month on Planet Hebron. Not very long really. Long enough. I studied up on the political developments that had shaped the city: its religious history, the 1929 massacre of the city's Jews, the rise of the messianic Zionist hard right, the 1994 massacre of worshippers at the Ibrahimi mosque, the subsequent closing of Shuhada Street, the division of the city in 1997 into Israeli- and Palestinian-controlled zones, the multiplication of checkpoints and the endless closures of the Second Intifada. It all made sense, kind of, but none of it added up. None of it seemed sufficient to explain the reality of the place. Nor did contemporary terrestrial analogies hold. Hebron wasn't Belfast or Soweto, Sarajevo or Beirut. It bore occasional and glancing resemblances to all of those places, and to the often violently segregated cities in which I had lived in the United States. In the end, though, it was works of science fiction that helped the most. Two of them in particular: Samuel Delany's *Dhalgren*, an epic novel set in a hazy, dreamlike city, perhaps entirely a dream, separated from and forgotten by the world, where time skips and space rearranges itself without warning; and China Miéville's *The City & the City*, an extraordinary work of speculative fiction about two cities, Besźel and Ul Qoma, that, interpenetrating one another, occupy the same geographic space. The citizens of each city are trained from infancy to *unsee* the other city and its residents, to not acknowledge even to themselves the existence of half the people and half the buildings that they walk past in the street.* Any failure to do so, however brief—a

---

*"As kids we would assiduously unsee Ul Qoma, as our parents and teachers had relentlessly trained us. . . . We used to throw stones across the alterity, walk the long way around in Besźel and pick them up again. . . . We did the same with the local lizards. They were always dead when we picked them up, and we said the little airborne trip through Ul Qoma had killed them, though it might just as well have been the landing."

gaze that lingers on the façade of a building that belongs to the other city, a moment's acknowledgment of the wrong human being—is the gravest crime that any resident of either polity can commit. So it was in Hebron.

I don't want to exoticize the place. Hebron *is* different from other earthly cities, but the painful truth is that Planet Hebron is not far off at all. I don't just mean from Beersheba or Nablus, but also from Washington, London, Los Angeles, or New York. It's our planet. We made it what it is. And by *we* I mean all of us—those of us who acted, and those who do not act. Another sci-fi hero, Philip K. Dick, once wrote, "I would not want to make you unhappy by detailing pain, but there is a crucial sort of difference between pain and the narration of pain. I am telling you what happened. If there is vicarious pain in knowing, there is actual peril in not knowing." Hebron's realities are the same as those in the rest of Palestine, only boiled down under tremendous pressure until they have been reduced to a thick and noxious paste. And Palestine's realities are not different from our own.* They are just starker, denser, more defined. The people I encountered in Hebron—the Palestinians, the settlers, the soldiers—were no different from people anywhere, except to the degree that the place and the maddening intimacy of its violence had coarsened and sometimes broken them.

That's not quite right. A number of them were completely insane.

ISSA WAS in a bad mood. We had arrived in Hebron a few hours earlier— me, the photographer Peter van Agtmael, and the Italian photographer and videographer Gaia Squarci. We followed Issa up the stairs behind the center, past the soldier posted there, to the office and classroom on the second floor. Issa's back was hurting, he said, but he was twitchy too, and more short-tempered than usual. (In answer to one of Gaia's questions, he

---

*As I write this, demonstrators are shutting down freeways to protest the killings of Eric Garner and Michael Brown by police in New York and in Ferguson, Missouri. Police helicopters buzz the sky above my office.

snapped, "When I say something, it means I'm one hundred percent right.") He powered on the Macintosh in the back room, tapping at the desk as the computer warmed up. This would be our orientation. Issa clicked open a link to a map of Hebron. The color coding was almost dizzying. H1—the part of the city governed by the PA, in which 80 percent of Hebron's Palestinian population lives—was one tone of beige. H2—the zone shared, if that is the right word, by about 850 settlers and 40,000 Palestinians,* and in which nearly all aspects of life fall under the control of the Israeli security forces—was another. H2 was further subdivided: the buildings and neighborhoods that had been taken over by settlers were shaded blue; a wide U-shaped expanse of violet covered the areas in which Palestinians could walk but were not permitted to drive; and the streets that Palestinians could not even cross on foot were marked in a dark, orangey red. The Israeli military refers to such thoroughfares as "sterile," as if the presence of Palestinians were a form of infection.

With the mouse, Issa circled Tel Rumeida. "We're here." The settlers' plan, he said, was to take over everything from where we sat "all the way to here"—the cursor zigzagged diagonally across a large swath of H2, stopping at the big blue splotch in the northeast corner of the map. They wanted, Issa said, to connect Kiryat Arba, which, with a population of more than seven thousand, formed the largest concentration of settlers in the area, to their holiest site, the Tomb of the Patriarchs, and beyond it to Tel Rumeida, which for now remained a small island inhabited by a few particularly zealous families of settlers and a shrinking community of Palestinian Hebronites.†

"We have," Issa went on, "eighteen checkpoints and more than one hundred movement barriers—metal gates, concrete and razor wire barricades, and other obstacles—between Kiryat Arba and here." He circled the

---

*About five hundred Jews reside permanently in Hebron—the rest are yeshiva students, who come and go.

†I later asked David Wilder, the settlers' spokesman, if this was in fact their plan. He shrugged. "We wouldn't frown on it."

checkpoint at Bab al-Zawiya, the neighborhood that forms a sort of gateway between H1 and H2, separating the more ancient sectors of the city from its newer downtown. We had passed through it a few hours earlier. (At the time, the checkpoint was just a metal detector inside a beige shipping container manned by two unhappy soldiers. Checkpoint 56, it was called.) "Right outside of it," Issa continued, "is the Rachel Corrie Restaurant and Coffee Shop." The proprietor was a friend, he said. "He charges internationals twenty-five shekels, but tell him Issa said it's fifteen."*

Issa pulled up a photograph of a bearded, middle-aged man in a large black skullcap tugging with both hands on the face of an Israeli solidarity activist. "This is Baruch Marzel," he said. "You should know him." Soon we would. Issa did a Google image search and came up with several shots of David Wilder, gray-bearded, with a warm, paternal smile. "He's the smooth one," Issa said, and opened photos of Noam Federman, who was arrested in 2002 for plotting to bomb a Palestinian girls' school in Jerusalem; Menashe Levinger, who was arrested with him and whose father was among the first Israeli Jews to stake a claim to Hebron in 1968; Menashe's brother Shlomo, who two days earlier had barged into the kindergarten that YAS was building just down the hill. The incident had been recorded. I had watched it on YouTube. Levinger had another settler with him. Issa told them to leave: "You're disrupting our work here."

"Nothing here belongs to you," Levinger responded.

Soon three more settlers came, one with a rifle, then soldiers, and finally police. Inevitably, Issa was arrested, as was a fifteen-year-old YAS volunteer named Ahmad Azza. It would be Issa's tenth arrest in 2013. "Last year it was twenty," he said. "I'm good this year."

He continued. "This is Anat Cohen." The photo depicted a thin, rather

---

*The restaurant was named for the twenty-three-year-old American solidarity activist killed in 2003 by an Israeli military bulldozer in the Gazan city of Rafah. I ate there only once. The owner wanted 40 shekels, or about $11, for what turned out to be a small plate of oily liver. I got him down to 20.

avian woman with severe and deep-set eyes. "She is a very dangerous person. She is the worst maybe." I would meet her too.

One of the younger guys came in and whispered something in Issa's ear. Issa stood, wincing as he rose. "I have to go outside," he said. "There is a settler." In fact there were two. They were young, teenaged, a boy and a girl. They were sitting on a swing hanging a few meters from the center's back patio. Not just sitting really—they were making out. The boy broke the embrace when Issa arrived. Issa yelled to the soldier that the young lovers were on Palestinian property and not allowed to be there. The soldier told him not to speak to them.

"By his own religion he's not allowed to do this!" Issa shouted. But the boy had lost interest in his paramour. Issa's anger was much more fun. The boy didn't say a word. He just kept grinning, pulled his girlfriend closer to him, and kicked the swing higher in the air.

Before we left, Issa informed us that we would sleep that night at the center. The place he had arranged for us wasn't ready yet. But we would like it, he assured us. "It is a special place," he said, and smiled for the first time that night.

It was later that evening that we came back late from a walk out into H1, the PA-governed section of the city, and crossed from Bab al-Zawiya through Checkpoint 56 back onto Shuhada Street. On the H2 side, where the IDF held sway, the streets were as haunted and empty as always, but the checkpoint was crowded with settlers, maybe a dozen of them, all of them teenage boys. They were hanging out with the two soldiers who were stationed there that night, and who looked a little uneasy as the settler teens laughed rowdily beside them, crunching pretzels and drinking tea. The settlers regarded us with amusement as we looped our belts back on and returned our passports and phones to our pockets. It wasn't entirely friendly, but it wasn't qualitatively different from the mildly aggressive adolescent mirth with which they seemed to regard everything around them.

One of them explained that they had brought snacks and warm drinks for the soldiers. "Because they protect us," he said.

"From the Arab killers," another one added.

"It's dangerous here," a third explained.

He was right about that. Or at least not wrong. Most of the dangers were endured by Palestinians, but a few weeks earlier, on the Jewish holiday of Sukkot, a twenty-year-old Israeli staff sergeant named Gal Kobi had been shot in the neck at a checkpoint at the other end of Shuhada Street, presumably by a sniper. Kobi died in the hospital soon after, becoming the first Israeli to be killed in Hebron since the end of the Second Intifada. During the same period, sixteen Palestinians had been slain in the city by Israeli forces.

Peter raised his camera. The teens gathered close and put their arms around one another's shoulders.

"Cheese," one of them shouted.

Another yelled, *"Sharmuta,"* which is Arabic for "whore."

All of them smiled.

EARLIER THAT NIGHT, at Issa's suggestion, we had gone to see a man named Mufid Sharabati. As far as I knew, I hadn't met him before. We walked down the path from the center, opened the gate and turned right at the old abandoned delivery truck with the painted word "SCHWEPPES" still legible on its door. The truck was one of the invisible nodes that Hebron was full of. To the uninitiated it was just an old American 1950-something truck, a weird anomaly that would make more sense rotting on the edge of a small Mojave town than here, far from any drivable road near the top of Tel Rumeida. Palestinians who lived in the neighborhood, though, knew that the truck marked a boundary. There was no sign of course, and no warning, just the rotting truck, but they knew they could not continue past it on the path, because in that direction lay the settlers' houses, which made it the settlers' path, which meant that if Palestinians continued on, or if they turned left from the center's gate rather than right, they risked arrest or something worse, depending on whether the soldiers or the settlers reached them first.

But that night the path was empty and dark. The yellow lights posted by the army on the rooftops above the olive groves* cast harsh, shifting shadows beneath the trees. We climbed down a metal staircase, past two abandoned houses and a flight of broken stone steps past another empty house with a military watch post, also abandoned, on its roof. We walked through the courtyard of the home that YAS had recently converted into a kindergarten for the neighborhood children and crossed from one rooftop to the next, balancing along the edge of a wall, until we arrived on the roof of Mufid Sharabati's home.

He was waiting there for us beneath a torn, green tarp. He looked familiar, but I couldn't remember where or under what circumstances we might have met. He was gray-haired and unshaven, with a thick mustache and a heavy, aquiline face that must have once been very handsome. Wearing an old and pilled blue sweatsuit, he sat, smoking, bent and with his shoulders slumped, on four plastic chairs stacked one atop the other. Presumably the added height made it easier for him to stand. Soldiers had recently beaten him on the same spot on his back where he had been injured years before, he explained. He had spent the day at the hospital. The doctors wanted to operate.

The Sharabati house was the last inhabited Palestinian home on this part of Shuhada Street. That is a more complicated statement than it sounds. A few Palestinians still lived farther down the street, on the far

---

*The trees were so gnarled and thick-trunked that people called them "Roman trees" and insisted that they were thousands of years old, which was unlikely—though hundreds was certainly correct—but it was surely comforting to think that any living thing could survive the fall of one empire, and another, and another, and that the pain and misfortunes that twisted its limbs would as the decades passed render it nobler and more beautiful and worthy of respect.

side of Beit Hadassah and the settlers' apartments, but they were not allowed onto the street outside their doors and had to come and go through the rear, or over the roofs and out through their neighbors' doors. The stone, three-story Sharabati house—which Mufid's family shared with that of his brother Zidan and with the al-Salayma family downstairs—was the last building on the short stretch of Shuhada Street between Checkpoint 56 and Beit Hadassah on which Palestinians were permitted to walk. Most of the others were abandoned. The storefronts were closed and welded shut, their doors graffitied with Jewish stars, "DEATH TO ARABS," and other similar messages in Hebrew. Signs in faded Arabic still hung from a few of the rusted green awnings advertising a health club or a doctor's office that had been closed for almost a decade and a half.

At the end of the block stood Beit Hadassah, a large and impressive stone structure, its façade a delicate lattice of Stars of David, originally built in 1893 as a clinic for Hebron's Jewish community. It was Jewish again—settlers lived there now—and a soldier was posted at all times just outside the building, and hence just outside the Sharabatis' door. The staircase beside Mufid's house, which was used by both settlers and Palestinians to climb to the old neighborhood of Tel Rumeida, formed another secret node. Descending the stairs, Israelis and foreigners could turn in either direction. Palestinians could only turn left.

It wasn't always this way. Mufid had been born in this house, he said, forty-seven years before. He looked easily fifteen years older than he was. When he was a child, Shuhada Street had been the commercial spine of the city and its liveliest thoroughfare. Beit Hadassah was empty then, as most of the Palestinian homes are empty now. A Jew named Jacob Ezra—one of the very few who stayed in Hebron after the 1929 massacre, in which sixty-six of the six hundred Jews who then lived in the city were killed*—used

---

*The unrest that shook the region that August was particularly ugly in Hebron. In all of Palestine, 133 Jews were killed, and 116 Arabs.

the old building as a dairy which he ran with a Palestinian partner from the Abu Aisha family. Ezra stayed until 1947, when the UN partition plan for Palestine was approved* and he decided that it was time to move to Jerusalem. The next year Hebron became part of Jordan. In May 1967, a year before Mufid's birth and three weeks before Israeli troops took the West Bank, Rabbi Zvi Yehuda Kook, who would become the spiritual father of the Gush Emunim movement, delivered a sermon lamenting Israel's failure to conquer all of the biblical lands of Israel. "Where is our Hebron—have we forgotten it?" he asked. "And all of Transjordan—it is all ours, every single clod of earth, each little bit, every part of the land is part of the land of God—is it in our power to surrender even one millimeter of it?"

Less than a year later, with Kook's prayer answered and Hebron under Israeli occupation, a group of Kook's former students led by a young rabbi named Moshe Levinger informed the city's new military governor that they wished to celebrate Passover near the Tomb of the Patriarchs, and that to do so they would have to stay in the city overnight. The governor consented. The soon-to-be settlers rented rooms in Hebron's Park Hotel. Passover came and went. The settlers announced that they had no plans to leave. The generally accepted Israeli narrative of the incident is that Levinger and his followers deceived the authorities about their intentions and that the settlement of the West Bank began with this subterfuge, a sort of original sin, the commission of which left the state embarrassed but unsullied. The scholar Idith Zertal and the journalist Akiva Eldar, though, have extensively documented the military and the Labor government's foreknowledge of and complicity with Levinger's plans: though not without its tensions, the settlement enterprise has been a state-sponsored project from

---

*The plan, which was rejected by the Arab leadership, would have created a far larger Palestinian state than any conceived of since, including all of the West Bank and Gaza, the city of Jaffa, the upper Galilee and the Mediterranean coast north of Acre, and a wide strip of land bordering Egypt.

the very beginning. Within days of the settlers' arrival in Hebron, the army had provided them with weapons. In a Knesset hearing that summer, Defense Minister Moshe Dayan confirmed that Levinger's group had "acted in accordance with orders that were issued by the military administration." Soon thereafter, the Israeli government confiscated a large plot of land on the eastern edge of the city and began construction of the settlement that would be called Kiryat Arba. Just before the high holidays in 1971, fifty Jewish families, including Levinger's, moved in.*

For most of the next decade, the settlers stayed put. But late one night in the spring of 1979, a group of ten women from Kiryat Arba, led by Levinger's wife Miriam, broke into Beit Hadassah. The Sharabatis had new neighbors. Mufid was still a child, but he remembered their arrival. The settlers brought their children with them, and once again refused to leave. The government—now Likud—did not approve, but neither did it expel them. A few months later, in January 1980, after a yeshiva student named Yehoshua Saloma was killed in the market a few blocks to the north, settlers took over four other buildings that had half a century earlier belonged to Hebron's Jews. The Israeli government lent its official blessing to an expanded Jewish presence in the heart of Hebron. A pattern had been set that would eventually become a hallowed principle of Israeli rule in the West Bank. Years later, the spokesman for the settlers' council put it succinctly: "For every drop of our blood, they will pay in land."†

The cycle continued: In May 1980, Palestinian gunmen retaliated for

---

*Levinger remained an irritant, but his relation to Israeli state institutions was always cozier than it was fraught. When in 1988 Levinger shot a Palestinian shoe-store owner named Khaled Salah, killing him and wounding one of his customers, Israeli authorities initially declined to prosecute. The case was not brought to court until nearly two years later. Levinger ultimately served thirteen weeks of a five-month sentence.

†Hours after the shooting of Gal Kobi in September 2012, Netanyahu announced that settlers were free to move back into a Palestinian house near the Tomb of the Patriarchs from which they had been ordered evicted. "Those who try to uproot us from Hebron, the city of our forefathers," the prime minister announced, "will only achieve the opposite."

the takeovers by killing six settlers outside Beit Hadassah. Yitzhak Shamir attended the funeral. So did the IDF chief of staff and the head of the army's Central Command. Meir Kahane, the Brooklyn-born ultranationalist rabbi whose Kach movement advocated for the expulsion of all Arabs from "the Land of Israel,"* spoke at the service. "Anyone who says that vengeance is not a Jewish virtue," Kahane said, "is simply wrong."

Most of Hebron was placed under curfew and the neighborhood was evacuated for fifteen days. Only the Palestinian residents had to leave. When Mufid's family returned to their home, they found that the army had taken over the house. The Sharabatis were allowed to stay in just one room, which had to function as kitchen, bathroom, bedroom, everything. Eighteen days later, the soldiers left. Things returned to what they then regarded as normal, until 1994.

That year seared itself onto the consciousness of Hebron's Palestinians much as 1929 had been burned into the collective memory of Hebron's Jews. It was Ramadan and a Friday. The Ibrahimi mosque was full. Baruch Goldstein, another ex-Brooklynite and a physician residing in the Kiryat Arba settlement, put on his army reservist's uniform and walked past the soldiers outside the mosque carrying an Uzi submachine gun. He entered the mosque and began firing at the men and boys praying within. None of the soldiers stationed outside attempted to intervene. Goldstein fired at leisure, emptying four magazines, killing 29 people and wounding another 125 before the surviving worshippers were able to disarm him and beat him to death. Hebron's settlers would venerate Goldstein as a martyred hero. The killer's grave, in Kahane Park at the edge of Kiryat Arba, became a pilgrimage site. "Here lies the saintly Baruch Goldstein," his monument reads, "who gave his life for the people of Israel. His hands are clean. . . ."

---

*"Israel" and "the Land of Israel" do not occupy the same space, or even the same type of space. The former can be found in any atlas. The latter lives only in the realm of myth: it comprises all of the lands promised to the Jews in the Old Testament, which, depending whom you ask, include the territory of the current state of Israel, plus Gaza, the West Bank, the Golan, the Sinai peninsula, most of Jordan, and parts of Syria and Lebanon.

In the days of outrage that followed the massacre, Prime Minister Yitzhak Rabin considered uprooting the settlement and evicting Hebron's Jews. The experiment, clearly, had failed. But Rabin vacillated, and did nothing. A year later he would be assassinated by another of Kahane's followers. In the meantime, Ehud Barak, then the IDF's chief of staff, imposed a curfew—not on the settlers, but on Palestinian Hebronites, who would be confined to their homes for weeks. Schools were shuttered. Shuhada Street was closed to Palestinian cars and sixty shops were ordered closed. "The victim was punished," said Mufid. The settlers were still free to drive where they wished. The curfews and closures did not apply to them.

When in 1995, in accordance with the Oslo agreements, Israeli troops pulled out of the West Bank cities and towns that they had occupied since 1967, they stayed on in just one city: Hebron. Israel was not ready to let go of the Tomb of the Patriarchs, or of its settlements. Two years later, Mufid was arrested. He was accused, he said, of "really, really big things": possessing firearms, preparing explosive devices, throwing a grenade at Israeli soldiers. He was taken to the Russian Compound in Jerusalem, the old Russian Orthodox mission and hostelry that now houses an Israeli courthouse, prison, police station, and, several floors below the street, a notorious interrogation center used by the Shabak,* where, Mufid said, he was beaten so severely on his genitals and thighs that his skin went black from his knees to his waist. "Like your jacket," he said. "They put me in a place called the cupboard." It was a tiny cell containing nothing but one very small chair, its seat slanted down and tilted forward. His arms were cuffed behind him, his legs shackled. A bag, dirty and foul-smelling, was pulled over his head. They kept him like that for twenty-nine days. When they let him out, he couldn't stand, or move his legs at all. They held him for another month and a half, until he could walk again, and then released

---

*Notorious, at least, to Palestinians. The Compound is in the center of Jerusalem's downtown. In the evenings, Israelis and tourists, dressed for a night out, use the empty streets of the prison complex as a shortcut to the restaurants and bars of Jaffa Road and Ben Yehuda Street.

him. He had never seen a judge, or spoken to a lawyer. The specifics of Mufid's story are impossible to confirm, but the use of torture at the Russian Compound has been extensively documented by journalists and Israeli and international human rights groups from the 1970s to the present. Other prisoners have described similar treatment in the small cells known as "cupboards." The position Mufid described is so commonly employed in interrogation that it has a name: the *shabach* position, from a Hebrew word meaning "praise." All of these practices have been legal under Israeli law since 1987, and are considered forms of "moderate physical pressure."*

Not long after Mufid underwent surgery to repair the damage done to his back, the Second Intifada erupted. A new era of curfews and closures began. Most of Shuhada Street—all but the short block between Bab al-Zawiya and Beit Hadassah—was closed to pedestrians. Palestinian pedestrians, that is. The army closed every shop along the length of the street, soldering shut the doors. More than 1,800 businesses closed. Most of the residents of what had been the busiest and most vibrant street in the city were evicted or moved out. By the end of 2006, more than 1,000 homes had been abandoned. "You could never imagine that this would happen," Mufid said. He swiped at the air with his cigarette. "If they could take the air from us, they would."

His most recent troubles had begun a few months earlier, when he drew up plans to expand his home by building out onto the roof. "As you can see," he said, gesturing at the door behind him, "my apartment is very small." Seven people shared it: Mufid, his wife, and their five children. We were sitting in what he had hoped would be the new kitchen. He applied for construction permits from both the Palestinian municipal authorities and the Israeli Civil Administration. Both, he said, were granted. He showed me the documents in Hebrew and Arabic. In September, he had begun to

---

*A 1999 High Court ruling banning such practices preserved their legality in cases of "necessity," which it has been left to the Shabak to determine. "Of the hundreds of complaints that have been lodged in the past decade," wrote Israeli human rights lawyer Irit Ballad in 2012, "not even one has been found worthy of a criminal investigation."

purchase cement blocks and bags of concrete. One morning, he began carrying them in. A settler saw him working and phoned the police, the army,
and the Civil Administration. Representatives of all three bodies came to
the house. "A lot of them," Mufid said. Palestinians are supposed to abandon their homes, not expand them, but Mufid had the necessary permits.
The officials left. He went back to work and kept at it until evening.

At six o'clock, the soldiers returned. Their commander told him he
would be arrested if he didn't immediately get rid of the construction
materials. Mufid argued: the work was legal. "Arrest me if you want," he
told the soldiers. They did. They brought him to the military base on Shuhada Street, which had once been the city's main bus station. "They began
to beat me," he said. "I fell unconscious. I remember waking in a very dark
room, waking and vomiting and passing out again." He spent ten days in
the hospital. Two months had passed since, but he had to go back to the
doctor almost every day for more tests and consultations. The blocks and
the bags of concrete still lay in piles on the edge of the roof.

He stubbed out one cigarette and lit another. "We will stay here," he
said. It didn't sound heroic, just resigned. "We will live here and we will
die here because these are our houses and we don't have the money to buy
houses somewhere else."

It was a little earlier, while he was talking about the police and the soldiers first coming to his roof, that I realized why Mufid had looked familiar, and why I hadn't recognized him. I felt like I had been punched in the
stomach: We had met before. He had been at the center the previous summer when the *tawjihi* results were announced and a bullet hit the steel
shutters and sent us all scattering. He was the handsome one in the spotless
white *galabiya*, the one who had seemed to breathe elegance. A lot can happen in four months.

We slept that night at the center. I had the sitting room to myself, and
my choice of four bruised green couches. The walls were decorated with a

large Palestinian flag, a tourist map of Hebron, and no fewer than six handmade no-smoking signs in Arabic and English, variously illustrated. (Almost all of YAS's volunteers, even fifteen-year-old Ahmad, smoked cigarettes or *arghile* or both: only Issa objected.) A poster hung on the door, a black-and-white grid of the faces of the men and boys killed by Baruch Goldstein. Down the hall was the kitchen, one wall given over to messages of hope and solidarity scrawled in magic marker by various international visitors. ("Free Palestine," "Never Give Up," "Love Wins.") The floors were stone, and cold, the windows protected by bars and thick metal screens of a sort that let mosquitoes in but kept stones out.

The house had been abandoned during the Second Intifada, its owners having fled the closures and curfews and constant violence. Soldiers took it over as an impromptu base. They stayed until 2006. Settlers moved in a month later, but the house had been wrecked—it had no electricity or functioning plumbing and the rooms were filled with trash—and they didn't stay long. Issa contacted the owner and offered to repair the place, and to keep the settlers out. "He was scared," Issa said—he feared the Israeli authorities would retaliate against him for the transgressive act of renting his home to another Palestinian. In the end, Issa persuaded him. Armed with a lease, he arrived with a few dozen volunteers and began to clean the house. Predictably, soldiers showed up. They told him the property was a closed military zone. "I said, 'What are you talking about?'" Issa recalled. "'It's my house.'" They showed him the order. It expired after twenty-four hours, so he and the volunteers came back again the next day, and worked on the house until the soldiers returned with a fresh order.*

---

*The ability of local military commanders to declare any area of their choosing a "closed military zone," in which all civilian trespass is forbidden, dates back to the British Defense Regulations of 1945, which were preserved after the foundation of the Israeli state. Article 125 of the Defense Regulations was used extensively in the Arab north of Israel well into the 1960s to prevent displaced Palestinians from returning to their homes, to quash demonstrations, and to confiscate land for Jewish settlement. It is perhaps unnecessary to state that Jewish Israelis were rarely arrested for violating the orders, which continue to be used, and for the same purposes, in the West Bank today.

So it went. It took nearly six months to render the house inhabitable. For two of those months, Issa slept outside the house each night. The soldiers detained him many times, he said. The settlers threw rocks and tried to break in. Hence the bars and grates on the windows and the steel shutters on the walls outside. But it was comfortable now and almost homey, tidy if not spotlessly clean. Little Ahmad swept the patio at least once each day, and stacked the white plastic chairs in the hall. There was even a garden outside the patio, a few untended rose bushes, a stray tomato plant and yellowed cucumber vine beneath the two old olive trees. Around the garden was a low stone and concrete wall, at the bottom of which wound a length of coiled razor wire. In red paint, just beside the door, someone had stenciled the words "THIS IS PALESTINE," as if it were possible to forget.

SHORTLY BEFORE I arrived in Hebron, hours after the release of the first batch of twenty-six Palestinian prisoners whom John Kerry had convinced Netanyahu to free in order to lure Abbas to the negotiating table, the Israeli government announced that it had issued final approvals for 1,500 new apartments to be built in the East Jerusalem settlement of Ramat Shlomo, and had begun advancing plans for another 3,360 homes for settlers in the West Bank. Already, in the first half of the year, as Kerry had been orbiting between Jerusalem and Ramallah like a dim but frantic satellite, settlement construction in the West Bank had accelerated by 70 percent. A State Department spokesperson issued a tepid statement of disapproval, the UN a slightly stronger one. Palestinian news outlets reported that the PA's negotiators, Saeb Erekat and Mohammad Shtayyeh, had in protest submitted their resignations to Abbas. The next day Erekat denied that they had done so. The negotiations, in other words, were going about as well as anyone had expected.

THE "SPECIAL PLACE" that Issa had arranged for us turned out to be the Sharabati house. Not Mufid's apartment, but his brother Zidan's downstairs.

We stayed in the dome-ceilinged sitting room on the ground floor. A ceremonial sword hung from one wall above a reproduction of a painting depicting the Goldstein massacre: the killer standing with his submachine gun, bloodied bodies in a pile, a weeping woman in a white scarf, her hands raised to the heavens. The room's one window opened to Shuhada Street, and Beit Hadassah, and the soldier at his post. It was grated of course. Stones, in Hebron, were like weather.

Zidan was a quiet man, bone thin, with a creased and heavy face and one dead eye. That happened in 2006, when the windows were still unscreened. He heard noises in the street, looked out and saw settlers throwing stones at the house. As he rushed to move his mother to safety, a large rock hit his face. The surgeons couldn't save his eye. He had also had his teeth knocked out, he told me once, lifting his dentures to show me his gums. That was back in '94. He had found work doing construction in the settlement of Beitar Illit, a few miles south of Jerusalem. He didn't like it, he said, but "You worked there or you didn't work."* A tool went missing, a long knife-like blade used for cutting concrete blocks. The boss sent Zidan out to buy a new one. Soldiers stopped him on his way back to work. They found the blade, arrested him for possessing a weapon, and beat him severely. He spent eighteen days in prison.

It was hard for him to work now. Sunlight caused him headaches and the slightest breeze hurt his eye. He had problems with his nose too. It was broken in another beating. He had been working in the street, repaving it, and attempted to intervene when he saw soldiers harassing one of his brothers. A few days later the same soldiers stopped him and beat him with their rifles. He showed me a series of photographs of himself, glossy prints of a younger Zidan, his hair fuller and his mustache blacker, his face

---

*The occupation has hit Hebron's economy particularly hard. The official unemployment rate in the city and its surrounding towns was 25 percent. Most of the men I met there were only sporadically able to find work, usually in construction, though many had advanced degrees.

equally forlorn. In the photos he stood in front of a red curtain as if on a stage, displaying the bruises on his legs and his back, naked but for his white underpants.

Every morning, Zidan knocked at the door with four coffees on a tray, one for himself and one for each of us. He would sit in silence, his legs crossed, drinking as we drank, smoking, lost in thought. Zidan was mostly quiet. Not just with us, but with everyone. He spent the evenings sitting outside the center with the other guys, his body bent as he chain-smoked the unbranded local cigarettes that he bought in the market in clear, cellophane bags. He would answer a question if one was asked of him and would sometimes smile for a moment if someone told a joke, but he rarely said a word unprompted. Once, after I had left Hebron, I asked Issa how he was. "Zidan?" he answered. "He is like always. He is in space. He is very far away." But for all his evident despair and the almost unearthly quality of his presence, Zidan seemed more precisely grounded than many of the people around us. He didn't fly into rages or lose himself in long, wandering stories about how things once were and how they should be, but he had been a steady part of YAS from the beginning. In his lost, laconic way, he had not stopped fighting. He almost always carried a video camera and, at considerable risk and with a stubborn dedication, documented every act of violence or harassment that he witnessed. In the end, Zidan and his camera would save me a great deal of trouble too.

I once asked him if he didn't sometimes lose hope. Even as I asked it, I knew it was a foolish question, but I needed to know how he kept going. The darkness in Hebron was so complete and overwhelming. ("How can one emerge unharmed from this daily schizophrenia?" asked the Spanish novelist Juan Goytisolo after a visit to Hebron in 1995, half a decade before things got really bad.) I wanted light, just a little. Of course he lost hope, Zidan answered. He looked annoyed.

"It's not a matter of hope," he went on. It was just that he didn't have any alternatives.

———

JAWAD ABU AISHA offered to show us around the old city. He was one of
the center's regulars, in his early forties with a round, boyish face and a
mournful sparkle to his eyes. He walked and talked slowly, not depressed
but determined, as if he were carrying a heavy burden and thinking hard
about where to put it down. It was Jawad's grandfather who had partnered
with Jacob Ezra. He kept sheep and supplied Ezra with the milk that he
sold as cheese from Beit Hadassah. When Ezra's wife died, Jawad's grandmother nursed the Ezras' infant daughter. When Ezra finally decamped
from the city in 1947, Jawad said, he left the business—and the building—
to Jawad's grandfather, who one year later turned it over to the UN so that
it could be used as a shelter for refugees fleeing villages in what had overnight become the state of Israel. Jawad told me that he had gone to the
wedding of one of Ezra's grandsons in the early 1990s, when it was still
possible for him to travel freely to Jerusalem. He was proud of the connection, of his stake in the alternate history that it pointed toward—something
more than the "tolerant" coexistence of liberal cliché, a vanished past of
genuine diversity in which Jews and Arabs, whatever their differences and
the occasional catastrophic breakdowns of relations between them, shared
a single culture, one that was not Jewish or Muslim or Christian, but
Hebronite, and Palestinian.

We walked down from the center and out to Bab al-Zawiya through the
checkpoint, one of four that we would pass on a walk of perhaps a mile.
Jawad was born in Tel Rumeida, not far from where the center now stands.
His father owned a brass factory there and he worked as the factory's manager until it was closed by the Israeli military in 2001. Jawad moved out to
the relative quiet of H1 and found work with the municipality. His uncle's
family still lived in Tel Rumeida, in a building known as the "cage house."
It was stuck between two checkpoints right across from the settlers' apartment complex and had been veiled almost entirely in thick, steel mesh to

keep the rocks out. The only Palestinians allowed through the checkpoints were the ones who actually lived in the house, which meant that I was able to visit Jawad's uncle and cousins, but Jawad was not. "Even prisoners are allowed to have visits," his cousin's wife Rima complained.

We passed the Rachel Corrie Restaurant and the chicken market—the old one, Jawad said, was much bigger, and took up an entire block. In one of the two open shops, with great deftness and consummate boredom, a butcher slit the throats of one silent bird after another. The street narrowed. Next came the clothing market, though the vendors' tables that clogged the street were piled with toothpaste, combs, and hair dye as well as stacks of garments. A heavy mesh screen had been mounted above the street to shield the merchants and shoppers from objects thrown by the settlers who lived above them in Beit Hadassah and the buildings around it. The screen sagged with trash, bottles, bricks, and concrete blocks. Sometimes they threw acid, Jawad said, sometimes urine.

Though it was invisible from the market, the upper floors of the buildings to our right opened onto Shuhada Street, or used to. Now they didn't open at all, and their inhabitants could only exit their homes through rear doors onto the street in which we walked. We peeked down an alley and through a rusted steel gate topped with razor wire. Behind it was an empty, garbage-strewn alley of closed shops, their green metal doors welded shut like the ones on Shuhada Street above. It used to be the gold market, Jawad said. Hebron's wealthiest families had lived nearby. "Now it's the rubbish market," he joked. He wasn't laughing.

Farther down, the road narrowed even more. Most of the shops were closed. Official closures hadn't been necessary here: the curfews had done the trick. During the first three years of the Intifada, central Hebron was under curfew for a total of 377 days, including one order that lasted for 182 straight days, during which no one was allowed to leave their homes, not to work or go to school or to the doctor. ("No one" applied only to Palestinians.) The army would lift the curfew for a couple of hours every few days so that people could buy supplies to get them through the next period of what amounted to house arrest for an entire population. Few shop owners could afford to stay in business. Most left.

We walked through a stone archway into the alleys of the old city. Some of the buildings around us, Jawad said, were as much as eight hundred years old. The devastation here was more complete. Perhaps one out of every eight or ten shops was open. Their offerings were sparse: a few milk crates piled with drooping parsley, mint, and spinach; a sad display of sponges and dustpans; a single bin of raisins and another of dried figs. "It used to be very crowded," Jawad said. "My father would have to hold my hand."

We had reached the entrance to the Ibrahimi mosque: two turnstiles at the end of a stone tunnel, a soldier waiting on the other side to check our IDs. Beyond it rose the ancient stone walls of the shrine that Muslims called al Haram al-Ibrahimi and that Jews referred to as Me'arat haMachpela. After the Goldstein massacre, the building had been divided, with separate sides for Muslims and Jews. I had been there before. From the carpeted silence of the mosque, I could hear Jews praying on the other side of a thin partition. Both sides had windows looking onto the small, octagonal rooms that housed the green, silk-draped cenotaphs of the patriarchs. The windows were barred of course, and positioned at an angle to each other, so that no one could shoot from one side to the other.

JUST OUTSIDE THE old gold market, now the rubbish market, a heavy man named Abd al-Khaleq Sedr had invited us in for tea. He took us first to his roof. None of it was visible from the market below, but from the rooftop it was possible to see that Sedr's house was right next to Beit Hadassah and across the street from the Sharabatis. It was a perilous location: Soldiers had welded shut not only the Sedrs' door to Shuhada Street, but all their windows facing south. The other windows were blocked by the same thick screens that covered every vulnerable aperture of every inhabited Palestinian dwelling in H2. "All the time, they throw stones," Sedr said of the settlers. "If I say good morning, they say *sharmuta*." He smiled grimly and told a few stories. Nothing extreme, the kind I would hear in almost every house I visited in Hebron. Every Palestinian house, that is. A month and a half earlier, Sedr said, the soldiers claimed a child had thrown stones from his roof. They came in to search the house, shoved his brother's four-year-old daughter, and, when he became angry, beat him. They ended up breaking his arm.

A few months later, after I left the city, I found a link to a video shot by Abd al-Khaleq's brother Shadi. The incident it recorded was not anything out of the ordinary—it was, in the local parlance, *normal*—but it managed to capture a great deal in a few short minutes, not just about Hebron, but about the whole sad comedy in which everyone was caught. The video began with a settler appearing on the edge of the Sedrs' roof, which was protected from its neighbors with a fence and a single coil of razor wire. A Palestinian flag flew from a low pole on the corner closest to Beit Hadassah. The settler, a thin bearded man in a white shirt and a wide, white skullcap, had climbed up from the adjacent rooftop. He was clinging to the fence, and appeared to be struggling.

"Why are you coming onto my roof?" Shadi asked.

The settler answered in a stilted Hebrew accented heavily with Russian. "Just to take down the flag," he said, coolly, as if he had come to fix the cable.

Shadi repeated his question in a Hebrew that was equally stilted, and heavily accented with Arabic.

"Okay," said the settler, who appeared to be stuck, "I won't come over. I just want to talk to you."

"The entrance is over there," said Shadi. "Come through there."

The settler asked for the flag. He even said please.

Voices echoed up from below, egging him on: "Take the flag!" The camera panned. Dozens of settlers had gathered behind Beit Hadassah.

Some were shouting and making obscene gestures. "Film this, you son of a whore," one yelled.

The settler, it was now clear, was standing on top of a ladder, fully snarled in the razor wire, unable to go up or down. Shadi reached out to untangle him. "It's okay," he said, "let me help you. You are welcome."

Another settler, standing at the base of the ladder, yelled up: "Don't touch him!"

Shadi pulled his hand back. The settler wanted to talk. He was earnest and composed, as if he and Shadi Sedr had casually struck up a conversation while standing in line at the post office and had raced past the small talk to what really irked them. He objected to the flag again. He thought it was Jordanian. Or, more likely, he knew exactly what it was but couldn't bring himself to say the word "Palestinian."

"You live in Israel," he said, "not in Jordan."

It wasn't an issue Shadi seemed interested in pursuing. "What if I came onto your roof," he asked, and took down an Israeli flag? "Would that be good?"

The settler thought about it. He shrugged. He even said, "Sorry." Then he appeared to reconsider.

"This roof is mine," he said. "It is all mine. The whole country is mine."

He was still stuck, still tangled in razor wire. He couldn't advance, but he couldn't back down either. He couldn't move at all without tearing his own flesh, but he was sure of himself and apparently oblivious to the precariousness of his position. A soldier had arrived and had begun yelling up at Shadi in Arabic, ordering him to go back inside his house. The settler kept talking.

"This is the Land of Israel," he insisted. "This is my country. And everything that is here is mine."

ISRAELI FLAGS FLEW from the roof of the old bus depot on Shuhada Street. Once upon a time, Hebronites could catch a ride here straight to

Jerusalem—and until 1967 to Amman and beyond—but all of that was now a world away.* Some things didn't change much: Before 1948, the station had served as a British police headquarters. In 1983, the IDF seized the compound and returned it to its original purpose. The bus station became a military base. On the walls outside, murals depicted one version of Hebron's history.

The paintings, crude but colorful, broke the past into four discrete epochs, starting with "The Biblical Era": a white-robed Abraham stared into a dark opening in the earth; King David stood nearby on the steps of his palace. Abraham, the legend has it, bought a cave here from the Hittites as a tomb for his wife Sarah, and David ruled from Hebron for seven years before marching on Jerusalem. Is it worth mentioning that there is no archaeological evidence for the historical existence of Abraham, or any scholarly certainty that David ever built anything sturdier than a lean-to? Probably not. This was not that kind of history. The murals' chronology jumped a gap of some two millennia, skipping the Assyrian and Babylonian conquests, 1,100 years of Persian, Hellenistic, and Roman rule, and the early centuries of the Islamic era. The next panel depicted the long golden age of Hebron's "Pious Community," which apparently persisted in unvarying bliss from the tenth century to the nineteenth. A single man in Arab garb stood at the center of the mural. Nearly everyone else wore the long, black coats and wide-brimmed hats favored by the Jews of Eastern Europe.

The riots of 1929 merited a mural of their own. "Destruction," it was called. "Arab marauders slaughter Jews," the legend read. "The community is uprooted and destroyed." The painting—an empty courtyard, crumbling homes—looked a lot like central Hebron did today. But this was a happy story: the final era was titled "Liberation, Return, Rebuilding." It was a portrait of the post-1967 present, and hard to recognize. An Orthodox

---

*For some, at least. Every half hour or so, segregated "settler buses" barreled down Shuhada Street. Transportation to West Bank settlements is heavily subsidized by the Israeli state: the trip to Jerusalem from Hebron took about an hour and a half, but cost only a few pennies more than a ride from one Jerusalem neighborhood to another.

woman pushed a pram while joyful settler children played in the streets accompanied by three beaming soldiers. There was not an Arab to be seen. From a far corner, a purple-robed king rode in on a white donkey—the messiah!—announced by a bearded figure blowing a ram's horn.

I did hear something. It wasn't a shofar. Two shots rang out in the distance to the east. Peter and Gaia and I hurried toward the blasts, walking down the middle of the empty street beneath the caged balconies of the remaining Palestinian homes. Five soldiers passed us, ribbing one another and laughing as they strapped on their helmets. Another bang split the air, and another. The soldiers were running now. We passed the old produce market—empty except for a soldier posted on the roof—and another mural depicting Solomon's temple rebuilt and glowing with divine light. Beyond it was a long-shuttered grocery store with a faded cigarette ad still legible above its awning: "Have a Good Time," it said. I could smell the gas already. We reached the Qeitun checkpoint, where Gal Kobi had been shot in the neck two months earlier. Three boys sat watching as the soldiers on the other side huddled behind concrete barriers, stepping out to fire off the occasional gas grenade. I asked the boys what was happening. "Stones," one of them said, and mimicked a soldier firing a machine gun in response.

But really it was normal. School had just let out. It was clash time. A man stood with his donkey outside the checkpoint, waiting for the trouble to pass. A taxi drove through the clouds of tear gas on the other side, stopped to let out a little boy and sped off. The wind blew the gas back and the soldiers retreated, retching and spitting. The three boys laughed. The man with the donkey took advantage of the pause to rush through the checkpoint.* We crossed behind him. I could see children gathering in the next intersection, a midget army of twelve-year-olds with stones in their hands,

---

*Going from H2 into H1, the soldiers don't bother to check IDs. It's like crossing from San Diego to Tijuana: only the flow from poverty to power requires vigilance. No one cares who goes out the other way.

their backpacks sagging with schoolbooks. To my left, in a narrow lot between the buildings was a small grove of olive trees. A man stood balanced on a branch in the tree closest to the street like a strange bird, only his head and shoulders protruding from the leaves. Women and children stood beneath him with sticks and rakes. They had spread tarps on the ground to catch the falling fruit. The kids on the corner unleashed another rain of stones. The soldiers had recovered and were throwing stun grenades again. Rocks clattered on the pavement. The man in the tree noticed me staring, winked, and went back to shaking the branch.

NARIMAN HAD A court date for her arrest four months earlier, so I left Hebron, met Irene in Jerusalem and drove with her to Ofer, just across the Green Line a few miles north of the city. If you entered the prison complex from the Israeli side, the process was easy enough: a gate, a metal detector, a window of mirrored glass to hand your ID through, another metal detector and an X-ray machine, a turnstile and a long, fenced corridor to a fenced-in yard. There was a bench of seats, a water fountain, a toilet, power lines crisscrossing overhead. Bassem and Nariman were there waiting when we arrived. So were about thirty other people, all with hearings or imprisoned family members of their own. Bassem seemed strangely relaxed, happy even. Nariman too. No one else did. I asked after the kids. "They're fighting each other," Bassem said, grinning widely. Ahed had called just before he got there. She was crying and complaining about her brothers. Bassem laughed: "They are without authority."

On the other side of a chain-link fence hulked the courtrooms themselves: a line of converted trailers painted a dull, institutional beige, like portable classrooms at an overcrowded elementary school. The whole thing had a slapped-together feel, an impromptu, careless informality. I've spent a lot of time in courtrooms in the U.S. covering one case or another and have always been impressed by the sheer theater of it, the polished wood, the flags and gilded seal of the state, the judge's robes, the entire elaborate stage set, blocking and costuming contrived to reinforce the legitimacy of the lurking violence of the state. The Israelis didn't bother. These were military courts. Brute force was on display. The judges and prosecutors were uniformed soldiers, the interpreters too. Only the defendants and their lawyers and loved ones were civilians. Everyone's role was clear enough without further ritual ado.

But we spent very little time in the courtroom. Mostly we waited in the yard, filling the hours with stories and jokes. "The first time I was in jail at Ofer was 1988, May 1988," Bassem recalled. It was new then, freshly established for the influx of prisoners during the mass arrests of the First Intifada. "It was just a tent," Bassem said. He was back again in 1990, 2004, 2011, 2012. He counted off the years on his hands and told a story about Nizar Tamimi, who was arrested with him in 1994 and released in the Shalit swap in 2011. Before they let him out, the prison authorities gave Nizar a sealed plastic bag containing whatever belongings had been confiscated from him at the time of his arrest. Nizar felt the bag before he opened it, unable to remember what it might contain. He detected the contours of a wristwatch and realized it was the plastic, digital watch he had worn in another life, seventeen years earlier. But the moment he unsealed the bag, exposing its contents to the light and air, the watch turned suddenly to powder. It was like a fairy tale, time itself collapsing.

"The same thing happens to your emotions," said Bassem.

The lawyer came to fetch Nariman and we hustled through the gate into the courtroom, three rows of plastic chairs on a grubby tiled floor, two wooden desks stained the same reddish color as the wall behind the judge. The proceedings were quick. Nariman was facing a single charge of violating a closed-military-zone order. No one was disputing the facts of the case, explained her lawyer, an Israeli named Neri Ramati: "They asked her to leave. She didn't leave. They arrested her." But he had argued in a previous hearing that no Palestinian had ever before been charged solely with refusing to leave a closed military zone during a demonstration—usually the prosecution could find something else to throw at them—and that the law was being selectively enforced to punish Nariman for her leadership in the protests. So the judge had ordered the prosecution to search for precedents, which meant sifting through thousands of cases by hand. The chief military prosecutor for the entire West Bank had made a personal appearance to protest that the search would take 307 twelve-hour workdays. "We are not even close to the beginning," Ramati said, and smiled.

When it was over, nothing had been decided, not even the date of the next hearing, but Nariman was crying, and Bassem was hugging her. The three dates the judge had offered were all clustered around the 19th of November, the first anniversary of Rushdie's death. "I hate this month," said Nariman.

POSTSCRIPT TO THE FABLE of the settler on the roof: Later that same day, five soldiers arrived at the Sedr family's door. Three of them climbed the stairs to the rooftop, smiling bashfully as they emerged into the open air, like children whose drunk father has assigned them a task they know to be absurd but cannot shirk. "You either take down the flag or we have to place you into custody and I don't want to do that," the one who appeared to be their leader told Shadi.

Actually, there were two flags. The Sedrs had doubled down since the Russian settler's attempt at infiltration. Abd al-Khaleq came up. Both brothers argued with the soldiers. Dozens of Israeli flags were flying from their neighbors' windows and roofs. The Sedrs wouldn't remove theirs, they said, unless the soldiers came back with a court order.

This went on for a while. The soldier in charge kept walking off to consult with his superiors on his cell phone. The roof was getting crowded. A few friends and neighbors came up, two of them with video cameras, as well as two international observers. The soldiers conferred with one another. Should they arrest him? They couldn't decide. Their leader made one last phone call. The decision was made. "There is no reason to re-move him by force in front of the cameras," he told his comrades. And with that, they left.

Issa grew up just off Shuhada Street, a few blocks east of Beit Hadassah, "between the blacksmiths' market, the carpet market, the yogurt market, and the wholesale market." He assured me that it was a beautiful area, but he hadn't been there for years. I had. It wasn't beautiful anymore. Just haunted: where the rubble market and the rust market meet the dust mar-ket and the stray-dogs-barking-in-the-night market. Dry vines snaked up the welded doors. Weeds had taken root between the stones of the houses. In front of one stood a squat monument to Rabbi Shlomo Shapira, shot on that spot while visiting Hebron for the Sukkot holiday in 2002. Three of his children, standing beside him, were wounded.* There was no glass in the windows on the buildings' second floor. The shutters hung wide, as if the specters residing within had in their loneliness pushed them open to invite in the breeze.

Issa's father, a schoolteacher, had moved his immediate family out into what is now H1 during the First Intifada, when Issa was seven years old, but his grandfather held on until 2000. He left thinking he would be able to return as soon as the curfew was lifted. He couldn't. The fighting ended, but the neighborhood stayed closed to Palestinians. It was during that epoch, the long siege years of the Second Intifada, that Issa earned his political education. If you can draw an almost-straight line from the strug-gles of the First Intifada to the popular resistance demonstrations in Nabi Saleh and elsewhere, in Hebron it was the later uprising that mattered

---

*Over the course of the Second Intifada, seventeen soldiers and five Israeli civilians were killed by Palestinians in Hebron, more than half of them in a single battle in November 2002. During the same period, at least ninety Palestinians, the majority of them noncombatants, were killed in the city by Israelis.

most. The Second Intifada and the Goldstein massacre were like two heavy curtains drawn over the past beyond which it was difficult to see.

By Issa's account, when the Intifada erupted, he was a good student. He avoided politics and tried to stay away from trouble. Most of his cousins became fighters in a local cell of the Al-Aqsa Martyrs Brigade, an armed group allied with the Fatah movement. At some point in the early 2000s, one of them came to him. They had just lost their engineer. They needed someone to replace him, someone to make bombs, and Issa, who was studying electrical engineering, was an obvious candidate. He refused. They would lose, he told them. "I knew they didn't have enough weapons. They didn't have enough training. They weren't dangerous people."

Such things are relative, but Issa meant it literally. He told a story about seeing one of his cousins take shelter behind a wall to fire his Kalashnikov at an Israeli tank a few meters distant. "I might as well throw stones at it," his cousin cursed, and threw his weapon aside. Issa later saw his cousin killed in front of him. "I was in the window, watching," he said, when an Israeli helicopter fired a rocket and his cousin disappeared in the explosion. In the chaos that followed, Issa pushed past his father and ran outside to see if his cousin could be saved. He couldn't. The helicopter returned, Issa said, and fired again. At him this time. He dove behind a wall. The rocket hit the spot where he had been standing moments before. "You know what a rocket does? It destroys everything. I went crazy." And he realized, he said, that "there's no way you can fight them with their helicopters, their tanks." Not with Kalashnikovs at least.

In January 2003, the army closed the two main universities in Hebron. Their campuses, according to the IDF, were "a hothouse for terrorists and suicide bombers." Issa went to class one morning and found the gates to the university welded shut. The administrators, he said, were unwilling to confront the Israeli authorities. They simply rescheduled classes in public schools with inadequate facilities and tiny, child-sized desks. Being a good student suddenly required that Issa learn an entirely different set of skills.

He didn't know where to start, he said, so he read about Mandela, Gandhi, Martin Luther King. He began talking to other students, organizing. Then, as now, the Palestinian authorities were the first obstacle. The students demonstrated in front of the district governor's office and the mayor's office. They would blockade city hall, they threatened, "unless you join us and pressure the Israelis."

Issa emerged as a leader in the movement. When the students decided they could no longer wait for help from the local authorities, it was Issa who opened the campus gates. "I was the one with the hammers," he said. The dean and the administrators showed up. Afraid the soldiers would follow the students in and destroy the university, they tried to stop him. "I told them, 'Today the university will be open.'" But the campus was a mess, and it took the students weeks of labor to get it in shape. The administration still refused to help. "We said, 'Okay, you don't want to teach us, we'll teach ourselves.'" The students set up their own curriculum and worked with the few professors who were unafraid to teach.

"It was an amazing experience," Issa said. "Because we won."

He graduated. The Intifada ended. Not much else changed. The gates to the entire West Bank have been sealed and, with the PA's complicity, all the Palestinians therein sit at tiny desks, studying their own humiliation. Everything Issa had experienced convinced him that unarmed resistance, if sufficiently organized, tenacious, and bold, would achieve the results that guns and bombs could not. He at first embraced nonviolence— unlike Bassem, he wasn't shy about using that word—tentatively, "as a tactic, not a strategy," he said: "Let's use it and see if it works." He began to study the history of the First Intifada and, perhaps more influentially, the techniques of his adversaries. The Israelis worked hard, he observed, not just to crush any individuals who resisted their rule, but to create divisions within Palestinian society and break up any collectivity that formed outside of their control, "because community is resistance," Issa said. He studied the settlers too, "how they build community, how they build facts on the ground."

Establishing the center met both of those goals. The house in Tel Rumeida functioned to cement the Palestinian presence in an area the settlers badly wished to claim. It would serve as a locus for organizing, a classroom, a stage for future efforts, and most important, a gathering place where people could find strength in one another's company. In 2008, a year after rehabbing the center, Issa cofounded YAS with another activist. At first, the group followed the model employed by the popular resistance villages along the route of the wall. They organized marches every Friday in Hebron's old city. In one key respect they diverged from the village model— they decided early on not to allow stone throwing. Youth in Hebron had been hurling rocks at soldiers for decades and things had only gotten worse. YAS wanted to try something new.

The army nonetheless responded to YAS's protests with the usual methods—gas and projectiles, beatings and arrests—and began shuttering shops in retaliation. The merchants weren't happy. Neither was Issa. "We wanted to open shops, not close them," he said. And the protests too quickly became routine: "Weekly demos meant they knew what we were doing." They changed their tactics, abandoning the demonstrations except for one "Open Shuhada Street" march every February on the anniversary of the Goldstein massacre. Instead, YAS focused on building resistance through concrete and even banal tasks that were nonetheless perceived by the settlers and army alike as a threat: cleaning the streets, rehabbing houses, distributing food, offering Hebrew classes so that residents would not be helpless in front of the Israeli military bureaucracy, doing whatever they could to fight off fear and despair, and to keep the community intact.

The previous September, the PA, which all that summer had been unable to pay its employees their full salaries, raised the price of fuel. Strikes and demonstrations spread across the West Bank. Finally, Palestine appeared to be catching up with the rest of the Arab world. Most of the anger was directed at then–prime minister and former IMF economist Salam Fayyad, whose economic reform program based in "institution building" and "transparency" measures was beloved by American officials and commentators—when

Fayyad resigned in early 2013, *The New York Times*'s Thomas Friedman hailed him with blithe incoherence as "the Arab Spring before there was an Arab Spring." Most Palestinians, though, understood Fayyad's slickly technocratic rhetoric to mean little more than public sector cuts, full economic cooperation with Israel, and the squelching of all forms of resistance that threatened the emerging Palestinian elite's profitable arrangements with their occupier. On September 6, demonstrators in Hebron burned Fayyad in effigy. Issa helped to organize the protests there, and to focus their demands. The price of petrol was the least of it: they wanted the PA to rescind the entire Paris Protocol, the main economic component of the Oslo Accords, which codified Palestinian financial vassalage to Israel. The PA, Issa said, had become "the main obstacle to all types of resistance."

On September 10 of 2012, thousands took to the streets in Hebron—twenty thousand by Issa's perhaps generous estimate. The march ended with protesters throwing stones at municipal offices and at the police headquarters. PA security forces responded with tear gas. Dozens were injured. It was just another day in Hebron, except that it wasn't the Israelis shooting gas this time. The PA, Issa said, did everything it could to suppress the movement. The clashes, he insisted, were started by provocateurs to give the PA a pretext to crush the protests. Palestinian police arrested his spokesperson and media coordinator and threatened him repeatedly. People came to him, he said, warning him that he would be arrested, or shot, or that rumors would be spread to destroy his reputation. "They don't like things," Issa said, "that they don't control." But Fayyad got the message. Part of it at least: he called off the price hike. The protests dissipated and the momentum died. The spring thaw had once again been deferred. This winter seemed to have no end.

Issa's latest project was more modest, if in its way no less risky: a kindergarten. There had been no school for small children in Tel Rumeida. What better way to bring people together than to give them something they needed? As they had with the center, the activists repaired an abandoned home that had been too thoroughly trashed to interest the settlers for long.

It took months. They had to sneak supplies in, avoiding the checkpoints, working at night. Repeatedly, soldiers and settlers tried to stop them. "We kept going," Issa said, "until they gave up."

The kindergarten opened shortly before I arrived in Hebron. It was a small, one-story building, its outer walls decorated with colorful paintings of cartoon characters, Popeye and SpongeBob looming large among them. Jerry the mouse was in there too. Tom the cat was conspicuously absent. The teachers were volunteers, the toys and supplies donated, the classroom filled with boys and girls sitting cross-legged on the floor, fidgeting eagerly at their teachers' feet. The activists planned to build a playground, but they didn't have the money and had installed only one piece of equipment so far—a red and yellow plastic slide about a meter high. The yard was still just unpacked dirt strewn with broken glass, and the low wall around it was in urgent need of whitewashing. Vandals had spray-painted it with Stars of David and a single sentence in Hebrew: "DEATH TO ARABS," it said, followed by not one but three fat exclamation points. I passed it every day as I walked between Zidan's house and the center. I thought about it a lot, those Stars of David, the crude black letters, the tiny but colorful plastic slide. I thought about it weeks later, after I'd left Hebron, talking to Issa one evening over coffee in Ramallah. "I feel that I'm winning," he said to me then, leaning toward me over the table, speaking with his usual high dose of certainty and assurance. "We are winning," he repeated. I am almost certain that he believed it.

WE DID A LOT of walking. One night we were out on the edge of the city, just beneath the settlement of Kiryat Arba. The streets, hilly here, were empty. Or nearly empty, though Palestinians were allowed to walk (but not drive) in this particular zone. A family of settlers—two men, a woman, a gaggle of kids behind them—ambled by on their way home from prayers at the Tomb. They were laughing and chatting, and in no hurry. They were unarmed, or at least not obviously armed, in the middle of a Palestinian neighborhood in a Palestinian city in which their presence was regarded as hostile, and yet they seemed at ease. But then they had an escort. Where there are settlers, soldiers are never far: an IDF jeep, lights flashing yellow on its roof, inched along a few yards behind them, its presence laying the foundation for their good cheer.

We cut down through a valley and weaved our way through dark olive groves toward the house closest to the settlement's fence. Its yard, we could see from below, was strung with colored lights. We climbed toward it and back up to the road again. Three soldiers were approaching from the opposite direction. One of them was leading a Palestinian boy by the arm. By the time I had figured out what was happening they had already passed us. The boy didn't look older than twelve. He was clearly terrified. Three more boys trailed a safe distance behind. We asked what had happened. They had been playing and, they swore, not throwing stones or anything. The soldiers thought their friend was cursing them, so they grabbed him and took him away. They told us his name: Nader Ghazzala. We left them standing beneath a streetlamp, looking lost and scared in its thin yellow light.

We kept walking. Just around the bend, we passed a monument to nine Israeli soldiers and three members of Kiryat Arba's security squad who had died here in a battle that had also killed three Islamic Jihad gunmen in November 2002. Among the dead was the commander of all IDF troops in Hebron, the highest-ranking Israeli officer to lose his life during the Second Intifada. Immediately after the skirmish, the army put all of H2 under a curfew that remained in effect for six continuous months, and announced plans to demolish twenty-two homes, some of them more than five hundred years old, and to confiscate a strip of land nearly a kilometer in length in order to widen the road from Kiryat Arba to the Tomb of the Patriarchs.*

We climbed a long driveway toward the house with the festive lights.

---

*The Israeli High Court ultimately approved the demolition of just two homes. In the end, three were leveled and eleven others badly damaged. Their ruins remain. The old, domed rooms are exposed to the street, their walls and painted ceilings crumbling.

There was music playing. Plastic bunting hung from the trees. The owner's son was getting married. The wedding wasn't for a few days, but the party had begun. A dozen men sat in a circle on the patio, clapping out the beat as an eight-year-old boy in a black and gold tracksuit danced in front of them, his eyes half closed in concentration. The groom's father, Qa'ed D'ana, would later tell me the usual excruciating tales about humiliating raids and assaults and settlers throwing stones and even grenades at the house from the other side of the fence in Kiryat Arba, which was just a few meters uphill. The boy in the tracksuit was his nephew. The rest of the children were wrestling and giggling behind him, but the boy danced on as if in a trance, sliding across the patio in a stilted almost-moonwalk.

We walked down into the valley beneath the settlement and talked to a man named Jamal Abu Seifan about the day in 2008 when Israeli police evicted settlers from the Rajabi house, which they had occupied the previous year and renamed the "House of Peace." The settlers responded to the eviction by attacking the surrounding Palestinian neighborhoods, burning cars and torching houses with sponges soaked in oil. "It was like hell," Abu Seifan said. On his cell phone, he showed us a blurry, shaky video he had recorded of a settler shooting his uncle and his cousin. It got even shakier when another settler firing an M16 began aiming at his feet.

We walked up past the Rajabi house, which that November was still being used as an army post.* Behind it, we climbed the hill to the police station. I pushed the buzzer on the intercom beside the gate. Eventually a voice answered in Hebrew. I explained that I was a journalist and wanted to know what had happened to a boy named Nader Ghazzala who had been arrested earlier that day. A minute or two later a gap-toothed Druze policeman appeared on the other side of the fence, in the yellow light of the police station's yard. The boy had been let go, he said. He had been the one

---

*Israeli authorities initially found that the documents the settlers submitted to prove that they had purchased the house were forgeries, but in March 2014, the High Court ruled that the purchase was legal and that the settlers should be allowed to return.

to release him. He seemed amused by our presence. His name was Sami Hamza. I asked if the boy had been charged. He hadn't. I asked why he had been arrested.

"He shouted to the soldier," Sami Hamza said. "He said bad things in Arabic."

I asked if that was against the law.

He smiled, amicably. "Sure it's against the law. But because of his age, and because it's the first time, I released him," he said. "When we can help, we help."

That was that. All was well. We said good night. Sami Hamza retreated through the yellow light of the yard and went back inside the station. A shooting star streaked white across the sky, enormous and bright. All around the city, dogs were barking about matters of concern to dogs.

ON THE MORNING of November 8, a Friday, Zidan knocked on the door, as he always did, with coffee. "Did you hear?" he said, sitting down to light a cigarette. "There was a martyr from Hebron." Late the night before, a young man named Anas Fouad al-Atrash had been killed at the Container checkpoint above Wadi Naar. He was twenty-three, and had lived in Abu Sneineh, the neighborhood in H1 overlooking Tel Rumeida. The official story was that he had stepped out of his car and attacked a soldier with a knife and that the soldier had fired once in self-defense, killing him. It had been a bad night. Earlier that same evening, another young man named Bashir Sami Habanin had been killed by soldiers at a checkpoint a few miles south of Nablus.* He had been on his way home from Tulkarem, where he worked as a professor at a local technical college. The IDF claimed

---

*Haaretz, the newspaper of the Israeli liberal left, mentioned the two killings three paragraphs into an article headlined "PALESTINIAN FIREBOMB ATTACK WOUNDS ISRAELI MOTHER, DAUGHTER"—elsewhere in the West Bank, near the settlement of Tekoa, someone had thrown a Molotov cocktail at a yellow-plated car, "lightly wounding" its Israeli passengers. The article named neither al-Atrash nor Habanin, and quoted no Palestinian witnesses.

he had aimed fireworks at Israeli civilians waiting for a bus and that soldiers had responded with gunfire.* He was twenty-eight.

The Friday clashes at Bab al-Zawiya didn't usually begin until after the midday prayer, but that day they started early. From Zidan's, we heard the first shots just before eleven. A few minutes later, as we left the house, the soldier stationed outside Beit Hadassah made a phone call. I had begun to notice such things. We passed through the checkpoint to Bab al-Zawiya. A few kids ran out from behind a building, hurled stones toward the soldiers, and hurried off to hide again. We flagged a taxi to the mosque near the Polytechnic, where the funeral of Anas al-Atrash would be held.

The street outside the blue-domed mosque was already packed with mourners. Dozens of PA policemen stood by, some in olive green, others in blue camouflage, all with AK-47s and body armor. Who, I wondered, were they there to protect? I ran into Imad, one of the guys from YAS. His family name, I hadn't realized, was al-Atrash. Anas had been his cousin. Imad's uncle, he told me, had a business manufacturing and selling shoes, and two of his sons, Anas and Ismail, ran the family's shop in Jericho. They slept there during the week, driving back to Hebron after they closed up each Thursday night. They had been on their way home when Anas was shot. Imad was a tough kid, a welder with hands like oven mitts who liked to boast of his defiance of Israeli laws, but that day he was near tears. The Israeli story didn't make any sense, he said. Anas hadn't been politically active and wanted nothing more than to get married and live his life. "He had a dream like all the youth in the world," Imad said, fighting to find words. "But nothing now."

---

*Representatives of the Israeli Military Advocate General Corps told the human rights group B'Tselem that after being shot in the legs, Habanin had stood up and resumed shooting fireworks at the soldiers and "in view of the menace he posed to the lives of the troops and civilians present . . . the forces fired additional shots which were the cause of his death."

———

JUST BEFORE NOON, the muezzin's call rang from the loudspeaker atop the minaret. Everyone went silent. "God is great," sang the muezzin, and the mourners pressed their foreheads to the asphalt. Across the street, a USAID billboard rose above a field strewn with trash and construction debris, rusted pipes and broken concrete. "INDUSTRIAL AREA ROAD, HEBRON," the sign read in English. "THIS PROJECT IS A GIFT FROM THE AMERICAN PEOPLE TO THE PALESTINIAN PEOPLE." So, it occurred to me, was the gun that killed Anas al-Atrash, and probably the bullet. The prayer ended. Several hundred men kneeled around me in silence, their eyes closed and their hands on their knees.

Later they carried out his body. It was wrapped in a flag, pink carnations beside a pale, unshaven cheek. His feet, in black socks, peeked out at the bottom of the bier. The mourners followed the pallbearers and the corpse they carried through the dusty streets toward the cemetery, past white, stone buildings in varying states of construction and collapse. Women stood in windows on the second and third floors, staring out from behind ornate metal grilles. The flag that wrapped the body began to sag, revealing Anas al-Atrash's hands folded on his chest. Two men in balaclavas stood in an olive grove below us, firing shot after earsplitting shot into the air, their M16s angled a bit too low for comfort. It was the Al-Aqsa Brigade paying tribute, announcing their survival with each shot, offering a promise of revenge that no one expected them to keep. Between bursts, I could hear the women ululating from the gravesite, greeting the corpse, shouting again that God is great. Anas al-Atrash's brothers stood at the cemetery gate, weeping in each other's arms.

When it was over we hitched a ride and then another ride and found a taxi to take us back to the center of the city. It was Friday, and the shops were closed, the streets empty of cars. From a few blocks away we could already see thick, black smoke pouring into the sky above Bab al-Zawiya.

6.

MUCH LESS A COUNTRY

Hebron, Jerusalem, Beitunia, Jericho, Ramat Aviv

Still, that was just the city; it wasn't an allegory. . . .

—CHINA MIÉVILLE

There were soldiers on the roofs in Bab al-Zawiya, and soldiers in the streets with their rifles at the ready. The market was empty, the stalls that earlier had been heaped with bananas and bright orange persimmons and pyramids of green *za'atar* dusted with purple sumac were bare now and tied off with dull white tarps. Still, the mood was somehow festive, if that is the right word. The guys threw stones at the soldiers, or toward them anyway. They laughed as they darted and dodged and kept laughing until a rubber-coated bullet took one of them down and they all gathered around and scooped him off the pavement and ran off carrying him and shouting until they finally heard him protesting that he was fine and they put him down and hugged and punched him as he limped off and they all went back to laughing and throwing stones again. One guy—older, in his thirties, perhaps a bit off—ducked around a corner and jumped out a few yards in front of the soldiers. He cocked his fingers at them like a little boy playing war, and shouted, "tok-tok-tok-tok-tok." The other guys cheered. The soldiers, thankfully, didn't shoot him.

"The boys are playing," the guy next to me observed. He was a pretty kid, with light eyes and long lashes. He laughed and touched my shoulder

and jogged off to join his friends. Someone delivered a giant box of rocks
and for a minute, until the soldiers started shooting again, they were clattering like hail. A thick-mustached old man in a blue suit stood at the entrance
to an alley, surveying the scene with tired disapproval. Life went on: a water
truck pulled up across the street and a minute later a worker lowered a hose
from the roof to fill the tanks four stories up. The pretty kid came back and
pointed to a boy standing alone on the corner, his face and neck disfigured,
one ear and most of his nose shorn off, his eyes watery and bright.

"You see this guy?" he asked. It was a rocket from an Apache helicopter
that did it to him, my new friend explained. "They were killing a Hamas
guy and he was nearby," he said. It was 2002. I did the math. He must have
been a small child. "He was a very beautiful boy," my friend said, and trotted off again.

A gray-haired man rode his bicycle through the middle of the melee,
smiling beatifically, taking his time. A garbage truck stopped and let two
workers off to gather the trash piled on the corner, but the driver panicked
and hit the gas, forgetting his companions, who ran, ducking and cursing,
after the speeding truck.

This was Hebron. There were clashes every day for the next two weeks,
the young men gathering in Bab al-Zawiya each afternoon and into the
night, the younger kids at the checkpoints on the other side of H2 every day
after school let out, swarms of them in their brightly colored backpacks.
They jeered each time the soldiers sallied forth and fired off a round or
threw a stun grenade, mocking them and chanting with unflagging glee.

"Container!" they shouted again and again. "Container! Container!
Container!"

ISMAIL AL-ATRASH SAT squeezed beside his parents in the sitting room
of their three-story house in Abu Sneineh. Ismail's hair was neatly gelled,
but his cheeks were unshaven and his eyelids heavy. An uncle sat sprawled

across an adjacent sofa, fingering a length of wooden prayer beads as Ismail recounted the events of the evening of Thursday, November 7. That night, he and his brother Anas had closed up the family's shoe store in Jericho and packed the car for the drive back to Hebron. Before they left, the brothers called their mother. "She asked me to buy tomatoes and lemons and oranges and cucumbers and potatoes," Ismail recalled. "We got in the car and headed for Hebron." It was normally about an hour's drive. They did it every Thursday. After a weekend's rest with the family, they would head north again to Jericho to open the shop for another week of work. That night Ismail drove. Anas was exhausted. "He put his head back, stretched his legs and went to sleep," said Ismail.

At 11:05 p.m., the brothers' blue Volkswagen lurched over the first speed bump outside the Container checkpoint. When it is not clogged with weekend traffic, Container—the English word is used in Arabic—is a desolate spot: a lonely stretch of asphalt, four dingy tollboothlike structures painted white and green, a few bored Israeli soldiers with automatic rifles. It's not a nice place to die. That night, Ismail said, the soldiers seemed agitated. They had stopped the car in front of him and were subjecting its passengers to an extensive search. One stood with his hands up, waiting to be frisked. A red dot of light bounced around the al-Atrashes' front seats as a soldier pointed the barrel of his weapon, and its laser-guided sight, at the two brothers. Anas slept through it all, his face resting in his palm. "He must have woken up confused," Ismail said, "and not known what was going on."

Ismail's father, unshaven like his son, stared blankly at a point perhaps a foot above the coffee table. He closed his eyes.

Without a word, said Ismail, Anas opened the door and stepped out of the car. Ismail called his brother's name. Anas didn't have a chance to walk away from the vehicle, he said: "By the second time I called him, the soldier had already shot him."

I asked Ismail if the soldier said anything first.

"No," he said.

I asked if Anas had anything in his hands.

"No," he said. "Nothing."

Ismail's mother, her face swollen with grief, reached for a tissue.

"I stepped out of the car," Ismail went on. Three soldiers, he said, ran up to him. "One put the barrel of his gun here, one here, one here." He indicated his head, his back, his hip. "They pushed me down on the ground," he said, and cuffed his hands behind him. He turned to look for his brother on the other side of the car. "I kept calling his name, 'Anas, Anas,' and I saw them dragging him away." He yelled out, asking his brother if he was all right. No one answered.

An ambulance arrived. "They put him in the ambulance. I thought maybe he was injured in his leg. I kept calling for him. A soldier came and pressed down on my shoulder with his boot and told me I wasn't allowed to say anything."

The father sighed. The room went silent except for the clicking of the uncle's prayer beads. A twelve-year-old boy opened the door—Anas and Ismail's youngest brother, Mohammad. He sat beside his uncle and tucked one foot beneath his thigh. Ismail continued: A man in plain clothes who he believed was an agent from the Shabak appeared beside him. "And the injured?" asked the agent. "Your brother?" Ismail said yes. The agent left. Ismail tried to drag himself along the ground to get a better view, but the ambulance's rear door was closed. He couldn't see anything. The Shabak agent returned. He asked a strange question: "Why is Anas so upset?"

"He's not upset," Ismail recalled answering. "He's in a good mood." They had been joking around all evening until Anas fell asleep. The Shabak agent asked if Ismail was certain, if Anas hadn't maybe had a fight with someone, perhaps a friend or a girlfriend, if maybe he was in love with someone who didn't love him back. Ismail told him no, nothing like that had happened.

Another strange question: "He said, 'Is he the kind who would carry a knife?' I said, 'No, he's not. We don't have any problems with anyone.'"

A third: the agent asked if Anas belonged to any of the Palestinian political factions, to Hamas or Fatah. Again Ismail answered no. The family
steered clear of politics, he said. Anas had never been arrested, had never
even been called in for questioning—a rarity for a youth from Abu Sneineh.
He was studying accounting, and hoping to get married in the spring.
"We're just busy with our work," Ismail told him.

The Shabak agent left him. Two policemen arrived with two men Ismail
believed were high-ranking Shabak commanders. They convened behind
the ambulance with the others. Eventually one of the commanders came
over. He sat on the ground beside Ismail. "What happened?" he asked.
"Did he have a knife?"

Ismail told him no, that Anas just got out of the car and a soldier suddenly shot him. The commander, he said, gave him water to drink and a
cigarette to smoke. "Then he went like this," Ismail said, smacking his
forehead with the heel of his palm. He asked the commander how Anas
was doing. The commander stood and walked away.

When he came back, he uncuffed Ismail's hands and recuffed them in
front of his body. He sat down across from him. "Please," Ismail said, "can
you just tell me how he is?"

"He's okay, thank God," the commander said.

"Thank God," said Ismail.

"If I told you Anas had a knife," the commander asked, "what would
you say?"

"I would say you're a liar," Ismail answered. There's no knife in the car,
he told him. "You can search it—you'll find tomatoes, lemons, oranges,
cucumbers and potatoes, some clothes, nothing else."

"He said, 'You're sure he didn't have a knife.' I said, 'I'm sure.'"

The commander led him to a spot on the pavement a few meters away.
A knife lay on the asphalt. "It wasn't even the spot where Anas was shot,"
Ismail said. "He said, 'This knife, have you ever seen it?' I said, 'No.' He
said, 'Are you sure?' I said, 'I'm sure. I've never seen it.'"

Beside him, Ismail's mother wept into her hands.

Again, Ismail said, he asked the commander, "Please, tell me what's happening."

"God willing, he'll be okay," the commander responded, and left Ismail again. He craned his neck to get a look at the ambulance. "All of a sudden I see them taking his body out. They put him down on the ground and put a sheet over him. I started going crazy and screaming and hitting my head on the ground. I don't remember what happened afterward."

By morning, Israeli newspapers had published the official version of Anas al-Atrash's death: A twenty-three-year-old Palestinian had run from his car and rushed at a checkpoint soldier with a knife. The soldier, fearing for his life, fired once, killing him. It wasn't much of a story, just another anonymous incident, one of a series of apparently uncoordinated assaults on Israeli security personnel. I called Micky Rosenfeld, the Israeli police spokesman, and asked to see any security camera footage from the checkpoint that might shed light on the incident. The footage, he told me, would under no circumstances be made public. A little while later, he e-mailed me a statement in which he clarified: "There is no investigation under way."

Tzipi Schlissel greeted us warmly. She was happy we had come, she said, because "no one in the world listens to our story." The settlers' story, that is. She was sure we must have heard "horrible stories about what the soldiers were doing to the Arabs," but we must have also seen with our own eyes, she said, how the Arabs threw stones and provoked them. She had been mopping the floor of her apartment when we arrived. It was small and somewhat cramped and smelled of oil and cooked meat. We hadn't had a chance to sit yet and Schlissel, abuzz with nervous energy, had put down the mop but hadn't stopped moving, and the smile hadn't faded from her face, and already she was talking about the organizations all over the world that "give money to spread the Arab narrative," and that support groups like Issa Amro's, which were devoted, she said, to training the youth to provoke the soldiers so they could film their responses and spread their propaganda around the globe. YAS, she said, was nothing but a "factory for making videos against the Jews."

Her circumstances were humble—the kitchen counter was cluttered with dirty dishes, the floor of the children's bedroom littered with clothing and stray toys—but Schlissel, with her lively eyes and sharp and sunburned features, was as close as anyone gets to settler royalty. Her grandfather was Abraham Isaac Kook, also known as Rav the Elder, or simply as *HaRav*, "The Rabbi," as if there were no other. Kook was the first Ashkenazi chief rabbi of Palestine under the British. In the late nineteenth and early twentieth centuries, most Orthodox Jews had been opposed to Zionism on theological grounds: The Exile was divinely ordained, and the messiah would arrive when God willed it. Until then, Jews were to stick to the Torah, and wait. Kook broke with this centuries-old tradition of political quietism, wedding Judaism's deepest mystical traditions to an agile pragmatism, grounding Zionism, and a devotion to the otherwise secular institutions of the state, in the numinous absolute.* Kook's son, Schlissel's uncle Zvi Yehuda Kook, continued his father's work, sacralizing every act of the Israeli state—including its wars—as "the embodiment of the vision of redemption," and placing a particular messianic emphasis on the obligation to conquer and control all of the Land of Israel. Kook the Younger's spiritualized nationalism would provide the theological basis for the Israeli settlement movement from the late 1960s on.

Through the windows, we could hear the booms echoing from the clashes in Bab al-Zawiya. Schlissel's father, the Rabbi Shlomo Ra'anan, had moved here, to the heart of the Tel Rumeida settlement, in 1992. He was killed six years later when "an Arab terrorist," as Schlissel put it, climbed in through a window and stabbed him in his bed. At the beginning of the Second Intifada, Schlissel and her husband moved to Hebron from a

---

*As early as 1920, he envisioned Israel as "a divine entity, our holy and exalted state!"

settlement outpost near Ramallah—not to Tel Rumeida, where her mother still lived, but to what was then the front line of the settlers' battle for Hebron, the old vegetable market on Shuhada Street, which had been closed by the army after the Goldstein massacre. In 2001, eight families of settlers had moved in, building their homes among the old market stalls. When they were evicted in January 2006 by Israeli police, most of the settlers went peacefully. Schlissel refused to leave. The police dragged her out, her youngest child in her arms. The eviction, she told *Haaretz* at the time, was a "national humiliation." The Schlissels moved to another contested site, a house a few blocks away that settlers claimed they had leased from its Palestinian owner. The state ruled that the documents the settlers submitted were forgeries, and that May Schlissel was again dragged off, again clutching an infant in her lap. For Hebron's settlers, these were battles for the soul of the Jewish state: settler youth threw rocks and Molotov cocktails during the eviction, injuring seventeen police officers. The Schlissels ultimately moved to a more tranquil environment—Tel Rumeida— where they have remained.

I only learned that history later. That day, Schlissel wanted to talk about the more distant past. She showed us an old, sepia-toned photo of her grandmother. "My story starts with her," she said. The woman in the photo was her mother's mother, who had grown up in Jerusalem but in August 1929 had been visiting an older sister in Hebron. When the family learned that the city's Jews were in danger, they barricaded themselves into her sister's home, pushing all the furniture against the door. "The Arabs threw a big, big stone through the window," Schlissel said. It crashed to the floor in precisely the spot where her teenage grandmother had been standing a moment earlier. "This is our family's private miracle," said Schlissel, her smile unflagging, "and this is why I can talk to you now."

It wasn't just a family story—the 1929 massacre, in which nearly 10 percent of Hebron's small Jewish community was slaughtered, formed a fundamental prehistory for the entire community of Hebron's settlers, an "absent-present, not a past event of almost eighty years ago," wrote Idith

Zertal and Akiva Eldar, "a motive that justifies everything." The blood that spilled that long-ago August mattered more than any abstract theology. It washed away, for the settlers, all curiosity about the concrete historic causes of the unrest, which had begun, familiarly enough, with a dispute over access to the Wailing Wall in Jerusalem's old city. The bloodshed was hardly timeless. Jews and Arabs lived in relative harmony throughout Ottoman-era Palestine. Overall, Jews enjoyed greater security and freedom in the Muslim Levant than they did among Christians elsewhere, particularly in Eastern Europe, but also in the West. In his official report to the British Parliament on the 1929 "disturbances," Sir Walter Shaw acknowledged that "there had been no recorded attacks of Jews by Arabs" in the previous eight decades and "representatives of all parties" had concurred "that before the [First World] War the Jews and Arabs lived side by side if not in amity, at least with tolerance." The aggravating factor, Shaw was forced to admit, was the 1917 Balfour Declaration, which promised British support for the creation of a Jewish homeland in Palestine, such that "the Arabs have come to see in the Jewish immigrant not only a menace to their livelihood but a possible overlord of the future."

Such empirical subtleties had no place in the settlers' martyrology, to borrow a term from Zertal and Eldar. For the settlers, the massacre was not a contingent historical event, it was history itself, and it was cyclical, stuck on eternal replay. Schlissel spoke at some length about the banker friend of the family who had offered to shelter her grandmother and her great-aunt, trusting that the esteem in which he was held by local Palestinians would keep his family safe. Instead they were slaughtered in their home.* When the city's Jews fled in the wake of the massacre, it was the first time in centuries that

---

*Schlissel didn't mention it, but it is worth recording that most of the Jews who survived the 1929 massacre did so because they were saved by Palestinians. Schlissel's neighbor across the street, Jawad's uncle Hajj Mohammad Abu Aisha, showed me an old document in Hebrew that recognized his father for the courage he had demonstrated in protecting Hebron's Jews in 1929. But Schlissel didn't talk to the Abu Aishas, she said, or to any Palestinians. Since her father's killing, she preferred "to have no contact with them."

no Jewish community lived in the "beloved and also rejected, terrible and pitiable town of Hebron," as one settler leader later dubbed it. A link the settlers viewed as vital, even sacred, had been broken. With their sacrificial presence, with their bodies and their lives, Schlissel and her neighbors were fighting to heal that rupture, to tear redemption from a history of loss. But they were caught by that past, trapped by it, condemned to keep dancing the same gore-spattered dance, dragging new and unwilling partners onto the stage, spinning and dizzy, refusing to fall. No matter what harm they perceived as being done to them—whether it was petty or profound, whether it was real or imagined or they had just finished provoking it themselves—they experienced the same eternal injuries, and were blind to the magnitude of the hurt that they inflicted.

Schlissel's understanding of her place in the city was like a funhouse-mirror version of her Palestinian neighbors', only not very fun: "If you're a Jew, you can't rent a house" in Hebron, she complained. "You can't buy a house, you can't build a house. We are in a ghetto. The Jewish community is not allowed to grow." I heard the same thing from every settler I spoke to in Hebron. It wasn't that they had successfully conquered Hebron's downtown and chased out most of its residents, it was that more than 90 percent of the city was not yet theirs. With great earnestness, they experienced this as a deep injustice. Oslo and the Hebron Protocol were not a victory but a terrible defeat, a surrender to persecutions that stretched back for millennia. When Gaia pointed out that Palestinians could not walk on the streets in their own neighborhoods, Schlissel explained that if the roads were open, "they will be able to attack and kill again." When we asked why her neighbors, the Abu Aishas, had to live as they did, she said the cages on their windows "are mostly for the media," part of the unending effort to defame Hebron's Jews.

She had more things to show us, aerial photos from 1945 and copies of old Ottoman documents that, she said, established the Jewish community's right to all of Tel Rumeida. One was a rental agreement signed in 1811, the other a land deed from 1816. They weren't in her name, or in the name of any of the current settlers or their forebears, but Jews had lived there, and the settlers were also Jews. That, in her mind, was enough. If so far the courts had not always agreed, she was confident that the settlers would prevail. Just outside her apartment was a fenced-off enclosure of the ancient stone walls unearthed by Israeli archaeologists during excavations in the 1980s and late 1990s. Among their findings, Schlissel reminded us, were ceramic jars, the handles of which were stamped in Hebrew, "For the King."* Her presence there, Schlissel said, was a continuation of the Jewish community that lived in Hebron more than two thousand years ago. Scores of other cultures had claimed this land in the centuries before and after, but none of them could be seen in the blinding, redemptive light of the Return. "As the Jewish nation had a redemption and we came back to the Land," she beamed, "I'm sure that one day all of Hebron will be Jewish."

What, I asked her, about all the Palestinians who lived there now?

"The people who want peace will stay," she answered. "And the ones who want war? They won't be here."

SOMETIMES HEBRON was beautiful. From the patio outside the center you could see the crush of the old city beneath you and empty Shuhada Street like a bare ribbon of stone, the high crenellated walls of the Ibrahimi mosque, and the crowded hillside neighborhoods above the holy site. The buildings were uniformly white and rectilinear and from a distance looked like cells in a hive. When the sun fell the whole city turned gold and the muezzins' cries rose in a clamor of exaltation from mosques to the east and west and north and south, always slightly out of synch and more

---

*The artifacts have been dated to the eighth century BCE, when Hebron was part of the kingdom of Judah. The king in question would not have been either David or Solomon, who about two hundred years earlier governed what archaeologist Israel Finkelstein argues was less a kingdom than a small and relatively impoverished rural chiefdom.

magnificent for its chaos and imperfection. The temperature would drop with the sun and the guys at the center would break up whatever boards or branches they had on hand and build a fire in an old steel drum. Big Ahmad would smoke *arghile*, Little Ahmad would stoke the coals, and everyone would talk and smoke into the night, the flames jumping in occasional explosions of spark, casting their faces at times into shadow, at times into glowing, orange light.

The clashes sparked by Anas al-Atrash's killing continued. As the days passed, the blasts from Bab al-Zawiya became ambient noise, like the howling of dogs at night on Shuhada Street. (The soldiers fed the strays, and all day the dogs slept in lazy packs around the watchtowers, their coats the color of the city at dusk.) Each morning the streets around Bab al-Zawiya were littered with thousands of stones, as if God had erred in the night and reached for rocks instead of rain. One day, Peter and Gaia and I walked out through Checkpoint 56 just as a cleanup crew was raking up the previous day's harvest of stones. Six workers with shovels and brooms were pushing them into the maw of a small bulldozer.* We stopped for a while to watch, but it was a big job, and we were too impatient to wait.

If you had time and didn't mind the trek, there were ways around most of the checkpoints. Like any border crossings, checkpoints are not primarily barriers so much as nodes of control. And however hard anyone may strive, control is never complete. If you knew the way, you could climb from Tel Rumeida into Abu Sneineh without passing a single soldier. We did it often, especially after the clashes in Bab al-Zawiya became constant and the adventure of dodging rocks and rubber-coated bullets while crossing through Checkpoint 56 had grown tiresome. You just walked out from

---

*Employment with the post-clash-checkpoint-rock-gathering crew places high on the list of absurd occupation-engendered professions, up there with the guys who drive the golf carts to ferry passengers through the kilometer-long cage between the Israeli and Palestinian checkpoints at the Erez Crossing into Gaza.

the center and through the old Roman olive trees above the cemetery and followed the path beside a series of giant ditches to an empty lot, and after that, the street, H1, Hebron.

The ditches were the only remaining evidence of excavations undertaken by an American archaeologist named Philip Hammond in 1963. Hammond was forced to abandon his project by the 1967 war, but in the meantime uncovered the fortifications of a Middle Bronze Age city (i.e., between 3,500 and 4,000 years old) with walls as much as thirty feet wide. You could still see the gargantuan stones he found buried beneath the dry dirt of the hillside, but the excavations were just holes now, overgrown with weeds and filling, slowly, with trash.

PERHAPS IF HE had remained in Boston, where he was born, Baruch Marzel would have been a calmer man.* Probably not. The unofficial leader of the Tel Rumeida settlement appeared to delight in giving offense, and also in taking it. The first time I approached him, he walked right past me and didn't turn when I called his name. We were on the path by the old Schweppes truck and he was walking home from the Tomb, dressed in Sabbath whites. One of the men with him stopped. "Remember *The Big Lebowski?*" he yelled. I didn't, but Peter caught the reference to the John Goodman character's insistence that he didn't "roll on shabbos." Peter laughed and the settler walked away.

Eventually I just knocked on Marzel's door. He lived a few apartments down from Tzipi Schlissel, and was considerably less hospitable. A plump and somewhat breathless man with an unruly beard, crooked glasses, and hands that seemed to never stop moving, Marzel did not hide

---

*I am thinking of Aimé Césaire's consideration of "how colonialism works to *decivilize* the colonizer, to *brutalize* him in the true sense of the word, to degrade him, to awaken him to buried instincts, to covetousness, violence, race hatred. . . ."

his contempt for journalists—the media, in his description, was a vast, anti-Semitic cabal—and, within moments of our arrival in his home, called us anti-Semites and launched into a tirade about the Spanish that somehow connected Isabella and Ferdinand's expulsion of the Jews in 1492 to the work of contemporary Spanish NGOs opposed to the occupation. Books by Meir Kahane—*They Must Go* and *Never Again* were among the titles—lined the shelves in his living room. Marzel, who was quite well known in Israel, had been a disciple of Kahane and was alleged to have led the movement Kahane founded well after it was declared a terrorist organization and outlawed by the Israeli government.

Marzel was a pugilist—blunt, combative, relentless. He had been arrested dozens of times—among other things for rioting, vandalizing Palestinian cars, and assaulting, in separate incidents, a Palestinian, an Israeli policeman, the prominent Israeli leftist Uri Avnery, and an Israeli TV crew. He had run for the Knesset repeatedly—always unsuccessfully—and was a frequent and vocal presence at anti-immigrant and antigay demonstrations in Israel. He once brought three donkeys to a gay pride march in Jerusalem and draped them in sheets that read "I am a proud donkey."

The narrative that Marzel spun—though it appeared to equally spin him—was a barer and more brutal version of the one that Tzipi Schlissel had offered up the day before. "I am a Jew that's coming back and doing what God wants me to do," he said with a bluster that defied any possibility of doubt. Hebron, he reminded us, was the place "where God promised the Jews the land of Israel in the Bible. If we don't have a right to live here, we don't have a right to live anywhere." (I didn't mention that my grandparents got on fine in Philadelphia.) By this logic, he went on, "If you believe that Jews should not live in Hebron, you're an anti-Semite." The latter term described for him all but a few human beings.

I asked Marzel how he would describe his community's relationship with its non-Jewish neighbors.

"Corrective," he answered. "When someone wants to kill, we'll kill him first.* If someone throws rocks at me, I'll throw rocks at him. We're not the religion that gives the second cheek to anyone."

Once he got going, Marzel could not be stopped. "Why are Arabs throwing rocks at us every day?" he asked, rhetorically. (Sometimes, but not always, Marzel's "us" appeared to include the soldiers.) "We're not dogs. We're not animals. Why are they throwing rocks at us?"

His glasses fogged. "Why did Arabs yesterday throw rocks at Jews here? And why a week ago? Why did they throw rocks two weeks ago? And why three weeks ago?" He kept going until he reached seven weeks. "And why did they kill tens of Jews here? Why did they massacre in 1929?"

Marzel had the answer: "Because they want us out of here. They want us dead or out of here."

It wouldn't happen. Of that, and everything else, Marzel seemed sure. A decade earlier, the movement to which he had devoted years of his life had been marginalized to the point of illegality. Now it was on the rise. Views that had once been expressed only on the furthest fringes of the Israeli right were aired openly and frequently in the local media, in the Knesset, in the streets. The KAHANE WAS RIGHT sticker on Marzel's cell phone, and the sentiment it implied—that no coexistence with Palestinians was possible, and mass expulsion the only solution—had become a mainstream position. Marzel was confident that it was only a matter of time. "The minute we will be allowed to build everywhere," he said, "Hebron will be Jewish."

I asked how he thought he would get there.

Marzel grinned. "By talking to you."

---

*This was something of a slogan. In 2011, Marzel was spotted hanging posters around town that depicted a Hebronite former prisoner named Hani Jaber, who had just been released in the Shalit swap. "KILL HIM FIRST," the caption read.

———

MOST OF MY ENCOUNTERS with soldiers in Hebron were less than cordial. They confined themselves to grunts and commands, neither of which bring out the best in me, but on a couple of occasions we managed to break through our mutual distrust, if only for a moment. Once, crossing back through the Qeitun checkpoint, I asked a soldier how he was and to my surprise got an honest answer. "Terrible," he said. His comrades were at that moment shooting tear gas at nine-year-olds a few meters away. "This place is terrible," he said. "This is the worst place." He shook his head and walked away. That was as far as we got.

Another day, tired of the after-school clashes, I hiked back down Shuhada Street and up the stone stairs toward the Tomb of the Patriarchs. A tall young Border Police officer stopped me, his rifle cradled in his arms. He asked where I was from.

"America," I told him.

"Are you Christian?" he asked.

I said I wasn't, and asked why it mattered.

He didn't answer. Instead he asked me my religion.

"I don't have one," I said.

"You must have one—Christian, Jewish, something?"

I knew what he wanted, but I didn't feel like playing along. "I'm not religious," I said. "Are you?"

He shrugged and thought about it. "I'm not either," he admitted, "but my mother is a Jew." He tried again: "What about your parents? They must have a religion."

"They aren't religious," I told him. "My grandparents weren't either." I wasn't lying. I come from a long line of people skilled at the art of refusal. But at this point we were both enjoying the absurdity of our exchange. Finally he gave in.

"Muslims aren't allowed here," he said. "I have to ask," he added, apologetically.

I told him I wasn't Muslim either. He nodded me past with a slightly guilty smile.

Nine months later I sat down in Jerusalem with an Israeli activist and former soldier named Eran Efrati. He had spent most of 2006 and 2007 stationed in Hebron. He was nineteen when he arrived there and at the time saw little reason to question the Israeli military's presence in the city. At his first briefing, he recalled an officer asking the troops what they would do if they saw a Palestinian running at a settler with a knife.

"Of course the answer was you shoot him in the center of his body," Eran said. The officer posed the question in reverse: What if it was the settler with a knife? "And the answer was you cannot do anything. The best you can do is call the police, but you're not allowed to touch them. From day one the command was, 'You cannot touch the settlers.'" This made sense to him, Eran said. Palestinians were the enemy. The settlers seemed a little crazy, but they were Jews.

A few days later, thousands of settlers arrived from all over the West Bank to celebrate a religious holiday. The army imposed a curfew to keep Palestinians off the streets. Eran's first task as a soldier in Hebron was to throw stun grenades into an elementary school to announce the beginning of the curfew. "I just did it, like everyone else," he said, "and within seconds, hundreds of kids ran outside. I was standing at the entrance and a lot of them looked at me in the eyes—that was the first time that it hit me. All of a sudden I understood what I was doing. I understood what I looked like."

That weekend, Eran recalled, settlers filled the central city. He was assigned to escort a group of them into the Patriarchs' Tomb. They were allowed into the Palestinian side too, into the mosque. What he saw there shocked him: children were peeing on the floors and burning the carpets. Their parents were there—the mosque was packed with settlers—but no one was stopping them. He and another soldier grabbed one of the children and took a cigarette lighter from his hand. "He started screaming at us," Eran said. "We laughed at him." Five minutes later, "one of our very,

very high-ranking officers came inside the mosque and said, 'Did you steal something from the kid?'" They tried to explain, but the officer only repeated the question. "We said yes." The officer ordered them to give it back and apologize. They found the child, apologized, and returned the lighter. The boy ran right into the next room, Eran said, and resumed setting fire to the carpets.

Things got weirder. Eran was put in charge of a checkpoint. He described it as grueling, mind-numbing work, standing in the cold for as long as sixteen hours, usually hungry and always sleep-deprived. Inflicting humiliation was part of the assignment. Schoolteachers would cross dressed in suits and ties. The soldiers would make them strip in front of their students. "Sometimes we would make them wait for hours in their underwear," Eran said.

The pretext was to check them for weapons. "Nobody thought that anything would happen to them," he said, but the troops were told again and again by their officers that all Palestinians were potential threats, that anyone might stab them if they dropped their guard for a moment.* That notion, Eran said, "made us very, very aggressive. So you would push them against the wall, undress them, take your weapon and hit them a few times. If he's saying something, hit him. If he turns around, hit him. Just make sure that you're completely in control."

His conscience began to nag at him. He started bringing bags of Bamba—a popular Israeli snack food, like Cheez Doodles, only peanut flavored and not phosphorescent orange—to the checkpoint and offering them to children. After a few days, "the first brave kid came up, grabbed a bag of Bamba, and ran away." Eran was thrilled. Not long after, a Palestinian boy of about eight years old asked him for a treat. This boy didn't run.

---

*The soldiers were also taught not to trust any foreigners they encountered in the city: "We were told not to react to any of the internationals because their job was to try to distract us so someone could stab us from behind. . . . They were the enemy."

He opened the bag, and offered some to Eran. They sat and ate the chips together. When the boy walked off, Eran felt ecstatic. He could finally be the man he wanted to be, a soldier who was loved for his kindness and who at the same time, as he put it, "was protecting my country from a second Holocaust."

When he got back to the base that night, he was ordered to eat quickly and prepare for another shift, not at the checkpoint but on a "mapping" expedition into H1. He was still so high from his success with the Bamba that he didn't mind the extra work. The routine was simple: "You go into houses in the middle of the night, get everybody outside, take a photo of the family, and start going around the house, destroying things." The idea was to search for weapons, "but we also needed to send a message," Eran said, to make sure the residents never lost "the feeling of being chased."* (It's awkward in English, but it's a single word in Hebrew. His officers used it a lot, Eran said.) His job was to draft maps of each house, charting the rooms, the doors, and the windows. "If at some point there was a terror attack from that specific house," the army would be ready.

That night, they searched, trashed, and mapped two houses in Abu Sneineh. It was snowy and cold. When they were done, the sun had not yet risen, so their officer chose one more house, apparently at random. They forced the family outside and into the snow and went in and started searching. Eran opened the door to a child's room—he remembered seeing a painting of Winnie-the-Pooh on one wall—and had begun sketching when he realized that there was someone in the bed. A young boy leaped out from under the covers. He was naked. Startled, Eran raised his gun, aiming at the child. It was the kid from the checkpoint that afternoon. "He started peeing himself," Eran said, "and we were just shaking, both of us,

---

*Like so many others, this tactic dates back to the British Mandate. During the Arab Revolt, "the soldiers went from house to house, searching for weapons," writes Tom Segev. "They would break down doors, smash furniture, and ransack pantries, ripping open sacks of rice, flour, and sugar and strewing the contents all over the floor."

we were just standing there shaking and we didn't say a word." The boy's father, coming down the stairs with an officer, saw Eran pointing a rifle at his son and raced into the room. "But instead of pushing me back," Eran said, "he starts slapping his kid on the floor. He's slapping him in front of me and he's looking at me saying, 'Please, please don't take my child. Whatever he did, we'll punish him.'"

In the end, the officer decided that the man's behavior was suspicious, that "he was hiding something." He ordered Eran to arrest him. "So we took the father, blindfolded him, cuffed his hands behind his back and put him in a military jeep." They dumped him like that at the entrance to the base. "He stayed there for three days in a very torn-up shirt and boxer shorts. He just sat there in the snow." Eventually, Eran summoned the courage to ask his officer what would happen to the boy's father. "He didn't even know what I was talking about," Eran said. "He was like, 'Which father?'" Eran reminded him. "You can release him," the officer said. "He learned his lesson."

After cutting the plastic ties that bound the man's wrists, untying the blindfold and watching him run off barefoot in his underwear through the streets, Eran realized that he had never given his commander the maps he had drawn. He hurried back to the officer's room. "I really fucked up," he told him, apologizing for his negligence.

The officer wasn't angry. "It's okay," he said. "You can throw them away."

Eran was confused. He protested: wasn't mapping a vital task that might save other soldiers' lives?

The officer got annoyed. "He says, 'Come on, Efrati. Stop bitching. Go away.'" But Eran kept arguing. He didn't understand.

When it became apparent that he wasn't going anywhere, the officer told him: "We've been doing mappings every night, three or four houses a night, for forty years." He personally had searched and mapped the house in question twice before with other units.

Eran was even more confused.

Bassem Tamimi in his living room. Nabi Saleh, April 2012. *(Keren Manor/ActiveStills)*

Ahed and Nariman Tamimi outside their home in Nabi Saleh, summer 2012.

(Peter van Agtmael/Magnum Photos)

RIGHT: Abu Yazan resting in the doorway. Nabi Saleh, summer 2012. *(Peter van Agtmael/Magnum Photos)*

Nariman filming soldiers. Friday in Nabi Saleh, summer 2012. *(Peter van Agtmael/Magnum Photos)*

LEFT: Israeli border police arresting Manal Tamimi. On the right with his back to the camera, Jonathan Pollak attempts to intervene. Friday in Nabi Saleh, January 2010. *(Oren Ziv/ ActiveStills)*

BELOW: Youth running from tear gas. Across the valley in the distance is the settlement of Halamish. Friday in Nabi Saleh, summer 2012. *(Peter van Agtmael/ Magnum Photos)*

Boy taking cover as soldiers fire rubber-coated bullets.
Nabi Saleh, February 2013. *(Peter van Agtmael/Magnum Photos)*

ABOVE: The view from Naji's living room. Nabi Saleh, winter 2013. *(Peter van Agtmael/Magnum Photos)*

LEFT: Bilal Tamimi filming. Nabi Saleh, winter 2012. *(Oren Ziv/ ActiveStills)*

Bassem's homecoming from prison, February 10, 2013. From left:
Salam, Waed, Boshra, Bassem, and Nariman. *(Oren Ziv/ActiveStills)*

Salam and the sea, July 2013. *(Ben Ehrenreich)*

LEFT: Bassem on a good day, July 2013. *(Ben Ehrenreich)*

BELOW: Mufid Sharabati on the roof of his home. Hebron, October 2013.

(Peter van Agtmael/Magnum Photos)

RIGHT: Hebron settler and her children on Shuhada Street, fall 2013. *(Peter van Agtmael/Magnum Photos)*

BELOW: The funeral of Anas al-Atrash. Hebron, November 8, 2013. *(Peter van Agtmael/Magnum Photos)*

ABOVE: A clash in Bab al-Zawiya. Hebron, November 2013. *(Peter van Agtmael/Magnum Photos)*

BELOW: The family of Anas al-Atrash at home in Abu Sneineh. Hebron, November 2013.
(Peter van Agtmael/Magnum Photos)

Olive harvest in Hebron. Soldiers were firing at schoolchildren a few meters behind the photographer, November 2013. *(Peter van Agtmael/Magnum Photos)*

Issa Amro in Tel Rumeida shortly after the Israel Antiquities Authority confiscated a plot of land to build an archaeological park and encourage Jewish tourism to Hebron, January 2014. *(Ben Ehrenreich)*

Bullet hole in the kitchen cabinet of Baruch Marzel's home in Tel Rumeida. Hebron, November 2013. *(Peter van Agtmael/ Magnum Photos)*

Old man, Hebron. A few minutes after this photograph was taken, he dragged the tree through an intersection in which soldiers were clashing with schoolboys and did not pause when a cloud of tear gas enveloped him, November 2013. *(Peter van Agtmael/Magnum Photos)*

Mo'atassim Suleiman al-Hathalin displaying the infamous oven of Umm al-Kheir, April 2014. *(Ben Ehrenreich)*

ABOVE: Suleiman on the mountain with his flock. Umm al-Kheir, April 2014.

(Ben Ehrenreich)

LEFT: Hassan al-Hathalin. Umm al-Kheir, April 2014.

(Ben Ehrenreich)

Eid Suleiman al-Hathalin at home in Umm al-Kheir, May 2014. *(Ben Ehrenreich)*

Eid's Blackhawk. Behind it, in the kitchen, stands his wife, Na'oma.
Umm al-Kheir, May 2014. *(Ben Ehrenreich)*

Eid's daughter, Lin, on her birthday. Umm al-Kheir, May 2014. *(Ben Ehrenreich)*

Wedding celebration. Qalandia, June 2014. *(Ben Ehrenreich)*

Outside the home of Mohammad Abu Khdeir on the day of his funeral.
Shu'afat, July 4, 2014. *(Ben Ehrenreich)*

Men sit beside a fire in the ruins of Shuja'iyya.
Gaza, October 2014. *(Peter van Agtmael/Magnum Photos)*

The officer took pity, and explained: "If we go into their houses all the time, if you arrest people all the time, if they feel terrified all the time, they will never attack us. They will only feel chased after."

That, Eran said, "was the first time I understood that everything I was told was complete bullshit." From then on, he said, "I didn't stop doing the things I did, I just stopped thinking."

THE FIRST WITNESS agreed to meet me at one of the main traffic circles in Hebron. It was night. Irene had found him, and driven down from Jerusalem. He spotted us walking out of a restaurant and flashed his lights. We got in his car and he drove for a few blocks until he found a spot that was sufficiently deserted. He pulled over, smoking out the open window.

There were three men in the car with him that night when he pulled up at the Container checkpoint, but all of them had families, he said, and none of them would talk. He asked me not to reveal his name or any detail that might identify him. He had been released from prison not long before and didn't want to go back. But Hebron felt small sometimes—he was certain that we had already been seen and an informant would get word to the Shabak that he had spoken to me and they would call him in for questioning. The risk, he said, was worth it. "This is a savage country. They have no shame."

The man's story closely matched Ismail al-Atrash's account. He was coming from the other direction, he said, and was stopped about ten meters from the al-Atrashes' car. "From here to that pole," he said, and pointed. He saw the soldiers searching the white car in front of the al-Atrash brothers'. The soldiers were very aggressive, he said, but that was normal. "We're used to that." Then Anas al-Atrash opened his door. "Maybe he was sleeping or something but he got out and stretched his arms and they just shot him. He didn't move quickly or anything." There was nothing in his hands, no knife. "We've heard that song many times," he said. The soldier was, "to exaggerate, two meters," away from Anas. He didn't think he would recognize the soldier if he saw him again, "but it all happened in front of my eyes," he said. "They shot him in front of my eyes."

The second witness also asked not to be identified. His concerns were identical. "The truth has to come out," he said, but "I don't want to wake up tomorrow morning and have to go talk with Israeli intelligence." We met him on the side of the road near Bethlehem. He pulled up beside us and got into the backseat of Irene's car. He showed us a video he had shot with his cell phone a little while after the killing, but there wasn't much to see or hear, just shouting and flashing lights in the dark. His story also closely matched Ismail's account.* He had been heading for Ramallah and waiting to cross the checkpoint. He saw soldiers searching the white car in front of the brothers. It was a Ford, he said. He saw one of the soldiers aim his weapon's laser sight at the al-Atrashes' Volkswagen "like he was preparing to shoot." And he saw a man open the passenger-side door of the Volkswagen and stand while lifting his hands in the air. The man was still "half in and half out of the car," he said, when "he was shot and he fell to the ground." There was nothing, he confirmed, in either of Anas al-Atrash's hands.

After the shooting, he said, he saw the car's driver—Ismail—step out. Soldiers ran over and threw him to the pavement. They tied his hands behind his back. Soon soldiers were everywhere. Blue-uniformed police arrived. The witness tried to get out of his car, but a police commander pushed his door closed. "Stay," he said. He asked the commander when he could leave. "Not until we can take you to Jerusalem and take your testimony about what you saw here," the commander answered.

"I didn't see anything," he said.

The officer corrected him: "You saw a guy attack a soldier with a knife."

---

*It differed in two details. He said "four or five" soldiers rushed to pin Ismail, while Ismail remembered only three, and he wasn't sure of the color of the al-Atrashes' Volkswagen. He thought maybe it was brown, but then dark blue paint could easily appear brown at night under yellow sodium lights.

In the end, they never went to Jerusalem. The soldiers held everyone at the checkpoint until the al-Atrashes' friends and relatives arrived from Hebron to claim Anas's body. There were a lot of them, and they were angry. Soon the soldiers were firing tear gas, the witness said, "and I drove away."

NARIMAN HAD ANOTHER court date. I left Hebron and entered Ofer, this time from the Ramallah side. The process for Palestinians was considerably less convenient. I walked with Nariman and Irene through the prison gate at the end of the road in Beitunia, through a turnstile and another turnstile and a metal detector, past a window of bulletproof glass where I showed my ID to the soldier and passed through yet another turnstile and into the open air again. The sun was low. We walked for at least half a mile on a single lane of asphalt limned on one side by razor wire. We bumped into a friend of Nariman's on the way, a woman she knew from the village of Dura, near Hebron, whose eighteen-year-old son had been arrested for throwing rocks at an IDF jeep. He had confessed, she said, but had refused to name the other boys with him. The prosecutor was asking for fifteen years.

The day before had been the first anniversary of Rushdie's death. Nariman wore black. We pushed through another turnstile and sat on dented seats in a small, grungy waiting area until we were buzzed through a gate and we passed through another metal detector and took turns being patted down by a guard in a windowless, closet-size room, and at last were allowed to enter the fenced corridor that led to the courts. As we waited between one turnstile and another, Nariman told us that the army had raided Nabi Saleh the night before and had arrested one man and one teenage boy. She was worried that they would be pressured to inform on Bassem, and that he would end up here once more, on the other side of the fence.

Again nothing happened. We sat in the courtyard and watched the men pace and the women stand with their arms crossed in the sun. It was afternoon, and cool, the shadows long. The hearing began. The prosecutor was still combing through old files, searching for precedents. The judge was annoyed. "What's going on?" he asked. "Why is it taking so long?" The prosecutor requested a postponement to discuss the matter further. The court interpreter, a young Druze soldier, sat slumped in his chair, only bothering when the mood struck him to translate a sentence or two of the proceedings—which took place in Hebrew—into Arabic for Nariman. She didn't miss much. I counted the fluorescent bulbs on the ceiling. Nariman's lawyer asked that she at least no longer be placed on house arrest every Friday, as she had been for four and a half months. There were thirty-two bulbs, two in each of sixteen fixtures. The judge announced that he was not ready to make a decision. The hearing was adjourned.

I DID NOT seek an interview with Anat Cohen, but in the end, in a way, I got one. Issa had warned us about her. Every Palestinian I spoke to in and around Tel Rumeida had at least one story about her. They were among the ugliest and most frightening stories I heard in Hebron, or anywhere in Palestine. If Baruch Marzel was a clumsy, ever-charging bull, Anat Cohen was a walking ember, a dark flame. The Internet overflows with accounts posted by international activists and observers of their encounters with Cohen, about how she kicked them or spat in their faces, about the horrible things she said. The stories usually end with Cohen accusing the foreigners of assaulting her, the police detaining the by-now terrified foreigners—most likely to save the officers the headache of further dealings with the Fury of Beit Hadassah—and Cohen, untouchable, remaining free.

If Tzipi Schlissel was settler royalty, Anat Cohen was of the high nobility. Her father, Moshe Zar, had been an old friend of Ariel Sharon's.* He

---

*Zar disowned Sharon after the 2005 forced evacuation of the settlements in Gaza. Sharon, he told *Haaretz*, "turned his back and became an enemy."

was one of the wealthiest Jewish land speculators in the West Bank* and one of the main financiers backing Gush Emunim. Samantha Shapiro, writing in *The New York Times Magazine*, called him "a sort of Wild West–style vigilante mayor of his stretch of the West Bank," namely the settlements outside of Nablus, which rival the Hebron area for their zealotry and violence. Zar was also a member of the Jewish Underground, a right-wing terrorist group active in the early 1980s and notorious for bomb attacks on Palestinian mayors, assaults on a grade school and an Islamic college in Hebron, and foiled attempts to blow up Palestinian buses and the al-Aqsa mosque.† He was convicted for his role in planting a bomb in a car belonging to Bassam Shaka'a, who was then the mayor of Nablus. Shaka'a lost both his legs. Zar served just four months in prison.

Moshe Zar's son Gilad, Anat Cohen's brother, was among the founders of Itamar, a particularly pugnacious settlement just south of Nablus. In 2001, he was employed as the head of security for the northern West Bank settlements when he was ambushed on the road and shot by Palestinian gunmen. He survived that attack, and in a rare statement told reporters, "We have to put the Arabs on their knees, send them back in time 15 years and make them grateful every day that we let them work for us." Two months later, Gilad Zar's car was again ambushed, and he was killed. Tzipi Livni, then a minister in Ariel Sharon's cabinet, attempted to speak at his funeral. Cohen grabbed the microphone from her hand. "You have tanks and planes," she shouted. "Start fighting and stop talking."

Three years later, when the American journalist Jeffrey Goldberg interviewed Cohen for *The New Yorker*, she had a framed photo of Baruch Goldstein ("The Saint Dr. Goldstein," it was inscribed) hanging in her apartment and referred to herself as a "soldier of God." Goldberg wasn't

---

*Zar began buying land from Palestinians in 1979 in deals that several later claimed were forged. One put an ax through his skull. Zar survived.

†"Nearly all" of the twenty-six men arrested for their roles in Jewish Underground attacks, according to a 1984 UN report, were "well known and highly regarded in the Gush Emunim movement." Several were from Kiryat Arba and the Hebron settlements.

buying it. He focused on the ill effects of zealotry on motherhood and was particularly disturbed that Cohen would endanger her children—she has, by most accounts, more than ten—by raising them in Hebron.* He invented a pathology for Cohen, diagnosing her with what he called Mount Moriah Complex, named for the site on which Abraham is believed to have bound his son Isaac and, to prove his faith, prepared him as a sacrifice to God. Cohen, in turn, dismissed Goldberg's secular, rationalist outlook with contempt. "You don't live just to keep living," she told him. "That's not the point of life."

Of course she was right. I find it strange that I am defending Anat Cohen, but she was a formidable woman, a ferocious soldier for her god, and it is too easy to dismiss her—or anyone else—as a fanatic. She was mad, but so was almost everyone in Hebron, and so was I while I was there. This is not praise, just acknowledgment: Anat Cohen had the courage to believe in something with the fullness of her being and no calculus to guide her save her own bottomless rage and inherited fear and the awe-drenched narrowness of her faith. A few weeks later, I would tag along on a tour of Hebron organized by the antioccupation veterans' group Breaking the Silence. For a while, Cohen walked beside us, her eyes aflame, hurling words like spears and darts, telling us alternately to go to Auschwitz and asking where, if not Hebron, a Jew could go. "Should Jews return to Auschwitz?" she shouted, as if that were the only other choice.

We had met earlier, one afternoon in the third week of November. Peter and Gaia had gone back to the U.S., and I was alone in the Sharabatis' sitting room when Zidan came to the door. We drank coffee and Zidan smoked and showed me the video he'd just shot of a twelve-year-old boy detained at Checkpoint 56. They held him there for two hours, Zidan said.

---

*He interviewed Moshe Levinger too, and several other male settlers, but did not mention their parenting skills.

His phone rang. Something was happening at the Qurtuba Girls School.* Zidan leaped up and I ran after him, past the soldier at his post, up the stairs beside the house and along the narrow trail to the school. The odor of aerosol hung in the air. A woman in a long skirt was scrambling down the hill beneath us. She walked slowly across Shuhada Street and washed her hands at a tap near the entryway to the apartment building beside Beit Hadassah. She noticed me watching her and, standing in the doorway, stared back.

The mural on the wall beside the school had been defaced.† A map of Palestine undivided by the 1967 line and an image of a giant key, the symbol of Palestinian refugees' dream of return, had both been painted over in white. The paint was still wet. Zidan filmed for a moment longer. As we walked back down the path, I saw a figure silhouetted in an open second-story window, watching us. Just as we stepped through Zidan's doorway, a voice called out. The soldier on guard outside the house approached. The woman we had seen scurrying off the path was standing in front of Beit Hadassah with another soldier. She had accused me, the closer soldier said in English, of throwing a stone at her. He corrected himself: of trying to throw a stone at her. She'd said I'd picked one up and had been about to throw it and when she turned and saw me I put it down again.

I told the soldier that she was lying, that I was a journalist and that I didn't throw stones.‡ Soon there were six soldiers around me, their young faces hard. I asked the one who had first approached me what the woman's name was. Zidan had already told me that it was Anat Cohen, but I wanted to hear it from the soldier too. He wouldn't say it. He said he didn't know.

---

*The school is named for the Andalusian city of Córdoba, famous for its tenth-century golden age, when Jewish poetry, philosophy, and scholarship thrived under an Islamic caliphate.

†When I first visited Hebron in 2011, I saw graffiti here in English that I have been unable to forget. "GAS THE ARABS," it said.

‡I've blushed more than once since then recalling the foolishness of those words. For the record, I retract them: Good journalists always throw stones. Even if only the metaphoric kind.

"You don't know?" I said. If she was accusing me of a crime, I said, I had a right to know who she was.

Another soldier barked out a "No." A third demanded my passport. I gave it to him. Cohen stood behind them, her dark eyes gleaming. Eventually a police truck rolled up and a jeep full of soldiers. There were at least a dozen of them, plus the cops. I didn't see Cohen slip away.

The police asked me what had happened. I told them. They didn't seem particularly interested. Zidan, who had been filming all along, showed them the video he had shot of Cohen scurrying down the hill and walking slowly across the street. She had a white object in her hand the size and shape of a can of spray paint. The police officer told Zidan he couldn't do anything unless he had filmed her in the act of defacing the mural. He couldn't arrest me either, he said. "It's not a crime to pick up a rock and put it down."

I puzzled over the incident later that evening, the pettiness of it. Was she lying, or was she so convinced that I meant to do her harm that her eyes conjured up a rock? If she was lying, why not tell the soldiers I had thrown the imagined stone? Whatever I said, they would have arrested me, and for the time being at least, she would have been rid of me. What calculus, if any, had coursed through the fear-carved runnels of her brain? It didn't matter in the end. The message was clear. She had shown me how things stood.

IT WAS ALREADY afternoon when I climbed from Zidan's house up the hill to the center to meet Irene and drive to the al-Atrash house in Abu Sneineh, and from there to Jericho, where a memorial ceremony would be held for Anas. Just as I arrived, three teenage settler boys were walking past. It was a Saturday, and they were dressed in white, in the loose, hip-pieish garments and wide, knit kippas favored by far-right settler youth. One of them carried an infant strapped to his chest with purple cloth. The boy with the baby began shouting. His name was Binyamin, Issa's brother Ahmad told me. "All the time, he's drunk," he said.

He didn't look drunk—his gait was steady and his speech unblurred—but he was certainly enthusiastic. "This house and every house, they are all ours," he yelled in Hebrew at the five or six activists standing on the patio. "We will conquer this whole city."

Ahmad, intense as always, stayed calm. He told the boy to be quiet.

"I'm not scared of you," shouted the boy called Binyamin. "I'm scared only of God."

"Go!" said Ahmad.

"I'm not afraid of you, Issa!" the boy shouted back.

Issa was in Europe. He and Ahmad were clearly kin, but they were hardly identical. Ahmad didn't bother to correct the boy. "Come on," he said. "Go."

But the boy kept yelling as he walked, protesting too much: "I'm not afraid of you, Issa!" he shouted again. Somehow the baby strapped to his chest slept through it all.

Ahmad grinned. "Come on," he said, teasing the boy. "You are afraid."

The boy stopped next to the soldier posted behind the house. He put his arm around the soldier's shoulders. The soldier looked unhappy, but stayed silent. "You're nothing," the boy spat at Ahmad. "Zero. Nothing, nothing, nothing, you son of a whore. I love God and I'm going to defeat you, Issa. I'm a proud Jew. I'm a real man, because I worship God."

Eventually he got tired. Irene and I hiked out past the old archaeological excavations to the empty lot in which she had parked her car. As we were leaving, I noticed two settler children, boys about nine or ten years old, standing beside a soldier on the hill above us. They looked almost angelic, dressed all in white, lit from behind, their blond hair and forelocks gilded by the sun. The one on the right held up his middle finger as we passed.

A banner had been strung over the street in front of the al-Atrash house in Abu Sneineh with a photo of Anas on one side and Yasser Arafat on the other. The process of absorbing him into the national mythos had begun. Anas al-Atrash was no longer just the bright young man whose laughter his mother and father would miss every day for the rest of their lives. Fatah had claimed him. He was Palestine's now, *al shahid wa al batal*, the martyr and hero, the collective property of a nation defined by its losses, its forbearance, its sacrifice, a nation that at times seemed only to exist through the medium of its suffering. We sat with the mourners and drank bitter coffee from tiny plastic cups.

Among the men who came to pay respects was an older fellow in a gray *galabiya* who was introduced to me as having been one of the gunmen who had killed six settlers outside Beit Hadassah in 1980. I never learned his name, but when he spoke everyone listened, or pretended to. He had a loose, arrogant posture and had rubbed a dark callus into the center of his forehead with fervent prayer. After the Beit Hadassah operation, he said, he had been captured and then released in a prisoner swap and exiled to Algeria, from where he made his way to Jordan and to Lebanon before being allowed to return to Hebron in 1999. He told stories of close calls and courageous escapes during the Lebanese war while under fire from Israeli F-16s. His voice was animated, his listeners morose. Of the two hundred fighters in his unit, he boasted, only seventeen survived. He turned to Anas's mother, Najah, who sat a few seats away from him, swathed in black, her face pale and bloated from eight days of weeping. He told her that he had sought death many times and never found it, that her son had been lucky, that the ones God takes are fortunate. She nodded, her hands clasped in her lap, but didn't look up.

The shadows were already growing long when people began heading for their cars. The rear window of the blue Volkswagen in which Anas al-Atrash had spent his last moments had been covered with a color print of Anas's face superimposed over images of the al-Aqsa and Ibrahimi mosques, the words "MARTYR AND HERO" above his name. His little brother, twelve-year-old Mohammad, was struggling to attach a Palestinian flag to the passenger-side window.

"The Jews will stop you," one of his uncles warned.

"I don't care," Mohammad said.

Another uncle came over and told the boy to take down the flag. "You think you're liberating the land," the uncle mocked.

"That's right, I am," the boy said, and shouted in protest as his oldest brother, Ra'd, snatched the flag from him and shoved him into the car.

They led the way to Jericho at reckless, breakneck speeds along the twisting, pitted roads out of Hebron, up through Wadi Naar to the Container checkpoint. The soldiers stopped us but waved us on and we didn't have to stare for long at the lonely spot on the asphalt—just past where the dog was sleeping, Anas's cousin told me from the backseat—where Anas's body fell. The moon, yellow, enormous, and full, rose in the sky to the east as we descended through the bare hills, past the sign marking sea level, into the desert and the Jordan Valley. The highway, used by Israelis and tourists on their way to the Dead Sea, was flawlessly smooth.

The memorial took place in an alley lit with streetlamps and lined with six long rows of plastic chairs. The local Fatah committee had sponsored the event. Palestinian flags and posters of Anas's face beside those of Arafat and Abbas hung between the lamps. A PA system broadcast nationalist hymns at earsplitting volume. The chairs slowly filled, each new guest shaking hands as they filed past Anas's father Fouad, his brothers and his uncles. Some of the men wore police uniforms. Others wore suits or mud-spattered work clothes. They sat and smoked in silence. A man in a yellow shirt took the microphone and, the speakers echoing with reverb, asked us all to stand for the national anthem. When it was over, he spoke of the "flower of resistance" that bloomed in every old man and every boy and girl in Palestine. "Because our tears are one tear and our blood is one blood," he said, Anas "is a martyr for all of Palestine."

A sheikh led a prayer and Anas's cousin Tamer, who had driven with us and whom I had met the previous summer—we had run into the olive grove together the night the *tawjihi* results were released—spoke on behalf of the family in the sonorous rhythms of formal Arabic. It was more of the same. "They killed him while the world was watching," Tamer said, though in fact its eyes were closed. "They killed him and silenced him,"

Tamer continued. "His blood has mixed with the blood of all the previous martyrs. How great this nation is. How great these people are."

We left as soon as Tamer finished speaking, as soon as we could without being rude, before the governor could take the stage and add to the platitudes. We filed past Anas's uncles and brothers and father again and shook their hands once more. His father looked weary and disoriented, as if he were still unsure of who we were, and what was happening, and where he was. We stopped on the highway as it climbed back into the mountains toward Jerusalem and got out at a rest stop to use the bathrooms and buy chocolate bars and water. The parking lot was filled with idling tour buses, the picnic tables outside the convenience store packed with young Israelis and European tourists sipping coffee and energy drinks and eating shrink-wrapped sandwiches from their cellophane wrappers. They looked tired but happy, worn out from a day of sightseeing and swimming in the bitter, hypersaline waters of the Dead Sea. Their laughter was free, their faces easy because they didn't know, apparently, and no one had thought to tell them, about the young man who at the end of a long week had woken from a nap in the car beside his brother and stood up and stretched his arms to the sky and without warning been transformed into something he had by all accounts never wished to be, the martyr and hero Anas al-Atrash, whose blood mixes with the blood of martyrs past, and who is not dead but will live forever in glory in the heart and the tears of his people.

In 2006, when the police evicted the Schlissels and seven other families of settlers from Hebron's old vegetable market, David Wilder had protested to *The Jerusalem Post* that the property belonged to the city's Jews. They had a bill of sale, the settlers' spokesman insisted, dating back to 1807, when a Hebronite Jew named Haim Bajayo bought a five-dunam plot just outside what was then the Jewish quarter. Wilder did not mention that one of the parties who had petitioned the Israeli attorney general to demand the settlers' removal was Bajayo's sole living heir, Haim Hanegbi.

With Irene's help, I arranged to meet Hanegbi in a café in the posh Tel Aviv suburb of Ramat Aviv.*

"I am a Jewish Arab," he said, enjoying the pause as he let the notion sink in. He hadn't said "Arab Jew," as Mizrahi Jews from Syria, Iraq, or the Maghreb are sometimes called. "Jewish" here was a modifier of the primary identification, "Arab." For Hanegbi, the unorthodox sequencing of those two words indexed an entire lost history. He had been born in Jerusalem in 1935, but his father and grandfather had lived in Hebron until 1929, and his family's roots in the city dated back centuries. The Bajayos were one of the oldest and most esteemed Jewish families there, and had arrived in the sixteenth century from Algiers after being cast out of Portugal. They had survived the 1929 massacre thanks to the intervention of friends from the Abu Haikal family,† and, though they left the city, they continued to regard themselves as Hebronites, and Jerusalem as an exile. The family spoke Hebrew at home, but Hanegbi's father and grandfather were equally fluent in both formal and colloquial Arabic. His grandfather, he said, "never wore pants in his life," just the traditional Arab *galabiya*.

As a child, Hanegbi remembered visiting Hebron with his father, who went back every year to pay taxes on his land there and on behalf of the city's entire Jewish community. Hanegbi recalled Palestinians in the streets and the markets greeting his father warmly, as a respected friend who had moved away. When Jacob Ezra, the only Jew who had stayed in the city after 1929, came to Jerusalem on the weekends to see his family, he would visit Hanegbi's father and catch him up on news from Hebron. Even

---

*I was coming from Ramallah that day, not Hebron, but Ramat Aviv, with its boutiques, salons, and glittering high-rises, still felt galaxies away. The customers in the café were dressed expensively, with Italian sunglasses and face-lifts. The waitresses were young and attractive. At one point, Hanegbi's wife, on learning that I lived in Ramallah, asked how I got there. By car, I told her. She seemed puzzled, as if she couldn't comprehend how such vast, interplanetary distances could be so easily traversed. "But aren't there checkpoints?" she asked. "Don't they stop you?"

†The Abu Haikals still live in Tel Rumeida, just across the street from Tzipi Schlissel and Baruch Marzel.

Hanegbi's name pointed to the family's identification with the city. As a municipal employee in Jerusalem, his father, he said, was pressured to Hebraicize his name after 1948, and abandoned the Sephardic Bajayo for the Hebrew Hanegbi, "the Negevite," as Hebron sits at the northern edge of the Negev desert.

The irony—that his family's Jewish roots had to be transformed and even disowned in order for his father to find acceptance in the new Jewish state—was not lost on Hanegbi. "Where is the homeland," he once wrote, "and where the exile?" In the early 1960s, Hanegbi became one of the founders of the socialist and anti-Zionist political movement Matzpen. The group dissolved into factional disputes in the early seventies and never numbered more than a few dozen members, but it briefly played an out-sized role in Israeli politics, and for a while after 1967 acted as the sole Israeli voice challenging not only the injustices of the occupation, but of Jewish privilege—and the corresponding repression and dispossession of Palestinians—within Israel itself. Hanegbi didn't have to reach far into his imagination to envision a single state in which both people shared a single culture and respected each other's differences. It was there in his memory, and in the memories he inherited from his father and grandfather. "This hatred isn't a fateful decree that we can't get rid of," I later heard him say in a documentary about Matzpen. "The hatred is new." Matzpen's political project had failed, Hanegbi told me, but his dream, "to return to a vision of people living together," was not, he insisted, dead.

The settlers' takeover of the Hebron vegetable market was, in a way, an opportunity. Hanegbi held the deed to the land on which the market was built and leases on two other parcels in Hebron, one of them in Tel Rumeida. The settlers' presence there had put the Israeli government in an uncomfortable position. They had argued in court that Jews had been expelled by force from Hebron and should be allowed to go back, and that the properties that had once been theirs should be returned to them. Disregarding the fact that they had no direct claim to the property in question, the settlers' arguments "opened a Pandora's box," Hanegbi's lawyer, Michael Sfard, explained to me later. If the judges agreed with the settlers that the ancestors of people who had been forced from their homes had a right to return to them, then in principle, at least, the courts would have a hard time denying Palestinian demands that the properties confiscated from them—not only in the 1990s and 2000s, but all the way back to 1948—should be returned. Legally speaking, the legitimacy of Israeli claims to huge swaths of the country—and in a real sense, of the state itself—hung in the balance.

Hanegbi insisted on consistency: unless all the heirs of the more than 700,000 Palestinians who had been pushed from their homes in 1948 had their property restored to them too, he didn't want his land. Until that happened, it was his wish that the Palestinian merchants who had been ousted from the market in 1994 be allowed back and the settlers, who were trespassing, be removed. The government chose not to let the issue hit the courts. The attorney general's office responded to Sfard's petition, saying that it had not reached a decision, and would inform Hanegbi when it had. Basically, they decided not to decide. In the meantime, to keep the lid sealed shut, the settlers had to go. So when Tzipi Schlissel spoke of "national humiliation," she wasn't being melodramatic. What the government's lawyers likely understood as a confounding legal bind, the settlers saw as a chance for clarity: the state had an opportunity to unequivocally declare that Jews had rights gentiles did not share, and it had backed away. To Schlissel and her neighbors, such bureaucratic face-saving was a treasonous disavowal of a sacred duty.

I asked Hanegbi if Hebron's settlers had ever contacted him or if he had ever talked to them at all. He scoffed.

"God forbid," he said. "We don't agree about anything—what is a house? What does a street mean? Much less a country."

THE MORNING AFTER the memorial in Jericho, Fouad al-Atrash, Anas's father, left Hebron for Tel Aviv. He had an appointment with a lawyer whom he wished to consult about a lawsuit. He didn't hope for anything resembling justice, only that the government might be forced to reveal the circumstances of his son's killing, that the truth might be told. He had a permit to cross into Israel, which he had routinely been allowed to do for more than twenty years. Between 80 and 90 percent of his family's income, he estimated, derived from business conducted there, distributing the shoes he manufactured and imported to Israeli markets and shops. When he reached the checkpoint that morning, he placed his hand in the biometric reader. The checkpoint soldier looked at her computer and asked to see his permit. He showed it to her. She consulted the screen again. "You can't pass," she told him.

He asked her why.

"You have no permit," she said.

Eventually he was told that the Shabak wanted to see him, so he went to Gush Etzion, between Hebron and Jerusalem, and waited in a corridor for four hours until someone called his name. The officer in charge of his interrogation asked him the same questions they had asked Ismail on the night that Anas was shot. "Why was Anas upset?" he said.

He wasn't upset, Fouad insisted. He wanted to live.

It went on for a while. His interrogator informed him that there was no question that his son had a knife. That wasn't at issue, but "we're a democratic state," his interrogator assured him, "and we really want to find out what happened." In the end, the officer told him that nothing could be done about his permit. "It's a routine thing," he said. They did it with everyone. Everyone, that is, unfortunate enough to have a close relative killed by Israeli troops.

I followed up with the Civil Administration, which is in charge of issuing work permits, and asked why al-Atrash's had been revoked. It took two days, but eventually I got an answer from Guy Inbar, the Civil Administration spokesman. It was short: "The permit was revoked," he wrote in an e-mail, "for security reasons."

AT SOME POINT in the second half of November, the clashes in Bab al-Zawiya stopped. Two vans filled with PA police in riot gear stayed parked just outside the checkpoint every day from morning till evening. The local merchants, apparently, had complained to the municipality. The clashes were costing them too much business, so the municipality sent the police, and the stone throwing and burning of tires with which the youth of Hebron had paid tribute to the memory of Anas al-Atrash came to an end. At that checkpoint anyway. The clashes were still as reliable as a good watch at the checkpoints on the other side of H2. School had been letting out early—the PA couldn't pay the teachers their full salaries, so the schooldays were cut in half. I usually heard the first blast at a little after eleven each morning.

One day, I walked down past the UN boys' school and watched the soldiers in their jeep and on the rooftops above the street, a gaggle of boys throwing stones in the distance, the rocks clattering to the asphalt ten or fifteen yards short of their targets. I chatted with one of the solidarity activists observing the action, a middle-aged British man in a bright new keffiyeh. He had just arrived in Palestine and was still sparkling with outrage. It would mellow, I knew, into a sustained, wounded simmer. One of the soldiers walked over and took our photos with his iPhone. The Brit and his two younger colleagues rushed to pull their keffiyehs over their faces. I took out my phone to photograph the soldier photographing me. He got back in his jeep. The other soldiers came down from the rooftops. The kids had gone home. The jeep left. I did too.

I retraced my steps, back through Checkpoint 209 and down Shuhada Street toward the Sharabati house. A few meters past the old corner grocery store ("HAVE A GOOD TIME"), a white Land Rover pulled up alongside me. It was the type of vehicle used by the DCO and the Shabak. Its front window was open. The driver wore no yarmulke. He wasn't a settler. He looked military. He was trim and muscular, and his head was shaved close, but he was older, in his forties, and he wore civilian clothes. He let the Land Rover idle slowly forward, its side mirror a foot or two from my right elbow, keeping pace with me as I walked and staring at me in silence, his eyes hidden behind his sunglasses, his face perfectly blank. I nodded to him. He didn't nod back and didn't say anything, just cruised along beside me long enough to check me out and convey whatever silent message he wished to convey. At last he turned the wheel, accelerated, and parked next to an IDF jeep holding two more military-looking men in civilian clothes. It was a Tuesday, and barely noon. I was planning to leave Hebron that Friday, to say my good-byes and return to Ramallah. It was time.

ON FRIDAY MORNING, I walked down to Shuhada Street toward Bab al-Zawiya to buy myself some fruit and bread for breakfast. A flatbed truck was parked outside the checkpoint, and an army jeep behind it. On the back of the truck were piled giant spools of chain-link. They had a crane there too, and a few soldiers were standing on the checkpoint's roof, welding a metal frame into place between the old empty buildings while their colleagues stood guard with their guns. The IDF had arrived at a solution to the problem of stone-throwing youth. When, I wondered, would the entirety of historic Palestine begin to sink into the earth from the combined weight of the concrete and steel that made up all of Israel's fences and walls? By the time I had packed my bags and said my good-byes and left for the bus station a few hours later, the frame was done and the soldiers had begun stretching chain-link to a height twenty or so feet above the checkpoint.

Twice in the year that followed, in August and again in November, the youth of Hebron found their own solution to the problem of the now fenced and reinforced checkpoint. They tossed Molotov cocktails inside, and burned it down.

PART THREE

LOW CLOUDS

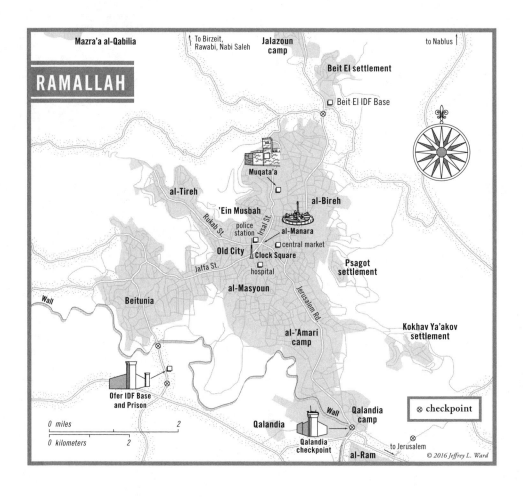

Mazra'a al-Qabilia

To Birzeit,
Rawabi, Nabi Saleh

Jalazoun
camp

to Nablus

RAMALLAH

Beit El settlement

Beit El IDF Base ⊗

Muqata'a

al-Tireh

al-Bireh

'Ein Musbah

police
station

al-Manara

Rukab St.

Irsal St.

Old City

central market

Clock Square

hospital

Jaffa St.

Psagot
settlement

al-Masyoun

Beitunia

Wall

Jerusalem Rd.

Kokhav Ya'akov
settlement

al-'Amari
camp

⊗

⊗

Ofer IDF Base
and Prison

⊗ checkpoint

0 miles   2

0 kilometers   2

Wall

Qalandia
camp

Qalandia

Qalandia
checkpoint

al-Ram

⊗

to Jerusalem

© 2016 Jeffrey L. Ward

7.

SNOW

Nabi Saleh, Ramallah, Jalazoun, Bethlehem, Za'tara

And yet joy was all around me.

—Jean Genet

The kids were getting restless. The winter's first rain had fallen two days earlier and the sun kept coming and going, bursting forth from behind low clouds and sneaking off again to hide. Plastic chairs filled the square in Nabi Saleh. The kids skittered out of theirs about ten minutes into the first speech while Bassem's nephew Mahmoud was still holding forth about martyrdom and resistance. They shrugged off all propriety and, relieved of its weight, were running and giggling to the left of the stage set up for the occasion. The guys slouched just behind them, their arms crossed, looking eager to be done with the formalities.

It was a Saturday, a special memorial for Rushdie and Mustafa. There had been a smaller ceremony the day before at the regular Friday demo. It had been cold and windy and the clouds were spitting mist and the villagers had marched in a slow and mournful procession from the square to Mustafa's grave to his mother's house and from there to the bend in the road where he had fallen two years earlier. The kids had gathered rocks—not to throw, but to mark the spot on the wet asphalt by spelling out Mustafa's name. They marched until the soldiers flooded the road with gas. The guys came out with their slings and their slingshots—not all of them, but at least a dozen, more than I had seen for many months. They had reached a détente with the elders, and the memorial had been important to them, this one even more so.

By noon, there were at least two hundred people in the square—all the usuals, plus the activists from Ramallah who had stopped coming when the guys dropped out, more guys from the surrounding villages, a few young European activists who had made the trip from Nablus and Hebron, the leaders of several of the other popular resistance villages, and a busload of Israeli leftists from Jerusalem. At last Mohammad took the microphone and invited everyone to march. The soldiers started shooting gas almost immediately. It was like no other demonstration I had been to in Nabi Saleh, as if everyone had woken up dancing and all the previous months of depression and despair had been one, long, restful sleep. Again and again, the guys picked up the smoking gas grenades and slung them back at the soldiers, scattering them. Again and again, the guys filled the hillsides in such numbers that the soldiers were forced to retreat. Stones flew through the air like flocks of darting birds. There was a standoff at the gate: Nariman, Shireen, and Mariam Barghouti sat down in the middle of the road and refused to leave. The unit commander ordered them to go home in what little Arabic he knew (*"Il beit,"* he kept yelling: "The house, the house!") and his soldiers tried to arrest them, but in the scuffle of shouting and shoving that followed, the army again did not prevail. "I am very, very happy," Nariman told me later, after another standoff in which she stood alone, refusing to be budged by the gas.

It wasn't all jubilation: Odai Tamimi, the less-shy of Mustafa's younger twin brothers, was hit in the face with a rubber-coated bullet. It broke his jaw. On the hill behind Bassem and Nariman's house, the guys sent the soldiers running again, but they came back and gassed us all and I ended up dashing blinded through the door and collapsing on the couch. When I was able to open my eyes, I saw one of the medics wrestling with Salam as Shireen and Mariam rolled laughing on the floor beside them. All afternoon, despite the gas and the ever-present danger nearly everyone was laughing, paying tribute to the fallen not with pomp but with the pure and exuberant mirth of resistance that they had left buried in grief for so long. The sun sank low and its light turned gold and pink and Nariman mocked the soldiers from her yard as they retreated past her down the road. The guys stood their ground on the hill, dozens of them watching with their slings in their hands until every last soldier had gone.

THAT NIGHT, Bassem and Nariman were late. They had promised the kids that after the demonstration, for a rare treat they would all go out to eat in Ramallah. The kids, being kids, wanted pizza, so I waited with a few activist friends at a place called Stones. We sat upstairs at a corner table beside a high plate-glass window. Everyone was hungry. Bassem called— he and Nariman had stopped at the hospital to visit Odai. Someone ordered garlic bread. The restaurant's name—written and pronounced in English, not Arabic—was decidedly not a patriotic reference to the favored symbol of the popular resistance. Stones, and perhaps a dozen other places like it, was a creature of Oslo: low light, clean lines, a full bar, a menu that catered to Americanized tastes and was priced to exclude. A dinner for two— perhaps a Thai chicken salad, hot wings, fettucine, a few cocktails or Coke Zeros and a shared slice of Oreo cake for dessert—would cost about the same as a comparable meal at an Applebee's in Dallas or Duluth, which would put the tab above the weekly income of all but a few Palestinians. In 2006, after PA police killed a teenager in an arrest raid on one of Ramallah's refugee camps, the guys from the camp launched a string of retaliatory attacks. They didn't march on the *muqata'a* or the police station or any of the PA offices or ministries. Instead they went to Stones. They trashed the place, along with a handful of other restaurants that had come to symbolize the class divides and corruption of post–Oslo Ramallah, in which a small and well-connected elite had managed to squeeze a profit from the occupation and, still more galling, enjoy relative immunity from the violence that afflicted the vast majority of their compatriots.

A waiter brought drinks, and news. Another martyr. A fifteen-year-old boy from the Jalazoun refugee camp, a few miles north and several galaxies distant from this placid corner of the city. The guys from the camp, the waiter said, were already downtown. They were marching from shop to shop, telling merchants they would smash their windows unless they closed out of respect for the dead. During the First Intifada, the practice of shuttering businesses following the death of a Palestinian at the hands of Israeli security forces functioned as a variety of strike, a barbed rejection of the everyday business of the occupation—the IDF was still directly administering daily affairs in the West Bank and Gaza then. In the post-Oslo era, the practice survived as a gestural form, a ritual nod to a mode of collective struggle that had otherwise been rendered largely obsolete.

Aboud, the activist sitting next to me, promised, "If they come here, we'll break the windows with them."

"I will too," the waiter said.

In the end, neither of them did. Aboud could be brave to the point of recklessness, but he wasn't the window-smashing sort, and the waiter needed his job. Bassem and Nariman arrived. The kids scrambled for seats. They ordered fries, chicken fingers, cheese sticks, a giant pizza. Salam's feet bobbed a foot above the floor. But the good mood that had lifted Bassem and Nariman all day had abandoned them. When they were leaving the hospital, Bassem said, he had seen a group gathered outside. He recognized an old friend. Wajdi al-Ramahi was his name. He was from Jalazoun. Bassem asked him what was going on. His son had been killed, he said, shot in the back by an IDF sniper posted outside Beit El settlement, which borders the refugee camp. When he heard, Bassem said, he could only cry.

"What could I say to him?" he asked.

The food arrived and soon the kids' faces were shiny with oil and cheese. The rest of us had lost our appetites. The waiters pulled down the window shades to avoid antagonizing passersby with a too-ostentatious display of indifference. A few minutes later, they turned off the lights as well. We heard people shouting in the street. The guys from Jalazoun had arrived. We pushed our way downstairs. There were thirty or forty of them and they were carrying sticks and yelling as the restaurant's staff tried to placate them. Somehow the waiters convinced the guys to let them stay open and the guys disappeared around the corner. Right behind them, several trucks of PA riot police pulled up and closed the road.

We drove to the hospital and found Odai lying sprawled across his bed, grinning slyly despite the bandages that swaddled his jaw. They had wrapped him up and taken X-rays, but the doctor wouldn't be back until ten the next morning, so Odai would have to wait, without painkillers, until then. His mother arrived and we said good-bye and walked out through the Qadoura camp to Clock Square and al-Manara. All the shops were closed— the groceries, juice bars, the boutiques and shoe stores and falafel and shawarma stands, the ice cream shop on Rukab Street. Only the pharmacies had stayed open, and the vendors selling boiled corn from carts. We drove back past Stones and past a posher place called Fuego that served Mexican food at American prices to customers who didn't mind paying to be seen. I thought they were closed at first, but they weren't. They had just kept the lights off. Through the windows, you could see the customers' faces lit by candles flickering on the tables over an unexpectedly romantic meal.

I ARRIVED IN JALAZOUN just before the bier bearing Wajih al-Ramahi's body made it to the mosque. It was raining again. In some respects at least, the circumstances around the shooting remained unclear. The boy's friends said they had been playing soccer in the yard of the school outside the camp and had left to buy a soda from a nearby shop when a sniper opened fire, hitting Wajih in the back. The soldiers shot him down, his father said, "as if he were a bird." Another witness claimed to have seen two groups of children throwing stones when the shooting began. The IDF conceded to *Haaretz* that a platoon had set up "an ambush meant to catch stone throwers" but insisted that they had "fired only into the air." No one claimed that al-Ramahi threw anything at anyone, that anyone besides the soldiers was armed, that the children were close enough to pose any danger, or that they were anything but children.

Whatever happened, Wajih was tiny. His face was bare, his cheeks smooth. He looked closer to twelve than fifteen. A flag covered his body from his narrow shoulders to his feet and a wreath of yellow and orange daisies quivered on his belly as the mourners rushed the bier into the mosque. Flags were everywhere: yellow for Fatah and red for the Popular Front. Most of the crowd—there were hundreds, maybe a thousand—was squeezed into the camp's small central square, where, beside a stone memorial to Yasser Arafat, a group of men with masked faces pointed the barrels of their guns in the air. Around them, people stretched their arms over one another's heads to snap photos of the gunmen with their phones. While I was looking elsewhere, someone pasted a poster of young al-Ramahi's face—his eyes frightened and his hair gelled up in spikes—over Arafat's image on the monument. Only the leader's hand was still visible, emerging from the shoulder of the fallen child and waving stubbornly to his people. The pallbearers carried the boy's corpse out of the mosque and the mourners filed after them through the camp's narrow streets in a long and solemn chain up the hill to the cemetery. At the front of the procession, I could hear people shouting chants and the gunmen firing their M16s and Uzis, but the men and boys around me walked in silence. Women looked on from windows, doorways, and rooftops. The rain fell harder. At the cemetery at the top of the hill, men walked from all directions through the rocks and the mud between the low, flat tombs, converging in a far corner around al-Ramahi's grave. It was pouring.

THE SNOW BEGAN on a Wednesday, paused, and returned in earnest the following evening, falling in soft and heavy flakes all through the night. The power in my apartment went out on Friday, which meant not only no light, but no heat, so my housemates and I hiked to a friend's place. It was normally a ten-minute walk, but that night it took an hour: the wind was strong, the snow blinding and almost horizontal. Men stood huddled around fires on corners and in the meager shelter offered by unfinished apartment buildings without windows or doors. The silhouettes of cars left abandoned by their owners in the middle of the street were steadily soften-ing and disappearing in the drifts. We arrived at my friend's building just as a transformer blew, lighting the night in a sudden, blue flash. His block too went dark.

By late morning, bulldozers had cleared most of the snow from the main roads. Few ordinary cars could get through, but the streets were passable for those with SUVs. And suddenly it was clear: Ramallah con-tained legions of SUVs. The side streets remained buried, or mainly bur-ied. One end of my friend's street—not the end on which his building stood—had been plowed. The bulldozer had stopped immediately after the home of a high-ranking Palestinian Authority functionary, blocking the rest of the road with a wall of snow. As we walked by, we saw the offi-cial pulling out of his driveway in a black SUV with red PA tags. Against the whiteness of the snow, Ramallah's class divide was starker than I had ever seen it. The wealthy and the powerful cruised the city in the heated cabins of their Land Cruisers and Range Rovers, as untouched by the inclemency of the environment as they were by the casual violence of the occupation. Groups of young men stood on the corners, throwing snow-balls at one another, enjoying the city's sudden bright, clean silence, warm-ing themselves in the sun or over fires once it set. Without power their homes were likely as cold as the air outdoors. Every few minutes they all pitched in, volunteering the strength of their shoulders and backs to help extricate a luxury car handicapped by lack of four-wheel drive.

On Sunday, I went back to my apartment. Tariq, the landlord, came by for a coffee. He lived upstairs with his wife and children. We sat in the liv-ing room, bundled up in coats and scarves. Tariq had lost a few fruit trees in the garden. He had been careful to beat the snow off the branches, but the cold had killed them anyway. Six of the chickens in the coop outside my bedroom window had also died. So, he said, had all the fish in his aquarium. Tariq was a serious, amiable man with small features and small hands. He had been active during the First Intifada and spent most of the 1990s in prison, where he had befriended Bassem and a few other men from Nabi Saleh and from Budrus. When the demonstrations started in those villages, his friends asked him to take part. He refused. He'd had enough, he said.

Tariq wore disillusion like other men wear hats. The world to which he had returned from prison was not the one that he had left. He found, for instance, that one of the biggest collaborators in Ramallah, someone everyone had known was working with the Israelis, was living around the block in an enormous house guarded by PA policemen. "I couldn't believe it," he said. "Now kids are growing up without any understanding of the past." They didn't know who was a traitor and who was a hero, he said, who sacrificed everything and who had arrived later, when the danger had passed, to pick through the spoils. After his release, Tariq had started a business. He depended on Israeli suppliers, he said, and couldn't afford to jeopardize his travel permit with political involvement. He was by no means rich by U.S. standards, but he had done well. He owned two cars and a comfortable home and his children were learning French and German at an exclusive private school. He was, in other words, part of the class that had managed to pull a profit from the unbearable status quo, however much he hated it. Tariq finished his coffee and laughed at the notion, at how things had turned out.

"There's not going to be a revolution," he said, and smiled, not without some sadness. In the meantime, the snow was still deep and his garden ravaged. He had more than enough work to keep busy.

KERRY CAME and Kerry left and Kerry came again. Unless you crossed paths with his motorcade, it was easy not to notice. In Ramallah, no one talked about the peace talks much, no more at least than they did the

weather, or the traffic at Qalandia. Back in Washington, the secretary of
state had enthused that the Israelis and Palestinians were closer to a deal
than they had been for years. He may have been right, but that didn't mean
much. Kerry delivered a speech at the Saban Forum—an annual gathering sponsored by the billionaire Democratic Party fund-raiser and staunch
Israel supporter Haim Saban—in which the erstwhile impartial deal bro-
ker boasted of his own "100 percent voting record for Israel" and, before
delving into his vision for peace, spent several minutes on the Obama
administration's unbreakable allegiance to America's favorite cousin—the
U.S., he said, was always "particularly prepared to be the first and fastest to
Israel's side in any time of crisis." His audience in Washington may have
required reassurance, but few Palestinians were ever unaware of this.

At the same conference, Avigdor Lieberman, Israel's foreign minister,
spoke with characteristic bluntness, cautioning that no one should get their
hopes up. But even if the dialogue was predestined to fail, as Lieberman
believed it was, it was important to keep the negotiations going in order, he
said, "to manage this conflict." This admission—that the point of Israeli
participation in the peace talks was not in fact peace—confirmed what
had long been a commonplace belief among Palestinians, as widely accepted as the corruption of the authorities and the whiteness of snow: that
"peace" was code for a sneaky sort of war, and that decades of U.S.-
brokered negotiations had served as little more than a useful spectacle that
enabled Israel to keep Abbas's leash tight and potential foreign critics distracted while the bulldozers and the army went about their daily tasks.

He wouldn't admit it for another few weeks, but Kerry had already
given up on his original ambition of reaching a comprehensive deal before
the scheduled conclusion of the talks in late April. His new plan was hum-
bler: to persuade both sides to agree to a "framework for negotiations"—
an unbinding agreement on how they might one day perchance agree. It
reeked of defeat, a hastily improvised two-step that would allow the talks to
continue and the show to go on. But even arriving at a mutually acceptable
"framework" seemed unlikely. Over the next few weeks, Netanyahu made

it clear that he had no intention of giving up the Jordan Valley or evacuating Hebron and Beit El, much less the main settlement blocs. He didn't even want to talk about Jerusalem. This didn't leave much to discuss. Kerry had enlisted General John Allen, who had just stepped down as commander of the U.S. forces occupying Afghanistan, to work out a security proposal with Netanyahu. In early December it was leaked to the press. Abbas, reportedly, was "boiling mad": The plan did not include anything resembling Palestinian sovereignty, or even an end to the occupation. Israeli troops would remain in the Jordan Valley for as long as ten years, Israel would maintain partial control over border crossings to Jordan, and the demilitarization of the Palestinian security forces would be monitored by American drones. The long-dreamed-of Two State Solution was looking a lot like more of the same.

Concrete proposals aside, Kerry's rhetoric had shifted subtly. The secretary, journalist Allison Deger observed, was no longer talking about Palestinian statehood but of building "effective state institutions" for what sounded like an indefinite trial period: "Israel and Jordan must know that they will have a reliable and responsible neighbor—not a failed state—living between them," Kerry had said. "It will take time to train, build, equip, and test Palestinian institutions." President Obama, Deger wrote, echoed Kerry's shift: "The Palestinians have to realize," the president said in his address to the Saban Forum, "that there is going to be a transition period where the Israeli people cannot expect a replica of Gaza in the West Bank." Full and democratic autonomy, in other words, would have to wait until Israel could be assured that Palestinians would vote in a fashion that would not make their occupiers uncomfortable.

You can't please everyone. Even in the face of concessions greater than those acceptable to any previous American administration, Defense Minister Moshe Ya'alon would complain a few weeks later to the Israeli daily *Yedioth Ahronoth* that Kerry was possessed with a naïve and meddlesome "messianic fervor."

"The only thing that can save us," Ya'alon went on, "is for John Kerry to win a Nobel Peace Prize and leave us alone."

A FEW DAYS after the snow stopped falling, an elite squad of Israeli paratroopers entered the northern city of Qalqilya and shot twenty-eight-year-old Saleh Yassin, an officer in the PA's intelligence service, as he walked home from work. The IDF claimed that their victim, whom the soldiers had left to bleed to death in the street, had fired first. Palestinian witnesses maintained that he did not fire at all. That afternoon, Israeli forces entered the Jenin refugee camp and raided the home of an imprisoned local Hamas leader. Clashes ensued, and soldiers opened fire, critically wounding two men and killing twenty-three-year-old Nafaa al-Saedi, the apparent target of the raid.

A pattern was emerging. Two months earlier, the army had killed a twenty-eight-year-old militant in the Islamic Jihad movement named Mohammad Assi. According to the official reports, Assi—who had been a suspect in a 2012 bus bombing in Tel Aviv that injured twenty-eight Israelis, the first attack of its kind in the city since 2006—died following a lengthy exchange of fire that concluded with soldiers shooting two anti-tank missiles into the cave in which he was hiding outside the village of Bil'in. The following month, Israeli special forces killed Mousa Mohammad Makhamra, Mohammad Fouad Nairoukh, and Mahmoud Khaled al-Najjar outside of Yatta, near Hebron. The three men, the official story went, were members of a "Salafist jihadi group" that the Shabak suspected was planning to kidnap an Israeli soldier. They allegedly shot at the soldiers pursuing them, provoking the soldiers to return fire. According to Palestinian witnesses, the soldiers fired without provocation. Nairoukh and Makhamra were both hit four times, and were both shot directly through the head. In all six deaths, the IDF claimed that its troops had been attempting to arrest terrorism suspects and that soldiers had been forced to kill them in self-defense. And in all six cases, local witnesses insisted that the killings had been unprovoked, that they had not resembled arrest raids so much as assassinations, "extra-judicial executions" as the Palestinian Centre for Human Rights put it in a report on the deaths in Yatta.

Targeted killings—by missiles fired from Apache helicopters, F-16s, or drones—had been a common Israeli practice for years, but only in Gaza, and occasionally in Beirut or Damascus. During the Second Intifada, Israeli special units and aircraft had carried out assassinations in the West Bank too. The hummus shop closest to the apartment I rented for the last few months I spent in Palestine had been the site of one particularly notorious broad-daylight execution. But since the end of that uprising, Israel appeared to have suspended its assassination policy within the West Bank. If only for its own purposes, the PA could be relied on to repress Hamas and any other potential rivals, armed or unarmed, whether from the Islamist right, the nationalist left, or dissident factions within Fatah. "Security coordination"—perhaps the two most reviled words in the contemporary Palestinian lexicon—meant that PA forces generally did Israel's bidding, removing any perceived threats from the territory under Abbas's extremely partial control. However much resentment and shame it provoked among the Palestinian populace, this arrangement had served both governments well for the better part of a decade.

Something appeared to be changing. The PA was as obeisant as ever, but the negotiations had been drawing tensions within Israel to the surface. To make up for yielding to American pressure and agreeing to consider any concessions at all, Netanyahu was being pushed by his rivals on the right into acts of greater and greater recklessness and bellicosity. The fact that Israeli security forces once again seemed to feel comfortable, confident even, conducting what appeared to be assassination operations within the West Bank, and in areas that the Oslo agreements had placed under the PA's direct control, pointed not only to the depths of Abbas's submission, but to a deeper shift—in heedlessness if not in substantive policy—one that would be felt with increasingly catastrophic consequences as the year progressed.

Early in January, Netanyahu revealed that, "according to official data," there had been fewer terrorist attacks in 2013 than in any year for a decade. Not surprisingly, he gave no credit to the PA's efforts on Israel's behalf or to any of the Palestinian factions that had on their own abandoned armed resistance. Nor did he credit the ennui, paralysis, and despair that the grinding realities of the occupation—and the Palestinian elite's complicity with it—had so effectively induced in much of the population. The drop, Netanyahu theorized, was "the product of a very clear policy of . . . continuous preventive action against those who seek to do us harm." The prime minister did not elaborate. Without a beat, he hurried on to discuss the latest cause for fear in the absence of actual attacks: the Palestinian Authority's record of "incitement" against Israel.

It was a drum he had been beating for several months already, and one that he would continue to pound throughout the bloody year that followed. To Palestinians, and to anyone paying close attention, the ruse was obvious, the charge absurd: it often seemed that Abbas's sole mandate was to crush and contain his people's every effort to defy the occupation, and that the PA, even more than the Israelis, was the strongest force standing in the way of the formation of any organized resistance. But on the far side of the Atlantic, where these realities remained invisible, and where the targets of Netanyahu's rhetorical gambit resided, the campaign found an eager audience. In the United States too, "security" was a religion, with a logic of its own. When Netanyahu's office prepared an illustrated, PowerPoint "Incitement Index," *The New York Times* published the document online and in an accompanying article repeated Netanyahu's claims with a lack of skepticism that should have been astonishing. Given that Palestinian violence against Israel had reached a record low, it was never clear exactly whom or what Netanyahu thought Abbas might be inciting. It didn't have to be. It was implicit in the reasoning, perfectly circular, by which each act of actual Israeli violence prevented another purely conjectural act by Palestinians, and all those imagined acts of terror, hypothetical though they may have remained, justified the next Israeli assault, and the next one, and the one after that, and the eventual, inevitable response by Palestinians—and it would come before the year was out—would justify all the killings of the past as well as future slaughters of far greater magnitude and horror.

CHRISTMAS CAME. I went to Bethlehem and crossed by car from Jerusalem through Checkpoint 300, a gaping rectilinear mouth in the eight-meter-high wall.* "THE ISRAELI MINISTRY OF TOURISM WELCOMES YOU" read the sign outside the checkpoint: "MERRY CHRISTMAS." The wall's concrete expanse was decorated with giant posters depicting the centuries-old stone fortifications surrounding Jerusalem's old city, as if this newer wall were some near kin of that more ancient one, and building walls was a peculiar indigenous tradition, unsightly in its contemporary registers but with a grand and storied history.

I waited with the worshippers—throngs of pilgrims from Kenya, the Philippines, Poland—to descend the narrow staircase that leads from the 1,500-year-old basilica of the Church of the Nativity into the cave below where, tradition has it, Jesus was born in a feeding trough for livestock to parents who would soon be in flight from the violence of the state. The cave was lit with candles. The pilgrims were singing down there, and praying, and strumming guitars. Some of them were moved to weep. I doubt any of them knew it, but earlier that day, Israeli warplanes had launched a series of strikes against Gaza, wounding nine people and killing a three-year-old girl.† And IDF bulldozers, accompanied by dozens of sol-

---

*"And in its wedge of shadow the long stupid zigzag of the checkpoint between Bethlehem and Jerusalem is indicated with a sign, there on the Bethlehem side. Entrance, it says," wrote China Miéville after crossing through 300. "Entrance, entrance . . . into Israel's eternal and undivided capital, CheckPointVille, at which all compasses point. . . ."

†Israeli soldiers had shot and killed a man just inside the border fence surrounding Gaza. Five days later, in apparent retaliation, a Palestinian sniper killed a laborer contracted by Israel to maintain the fence, a Bedouin on his first day at work. Israel, in response, launched airstrikes against a series of targets across Gaza on December 24. The girl was playing in the courtyard of her home when the missile struck. Her name was Hala Abu Sbeikha.

diers, had arrived in the Bedouin communities of 'Ein Ayoub and Fasayil al-Wusta. They leveled more than a dozen homes, displacing sixty-eight people, nearly half of them children. The snow was mainly gone, but it was cold that night, and cold the next night too.

I had moved out of Tariq's place and was house-sitting for some friends in the same rooftop apartment that I had rented the previous summer. There was no heat there either. I stayed bundled up indoors and dragged the space heater with me from room to room like a silent, glowing dog. But I had a roof and a bed and little else to complain of, and that Friday I missed the demonstration in Nabi Saleh because I was in Ramat Aviv, enjoying the coastal warmth while Irene and I interviewed Haim Hanegbi. On the drive back into the hills beneath Jerusalem, Abir called. Shireen and Nariman were in the hospital. They had both taken direct hits at short range from the skunk truck's water cannon. (Later, I became friends with one of the emergency room physicians. Whenever he smelled skunk in the ER, he said, laughing, he thought to himself, "Oh no, it's Shireen and Nariman." And usually it was.) By the time I reached Ramallah, Nariman was on her way back to the village and Shireen was at home in her apartment, showered and scrubbed and drowsy from the morphine they had given her.

For a while, Shireen told me, she had stopped going to Nabi Saleh. She had been at Mustafa's side when he was killed and couldn't stand to watch the movement he had died for collapse over what seemed such petty disputes. She loved Nariman and Bassem, but she had been mad at them too, angry that they had not been able to overcome their pride and do whatever was necessary to hold the movement together. Bahaa had called a few weeks earlier and asked her to come back. She had gone to the village for the memorial demo, and returned every Friday since. That afternoon, she said, had been like the old days. All the guys were there.

As part of the deal to which Netanyahu had agreed before entering the talks, another batch of twenty-six prisoners—the third of four—was scheduled to be released that Sunday. Said Tamimi was on the list. His turn had come. Everyone in Nabi Saleh, even those too young to have known him, was overjoyed. He was their cousin, brother, uncle, nephew, son. To them he was a prisoner of war who had been incarcerated unjustly while fighting for his country—thousands of Israeli soldiers had committed graver acts of violence and been welcomed home as heroes. And Said was more than a relative and a dimly remembered face. He was a prisoner. Scratch any surface in the West Bank and you'll find prison lurking just below. "Those who enter jail in our country," wrote Emile Habiby in 1974, "become like a shuttle in a weaver's hand, forever coming in and going out." Bars and cells hide beneath all visible reality, and not just as a potential fate. Forty percent of Palestinian males have been confined in Israeli jails. Nearly everyone had someone in prison. Their absence was a hidden ache that marred every present joy. In Nabi Saleh, Said, gone these twenty years, stood in for all the others. His release would be no ordinary homecoming.

But the soldiers stationed in Halamish had apparently seen things differently. To them he was not an enemy soldier and hence a sort of equal, but a terrorist and a murderer. To welcome him, they drenched his family's home with skunk water. The blasts broke the windows, soaking the carpets and furniture inside. For the people of Nabi Saleh it was one insult too many, and too deep. Said's nephew leaped onto the truck's front bumper, gripping the grate that covered its windshield, refusing to let go. Nariman, enraged, did the same. And Shireen—who had only recently recovered from surgery on a broken neck that had left 30 percent of her body paralyzed for weeks—joined them, clinging to the grate. It worked. They stopped the truck. The guys rained rocks on the jeeps and soldiers that accompanied it. Women who normally took no part in the demonstrations ran out of their houses and joined the young men in hurling stones. Manal charged at the soldiers in a fury, Nariman beside her screaming at them: "Get out!" From a distance of less than six feet, a soldier shot Manal in the legs, hitting her with four rubber-coated bullets. Almost miraculously, they neither pierced her skin nor broke her bones.

A FOG HUNG OVER the *muqata'a*. The streets were shining from the rain that had fallen earlier in the evening and the mist surrounding the presidential compound was glowing blue with the flashing lights of police motorbikes. The prisoners were coming, just one day late. It was after midnight and the kids were shy with sleepiness. Bassem was buoyant at the prospect of being reunited with one of his oldest friends. Nariman claimed to have recovered from the previous Friday's injuries, though if she were in pain, I doubt she would have said so. Abu Yazan was taciturn as always, but soon Shireen was dragging him across the pavement, both of them shrieking with laughter.

An hour passed and the courtyard slowly filled. Most of Nabi Saleh was there. "This is our great day," Mohammad told me, though he was too young to remember Said at all. Said had been in prison since before the PA, before the wall and the checkpoints, before the West Bank had been sectioned off and garlanded with thousands of tons of concrete and all those miles of barbed wire. A stage had been set up on the other side of the courtyard beneath the dull, steel-shuttered stucco building in which Arafat spent the last two years of his life. It was the only part of the compound that had survived the siege of the Second Intifada. Said had missed that too. At two a.m. word spread that the prisoners had left Ofer. The guys from Nabi Saleh started to chant. Said's sister was in tears. Half an hour passed. People were whistling and running toward the stage.

It was a false alarm. The first of several. Bassem pointed to the old stucco building—the new sections of the compound were faced with stone. It was there, he said, that he had last seen Said, shortly after they were arrested in the village. The PA had not yet taken over and the Israelis were still using the *muqata'a* as a prison and court. Both men were in shackles. They were being led in opposite directions down the same hallway. They couldn't speak, so Bassem bumped Said with his shoulder as he passed. That was twenty years ago. Another half hour went by. Manal, grimacing, admitted that it was painful for her to stand. The whistling resumed, then turned to shouting. The guys were yelling Said's name.

It was three a.m. when Bilal ran to the stage, his camera in his hand. Abbas was up there in an overcoat. There were more than a thousand people in that courtyard from at least a dozen cities and villages around the West Bank, but none of them were as lively as the crowd from Nabi Saleh. "From Ofer to Megiddo, we will tear the prisons down," yelled Bahaa, and the villagers yelled it back to him. Abu Yazan was jumping up and down. The chanting collapsed into cacophony and then reformed itself around Said's shouted name. This was how it went, how it still goes. Anticipation, exultation, disappointment, heartbreak, anticipation again. Despair is not solid. Neither is joy. They alternate, and contain each other. There is no joy that is not also touched by sorrow, no grief that is not rendered sharper by the memory of bliss. If things move forward in one direction and not another, they do so by rolling there, passing through the same tight orbit, touching here an ecstasy, there another shattering loss.

A prisoner floated by on the shoulders of his loved ones, and then another, and then three more. Some looked giddy, others terrified and fragile. Whatever else it may have been, freedom was a shock. And there he was, Said Tamimi, his arms outstretched, his face frozen as everyone rushed to embrace him. If he didn't recognize them, he didn't let on. Soon he was on their shoulders again, a keffiyeh draped over the thin jacket of his tracksuit, dark circles beneath his eyes. His sister fainted. Somehow everyone made it out of the *muqata'a* and drove in a caravan of nearly forty honking cars back to Nabi Saleh, waving flags and leaning out the windows all the way until at last they got out and Said, looking dazed in a new leather jacket, greeted all the men by kissing their cheeks, and the women with hugs and more kisses until finally it was his mother standing in front of him, an old woman who had not been old when he had seen her last. He kissed one cheek and then the other and then her brow as tear after tear rolled from her eyes.

WITH HIS HUNCH, his sunken eyes, and prominent nose, Said looked a bit like a crow perched on the edge of my sofa, a crow that smoked Marlboros. He sounded, though, like a time traveler. "Everything is different," he said, marveling. All the familiar places had changed in his absence, the people too. Bassem had been a young man, he laughed, placing his palm on his old friend's knee. He couldn't have imagined him married, much less a father of four. The village had been smaller and more close-knit when he left, but somehow in his memory it had also managed to expand: the first morning he woke up in the village, he stepped outside and thought the road had been moved closer to his house. And it wasn't just Nabi Saleh. The whole culture felt distorted. In the Palestine he had left, he said, "Nobody was separate. Everyone worked together."

There was surely a rosy tint to Said's memories, but perhaps not much of one. His father had been killed by the Israelis, and Said spent most of his childhood in a school for orphans in Jerusalem's old city. The slender piece of his adulthood that he spent in freedom had coincided with the First Intifada and the years immediately after it. He was arrested for the first time in 1990 and jailed for a year for "the things everyone was arrested for then," he said—for "being active and throwing stones." A year was an easy sacrifice to make. He was "one hundred percent" confident, he said, that victory was near. "When I was out there in the streets and we would face the soldiers, we were sure we would defeat the occupation."

Beside him, Bassem grinned: "With the throw of one stone."

After his arrest two years later for the killing of Chaim Mizrahi, things got serious. During his interrogation, Said was beaten, though not as severely as Bassem was. He had expected that. "Later the issue was clear," he said. "They were taking vengeance on us." He was sentenced to life in prison and brought to a windowless cell several floors beneath the ground in the jail at Ramla, inside Israel. They kept him in solitary confinement, he said, for more than seven months. "They would search the cells every day and for any infraction they would throw gas grenades in. Right before they thought people were going to die, they would pump in oxygen." Even that, he said, was bearable. He always believed he would get out, that some deal would be struck to free him, that he would not be forgotten. "I knew I was in prison for something just, the Palestinian cause, that I had to remain strong."

About Mizrahi, Said expressed no remorse. "I didn't know him personally," he said. "Those were the means that we used. It was part of the resistance and part of the struggle. I was considered a fighter, a soldier. The role of a soldier is to kill or be killed."

Bassem interrupted: "This was not a personal issue," he said.

Said nodded and agreed. "It wasn't personal," he repeated. "My father was killed in a battle. I killed in a battle."

I asked him where it happened.

Bassem answered for him. "Near Beit El," he said.

I asked him how.

Again Bassem answered. "With a knife," he said.

Out the window, the muezzin's cry was rising from the mosques. Said stubbed out his cigarette, excused himself and kneeled in the corner to pray.

I poured Bassem another coffee. "Ben," he said, laughing, "fuck you. Why do you ask all these questions?"

A FEW WEEKS LATER I caught a taxi north out of Ramallah toward Nablus. The drive was uneventful. The landscape in the northern West Bank is wider and more open than in the south, the hills less sharp, the valleys lusher and more expansive. The highway curved beneath Gush Emunim's early settlements—Ofra, then Shilo and Eli. They had once been radical in the same way that the Hebron and Nablus area settlements are today: one of

Ofra's founders had gone on to lead the Jewish Underground cell responsible for planting bombs in the cars of Palestinian mayors and conspiring to blow up the al-Aqsa mosque.* Now they were staid, semisuburban communities, red-roofed "facts on the ground" that had altered the political geography of the entire region. In Ofra, they didn't need to be radical anymore. Their battle was won, and the settlers' presence in their thousands on hilltop after hilltop—Eli alone covered six adjacent peaks—was a monument to that victory, an ostentatiously clear declaration that however John Kerry chose to spend his time, the two-state solution had been a cadaver for years. The West Bank's settler population had more than tripled since the beginning of the peace process in 1993. There were too many of them now, more than 350,000, and they were too well established—not only in these hills but in the centers of Israeli power. No Israeli politician who valued his or her career could dream of forcing them out, or of mentioning their evacuation as a concrete possibility.

"No one today doubts that the people of Gush Emunim have distanced themselves greatly from the center of the Israeli consensus," wrote the novelist David Grossman in 1988. Even then, Grossman's claim was hyperbolic. In practice if not in rhetoric, successive Israeli governments of both the left and right had, sometimes begrudgingly but nonetheless with overwhelming consistency, thrown their institutional and military weight behind the settlement enterprise. The most wild-eyed settlers worked then, as they continued to, as an advance guard for the state, and a convenient scapegoat for its ambitions. Grossman's claim could now be safely turned on its head. The old settler fringe had grown respectable. They were the center. The ideological heirs of Gush Emunim controlled the Knesset and the media, the army and the ministries. On the road to Nablus, beneath Ofra, Shilo, Eli, Yitzhar, and Itamar, the liberal Zionist vision for which

---

*"It was my right to participate in cutting short the legs of a few murderers," he said at trial. "I insist that this action was taken justly." He was sentenced to seven years in prison, of which he served five.

Grossman had for so long stood as champion seemed a quaint and sentimental anachronism.

At Za'tara checkpoint, two Border Police officers waved the shared taxi
in which I was riding to a stop. They ordered the young man in the front
seat out of the minivan and shoved him up against the door. He knew what
to do. He put his hands on the roof and spread his legs apart. One officer
roughly searched him while the other collected our IDs. Across the street,
two teenage settlers waiting at a bus stop looked on, giggling. The Border
Police kept us for another ten minutes before handing back our documents
and indicating to the young man with a grunt that he could get back in the
van. He and the driver laughed about it as we drove away. What else could
they do?

INTERLUDE

OCCUPATION CABINET
OF CURIOSITIES

EXHIBIT FOUR: THE HUMILIATION MACHINE

Qalandia

The first time I crossed Qalandia by foot was in the spring of 2011. I was staying with a friend from Jayyous. The wall had wrecked the economy there. Among other things. There was no work, and the horizon had been literally cemented off. He and his brothers moved to Ramallah, where they shared an apartment not far from the al 'Amari refugee camp. I slept in their dining room on a narrow bed pressed up against the wall.

One morning, a few minutes before my alarm was set to ring, I woke to a door squeaking open. Two bare legs shuffled past me toward the bathroom. I heard water running, the toilet flushing. When the bathroom door opened, a light-haired woman in her twenties walked by and disappeared into one of the brothers' bedrooms. I got up, pulled on a pair of pants, and lit the stove to boil water for coffee. The woman emerged from the bedroom. I mumbled a good morning. She nodded, miserably, and made a small show of pulling her key to the apartment from her pocket and placing it on the coffee table.

"The key," she said. Then she opened the apartment door, and left.

I hadn't seen her before and if I ever met her since that day—which I very likely did, because Ramallah is an overgrown village—I didn't recognize her, so I never learned what happened. It was clear enough from her eyes, though, and from the tense slump of her shoulders, that I had been the unwanted witness to a breakup, and the beginning of a very bad morning. I choked down a cup of coffee, grabbed my bag, checked my pockets for my wallet and passport, and locked the door behind me.

I had an appointment in Bethlehem, which meant that I had choices. I could flag a taxi to the center of Ramallah and take another shared taxi from the bus station there straight to Bethlehem. Or not straight exactly— Jerusalem lay between the two cities, which meant that long, wide loop through the Container checkpoint and Wadi Naar. Which meant it might actually be faster to hop a taxi to Qalandia, cross the checkpoint on foot, and take a bus from the Jerusalem side to the main depot on the Nablus Road in East Jerusalem, where I could catch another bus to Bethlehem. Such conveniences, of course, were not available to everyone.

So it was that I ended up weaving my way between the cars idling as they waited and inched and inched and waited in the shadow of the wall. Maybe it's the stonecutters' yard a few hundred meters away, or the exhaust from all the idling cars and trucks and buses, or the black powder left by burning tires, but I do not believe there is any spot in Palestine dustier than Qalandia. Until 2000, there was no checkpoint there at all, just a road like any other leading from one city to another. That year, the monster was born. It began as a humble mound of dirt where Israeli soldiers occasionally stopped cars to check their drivers' papers. In 2001, concrete barricades appeared. In 2003, the watchtower. Two years later, the Israelis razed a hill and built the wall. Tollboothlike structures went up, and a vast and well-named "terminal" sheltering a warren of caged passageways, turnstiles, and inspection booths behind bulletproof glass. It kept growing, mutating, the barriers moving, the routes and rules shifting week by week and sometimes day by day. Uncertainty was part of the point, the constant reinforcement of "the radical contingency at the heart of daily life," to borrow a phrase from the scholar Nasser Abourahme. Despite its ever-shifting face, the checkpoint would come to feel like a permanent feature of the landscape.

Technically, Qalandia fell within the municipal boundaries of Jerusalem, but when the wall was built, it became a border crossing between Israel and the West Bank. It developed its own ecosystem, as borders do. You could buy cigarettes without leaving your car, or SpongeBob bedspreads, or plastic jugs of purple pickled eggplant. Men sold coffee and kebabs from carts. Women sold produce or stood begging with their infants in their arms. Kids hawked chewing gum and Kleenex and pirated CDs to the waiting cars, or smeared their windshields clean with dirty rags. Outside, Qalandia was its own market, its own world.

Inside it belonged to Israel. That morning, I walked past the concrete blast walls and through the parking lot into the terminal. I stood beneath its high, corrugated metal roof and tried to guess which of the half dozen or so lines was moving fastest. I chose the shortest one and stood, inching forward into a sort of oblong cage about twenty feet long and just wide enough for a slender adult to stand without touching the steel bars on each side. There were people packed in ahead of me, and people squeezed in behind. We waited, wedged together and barely moving. This was new to me then, but it was part of everyone else's routine. Most were going to work. Crossing Qalandia was one stage of their commute. I'm not sure how long it took before we reached the turnstile at the end of the cage—not long enough for claustrophobic panic to set in, but long enough that I could sense it hovering nearby, a palpable presence a few inches above and behind my skull.

After the turnstile came another turnstile. We were being sorted. Some of the turnstiles were more than six feet tall and barred from top to bottom, a sort of revolving door-cum-cage. Some were the waist-high kind you pass through in subways or public libraries. Except that military engineers had these ones custom-built for checkpoints, specially fitted with arms more than 25 percent shorter than the ones used in Israel. The pre-text, as always, was security, so that no one could sneak by with bulky explosives. But the turnstiles served another function as well, a more important one, and it was standing between them in that dank, longitudinal cell—pressed against the people in front of and behind me, smelling the smoke of their cigarettes and the anxiety and irritation in their sweat and their breath—that I understood for the first time that in its daily functioning, the prime purpose of the occupation was not to take land or push people from their homes. It did that too of course, and effectively, but overall, with its checkpoints and its walls and its prisons and its permits, it functioned as a giant humiliation machine, a complex and sophisticated mechanism for the production of human despair.

That was the battle. The land mattered to everyone, but despite all the nationalist anthems and slogans, the harder fight was the struggle to simply stand and not be broken. It was no accident that clashes tended to occur at checkpoints, and it wasn't just at the soldiers manning them that people threw stones. It was at the entire, cruel machine that the soldiers both guarded and stood in for, and its grinding insistence that they accept their defeat.* They knew—even the kids knew—that they couldn't break it or even dent it and they usually couldn't even hit it, but by fighting, by dancing and dodging fast enough and with sufficient wit and furor, they could avoid being caught in its gears. For a while they could, or they could try to.

After the second turnstile, we entered a slightly wider enclosure. The walls in front of us and behind us were barred. The ones to the sides were a dingy white scuffed black by the soles of thousands of shoes. Above us hung a long fluorescent bulb, furred with dust, and a surveillance camera splashed with coffee grounds. The floor was littered with cigarette butts

---

*"What checkpoints reinforce," the scholar Helga Tawil-Souri writes, "is Palestinians' loss of orderly space-time, of the missing foundation of their existence, the lost ground of their origin, the broken link with their land and with their past."

and empty bags of chips. There were twenty or thirty of us in there, crowded together, shoulders and elbows touching. We weren't advancing so much as being pushed forward by those behind us.* A baby was crying. Every few minutes a soldier, invisible behind a bulletproof panel in the next room, pressed a button and a buzzer sounded, a lock clicked, and three people were allowed to pass through the turnstile at the far end of the enclosure.

So it went. Each group of three that filed into the inspection room was replaced by another three. Usually, someone got stuck between the bars of the turnstile just as it locked again. This time, the person caught inside it was the woman I had seen leaving the apartment earlier that morning. Her eyes were somewhere on the other side of patience, so exhausted by rage that she looked almost calm. She didn't see me. I didn't shout hello. I doubted that she would welcome any reminder of her morning, which was only getting shittier. Finally the buzzer freed her. She pushed out of the cage into the next enclosure. Inside it was an X-ray machine and a metal detector like the ones at airports, only far grimier, and an inch-thick pane of Plexiglas in one wall, behind which a soldier sat in front of a computer screen.

The woman placed her purse on the conveyor belt, removed her earrings and her belt, and stepped through the metal detector. A voice barked out in distorted Hebrew through the intercom. She kicked off her shoes and tried passing through again. The machine went off again. She stood in front of the window, making an obvious effort to contain her anger, spreading her arms and opening her hands to show that she was not carrying or wearing anything made of metal. The loudspeaker issued another staticky command, and she stepped back through the metal detector. This time the machine stayed silent. She collected her shoes, her earrings, her belt and

---

*I didn't know it then and couldn't appreciate the irony, but Qalandia was once primarily associated with flight. It was the site of Palestine's first airfield, and its only one until what is now Ben Gurion Airport opened sixteen years later in what was still a small Palestinian town called Lydda, which would become the scene of one of the most notorious massacres of the 1948 war.

purse, and pressed her ID against the glass. The soldier stared at it and, after a minute's inspection, waved her through. She wasn't done. She had to wait to be buzzed through the final turnstile. Only when the two people behind her had gone through the same routine and also been cleared did the exit finally unlock. She pushed through it without a glance back, shoving her hair from her face.

8.

POKER

Jerusalem, Nabi Saleh, Sha'ar Binyamin,
Beitunia, Ramallah

Oh, there is so much less truth in the universe than
anything else.

—SAMUEL R. DELANY

It was spring still, but that summer would be a long one. Worse than long, disastrous. Looking back it's hard not to see signs, omens, hints of what was coming. At the time they were invisible. Days were just days. Momentum gathered once more. Activists established another protest camp on the model of Bab al-Shams and al-Manatir. This one was called 'Ein Hijleh and was erected in the Jordan Valley as an explicit rejoinder to Kerry's proposal that the valley remain in Israeli hands for another decade. It lasted a week. I was back in the U.S. and missed it, but some of the guys from YAS in Hebron were there for a while, and a crew from Nabi Saleh. Ahed celebrated her birthday by the fire in 'Ein Hijleh, blowing out the candles on a cake decorated with the famous photo of her shaking her fist at a soldier. A few hours later, the army arrived. Soldiers hit Waed with a rifle butt, pushed Shireen into a fire, and shoved and herded two hundred activists onto buses. They drove them to the Allenby Bridge, the border crossing to Jordan, and handed them over to Palestinian police, who loaded them onto their own buses and dropped them all in Jericho. The buses were there waiting: the protest camp's eviction had been coordinated with the PA.

The momentum waned. Resistance was cyclical, just like the violence. It rose and peaked and faded and died and pulled itself up to climb again. There were more killings. On February 27, soldiers entered the town of Birzeit, about halfway between Ramallah and Nabi Saleh. They surrounded the home of a twenty-four-year-old PFLP activist named Mua'taz Washaha and ordered the occupants out. Washaha refused to go. Soldiers fired antitank missiles into the building, knocked down an outer wall with a bulldozer, and shot Washaha repeatedly. His photo joined Rushdie's and Mustafa's on the wall of Bassem and Nariman's living room. The more I stared at it—at his long, dark face and sleepy eyes—the more certain I was that I remembered him. He had come to a few protests in Nabi Saleh and had been there two years earlier the day the marchers made it to the spring.

A week and a half later, six Palestinians were killed in one day, three in an airstrike on Gaza and three more in the West Bank: an eighteen-year-old university student named Saji Darwish was shot on the side of a road near Beit El; Raed Zeiter, a Palestinian with Jordanian citizenship who worked as a judge in Amman's municipal courts, was killed while waiting to cross into the West Bank to visit his family; and Fida' Majadla, who was twenty-three, died after soldiers opened fire on his car at a checkpoint near the northern city of Tulkarem. Darwish, the army claimed, had been throwing stones at Israeli cars. The IDF's official line on Zeiter was that he had run at a soldier screaming *"Allahu akbar,"* and tried to grab the soldier's gun. According to witnesses interviewed by journalists and by the human rights organization Al-Haq, Zeiter had been smoking a cigarette outside the bus that ferries Palestinians from one inspection point to the next when a soldier, irritated that Zeiter was delaying the process, shoved him to the ground. Zeiter stood up and shoved the soldier back, after which three soldiers shot him in the chest. No official explanation was given for Majadla's shooting, nor was his death reported in the Israeli press.

Nine days went by without a killing until fourteen-year-old Yusef al-

Shawamreh and two friends, out early one morning to pick wild thistle in the fields, took a shortcut through a gap in the separation barrier, which cut off their village from its agricultural lands. Soldiers, waiting in ambush, opened fire. Al-Shawamreh was dead before the ambulance reached the hospital. Three more days passed and three more died in an IDF raid on the Jenin refugee camp. Reporting in *Haaretz*, Gideon Levy wrote that soldiers had come for twenty-two-year-old Hamzi Abu al-Haija, whose father had been a Hamas leader in the camp. They came in shooting, Levy wrote. Abu al-Haija returned fire, and was killed. According to Levy's sources, IDF snipers then shot the two young men who attempted to retrieve his body, Mahmoud Abu Zeina, seventeen, and Yazan Jabarin, twenty-three, killing them both. New numbers came out: settlement construction had more than doubled over the previous year. In 2014 it would jump by 40 percent again. If the violence was cyclical, it was not like the seasons. It had direction, purpose. It was going somewhere, and it appeared to be accelerating.

I RETURNED TO Ramallah and called Bassem on a Tuesday. The new IDF unit stationed in Halamish was a particularly aggressive one. They had raided Nabi Saleh every night that week. There had been clashes every day, and the soldiers had been making liberal use of live ammunition. Bassem sounded exhausted. I promised to come to the village that Friday.

It was a strangely intimate demonstration. A dozen soldiers spread out at the base of the hill across the road from the spring. The activists lined up just a few feet away, too close for the soldiers to risk using gas. They did throw the occasional stun grenade and a fragment of one hit a young French activist in the head, cutting her. She spent the next hour with a bandaged brow, insulting the soldiers. "I hope you will never be married," she shouted in French-accented English. "You have never seen the meaning of love." Later she started calling them Hitlers.

Eventually the soldiers got bored with this. At about twenty to three, one of them announced through a bullhorn that the protesters had five minutes to disperse. "Four minutes," he said, about ten seconds later. Nariman was out in front, yelling at the soldiers. Bassem, who had come down to look after her, realized he could do nothing but get himself arrested too, and left. The soldiers advanced. Most people fled. Bilal didn't. They grabbed him. Out of nowhere, from far across the field, his son Hamada, who was then about fourteen, came charging straight at the soldiers, his face wild, screaming, "Daaaddyyy!" The soldiers forgot Bilal and took off after Hamada, who kept running toward them until something clicked in his eyes and, like the cartoon coyote who has already raced off the precipice, he became suddenly conscious of what he was doing, reversed his course, and fled. Later the guys came out in force and pelted a jeep with so many stones at once that they managed to knock off its bumper even as it fired tear gas at them from the launcher on its roof.

Abir was my ride back to Ramallah, and she was eager to get home, so I jogged up to Bassem's to retrieve my backpack. I found him lying alone in the dark. He didn't get up. At the gas station, Mariam Barghouti was already in the front seat of Abir's car. Almost two years earlier, the day the demonstrators made it to the spring, it had been Mariam and Abir who held tight to little Ahed and Marah as they marched down the road, refusing the soldiers' orders to disperse. Mariam, at twenty, wasn't much older than the two Tamimi girls, but was so poised that I was always shocked whenever I was reminded of her age. She was a student at Birzeit University, idealistic, angry, and smart, and had lived in the U.S., in Georgia, for much of her childhood. In her public persona, on her blog and on Twitter, it was the anger that dominated, with all the hard righteousness of youth. In person she was warmer, thoughtful and funny in a self-deprecating way. Abir's little Ford was almost full. I piled into the back with two other journalists, an American man and a French woman.

It was nearly four when we pulled out from the gas station. A group of soldiers stood beside the gate at the edge of the village. As we approached, a tall soldier stepped toward the road. He raised one hand, indicating that we should stop. He was tall and thin, with a small, pinched face and a sergeant's stripes on the shoulders of his uniform. Abir stopped the car. Lazily, without ceasing his conversation with his comrades, the soldier waved his hand to indicate that we were free to go. Abir released the brake. The second the car began to inch forward, the sergeant tore open the door, pushed her aside and yanked the keys from the ignition. Suddenly the soldiers were surrounding us, shouting at us to get out. They fell on the car, searching it, throwing our bags in a pile in the dirt.

I counted the soldiers. There were fourteen of them. They shoved us to the edge of the road beside a large concrete block and yelled if we stepped more than a few feet from it. I asked why we had been stopped. The soldiers ignored me. One of them pushed the other American journalist up against the concrete block, indicating that he should bend over and grab its corners with his hands. My cell rang. It was Bassem, wanting to know what was going on. Before I could tell him a soldier shouted, "Get off the fucking phone," and tore the device from my hand. My turn came next. The soldier assigned the task of frisking us—a chubby kid with slow eyes—told me to take off my shoes. I held the corners of the concrete block as he pawed me roughly from my wrists to my ankles. I asked him why I was being searched. Another soldier, a few feet away, answered. "Because we want to," he said.

Abir approached the soldier who appeared to be in charge, the sergeant who had initially stopped the car. As soon as she began speaking, a private, red-faced and blond, rushed toward us and shouted, in perfect American-accented English, "Shut the FUCK up! Get the FUCK back!" A police van arrived. We listened as the tall, pinch-faced sergeant explained to two police officers that Abir had tried to escape and had driven straight through the checkpoint without stopping, and that Mariam had been throwing stones. Around us, the soldiers began strapping on their helmets and picking up their riot shields. The guys had appeared on the field behind them and begun slinging stones at the guard tower above the gate. One of the policemen asked us where we were from and what we were doing there. I explained what had happened. He nodded toward the pinch-faced sergeant.

"That soldier," he said, "said that four soldiers were standing in front of the car and you tried to drive through them."

The sergeant, a few yards away, pointed to Abir and added, "She was throwing stones too."

I had been within a few meters of Abir and Mariam for the entire demonstration. Neither had thrown a stone. Neither threw stones. They weren't against it, but it wasn't their thing. And no soldiers, not four or three or even one, had been standing in front of the car. The pinch-faced sergeant was strutting now, looking inches taller than he had a few minutes earlier. When the policeman walked off to confer with his partner, the sergeant strolled over to Abir and, grinning, told her in Hebrew, "I'm going to mess up your life."

And just like that, he did.

Eventually, after about an hour, the police handcuffed Mariam and Abir and put them in the van. I drove the other journalists back to Ramallah in Abir's car. Later that night, Irene and I went to the police station in the gated settlement shopping center of Sha'ar Binyamin, beside the grocery store where Bassem had been arrested more than a year before. Almost as soon as we arrived, they let Abir go. She was from Nazareth, inside Israel, and hence had Israeli citizenship, which meant that she was not subject to military law. She would not be charged. But they had kept Mariam, who had a West Bank ID, and Abir was crying, trying to hold it together but blaming herself for her younger friend's arrest. The police had said they still might release her, so we waited in the harsh cones of light cast by the sodium bulbs above us in the parking lot outside the police station. A few feet from the window of the interrogation room in which Mariam still sat was the door to a bakery. There was a health food shop too, and a fish store. They were dark now, but on Sunday morning the whole place would fill with shoppers restocking after the Sabbath. We waited another hour before the police told us they would not release Mariam that night. Abir wept in the car all the way back to Ramallah, and kept crying there, over mint tea at a friend's kitchen table, late into the night.

———

THE TALKS, BY THEN, had already collapsed. Two weeks earlier, on March 29, the deadline for the release of the final batch of twenty-six prisoners came and went without the release of a single Palestinian. No deal would be made to free them, Netanyahu announced, "without a clear benefit for Israel in return." Of course a deal had been made, and benefits calculated, the previous July 28, when Netanyahu's cabinet voted to approve the release of 104 prisoners in four stages over nine months. Now even Kerry's "framework" strategy was in tatters, but two days after the prisoner release deadline passed, the secretary of state was reportedly about to seal an agreement that would keep the process limping forward. Kerry had persuaded Obama to agree to free convicted Israeli spy Jonathan Pollard, who was serving a life sentence in a U.S. prison. In return, Netanyahu would release the last twenty-six prisoners and Abbas would commit to another nine months of negotiations. Kerry had apparently not noticed the date. It was April first. That afternoon the joke was on him: the Israeli Ministry of Housing published a tender for the construction of 708 apartment units in the East Jerusalem settlement of Gilo. A few hours later, in a formal ceremony, Abbas officially signed fifteen international treaties, as he had been threatening to do for years. Only pressure from Kerry, and the promise of a prisoner release, had prevented him from signing them the previous summer. But with Netanyahu discarding the deal that had brought Abbas to the negotiation table in the first place, and with the Gilo announcement flaunting the Israelis' contempt for the entire process, Abbas had little to lose. "This is our right," the Palestinian president said. "All we get from the Israelis is talk." Taken by surprise, Kerry canceled a meeting he had scheduled with Abbas and flew to Brussels. Only three days later, after a seven-hour emergency parley had ended, according to *Haaretz*, in "stormy failure," did the secretary's titanium-clad optimism begin to show signs of wear. It was, he suggested, about nine months too late, time for a "reality check."

Before the week was out, Israeli commentators were already discussing the peace talks in the past tense, and with little nostalgia. On April 8, employing a highly diplomatic use of the passive voice, Kerry suggested that Netanyahu's decision to renege on the prisoner release might have had something to do with the talks' collapse.* Another month would pass before a frank American narrative of what had occurred in Jerusalem and Ramallah hit the press. In May, the Israeli daily *Yedioth Ahronoth*'s Nahum Barnea published an interview with anonymous senior U.S. officials who, he wrote, had been closely involved in the talks. The story that emerged from what Barnea called "the closest thing to an official American version of what happened" was one of Israeli cynicism and an almost astonishing American naïveté. "We didn't realize," said one of Barnea's sources, that "Netanyahu was using the announcements of tenders for settlement construction as a way to ensure the survival of his own government. We didn't realize continuing construction allowed ministers in his government to very effectively sabotage the success of the talks." If true, this is a shocking admission: the Americans, with all their vast data-collection capabilities, did not know what even the least observant reader of Israeli newspapers had for months understood to be self-evident.

Abbas emerged from the wreckage of the negotiations not as the demonic inciter portrayed by Netanyahu, but as something rather less dignified. He had bent to almost every wish expressed by the Americans, and had considered giving up or profoundly compromising on nearly all of the historic demands of the Palestinian struggle. Abbas had been willing to make the return of refugees dependent on Israeli consent, to give Israel sovereignty over the parts of East Jerusalem already taken over by settlers, to allow an Israeli military presence in the Jordan Valley for years to come, to accept an entirely demilitarized state, and to consent to borders that would cede to Israel areas of the West Bank on which 80 percent of the

---

*"Unfortunately, prisoners were not released on the Saturday they were supposed to be released," Kerry had said. "And then in the afternoon, when they were about to maybe get there, 700 settlement units were announced in Jerusalem and, poof. . . . We find ourselves where we are."

settler population lived. Despite these concessions, which were deeper than those offered by any previous Palestinian leader and would almost certainly have been unpalatable to the Palestinian public, the Israeli team, the officials said, "demanded complete control over the [occupied] territories . . . its control of the West Bank would continue forever."

In the end, the officials pinned the blame for the negotiations' failure squarely on Israel, and on Netanyahu's insistence on continuing settlement expansion throughout the talks: "The Palestinians don't believe that Israel really intends to let them found a state when at the same time it is building settlements on the territory meant for that state. We're talking about the announcement of 14,000 housing units, no less. Only now, after the talks blew up, did we learn that this is also about expropriating land on a large scale."

When I first read that line, I nearly coughed up a small piece of my kidney. "Only now," the unnamed official said.

Nearly half a century into a massive state-supported settlement enterprise that had, at the cost of thousands of lives, pushed Palestinians from as much as 60 percent of the West Bank?* Only now? After nearly half a century of evictions, demolitions, confiscations, mass arrests, targeted killings, and the steady and methodical disenfranchisement, dispossession, and humiliation of an entire people? Only now do they realize that this is *also* about expropriating land?

Six weeks after the talks collapsed, after almost a year of near-constant deception, insult, and bad faith on the part of the Netanyahu government, Obama dispatched his secretary of defense, Chuck Hagel, to meet with Hagel's Israeli counterpart, Moshe "Bogey" Ya'alon, who perhaps more than any other member of Netanyahu's cabinet had been open in his scorn for John Kerry personally and for the peace effort that Kerry had so

---

*In 2010, basing their calculations on official maps created by the Civil Administration, B'Tselem researchers reported that 42 percent of the landmass of the West Bank fell under the control of settlers. An additional 18 percent has been seized by the IDF as "closed military areas" for purposes of "training."

earnestly led. If the two men's discussions were marred by any tension, they kept it to themselves. "Nothing speaks more clearly," said Hagel at a press conference, "than America's concrete support for Israel's defense. That includes $3.1 billion per year in foreign military financing, which is not only more than we provide to any other nation, but the most we have provided to any nation in American history." Whatever else might happen, Hagel went on to reassure, "Military-to-military cooperation between the United States and Israel is stronger than ever and Minister Ya'alon and I are both committed to ensuring that it not only stays that way, but it grows stronger. America's commitment to a strong and secure Israel has not and never will be anything but complete and unwavering."

ON THE WALL of the inspection room at Ofer, just above the X-ray machine, hung four framed prints of dogs playing poker. You know the ones. You can find them in almost any thrift store in dusty, faded prints, a motley collection of bulldogs, collies, St. Bernards sitting around a card table. I don't know how many times I passed through that room on my way to Nariman's hearings* or to Mariam's. Always with some edge of anxiety. It was there that you were required to surrender your ID, and it was in the next, tiny, closet-size room that you stood alone with a guard and, without other witnesses, submitted to a search that if the guard wished could be considerably less than pleasant. I don't know how many times how many thousands of others passed through that room en route to their own hearings or those of the people closest to them, suffering an anxiety that surely went deeper than mine, those poker-faced dogs staring down at all of them.

Who bought them and framed them and nailed hooks to the wall to hang them from? With what intention? What game was being played? If it was a joke it was a cheap one, the kind that goes stale in the mouth before it's even

---

*A few weeks after Mariam's arrest I asked Nariman how things were going with her case. She shrugged, bored with the topic. It was still moving along, slowly. "It will take years," she said.

told. But Ofer was, after all, not just a prison but a workplace, and not a very nice one. For the guards time spent here was dead time, windowless hours to be endured before they could punch out and attempt to live again: drive home, peel off their uniforms, maybe eat something that didn't taste of other people's grief. What did the dogs tell them? To laugh at it all? To keep their emotions hidden? Did they really need to be reminded? Or was it a message to everyone—guards and attorneys and observers, prisoners past and future, their parents and their siblings and their spouses—a reminder that all of us are ridiculous animals playing a high-stakes game, the rules of which we can't hope to fully understand? Of course some dogs hold flushes and others not a pair, and there is no reason, really, for any of us mutts to keep sitting in these ill-fitting human clothes on these uncomfortable chairs instead of over-turning the table and spilling all the cards, the chips, and the drinks, and running and howling and fighting to invent some new game, a better game, one that's not so ugly and that doesn't stink of despair.

In any case, we waited all day. In the courtyard, under the sun. It was okay though. There was a water fountain and it wasn't entirely broken. Mariam's father and sister were there, and Irene and Shireen and a few more of Mariam's friends, and a polite young man from the U.S. consulate. (Mariam had American citizenship.) We arrived at about ten and waited there until four that afternoon, when the lawyer finally called us in to one of the cramped containers that served as a military court. Mariam stood in shackles, her face shining with tears. Later, Shireen would be angry that Mariam had let them see her cry.* But Mariam was smiling when she saw her friends, her chin shaking with emotion. I had never seen her look so young. The hearing lasted five minutes. Just before it began, the prosecutor had submitted new evidence that Mariam's lawyer had not been able to

---

*Mariam kept a journal at HaSharon prison. She sent me excerpts later. In one, she wrote, "I saw friends and family in the court and I wanted nothing more than to cry in their arms. I felt weak. Weak and guilty. Guilty, because I am showing my weak side publicly. We have an indoctrinated dogma that we should always be strong. Never weak. That's what's fucking us up."

review, so he had no choice but to ask for an extension. We could leave. Mariam was led off in chains.

EARLIER THAT AFTERNOON, while we were waiting in the courtyard, I was standing beside Mariam's lawyer and overheard his conversation when he answered a call from Hebron. Dozens of settlers had forced their way into a Palestinian home and the owner of the home, terrified, had allegedly picked up a propane tank and held his lighter to it, threatening to ignite the tank if the settlers didn't leave. The man was arrested. The settlers were not. I asked the attorney what the man's name was. It was Zidan Sharabati, he said.

Later I called Issa. Zidan, my silent host in Hebron, had been released on bail. The soldiers, Issa said, had also beaten his brother Mufid. In the end no charges were pressed.

IT HAD BEEN a bad week. The morning after Mariam and Abir's arrest, soldiers had closed the gate at the base of the village, sealing Nabi Saleh and preventing anyone from coming or going. There had been clashes every day since. Odai had spent Saturday in the hospital having bullet fragments removed from his face and his chest and soldiers at the gate had beaten Bahaa's mother in front of her three-year-old nephew. Anticipating raids, none of the young men had been sleeping at home. Bassem had tried to persuade Waed to leave the village until things cooled down, but he refused. On Monday, while I was at Ofer, the villagers marched to the gate. Soldiers shoved them, threatened them, threw stun grenades at them, and made arrests, but they refused to back off. I saw the tall, pinch-faced sergeant in Bilal's video later, making frantic calls on his radio. The villagers—women and girls leading the way—managed to pull the gate open. The soldiers pushed it closed. The villagers opened it again. Finally, the soldiers gave up. The gate stayed open.

That Wednesday, Mariam had another hearing. It didn't look good, her lawyer told me. "We have three soldiers saying she threw stones from five meters away and that she hit one of them in the foot," he said. At some point, the lawyer said, my testimony might be needed, but it wouldn't count for much against the soldiers' declarations: "At this stage, we have a presumption of guilt."

Mariam was looking better. She mouthed the words "I love you" to Shireen and only cried a little. The lawyer did his best. In the soldiers' statements, he pointed out, they had all described the clothing Mariam had worn after the protest, and none had mentioned the bright red scarf she was wearing in video shot during the demonstration itself. And from five meters away, would she really have only hit one of them in the ankle? (She *is* a girl, cracked the judge.) And if she had been throwing stones from so close, why hadn't they arrested her right then? To everyone's surprise, the judge was sympathetic. Maybe he noticed the journalists and consular officials in the back rows of the courtroom. Maybe he had a daughter Mariam's age. In any event, he ruled that there was insufficient evidence to keep her imprisoned until the end of proceedings, as the prosecutor had requested. The trial would move forward, but Mariam could post bail, and, for now at least, be free.

I rode back to Ramallah with Abir. Even outside Ofer's gates, prison seeped into everything, inserting itself invisibly beneath the skin. Abir was tormenting herself with guilt, telling herself again and again that she shouldn't have been in such a hurry, and should have waited to leave until the soldiers had retreated to their base. I pointed out that it was the soldiers who had arrested Mariam and lied to the court, not her, and that an entire system had been erected that allowed this to occur. It didn't help. She knew all that and blamed herself anyway.

IT WAS STILL light out when we drove from my apartment to the parking lot at Ofer, past the shiny new Coca-Cola plant and the fields of grazing sheep. Shireen's car was already there. Mariam's sister arrived with her five-year-old son, her mother, and an aunt. More friends and relatives parked and gathered in the dirt lot outside the prison. We waited. The light was low and warm and strangely crisp. There were clashes in Beitunia somewhere just out of sight and every few minutes a blast would echo from the other side of the hill. A yellow minivan arrived and sat there idling: a taxi awaiting Ofer's daily crop of prisoners. Finally, at a few minutes before six, a white bus pulled up on the far side of the prison gate. Eight or ten men got out, looking dazed but happy, carrying their belongings in sealed plastic bags. A few had to wait in the street until their relatives arrived, but none took the taxi. It drove away. At six-fifteen the bus returned, carrying women this time. Just one woman actually: Mariam. Everyone cheered when they saw her and Mariam ran, sprinting through the yellow gate, literally racing toward freedom. She leaped into her sister's arms and gripped her fiercely, her face wet with tears. She hugged her friends and hugged her cousins and hugged her little nephew tight.

"Come to the car and see your mother," one of the cousins said.

"No," Mariam answered. "I want to hug everyone!"

And she did. Her mother waited in the front seat. Mariam hugged her there, the older woman weeping, and then she got in, and her sister got in, and her aunt and her nephew, and they drove away together, home.

A WEEK LATER, I met Bassem in Ramallah. He had promised to introduce me to a friend of his who had grown up in the Jalazoun refugee camp. I had met some guys from the camp who told me that Israeli snipers had been using .22 caliber ammunition (English had infiltrated the Palestinian vernacular: *tutu*, the bullets were locally called) and shooting Jalazoun's young men and boys in the knee. Lots of them. Rajai Abu Khalil, a doctor friend who worked in the ER of Ramallah's hospital, confirmed it. He had seen dozens of cases with nearly identical injuries, all from Jalazoun. The shots were almost surgically precise, he said, and aimed for maximum damage. A couple of inches higher or lower and the wounds would heal fairly easily, but not the knee: a generation of young men was being systematically hobbled.

I had spent the previous day with Bassem and Nariman, and had left Nabi Saleh in the evening. "I have to get up at four," Nariman had groaned. Waed had an exam, and she had to be up to wake him and make sure that he studied. It didn't work out though. A few hours after I left for Ramallah, soldiers raided the village. When we met in the square a block from my apartment, Bassem was wearing the same jeans and V-neck sweater he had worn the night before. He hadn't slept, he said. I asked what had happened, but he didn't feel like talking. Only later, after we had eaten and hopped in a taxi, did he begin to open up. He told me that the soldiers had arrived in the center of the village at about one in the morning. The guys went out to greet them and the clashes lasted until four. Stun grenades and tear gas, but also live ammunition. Two boys had been arrested.

I asked if Waed was okay. Bassem shook his head. "He was almost killed," he said. "He came home with a hole in his jacket, here." He tugged at the left shoulder of his sweater and fell silent. I asked if Waed was frightened. Bassem said that he was. I asked if he thought that might make it any easier to persuade him to leave the village until things cooled down.

"I don't think so," Bassem said. "And how can I convince him when he sees what I do?"

ON APRIL 23, 2014, the day before Waed was nearly shot, Hamas and Fatah issued a joint statement announcing their formal reconciliation after seven years of strife. A unity government would begin working within five weeks. So they said. And national elections, already five years overdue, would be held in six months' time. "This is the good news we have to tell the people," announced Hamas leader Ismail Haniyeh at a press conference in Gaza City: "the era of discord is ended."

No one I spoke with had much faith that the deal would last. Whatever the leadership said, the rancor between the factions went too deep. For the Israeli prime minister, though, the reconciliation provided a perfect alibi. Calling the announcement "a great reverse for peace," Israel took the opportunity to withdraw from the talks, which had already effectively collapsed and were due to officially expire six days later. But now, after the fact, Netanyahu could blame their failure on Abbas. The United States, which still regarded Hamas as a terrorist organization, would have no choice but to back him. "Whoever chooses Hamas does not want peace," Netanyahu said. It was a refrain that he would continue to repeat throughout the months that followed.

That same day, just after Haniyeh's announcement, Israel launched an airstrike on a densely populated area of the northern Gaza town of Beit Lahiya. Israeli media reported that the missiles missed their target, an Islamic Jihad militant on a motorcycle. According to the United Nations, thirteen people were injured in the blast, five of them children. It was the second strike that week.

MARIAM'S FINAL HEARING did not come till early June. The prosecutor offered her a deal: if she pleaded guilty to taking part in an illegal demonstration, all other charges would be dropped and she would get a two-year suspended sentence. No jail time. Or she could go to trial. She knew the odds: 99.74 percent of Palestinians tried in the military court system were convicted. Three soldiers had testified against her. There was no reason to think she would be part of that lucky .26 percent, and the stone-throwing charge could send her away for two years. Still, when I saw her a few nights before her court date, she was feeling bold. She had been going back and forth all week, but that night at least, she was determined to refuse to cooperate with a system she knew to be unjust. How else could it ever be defeated?

Another hearing was still in progress when we walked into the courtroom. Five young men in brown prison jumpsuits stood shackled in the dock. The whole room smelled of sweat and fear. The guard escorted the young men out, the chains on their ankles clanking as they shuffled off. Mariam was next. She stood beside her lawyer, answering yes or no to one or another question from the judge. She didn't look bold anymore, or even as proud and scared as she had when she had been up there in shackles a few weeks earlier. She took the deal. There was no point, she told me later. Even by showing up, she was playing along with the system and she would be convicted either way in the end. If she fought it she would only serve more time, and for what? Her pride? She did the right thing, the smart thing. All her friends told her so. Still, it was a blow. Mariam's plea was a small and ordinary defeat of the sort that was repeated in that and other courtrooms dozens of times each day, but as she stood there beside her lawyer with her shoulders slumped, I could see that it would not be small for her, that something inside of her had broken. She learned that she wasn't as strong or as brave as in the furor and innocence and righteousness of youth she had imagined herself to be. And for a while at least—until she learned to make of it something else—that knowledge would sit in her heart like a sharp little stone.

"The one thing that hurts," she said a few minutes before the hearing began, "is that I can't ever tell anyone to just fight harder again."

INTERLUDE

OCCUPATION CABINET
OF CURIOSITIES

EXHIBIT FIVE: WHAT YOU SEE

Rawabi

was with Bassem the first time I saw Rawabi. We were standing beside the old domed shrine on the edge of the village and I could just make out a blur of towers and cranes in the distance to the east. I asked Bassem what it was. "A new Palestinian city," he answered. "Like a settlement." Later, on a whim, on our way from Nabi Saleh to Ramallah one day, Irene and I turned onto the immaculately smooth road leading to the new city. Half-built high-rises emerged out of the fog, rebar still protruding from the top floors of the buildings' concrete frames. Inside the showroom we found a scale model of the planned development. It was big enough to walk through. Five thousand new apartments were going up. The entire hillside would be covered in towers faced with white stone and broken into twenty-three neighborhoods with their own shopping centers, offices, schools, pools, gyms, a mosque, and a church. The community's design was inspired, we were told, by the old cities of Jerusalem and Nablus, but it felt like the antithesis of the twisting, crumbling chaos of those ancient city centers. Rawabi was all monochrome order, clean edges, light. If anything, it looked like the Israeli planned city of Modi'in a few miles to the west, a suburban fantasy of urban life denuded of all offending heterogeneity, serendipity, and dirt.

A sales representative whisked us into a screening room designed to resemble a mini Roman amphitheater. Another employee handed out 3D glasses from a wicker basket. A third spritzed the air with eau de cologne. The video began with a family picnicking on a bucolic West Bank hillside. Suddenly, buildings began sprouting from the earth, roofs and windows falling into place from above. Like Athena from Zeus's forehead, Rawabi was born fully formed and already populated with slender, stylish residents in European dress. Women shopped and sat in outdoor cafés. Men shook each other's hands and went to work. Everyone was smiling. The streets, parks, and courtyards were bright and uncrowded, the interiors sparse and sleek. The apartments would sell, a man who introduced himself as Jack told us later, for between $75,000 and $140,000, which sounds reasonable until you remember that the average wage in the West Bank was just over $25 a day. For the lucky few who might qualify—Palestinians from the diaspora or members of Ramallah's small but hungry professional class—Rawabi was all set up, Jack said, for "one-stop shopping." At the center of the showroom, beneath high windows looking out over the construction site, iPads were arranged on pedestals—all you had to do was select a floor plan and sit down with a mortgage lender on your way out. The Cairo Amman Bank, the Arab Bank, and the Bank of Palestine had shiny, glass-enclosed booths on the wall to the left.

Over the years that followed, the towers kept rising. Ads for the new city hung from every lamppost between Ramallah and Birzeit—images of elegantly minimalist bathrooms and bedrooms, each emblazoned with Rawabi's logo and a single, seductive adjective: "classy," "stylish," "sophisticated." Between them billboards hawked mortgages and loans for household appliances: TVs, washing machines, computers. People talked about Rawabi. Everyone had an opinion. I encountered a few who were pleased with it, who saw in the development a model for a different kind of Palestine, one that could keep pace with any country in the world. Most of the people around me, though, pronounced its name with a groan. The contractors were all Israeli, they said. Many of them were. By the summer of 2013, Rawabi's developer had made a direct contribution of between $80 and $100 million to the Israeli economy. The architect was Israeli too, people said, the same guy who built Modi'in Illit—a settlement! That wasn't true, but the project's developer, Bashar al-Masri, had consulted with the architect behind Modi'in, the settlement's neighbor on the Israeli side of the wall. The money came from abroad, people said, from the Gulf. Al-Masri had secured a giant investment from Qatari Diar, the real estate arm of Qatar's national investment authority. Rawabi was built on stolen land, they said—just like a settlement. In 2009, Abbas had at al-Masri's request ordered the confiscation of more than four hundred acres of land belonging to the villages of 'Ajjul, 'Atara, and 'Abwein. It was all legal, said a PA spokesman, because Rawabi's construction "is for the public good and falls in the framework of economic development."

That was the magic word: development. It had the same power that saving souls had in a previous era of commerce with the Holy Land, and it won al-Masri's project near unanimous praise in the Western media. Headline writers reached for the transcendent. *Time* magazine called Rawabi a "shining city on a hill." The *Financial Times* went with "city of hope." It all fit neatly into the discourse of Fayyadism,* then–prime minister Salam Fayyad's vision for a shiny, technocratic Palestine in which such buzzwords as "institution building," "economic reform," and "good governance" would build the basis for a state in the absence of concessions from Israel—and, it

---

*As an economic policy, Fayyadism both preceded and outlasted Fayyad's six-year term. *The New York Times*'s Tom Friedman, Fayyad's biggest booster, had coined the term in 2009, defining Fayyadism as "the simple but all-too-rare notion that an Arab leader's legitimacy should be based not on slogans or rejectionism or personality cults or security services, but on delivering transparent, accountable administration and services." The journalist Ali Abunimah, to whose reporting this interlude owes a great deal, has pointed out that "Friedman couldn't and didn't say that legitimacy should be based on winning elections." Fayyad had become prime minister by appointment in June 2007, eighteen months after a parliamentary election in which his party earned 2 percent of the vote.

went without saying, of popular defiance to military rule, organized or no. Netanyahu seemed to like Rawabi too: "It's crucial that you augment the peace process with tangible economic steps," his spokesperson told CNN in 2013, "and Rawabi is definitely a tangible step that we support."*

Unanimity makes me itchy. It almost always hides a grave. I started digging. Rawabi began making headlines in the fall of 2009, shortly after the PA started confiscating land from villagers who had been reluctant to sell to al-Masri. But none of it had been possible until April of the previous year, when Abbas announced the creation of the Affordable Mortgage and Loan Corporation, which went by the acronym AMAL, Arabic for "hope." AMAL would function as a sort of Palestinian Fannie Mae, backing private-sector loans in a region where political and economic insecurity, and a long-standing cultural discomfort with borrowing on credit, had made long-term mortgages impossible. Who could plan thirty days ahead in the West Bank, much less thirty years? Without the availability of mortgages, projects like Rawabi didn't stand a chance. Nor did "development" in Palestine. But with AMAL backing loans, a market in Palestinian mortgages could emerge, and with it, a market in real estate. Half the money would be provided by the U.S. Overseas Private Investment Corporation, the American government's quasi-public development finance agency, which, per its Web site, "mobilizes private capital to help solve critical development challenges and in doing so, advances U.S. foreign policy."

In 1990, the anthropologist James Ferguson published *The Anti-Politics Machine*, in which he argued that "development," the West's great gift to the poor countries of the world, rarely resulted in the reductions in poverty that it was intended for but nonetheless consistently produced side effects that would prove beneficial to some. "The way it all works out," Ferguson wrote, "suggests an analogy with the wondrous machine made famous in Science Fiction stories—the 'anti-gravity machine,' that at the flick of a

---

*That support only went so far: Rawabi's official opening was delayed for a year because Israel refused to supply the development with water.

switch suspends the effects of gravity . . . the 'development' apparatus sometimes seems almost capable of pulling nearly as good a trick: the suspension of politics from even the most sensitive political operations." So it was with Rawabi, and more generally with the PA's economic policies under Salam Fayyad. Accepting the economic terms of the occupation, avoiding any substantive confrontation with their occupier, and seeking to expand private profits within that highly exploitative framework became, via the magic of development discourse, a strategy that somehow transcended politics, and that even provided "hope" for a new and less rancorous form of engagement between the two sides.

AMAL would open up a new market not only in land and housing but in debt, in loans that could themselves be broken into pieces and bundled with other financial instruments to be bought and sold for further profits. At the very moment that AMAL's launch was announced, such financialization was wreaking havoc on the American banking system. The investment giant Bear Stearns had gone under one month earlier, yet it was from the U.S. that the idea for an American-backed Palestinian mortgage market emerged. Specifically, from a group called the Middle East Investment Initiative, a Washington-based nonprofit with intimate ties to the highest echelons of political and corporate power. Its president, chairman, and several of its board members had close links to the elite centrist think tank the Aspen Institute and to DLA Piper, one of the largest corporate law firms on the planet. Former secretary of state Madeleine Albright was on the MEII board, as was former U.S. ambassador to Israel—and later to the United Nations—Thomas Pickering, and former Reagan administration labor secretary Ann McLaughlin Korologos, whose husband Tom was a lobbyist so influential that he had been nicknamed "the 101st Senator." Why would laying the financial groundwork for a housing development outside Ramallah—even a very big one—make it onto such people's radar?

Less than a year before AMAL's launch, Hamas successfully pushed Fatah out of Gaza. The Islamist party had won the 2006 legislative elections and had since been fighting a brutal U.S.-backed Fatah effort to dislodge it from power.* Covert military means had failed, but the U.S. wanted to guarantee that Hamas's victory would be contained. OPIC's president, Robert Mosbacher, was candid about AMAL's purpose from the start. "Our role is to deploy private capital as a soft power tool," he told *The New York Times* in 2008. Korologos, Albright, and MEII director Jim Pickup—also a partner at DLA Piper who served as general counsel for the Aspen Institute—hoped, according to *The Washington Post*, that the availability of mortgages and small business loans would help build "a Palestinian middle class that will have a direct financial stake in the economic and political success of a future state." People who had cause to fear political insecurity, in other words, would be more likely to vote for the status quo.

Late in the summer of 2013, a billboard went up outside Ramallah depicting a giant key—the old skeleton kind that for sixty-five years had been the primary symbol of Palestinian nationalism, of a return to the houses from which Palestinians were driven out in 1948. The billboard was not political, or not in the ordinary sense. It was an ad for mortgages, and the key it depicted was a symbol not of the long-dreamed-of redemption of the Return, but of individual home ownership. This was the sleight of hand that AMAL hoped to work, replacing collective political ideals with an antipolitics based in the desires of individual consumers. Between 2008 and 2014, consumer credit in the West Bank would increase by a factor of thirteen, from $70 million to $922 million.

I did some more digging, tracing out contacts, associations, networks. Both Tom Korologos and MEII board member George Salem had contracted with DLA Piper to lobby Congress on behalf of Al Jazeera, the media network owned by the ruling family of Qatar, one of Hamas's only state sponsors. DLA Piper also did lobbying work for the American weapons manufacturer Raytheon, which produced the "Iron Dome" defense

---

*Writing in *Vanity Fair* in 2008, David Rose documented the Bush administration's attempt to spark a civil war and overthrow the democratically elected Hamas government by secretly funding and, with Israeli assistance, arming forces led by Mohammad Dahlan, the onetime head of the PA's notorious Preventive Security Service.

system with which Israel shot down Hamas's rockets. And the Qatar Investment Authority held a large stake in the British bank Barclays, which in turn owned a substantial chunk of the Israeli defense company Elbit Systems, which manufactured the drones that the IDF used to launch missile attacks on Gaza. The Qatar Investment Authority was also the parent company of Qatari Diar, Rawabi's main outside investor. So some of the same people who were pushing the sale of mortgages in the West Bank in an attempt to contain Hamas were also lobbying on behalf of the media conglomerate owned by Hamas's largest backer, which in turn hoped to profit from the production and sale of weapons used against Hamas—and against Palestinians generally—in Gaza.*

Stay with me. This will get a bit dizzying. There was also the fact that Bashar al-Masri, Rawabi's developer, had hired a former Ariel Sharon adviser named Dov Weisglass to help him navigate his legal dealings with the Israeli government. Weisglass, who had done business with al-Masri since the late 1990s, famously explained the Israeli blockade on Gaza with the words, "the idea is to put the Palestinians on a diet, but not to make them die of hunger." Al-Masri, who faced no such danger himself, had also worked with the Israeli-Palestinian Chamber of Commerce, which was, despite its name, an entirely Israeli-run NGO devoted to creating investment opportunities for Israeli businesses on the Palestinian side of the Green Line. On its board was a man named Gadi Zohar, a former IDF military intelligence commander and onetime head of the Civil Administration in the West Bank who had upon his retirement from public service cofounded a security consultancy called Netacs. Among Netacs's clients was PADICO, a holding company controlled by Bashar al-Masri's uncle, Munib al-Masri, by most accounts the richest man in the West Bank. PADICO, which was incorporated and registered in Liberia one month

---

*Qatari Diar had also acquired a stake in the French conglomerate Veolia Environnement, which became the target of an international boycott campaign for its role in operating the light rail system connecting West Jerusalem to the East Jerusalem settlements.

after the signing of the Oslo Accords, owned 68 percent of the Palestinian stock exchange and controlled 75 percent of its market capital through enormous and sometimes monopoly stakes in almost every sector of the local economy: telecommunications, banking, electricity, tourism, real estate. Nabil Sarraf, the chair of PADICO's real estate subsidiary, also sat on the board of the Palestine Investment Fund, which had helped to fund AMAL, and hence Rawabi. And PADICO's chief executive, Samir Hulileh, served as the manager of the Ramallah office of the Portland Trust, a British NGO devoted to promoting "peace and stability between Israelis and Palestinians through economic development," which had helped design Rawabi's financing strategy. Until 2011, the Portland Trust's chief executive was a retired Israeli general named Eival Gilady, who had headed the IDF's Strategic Planning Division during the Second Intifada, and who also stood as the honorary president of the Israeli-Palestinian Chamber of Commerce, with which Bashar al-Masri worked from time to time, and which had previously been directed by a retired Israeli lieutenant colonel named Avi Nudelman, currently in charge of business development for Netacs, of which Munib al-Masri's PADICO was a client. Another of Netacs's cofounders was former IDF major general Danny Rothschild, who after a long career in military intelligence was placed in charge of the Civil Administration during the latter half of the First Intifada. In 2011, Rothschild was forced to flee England after being warned by the Israeli embassy that he faced a possible arrest on war crimes charges. Now some of the most powerful men in Palestine were paying him to protect them.

Some of these links are tenuous. Others are quite direct. But when you begin poking around the various institutions associated with Rawabi, or with any major development project in the West Bank, the same groups and individuals keep coming up, the same bewitching haze of associations among supposed enemies. I am not trying to sketch out a cabal, just to suggest the dimensions of a cloud, one that is difficult to see from the surface and low foothills of the earth: the cloud of money and of power that floats over and around Palestine, and over everything.

"What you see is not what is actually happening and what is happening is not what you see," Gadi Zohar told the writer Peter Lagerquist in 2003. On the crust of the planet people fight and die and are broken for their beliefs or their land or their dignity. Their leaders stoop to praise them and promise that their sacrifices will not be forgotten. Whole nations are made of such promises. But above and around it all moves money, which has no loyalties and no memory, and seeks solely to multiply itself. Its worshippers play all sides at once. Whatever uniforms they may wear and whatever oaths they might swear, their citizenship is with that ever-shifting cloud, which, moored to no rock, forms and dissolves and takes new shapes and evanesces yet again. It was not a question of betrayal—Palestinian businessmen and high officials making deals with the enemy, or Israelis doing the same. It was that when you floated high enough, those boundaries and distinctions could no longer even be seen.

Understanding this, I was not able to see Rawabi as an encouraging development, an innovative private-sector solution to dilemmas governments could not solve. I saw it as an extrusion in stone and glass shat out by the cloud, inhabitable scat deposited by capital on its way to a goal that excluded nearly everyone. The statistics were dismal: private-sector wages in the West Bank had been falling for years, unemployment remained stuck at 20 percent and was much higher for the young; poverty and food insecurity afflicted an approximately equal percentage of the population and were much higher in Area C, the more than 60 percent of the West Bank that fell under direct Israeli military control.* In Ramallah, such realities could be easy to forget: the cloud left droppings everywhere, mini-

---

*Fayyadist fantasies notwithstanding, development could work no magic within the framework of the occupation. As one UN report put it in the summer of 2014: "short of a wide ranging lifting of Israeli restrictions on the Palestinian economy and trade, and enabling greater access to economic and natural resources, the Palestinian private sector will remain unable to create jobs, and the severe unemployment crisis will worsen. . . . Long-term sustainable development cannot be achieved without addressing the fundamental weaknesses and structural distortions that were fuelled by decades of occupation."

Rawabis all across the hills and wadis in every direction not blocked by the wall. There was al-Reehan, a two-thousand-unit planned community developed by the Amaar Real Estate Group, which was owned by the PA's Palestine Investment Fund, the chairman of which was Abbas's economic adviser and deputy prime minister Mohammad Mustafa, one of AMAL's early boosters. Amaar was building Ersal Center too, an enormous office, mall, and hotel complex going up in the middle of downtown Ramallah, next to the grand new headquarters of the Palestinian Monetary Authority.* There were endless new restaurants and coffee shops, smooth extrusions like Zamn, where Ramallah's elite gathered over cappuccinos that cost one sixth the average daily wage. Zamn's owner, Ahmad Aweidah, was also the CEO of the Palestine Securities Exchange, which was, like almost everything, owned by PADICO and the al-Masri family. Salam Fayyad, Tom Friedman's favorite Palestinian technocrat, Aweidah boasted to Toronto's *Globe and Mail*, was among Zamn's regular customers.

All around the city, new apartment towers kept going up—in the center of town, in the new and wealthy neighborhoods of al-Masyoun and al-Tireh, and in the steep and rocky valleys stretching north from 'Ein Musbah. The odd thing was how many of these towers were left unfinished. Everywhere hulked hollow concrete shells. At night their windows stared like eyes. From the sunroom of the last apartment I rented in the city center, I looked out at the bare concrete supports of a six-story building missing windows, walls, a roof. "Goodluck Houses," it was called. No matter how many buildings were left empty, new ones were going up in defiance of any obvious economic logic. I asked everyone I could about it. I heard a lot of theories. People just ran out of money, I was told—they got started and couldn't afford to finish. But so many people? It was the bureaucracy, I heard. Palestinians who had made their fortunes abroad wanted to invest in something tangible, but, because they had no local connections in the PA and

---

*Why, you might ask, would a quasi-state without a currency of its own need a monetary authority? What you see is not what is happening, and what is happening is not what you see.

competed with those who did, their permits were denied, their projects left undone. Still—so many of them? I heard it was money laundering too. The many forms of separation imposed by Israel created almost infinite opportunities for smuggling, which meant there was a lot of money moving around that had to be made clean, so projects were created and abandoned as soon as the cash passed through them, like a filter that could be thrown away after one use. All of that was likely true, but none of it seemed sufficient to explain the sheer quantity of empty buildings.

The most interesting explanation I heard was from a man a friend introduced as the one of the most successful developers in Ramallah. Everyone wanted to live in his buildings, I was told. If anyone could untangle the perplexing logic of Ramallah's boom, I thought, it would be him. We met casually, sitting outdoors at a restaurant in al-Masyoun, watching the World Cup on multiple flat-screen TVs. He was polite and soft-spoken. Between games, I asked him my question. "I am afraid I disagree," he answered. "Maybe in the past there were such buildings here," he conceded, or perhaps I was thinking of some other and much poorer city, but no, there were no such empty buildings in Ramallah, or not more than one or two. Here, he assured me, everything was fine.

9.

SO EASY, SO HARD

Umm al-Kheir

. . . well, let it be only a dream!

—FYODOR DOSTOEVSKY

On April 30, the morning that the peace talks officially expired, I woke to the chatter of birds. It was more of a racket really, there were so many of them. I was in the village of Umm al-Kheir, in the desert hills south of Hebron, outside the tiny, two-room home belonging to the family of Tariq Salim al-Hathalin. I had slept outdoors beneath the stars again atop a concrete cistern a few meters from the settlement fence. Somewhere a donkey was braying loudly and the pigeons had awoken in the dovecote and all commenced cooing at once and the dawn was still a thin red line in the eastern sky on the far side of the Dead Sea and Tariq's cell phone, which he had buried beneath his pillow on the other side of the cistern, was ringing an alarm that had somehow, though it was inches from his ear and had already been sounding for ten minutes, failed to wake him. By seven, F-16s were splitting the sky with a near-constant rumble and I could hear a Bobcat working in the settlement next door. They had houses to build over there. Tariq didn't wake until it was after eight and already getting hot and his older brother and his cousin were mocking him mercilessly. "Tell them, Ben!" he beseeched me. "Tell them—I am not lazy. I just sleep heavy!"

It was true. Tariq, who was twenty, slept through that alarm every morning, and through all my attempts to shake him awake. Each night we laid out our bedding on opposite sides of the cistern, a hollow cube of concrete about five feet off the ground, and we lay there and watched the stars wheel and the meteors streak across the sky and the flashing blue light of the settlement security truck on its slow circuit around the perimeter fence. The yellow lights of the settlement were almost bright enough to read by and Tariq could pick up the settlers' Wi-Fi on his cell phone. Was it stealing? he asked me. No, I assured him, it was fine. He lay awake trading messages on WhatsApp with a friend in the U.K. and listening to Turkish love songs until the tiny speaker of his phone was drowned out by an Apache helicopter passing invisibly in the dark with a growing, directionless roar. There was no moon, and Mars gleamed red above us and I said something to Tariq about how gorgeous the sky was and he said yes, "but there would be more stars if we were farther away from the lights, in the blackness."

Later, during the day, I told him how beautiful I found Umm al-Kheir. He agreed that it was beautiful, this jumble of dusty, crumbling tents and shacks and the twisted ruins left by past demolitions. "Yes," he said soberly, "but it could change at any moment. We know this."

A few weeks earlier in Jerusalem, I had told an Israeli activist who worked often in the South Hebron Hills that I was planning to go to Umm al-Kheir and to stay for a while. She wrinkled her nose. "Why Umm al-Kheir?" she said. "Nothing happens there. Why not Susiya or al-Tuwani?" The settlers around those villages, just a few miles down the road, were more aggressive than the ones in Carmel, Umm al-Kheir's neighbor. There was more action there, but the "nothing" that happened in Umm al-Kheir—and that kept happening there, day after day—had become far more interesting to me than the by-now familiar dramas of God-crazed settlers beating old men, killing sheep, and throwing stones at foreign leftists. The nothing wasn't really nothing. Flashpoints of extremist settler violence like Hebron and Burin—or Susiya and al-Tuwani—represented one pole. Umm al-Kheir was another, with little drama but the steady curtailment of possibility, the gradual amputation of each and every condition of an entire way of life, the long and hard push into a deeper nothingness that with each passing month became more complete and irrevocable.

And there was Eid, Tariq's cousin. I went to Umm al-Kheir because Eid was there. The first time I visited, in 2011, Ezra Nawi brought me. An Iraqi Jew who lived in Jerusalem but spent most of his days in the South Hebron Hills, Ezra had spent a month in prison for refusing to leave a house in Umm al-Kheir that an Israeli bulldozer was attempting to demolish. He introduced me to Eid Suleiman al-Hathalin. Eid, he told me, was such a gentle and pure soul that he should not have been born in this world. By which he meant not only the specifically harsh and violent landscape of the South Hebron Hills, but the entire, unforgiving planet. Eid was an artist, a sculptor, and a vegan, Ezra told me. Imagine, he said, a Bedouin vegan!*

Ezra was right about Eid. He had alert, glowing eyes and an open, joyful face of a sort you don't see often on adults. His hair was shaved almost to his scalp and his forehead was unusually large, his skull round and slightly bulbous, which only accentuated his extraterrestrial quality. We didn't stay long that time. Maybe an hour. A black goat followed me around the village like a puppy, nibbling at my shoelaces. Another goat, four days old and born with deformed legs, bayed miserably, ceaselessly, dragging its crippled forelegs in the dirt. Eid showed me two of his sculptures: a perfect miniaturized Black Hawk helicopter and a yellow bulldozer. He had built them from scraps of salvaged plastic that he cut in strips and sewed together with wire. He had repurposed a motor from a child's toy so that the helicopter's rotors actually spun.

---

*Eid was actually just a vegetarian. "Sometimes I'm a vegan," he told me. "Mostly I'm a vegetarian man who is crazy."

I went back in the summer of 2013. In the two years that had passed, Eid had changed. He was just as eager and kind as he had been but he seemed shaky and distracted, impatient. Not with me or any individual, but with the shrinking confines of his life. I kept going back. Umm al-Kheir was hard to get to from Ramallah. The South Hebron Hills were yet another planet in the solar system of greater Palestine, or perhaps a distant moon, drier and poorer than any other. Even more than in the villages around Nablus, it was the Wild West. The settlers did as they pleased, and almost no one paid attention. Umm al-Kheir was small, and too far out of the way for even the local, fixed-route taxis to bother with, so when they had room in their bus I would catch an early-morning ride out of Jerusalem with the Israeli activist group Ta'ayush, and spend a Saturday with Eid, his brothers, and his cousins. Every time I went, things were worse. Not dramatically, but just enough that everyone there could feel the noose slowly tightening.

WHEN I VISITED that August, I spent a few hours with Eid's brother Khaire, who at twenty-three was about six years younger than Eid. Khaire was wiry, with a boy's thinness and a playful defiance to his eyes. Their family, he told me, was filled with engineers. Most of them worked as shepherds and could earn money only by crossing illegally into Israel and laboring in the fields there and on construction sites, but the men had all been to university and had degrees. "We are a smart family," Khaire said, but "in every family there is one whose head is not good. I am that one." He laughed, but he seemed to mean it. It wasn't true. Khaire was as quick and witty as they come. He had studied to be a teacher but hadn't finished and, like most of his brothers and cousins, he spent part of each year in Israel. "The work is hard and the people are not good people," he said, but he could earn in three months what it would take him all year to make if he could find a job in the West Bank, which he couldn't. In this way, he had saved enough to build himself a house and get married. The wedding was three days away. Khaire explained to me that Bedouin women could marry only Bedouin men and that he knew this rule might seem unreasonable but it was a tradition and could not be broken.* I did my best not to look up when a pretty, bright-eyed young woman entered the tent in which we sat to pour us tea.

We walked to the edge of the village. It didn't take long. Eid met us there. He seemed tense. Khaire pointed to the line of nearly windowless yellow stucco homes on the other side of the security fence in Carmel. They were barely a stone-throw away. The older part of the settlement, which dated to the early 1980s, was just to the north. Construction on the houses closest to us had begun in 2005. Since then, the village's shepherds had not been allowed to pass beneath them and had to take a long and circuitous path to reach land on which their goats and sheep could graze. In March, five months earlier, the settlers had erected a tent at the far end of a ridge-line perhaps two hundred meters to our south. They used it as a synagogue, walking every Saturday morning with their rifles to the end of a steep spur of rocky earth that extended out from the settlement into the open desert. The shepherds had since been forbidden from crossing, or even approaching, the ridge, and the circle which they were forced to make with their herds had widened dramatically.

In the years since Carmel's new neighborhood was built, several of Umm al-Kheir's families had given up and sold their livestock, depending entirely on labor in Israel or occasional work inside the West Bank. For Bedouins this was no small thing—it meant abandoning all that remained of an entire way of life and a connection to the past.

---

*Later, when I returned in April, he repeated the injunction, specifying that I was very welcome there, but that if any outsider came and spent too much time looking at the women in the village, there would be problems. You will understand, I hope, if in Umm al-Kheir I made conversation almost exclusively with the men.

"Our life in the future is going to change," said Khaire. "Maybe for the bad."

When I came back in January, the blizzard had destroyed the tent the settlers had been using as a synagogue. They had not bothered to rebuild it, but the ridgeline and the land beneath it remained off limits to Palestinians.

EID AND HIS brothers and cousins and all of the one hundred or so residents of this part of Umm al-Kheir were members of the Hathalin clan. There was another half to the village, with another hundred or so residents who lived about a ten-minute walk closer to the highway. They were also Hathalin, but for reasons no one would discuss, the two sides of the village avoided one another. Humans find ways to disagree. The Hathalins' grazing lands once extended from what is now the Israeli city of Arad, in the Negev desert between Beersheba and the Dead Sea, to these arid hills at the southernmost edge of the West Bank. After the 1948 war, tens of thousands of Negev Bedouin fled or were forcibly expelled from the new state of Israel.* Eid's grandfather, who died in the early 2000s, brought his family and his flocks to the rocky hilltop called Umm al-Kheir, which translates roughly as "Mother of Goodness." He purchased the land for the price of one hundred camels from farmers who lived in Yatta, the nearest city of any size. But when the Israelis occupied the West Bank in 1967, they began to selectively apply certain Jordanian laws based in the Ottoman Land Code of 1858, which ruled that any acreage left uncultivated for three consecutive years—hilltops were rarely farmed—would revert to the state, which could transfer the land to private owners. Meaning settlers. In

---

*In the mid-1940s, between 65,000 and 90,000 Bedouin lived in the Negev in what is now southern Israel. A decade later only 11,000 remained. "More than any other group," wrote historian Sabri Jiryis, "the Negev Bedouins suffered the full and unrestrained harshness of military rule."

this way, Israel had confiscated nearly 40 percent of the West Bank's land-mass by the early 1990s.

"Jordanian rules," Khaire scoffed. "Do we live in Jordan?"

"It comes from the Ottomans," Eid clarified. "The sultan can do what he wants."

"Fuck the sultan," said Khaire, and laughed.

The result, though, was far from funny: the entire village could be classi-fied as state land. Thus, under cover of law, the Israeli authorities had already confiscated a large portion of the plot that Suleiman's father purchased and turned the land over to Carmel. Eid's younger brother Mo'atassim took a sheaf of folded papers from the back pocket of his jeans. He showed me a color photocopy of Carmel's master plan, which the settlers had recently filed with the Civil Administration. "This is the situation now," Mo'atassim said, "and this is the future." The map showed the existing settlement in yellow and beige, a single Y-shaped stalk of houses. Two proposed extensions in yel-low and pink jutted to the south and to the west along the ridgeline where the tent had been. Surrounding them sprawled a huge, green-shaded blob several times the size of the existing settlement: that land, the hillsides and valleys, would remain undeveloped but would nonetheless become a de facto part of Carmel. Umm al-Kheir would lose what little farmland it had, and its shepherds would be forced to trek so far around the expanded settlement that their sheep and goats would expend more calories walking to and fro than they would be able to consume in the sparse and spiky foliage of the hills. It didn't say so anywhere in the map's legend, but the document was a death sentence. Umm al-Kheir appeared on it only as an absence.

The Israeli bureaucracy was slow. It might take two years, Eid said, before the Civil Administration signed off on everything. The villagers would challenge the settlers' plans in court, which might hold off construc-tion for another year, maybe two. "It's not much time," Eid said. "All of us just live here and wait." But the eventual expansion of the settlement's boundaries was not Umm al-Kheir's only or even most pressing problem.

The village fell entirely in Area C, which meant the Israeli military was the sole authority here. For Palestinians if not for settlers, all building was forbidden. When Eid wanted to install a toilet in his home and to dig a hole for the septic tank, he couldn't find a contractor willing to risk having his equipment seized, so he dug under cover of night using hand tools and a small generator. It took him twelve nights. Every structure in the village that had already been built was deemed illegal. Demolition orders had been issued for 80 percent of them, Eid said—not just the few tiny, two- or three-room cinder-block homes but the ragged tents and the scrap-metal shelters for the animals, the concrete cistern on which Tariq and I slept, and the communal oven in which the women baked bread every morning and again each afternoon.

"We call it the Chernobyl oven," Eid joked. Mo'atassim flipped to another sheet of paper printed in Hebrew. It was a complaint filed with the Israeli courts by two residents of Carmel, a couple named Yaakov and Bareket Goldstein, who were demanding 100,000 shekels (nearly $30,000) in damages and the immediate destruction of the oven, the smoke from which they claimed was damaging their own and their children's health. We walked over to the offending structure. Eid and his brothers seemed to enjoy the absurdity of it. A lot of important people had visited this oven, Eid told me. High-ranking military officers and officials from the DCO had come, and foreign diplomats, NGO chiefs, journalists. It didn't look like much: a low circle of heavy rocks covered with tattered shreds of cloth. Mo'atassim pulled back a tarp, revealing a heap of powdery ash, beneath which a layer of smoldering dung surrounded the clay oven itself. It was as simple and as cheap a kiln as could be imagined. Each time they baked, every morning and every afternoon, Mo'atassim explained, the women piled on a fresh layer of dried goat shit and covered it with ash. The fuel was free and the bread it produced—a rough and chewy flatbread specked with char—was a staple of the villagers' diet. Most meals consisted of bread, some goats' milk or dried and hardened yogurt, perhaps a fried egg and a salted tomato. For the villagers, Eid said, it wasn't a political issue: "The people need bread." The DCO had come by with a demolition order in 2010, but the villagers' lawyer had fought it all the way to the High Court, which had granted them a stay. "It's the funniest case," Eid said. "It's not even a building." Despite the court's order, the settlers still came in the night and poured water over the oven, flooding it. Come morning, the villagers would clear away the soggy ash and light it again.

I don't doubt that the Goldsteins, who according to their complaint moved to Carmel in 2008, were sincere in their hatred of that oven, but in truth it produced very little smoke. I was almost always closer to the oven than the nearly windowless Goldstein house was, and only occasionally, when the breeze was right, did I notice the sharp and slightly bitter odor of its smoke. It was hardly noxious and no more damaging than a neighbor's fireplace a few doors down, but I could imagine that it might drive certain settlers mad, that it might lodge in their nostrils and never leave, the stink not just of smoke but of poverty and stubbornness, of a relation to this land that predated them, a way of living that challenged the brittle, fearful tidiness of the suburban order that Israel was attempting to impose on these rough hills. Mainly the oven's smoke smelled of other people, others whom the settlers could not understand and did not wish to, and who refused— consistently and with a willfulness that must have been infuriating—to just die or go away.

WE TALKED ABOUT EVERYTHING. There was always work to be done— crops to be harvested, sheep to be brought to pasture, or washed and sheared, things to be built, maintained, or repaired. But people talked as they worked or as they rested between one task and the next, and in those intervals I learned that Khaire was a Nicolas Cage fan, that Tariq liked Bollywood, and Eid loved westerns. He wanted to know if there were still cowboys in America. Mainly we talked about weightier matters. There were always disagreements, usually with Eid, who consistently formed a minority of one.

There was the question, for instance, of whether people could be admitted to heaven if they did not pray as the Koran required. Mo'atassim didn't think so, and was concerned that, though he was a good man, Ezra Nawi, the Israeli activist who had first brought me to Umm al-Kheir, might end up in hell. But Eid insisted that God was merciful and that we could not see everything that God saw. This softened Mo'atassim's stance, and he recounted a hadith about a prostitute who gave water to a dog dying of thirst and was allowed to enter paradise for this one act of kindness despite all her previous sins. "Exactly," said Eid. "That is it." Still, Mo'atassim said, it would be better if I became a Muslim.

And there was the question of polygamy, which came up a lot. Islam permits a man to marry up to four women, and in Bedouin communities the practice was not uncommon. Suleiman had two wives—though they were brothers, Eid and Mo'atassim had a different mother from Khaire, and Khaire, though he had just been wed, was already thinking of taking a second bride. So were Mo'atassim and Tariq's older brother Bilal. They were crazy, Eid told them. (His wife Na'oma, I should add, was the only woman in Umm al-Kheir who worked outside the village. She was a schoolteacher.) Between one man and one woman there could perhaps sometimes be peace, Eid said, but only if they were very lucky. If a man took a second wife, the first one would become jealous, and would devote herself to tormenting the new arrival, and the strife between them would rob their husband of all possibility of tranquillity. If he married again, Eid said, the first and second brides would unite against the third, and the discord would only grow worse. It would happen again if he took a fourth wife: the first three would join forces to make the fourth as miserable as they could until finally, when they all got old and tired of fighting among themselves, they would together commit their final years to making sure their husband never saw a moment's rest. "He's going to get a heart attack," Eid said. "That's it."

Bilal objected that his father had four wives.

"And they killed him!" Eid said.

Bilal looked thoroughly annoyed.

"Yes," Eid said. "They killed him—they took all his energy and he died!"

THE FIRST TIME I asked Eid about his vegetarianism, he changed the subject. "I love animals, but it's not that." Meat, he said, was "very heavy." He put a hand over his stomach and made a face. Later he was more expansive. We were standing around at the edge of the village, chatting. Some of us were standing around. Tariq's mother was kneeling in front of the oven, baking bread, and his brother Bilal was lifting and piling heavy stones to build a wall just up the hill. Come winter it would shelter the animals from the wind. Bilal laughed. "The Israelis will say it's a house," he predicted, and issue demolition papers.

Eid had been talking about the PA's complicity in deepening the suffering of its people. "Sometimes the problem is inside us, not the Israelis," he said. "We have other diseases of our own. I am not afraid to say this in front of the world. They're going to say that Eid is a traitor, that he's not religious, that he's a communist, whatever. I am a Muslim actually. I pray. But this is the truth."

In Umm al-Kheir, one topic led to another just as the valleys adjoined the hills in the distance, and the hills led to other valleys, and other hills. "You know Buddhism is a very good religion," Eid said. "I don't know if the guys agree with me."

They didn't, and he knew it.

"You know why?" Eid asked. "No killing." He said it again. "No killing! This is incredible."

"Religion is a need for everyone," acknowledged his younger brother Mo'atassim, attempting to meet Eid halfway. "Everyone needs faith in something."

But Eid was in awe: "No killing! No violence! The Dalai Lama: he's the perfect one, I think." It occurred to me that Eid, with his beatific gaze and round, close-shaven skull, could easily pass for a monk.

Mo'atassim wasn't having it. The Koran was clear about this one: "God created humans as the perfect animal," Mo'atassim countered. "The other animals are here to serve the humans."

It had the feel of an argument they'd had many times before. Tariq joined in and asked Eid why it was okay to kill plants.

"If you don't eat any living thing, you will die of hunger," Mo'atassim said. "All of the things in the world are for human beings and you must share them with your brothers." He grinned. Eid, he knew, was just getting started.

Eid told a story. He had once gone to Yatta during Ramadan and seen "strong guys, very fat, with huge knives" slaughtering a cow in front of a truck filled with livestock. The other animals watched as the cow struggled, its blood fountaining against the walls of the building beside it. They panicked, and tried to leap from the truck. "I wanted to do something," Eid said, "but these big men had knives. What could I do?"

Some people beat donkeys, Eid continued, and made them pull loads too heavy for them. "Maybe you've seen it in Hebron," he said. The other guys let him go on. They disagreed with almost everything he said, but they loved him. "Maybe the donkey is weak," Eid said, "and they didn't feed him, and they beat him. What the fuck are you doing? Why don't you pull the cart yourself?" Farmers beat their animals as they plowed the fields. People kicked dogs all the time. "This animal is feeling," Eid said. "There is blood in it, and spirit and a heart." Then there was hunting for sport. He didn't understand it. And humans torturing one another, for pleasure or revenge. "But the animals are innocent," Eid said. They killed out of hunger and necessity. Humans killed because they liked to, "because they hate."

Eid fell silent for a moment.

"Humans, they're crazy," he concluded. "It's really pissing me off."

———

SULEIMAN SHOWED no sign that his energies were flagging. He was just over five feet tall, but Umm al-Kheir's patriarch often seemed a giant. He had a wild, gray beard and skin burned copper by the sun. Long gray curls of hair twisted out from beneath the white scarf he wore wrapped around his head and even when he was standing still he seemed to be in frantic motion. His hands carved and sliced the air as he spoke and his voice was a rough and barking yell. Ahead of me, he was tossing rocks to keep the flock together and shouting at the animals in a special, hacking, sneezing tongue reserved for sheep and goats, all throaty ikhs and akhs: *"Ikh ikh!"* Suleiman would yell. *"Akh akh akh! Tueey tueey ikh!"* The animals appeared to understand these pronouncements, and for the most part went where he directed.

It was early when we left the village. Suleiman carried only a small transistor radio and a water bottle in a bag sewn from the amputated leg of a pair of blue jeans. He had 120 or 130 animals, he told me, dust-colored sheep and velvet-eared goats with long and silky wool in white and brown or a black that was almost blue. His nephew, Hassan—sixteen, serious and shy—trailed behind us with a flock of 80 more. It seemed like a lot of animals, but before the settlers began to take their land, Tariq had told me, his grandfather had a flock of 1,500. The earth was uniformly brown and sharp, the sky an unbroken blue. There was little grass and nothing green. We hadn't walked a hundred yards before I was regretting having left my boots in Ramallah. Hassan had only sandals on. He was limping a little, and trying not to show it. A day ago, he said, a thorn had pierced his foot. We made a long circle around the ridgeline where the settlers had built their plein-air synagogue. Suleiman pointed to the new houses going up on the other side of the settlement fence. "They want all of this," he said, cutting a broad arc through the air with his arm. "The whole mountain."

Hassan caught up. Only when I asked how his foot was did his face betray his youth. He shook his hand in the air, palm down, to indicate that it wasn't great. In other words it hurt a lot. The settlement fence was almost out of sight up the hill to our right as we walked and to my eyes the land around us looked open and free, as if any route might do. But Hassan and Suleiman were taking great pains to keep the animals together and to confine them to a narrowly circumscribed path. Hassan's shepherd's argot was softer and more sibilant than Suleiman's, all *sssss* and *shhhh*. "All the land over there," he told me, indicating the hillside and the settlement above us, "is forbidden. And over there and there and there." He had pointed in every direction except the thin band of earth directly behind and in front of us. The valleys below us belonged to farmers from Yatta. We could see them in the distance, bent in their fields.

A few of the sheep left the track and wandered into the tall wheat. *"Akh! Ekh!"* said Suleiman. Reluctantly, the animals obeyed him, but the temptation must have been excruciating. Around us there was nothing but thistle. The goats' ears dragged in the dirt. An F-16 tore through the sky above us and Hassan hid a smile as I smeared sunscreen on my nose. It was barely nine and already blazing hot. We reached the highway. A green Israeli bus careened around the bend, followed by two settlers in a Japanese compact. From their windows, the highway must have seemed a narrow, asphalt strip of Israel, and the shepherds and their flocks in these burning hills just scenery. Hassan herded the animals across the highway. *"Shhhh,"* he said. *"Sssss shhhhh ssss."*

"Akhh," urged his uncle. *"Ikh tueey akh!"*

With a stick, Suleiman traced a circle in the dirt to represent the route we had just trekked. He drew a straight line across it to indicate the far shorter path we could have taken, the one he had used for years before the settlement's expansion. "Where will we go?" he asked. He pointed up to the sun and sky, as if he might find pasture there, or as if God might have an answer. We walked on along a slender strip of dirt between two fields of wheat. On top of the hill to our left sprawled five aluminum-sided barns ringed by barbed wire—a dairy farm owned by settlers. If we got too close, Hassan said, they would come down or send the police. So we zigzagged on across the dry, hard land, avoiding one obstacle here, another there. The goats were sneezing dirt. Hassan pointed to a yellow butterfly and pronounced its name in Arabic. (Neither he nor Suleiman spoke a word of English.) *"Farasha,"* he said, and pointed out two more, white ones, as they flitted by. He jogged ahead and beckoned to me from the top of the next hill. He had something in his hands. A butterfly, gripped gently between his forefinger and thumb. He gave it to me. I let it fly off.

"Farasha," I said.

Hassan grinned. *"Farasha,"* he agreed.

On the next hillside, when we had caught up with Suleiman, I heard Hassan boasting to his uncle that he had taught me the word for butterfly.

"Good," Suleiman said. "He's learning Arabic."

Hassan ran ahead and caught another and brought it to me. Again I let it go.

"Ah!" he said, and laughed for the first time that morning as the insect fluttered off.

THE PREVIOUS JUNE, officials from the Civil Administration, accompanied by more than half a dozen soldiers, had descended on the village to confiscate a portable toilet. With their M16s strapped over their shoulders, the soldiers lifted the toilet from its base and, as the village women cursed them, placed it on its side in a trailer hitched behind a Civil Administration SUV, which wasted little time in driving off. One older woman collapsed in the excitement.

The toilet had been installed for the use of Tariq's older brother, Mohammad. He was a tall man, and slightly paunchy, with his head nearly shaved. I saw him around a lot, but he looked away whenever I approached and answered my greetings with an absent wave. He was afraid of me, Tariq told me, because I was a foreigner. Mohammad passed most of each day sitting or standing in silence not far from the famous oven and the dovecote that his brother Bilal had built. The latter was an extraordinary bit of architecture, a ramshackle two-story apartment complex for pigeons, raised more than ten feet off the ground on metal poles and leaning concrete pillars. On two high shelves of repurposed wooden planking, Bilal had stacked plastic buckets with holes cut in them and old, dead televisions with their guts and screens removed so that the birds could nest in their bellies. I could understand why Mohammad liked it there.

In 2004, Tariq said, a settler from Carmel had beaten Mohammad, striking him in the head with the butt of his gun. The soldiers, Bilal said, held the villagers back while the settler beat him. They told me that Mohammad had lost 80 percent of his brain functioning and they may have been right, but there was clearly a great deal happening behind their brother's eyes. Mohammad haunted the place. He never wandered far from Bilal's house, and mainly lingered in one shady spot or another. Sometimes he would bend at the waist to inspect a rock or a scrap of trash, picking it up, putting it back, walking away and returning to inspect it again. Or he would stride suddenly and with great purpose, a lumbering giant, until he encountered some phantom doubt and stopped abruptly, turning around and retracing his tracks. His eyes were almost always on the ground, as if he had lost something important and couldn't remember what it was.

"They wait," wrote Mahmoud Darwish, "and waiting is steadfastness and a stand." But to stay in Umm al-Kheir and make that stand, to hold tight to the tiny and shrinking patch of land that still remained to them, they had to go away. Not permanently, but for a few months each year. No one in Umm al-Kheir could afford to live off their flocks alone. Tariq and Bilal's brother 'Adl had a job with the PA police in Bethlehem—they wouldn't even give him a gun, Bilal said, laughing—but for the most part, as Bedouins, they faced discrimination and had no way into the PA patronage system, so public-sector employment was closed to them. "When they make two states," Khaire said, "there will still be no place for us."

Eid had been hired by the HALO Trust, a Scottish-American NGO devoted to removing unexploded ordnance from former conflict zones. He spent his days combing the rugged landscape of the surrounding hills, talking to the shepherds and farmers he encountered, asking if they had seen any shells or strange metal objects. (In this part of the West Bank, the munitions were not leftovers from any of Israel's wars, but debris left behind by the army's endless exercises.) Whenever he found something—which at times he did daily—Eid called his contacts in the IDF and soldiers came out to destroy it. The work was difficult, but Eid liked it, and liked to feel that he was doing something good, something that would protect children, farmers, even animals from harm. As for the danger of working with explosives, he worried more about people thinking he was a spy because they saw him talking with the army. But Eid, bless him, thought in terms of individuals and not nations or sides. Of the soldiers he worked with, he said: "They're good guys. They shake my hand. I'm not ashamed when I do that."

For most of the other men in the village, periodic work on the other side of the Green Line was the only way to survive. "Our life is like people you see on TV, the Mexicans who go to America," Khaire said. "Their dream is America. Our dream is Israel." He found that very funny, and laughed hard. Finding jobs there was easy. He would get a call from a middleman, a Palestinian inside Israel who would let him know when there was work. Through most of the desert there was no wall and no fence, just open hills and valleys that the local smugglers knew better than the Israeli police. It was just a matter of paying one to drive you across: about $40 to Beersheba, more to points deeper inside Israel. If the police caught you, they just sent you back. The first two times at least. After that you went to jail. "There is some beating," Khaire said. "It's not a big deal."

"If I could leave I would leave," Eid told me the day I arrived in April. "I want to run away." We were alone, and he said it like it was a secret, a confession of weakness or of some inherent sinfulness that he knew others would condemn him for. But he was past shame, and didn't care. This world was closing fast, and suffocating him. And it wasn't just the heartbreak of watching his birthplace shrink and die that he found stultifying. It was the whole region and all of its endless, stupid violence, the impossibility of existing as anything other than a member of a specific tribe, be it Jew or Arab or Bedouin. It drove him crazy. "They say it's the holy land," he said. "It's not. It's the same land as Jordan. It's the same land as America. It's *land.*" This was heresy of course, but the others tolerated it as they did all his eccentricities. Eid was special, and everyone knew it. And he knew the world better than the rest of them. He had gone to Saudi Arabia twice on pilgrimages to Mecca. He didn't like it. The Saudis drove too fast and too aggressively. "They think the people are like goats," he said. He'd been to London too, and been disturbed by what he saw. Nobody spoke to anyone, he said, not on the metro or in the streets or the shops. "No speaking. It's quiet. It's industrial. It's so sad. Oh God, what happened?" It wasn't just London, he knew: the same crushing "industrial life," as he called it, had reached Ramallah and Hebron and every place ruled first of all by money. People were becoming "like robots, like a machine really," Eid said. "You can go two weeks without seeing your neighbor because you're working." Even Umm al-Kheir was being transformed. When a man finishes work, Eid said, he goes straight home. "He has a headache, he's under pressure. He tells his wife, 'I have no time.' He's going to kill himself!"

Still, Eid said, he would go to America if he could. "I tell you," he said, "it's my dream." Even though he knew that the U.S. was the originator and prime exporter of the "industrial life" that filled him with such horror. Even though he understood that it was a hard place to be an immigrant, and to be a Muslim. "If I have a chance," Eid told me, "quickly, I want to be far away from the Middle East."

Perhaps that's what had changed about Eid, the distractedness I had first noticed the previous summer. It wasn't just the dread and the sadness that everyone felt, the near certainty that they would lose what they had.

Something in Eid was straining toward a different life. He was already far away. His brothers and his cousins saw this. I'm sure it wounded them. Once, apropos of nothing, Tariq announced, "I will miss Eid very much. But I will be okay. This is my life. I think I will complete it. I think I will never leave here."

Eid regarded his young cousin with affection. "I think you love your Umm al-Kheir so much," he said.

Tariq pretended to take offense. "You don't know what's in my heart!" he said, but he couldn't keep from smiling.

ONE AFTERNOON, I joined Eid at his house, down the hill and away from the others. I had picked up a shadow: a silent little boy with a shaved head and a runny nose. His name was Ahmad Abdullah. His father was in Israel, working. He waited just outside the open door while Eid sat on the floor of his small living room, cross-legged, with his youngest daughter—the one he called the penguin—sleeping in his lap. His sculptures, gleaming and immaculate, filled five metal shelves beside the door. There were two bulldozers—one with wheels and one with treads—plus a dump truck and an excavator, all of them Caterpillars and painted a deep, glossy yellow. There was the old Black Hawk I had seen before, plus a white Volvo 420 big rig, and a green John Deere tractor hauling a trailer. Each piece was about two feet long and built to scale with an astonishing degree of perfectionism. Ahmad Abdullah gazed in at the sculptures longingly.

Eid laid the baby in her crib and lifted the excavator from its shelf. His face brightened as he handled it. He showed me how the machine's body detached from the treads, and the cab from the body. The cab was only slightly larger than his fist. "I didn't forget any details," he said, "even the ladder here that the operator can use." It had perfect little side mirrors too, and radio antennae, and its door opened on a tiny hinge and there was a seat inside for the driver, a gearshift in the floor, a tiny control panel complete with tiny dials. Eid had carved the chair from a bottle of shampoo and the windows from plastic soda bottles. The mirrors and lights he made from CDs and the reflective panel on the back of the machine was cut from a cast-off license plate. The whole thing was fully functional—the excavator swiveled on its treads, and its arm extended and bent at three joints. Eid was beaming as he showed me, lifting and lowering the bucket, scraping at the carpet on the floor as if digging in a quarry. Without either of us noticing, little Ahmad Abdullah had crawled into the room. He sat staring at the sculptures like a hungry cat.

When I had first met Eid three years earlier, I had seen only the bulldozer and the Black Hawk and based on that small sampling I had understood his work as a response to the occupation, a sly miniaturization and repurposing of the army's instruments of war. I was wrong. There was no critique at work here. He just admired big machines. A lot of people, he told me, wanted to impute some political comment to his work. It wasn't there. His wife, he said, had at first complained that his sculptures reminded her of the real machines she had seen used to destroy people's houses. They looked like scorpions, she said. "I tell her it's completely different," Eid said. "I see these machines in the fields working. I love these things."

Two months earlier, Eid had shown his work at a gallery in Ramallah. He was only able to bring four pieces, he told me—that was all he could fit in the car. I had been in the U.S. and had missed the show, but a lot of people came, he said, and they were enthusiastic about his work. Still, he seemed disappointed. Perhaps he had expected too much: "In the beginning all of the people came and they said, 'Oh, nice, very good,' but later they forgot it. They went quickly back to their routines and they forgot it." What Eid really wanted, he said, was to have one of his pieces added to the permanent collection of the Caterpillar museum at the corporation's headquarters in Peoria, Illinois. He had lovingly painted the company's logo on each sculpture. He knew that activists had called for a boycott of

Caterpillar because the company supplied the IDF with armor-plated bull-dozers used in demolitions. It was a Caterpillar that had crushed Rachel Corrie, the American solidarity activist killed in Gaza in 2003. When he heard about her death, he was terribly sad, Eid said, but he didn't blame the machines or their manufacturer. Besides, even if the army had some-times used Caterpillars to bulldoze homes in Umm al-Kheir, mainly, he said, they used Volvos.

We were at the birthday party for Eid's daughter Lin when his phone rang. It was a farmer named Ibrahim who was harvesting wheat just out-side the village with his son. Something had fallen from an F-16, he said, and landed in their field. It was a short walk. The farmers, who had come from Yatta to work the land, put down their scythes and showed Eid what they had found, a heavy, rectangular object wrapped in shiny foil and dented at one end. A sticker in Hebrew had survived the fall. "Flammable Material," it read. Eid didn't think it was dangerous. He photographed it anyway and logged the location on a yellow GPS reader. The farmers went back to their work and Eid and I sat on a stone wall. The conversation turned to animals, their genius and their strength, our blindness beside the power of their senses. "You know the camel can crush a car," Eid said. "If you make it angry, oh God—it will kill you." And of course there were giraffes. "What a miracle of an animal," Eid said. "Her legs are so long!

"Yes, my friend." He sighed. "That is it: so easy, so hard."

It was something he said often, a refrain he repeated, almost a tic. I thought about it later, lying awake on the cistern, staring up at the maze of the stars and at Mars glowing red in the sky. I remembered a Dostoevsky story called "The Dream of a Ridiculous Man." Walking home one gloomy evening, Dostoevsky's protagonist saw a bright star between the clouds and resolved to end his life that very night. But he fell asleep, his revolver on the table beside him, and dreamed that he had shot himself and in death traveled to the star he had seen and found a planet there, like earth but "undefiled by the fall." Its people knew neither cruelty nor grasping, only a love "increased as if to the point of rapture, but a rapture that was calm." And the protagonist, freed from his despair, saw how beautiful life could be, how simple it was to love. Of course it didn't work out. It was a Dostoevsky story. Without meaning to, the story's protagonist brought corruption with him. In jest or in flirtation, he told one small lie, and lies soon spread, and cruelty was born from them, and bloodshed and shame. "There began the struggle for separation, for isolation, . . . for mine and thine." No sooner had people turned on one another "than they began talking of brotherhood and humanity," and no sooner had they discovered crime than "they invented justice, and drew up whole codes of law." The protagonist awoke from his dream and resolved to devote his life to preaching, to telling everyone he could of the truth he had witnessed. His message was not so different from Eid's: "that people can be happy and beautiful without losing their ability to live on earth," that all they have to do is love—"that is the main thing, and that is everything." So easy, my friend, and so hard!

And that, I realized, was why the others regarded Eid with such gentle admiration no matter how heretical or nonsensical they found his views. It wasn't just his art or his intelligence that made him special. It was that something had stayed alive in him that had died or gone dormant in the rest of us, something delicate and perhaps even sacred, and though we could no longer always find it in ourselves, we could recognize it in Eid, could see its beauty and its truth, and also the pain that it caused him. Behind us, on the far side of the fence, three soldiers loitered outside their quarters. One of them walked off on patrol, not bothering to wear his helmet, and Eid talked about torture in the prisons of the Arab world, and the fear that prevented him from going to pray at the al-Aqsa, and the possibility of judgment day. "I believe in that," he said, though he didn't think it would happen soon. We talked about climate change and the war in Ukraine. "Bad world," Eid said. "Everything is going to be a problem." We talked about his first time on a plane and the city of Cambridge, which he had loved, and the fanatical settlers of Yitzhar. "A lot of crazy things in this world," Eid observed. "Where there are bad things, you find the good things actually."

For instance, there was a settler who lived in Carmel, the son of a Holocaust survivor. His name was Roan. He had called Eid to apologize the last time the army demolished homes in the village. "He's a very good man actually," Eid said. He didn't speak to him often because the other settlers would cause trouble for him if they saw him fraternizing with Arabs, but "in my mind," Eid said, "he's a friend of mine. I'm not concerned with the geography, whether it's an illegal settlement or not. I'm concerned with finding good men." Even the bad men—and Eid acknowledged that there were some of those—he didn't want to see them hurt. It pained him, he told me, whenever he heard that a settler had been shot.* The man's family would suffer, and so would whoever shot him, whether they were captured or not. The wheel of vengeance would keep on spinning, and dragging everyone along.

"I think this land is very big," Eid said. "It can take all of us without any problems. But because we are humans we are stupid and we do not see the truth. We do not want to speak to our neighbors and there is misunderstanding between us."

I was about to reply that he made it sound too simple, that good people did ugly things all over the world, and it was rarely a question of individuals and their choices or emotions, but of systems, machines that were larger than any of us. But Eid beat me to it and said it again, his refrain: it's so easy, he said, and so hard. He talked about other friends, Israeli friends whom he used to see but didn't anymore: Eyal from Beersheba, with whom he used to do tai chi, and another friend—"really a very good man"— who lived in Sderot, just outside of Gaza, and who had to deal not only

---

*Two weeks earlier, an Israeli police intelligence officer named Baruch Mizrahi had been killed on the road as he drove to Hebron for the Passover holiday. His wife and one of his children were injured in the shooting.

with the rockets falling but with the anger of his neighbors who didn't like it that he had Palestinian friends until finally he moved his family to America because he didn't want his children to grow up around such hate; and another friend, "a very good friend," who had moved to the U.S. too so that her son would never have to be a soldier. Yes, Eid said, they all moved away, and he was always sad when they did. But of course they moved, he said, everyone wants to go. I didn't mention that most people in the village wanted only to stay.

THAT NIGHT WAS my last in Umm al-Kheir. I would be sad to leave. Hassan sat beside me on the edge of the cistern, our legs dangling as we stared across the fence into Carmel. The sun was sinking, but the streetlights in the settlement had not yet blinked on. It was another world over there, orderly and clean, all right angles and smooth surfaces. Every half hour two soldiers would pass on patrol, chatting lazily as they walked. Or a young couple would stroll by hand in hand, walking in a straight line on a straight road. Beside it Umm al-Kheir looked like rocks against rocks against rocks with its few unpainted concrete structures and shacks of torn metal, everything else just tarp-roofed tents and cockeyed shelters cobbled together from scraps, here and there a stunted fig tree or a cactus, barefoot children and goats toddling about, cats and dogs lazing where they could, birds flying from tent to shack and back, singing from the rooftops and the crumbling stone walls. It occurred to me that whenever I returned, it would not look the same.

Hassan and I discussed the stars as they began to appear in the sky that stretched above both the village and the settlement and he asked me about America and how big it was. Very big, I told him. "Bigger than Jordan?" he wanted to know. We watched a dog sniff by beneath our feet and reappear a minute later on the far side of the fence. The dog looked cheerful and relaxed and unaware of its transgression. I asked Hassan if he recognized the animal, and if it was from Umm al-Kheir or from Carmel. It was from here, he said, and to prove it he tsssked softly beneath his breath. Over in Carmel, the dog stopped in its tracks. It looked toward us and wagged its tail. Hassan grinned and the dog trotted off again, in no hurry, to wherever it was going.

PART FOUR

A DEEP DARK BLUE

PROLOGUE: IF ONLY

Ramallah, Beitunia

Afterwards, everything happened.

—David Grossman

And it all fell down. When historians record the events of the summer of 2014 in the region currently known as Israel and the Occupied Palestinian Territories, they will likely begin with the 12th day of June, when three Israeli boys went missing from the Gush Etzion roundabout, if not the 23rd of April, when Hamas and Fatah announced their unity deal, or the first of that same month, when the peace talks breathed their last. If I had to choose a day, it would be that May 15. It was a holiday of sorts, but that's not why I would choose it. It was Nakba Day, the obverse of Israel's Independence Day, which that year marked the sixty-sixth anniversary of the uprooting of more than 700,000 Palestinians from what became the Jewish state. In Ramallah, black flags hung from the lampposts, but the sidewalks were packed as always. Commerce hadn't slowed. And why should it? There was a Nakba Day every year.

I was walking down Rukab Street with Irene when she stopped to greet an acquaintance.

"Did you hear?" he asked.

Good news rarely follows those words.

Someone had been killed, he said. At Ofer.

We rushed to the hospital. A crowd had gathered in the driveway. Just outside, I ran into a medic I knew from Nabi Saleh named Ahmad Nasser. He had washed his hands, but his pants and shirt were still covered in blood. Ahmad lived in Beitunia, not far from Ofer, and worked at a grocery store a few blocks from my apartment. On Fridays, he was either in Nabi Saleh or at Ofer, where teenage boys and young men from the area and from the villages surrounding Ramallah gathered on the long straight road outside the prison complex to throw stones at the gate and the wall and the jail behind it. Toward them anyway. They were like the clashes at Bab al-Zawiya in Hebron, only more dangerous because the road outside Ofer was so straight and there were so few places to take shelter. That day, Ahmad said, he had seen an Israeli officer peering through binoculars and pointing out targets for snipers to shoot. Nine had been hit, he told me, all with live fire. Two had died. Ahmad had treated the first one, or tried to. The boy had been shot through the heart. He was seventeen. His name was Nadeem Nawara.

The other boy who had been killed was shot in the back. The bullet pierced his heart too. His name was Mohammad Abu Daher. He was sixteen. In the crowd outside the hospital I found Mohannad Darabee, whom I knew from Nabi Saleh. He was a good friend of Mariam Barghouti's who, like Ahmad, worked as a volunteer medic at protests. He had just come from Ofer. Abu Daher had died in his arms. "He screamed and then he didn't say anything else," Mohannad told me, but he couldn't say much more. A little while later, he was standing alone beside me when he began suddenly to shake—not crying but convulsing as the trauma of Abu Daher's death settled physically into his body, a ghost that would not leave him soon. The two boys' classmates, many of them still in their school uniforms, were walking by in tears. Twice I saw a group of them carry a boy flailing with grief into the emergency room. A crowd gathered outside a low building of stained stucco down an alley in the hospital compound. The morgue. Nadeem Nawara's father was there. He was in his mid-forties, his curly hair prematurely gray. Cameras surrounded him as he waited to see his son. He called out to God. And to his son. "Oh my darling," he wailed again and again. "If only, if only," he cried, but he didn't finish the thought.

BEFORE THE DAY WAS OVER, Israeli and American media were repeating the IDF's claim that soldiers at Ofer had used only rubber-coated bullets and other "nonviolent means" of crowd dispersal. Before I left the hospital, I had talked to Dr. Rajai, my friend who worked in the E.R. He had no doubt that the boys had been shot with live ammunition. "There were exit wounds," he said. Even at close range, rubber-coated bullets could not pass through a human torso. When they opened Nadeem Nawara's chest, he told me, "his heart was just destroyed."

I went to the funeral the next day. There were too many people to fit inside the mosque, so prayers were held in a field just beneath the campus of Birzeit University. Giant blue and black tarps had been laid on the ground so that mourners would not dirty their clothes as they prayed, but the tarps weren't big enough for everyone. Some men kneeled on newspapers, or on their keffiyehs, on yellow Fatah flags or green Hamas ones. At the center of the crowd, the two corpses lay on biers, a yellow banner on Nadeem Nawara's chest, a green one on Mohammad Abu Daher's.

After the prayer, when everyone was on their feet again and the political speeches had ended, pallbearers lifted Nawara's body onto their shoulders and began to carry him down the winding road into the valley below, toward his family's village, Mazra'a al-Qabilia. Women watched from the balconies, weeping. Drummers in Boy Scout uniforms led the procession through the narrow streets of the village. Behind them bobbed Nawara on his bier, his eyes closed, cheeks smooth and slightly yellowed, lips parted just enough to show his teeth. Posters bearing his image hung from nearly every door and wall in the village: a short-haired boy in a T-shirt and hoodie, facing the camera, his jaw and mouth twisted slightly, as if he were about to break into a smile. Soon the posters would be all over Ramallah too.

I went to Beitunia two days later with Mohannad Darabee, and with a photojournalist named Samer Nazzal who had been a few feet from Nawara when he was shot. "It was exactly here," Nazzal said. We were standing in the middle of the street. The gates to the prison were not even visible. There were about sixty people there that afternoon, he said, ten or twelve throwing stones and the rest lingering farther back. It was, Nazzal said, a "normal" clash, even a calm one. Twenty or thirty soldiers had gathered behind a concrete blast wall at the edge of the prison parking lot two hundred meters down the road. A smaller group of Israeli Border Police stood on the hillside about fifty meters away. Both were too distant to be in any danger of being hit by stones, but the soldiers, Nazzal said, were using live ammunition from the moment he arrived. "Each time it was one shot," he said. "Like a sniper." When Nawara was hit, "he was just standing in the street," Nazzal said. "They were hunting."

Mohannad had arrived about fifteen minutes after the ambulance took Nawara away. No one yet knew that his wound was fatal. Abu Daher, Mohannad said, had just thrown a stone toward the Border Police position on the hill and was running to take cover when he was shot through the back. Mohannad remembered placing his hand over the exit wound on the boy's chest to try to stop the bleeding. "He put his hand on my hand," he said, and didn't move again.

The Beitunia killings didn't go away. There was video this time. The security cameras on the building outside which both boys fell had recorded the shootings. The building's owner, a man named Fakher Zayed, handed the recordings over to a local NGO, which posted the footage on the Internet. It was just as Nazzal had said. The road had been nearly empty. No one was throwing stones. Nawara was standing in the street and suddenly fell forward. Abu Daher was walking—not running as Mohannad remembered, but walking, calmly, slowly away from the soldiers when the bullet hit his back. It looked bad. Not crowd control but murder. The U.S. State

Department announced that it expected Israel to conduct a "thorough and transparent investigation." The UN called for an independent probe. The fight moved to the Internet, the newspapers, and the networks. The army was sticking to its story: no live fire had been used. As for the video, an IDF spokesperson said, it had been edited in a "biased and tendentious way" that did not "reflect the violent nature of the riot." B'Tselem released the full, unedited video, revealing no such bias at all. An analyst for Israeli television's Channel Two took things one step further and suggested that the footage had been staged. The IDF liked that line, and went with it: there was, an unnamed senior official told *Haaretz*, "a high likeliness of forgery."

More footage came out: video shot by a CNN crew of a Border Police officer aiming and firing at the precise moment that Nawara was killed. This was harder to dismiss. So you might think. Former Israeli ambassador Michael Oren, who was under contract with CNN as a "Middle East analyst," appeared on Wolf Blitzer's show on the very network that had recorded the incriminating footage. It was possible, he told Blitzer, that the two young men had not been killed at all. "We don't know that for certain," Oren said. "There are many, many inconsistencies. . . . You've got to ask some very serious questions."

Blitzer responded with his usual rigor. "All right," he said.

"I've had a lot of experience with this," Oren reassured.

That was enough for Blitzer. "All right," he said again. "Ambassador Oren, thanks for coming in."

WAED GRADUATED FROM high school and changed his Facebook profile photo to a shot of himself on the road outside Ofer where Nadeem Nawara and Mohammad Abu Daher were killed. Behind him, the air was thick with smoke from burning tires. His face was partially covered by a T-shirt, and his hands were filled with stones. Bassem paid me a visit. I asked how he was. "Half bad, half very bad," he said. He tried to laugh. I asked him what the very bad part was.

He sighed. "I was more motivated before. You saw that."

Everything was getting worse. He saw no hope, he said, and no way out. He knew almost everyone. He talked to people. Within Fatah circles at least, he knew what was going on, and what wasn't. And nothing was going on. People might plan individual actions here and there, but no one had a strategy. The foreign NGOs made things even more difficult—they offered help, but always on their terms, always with conditions, usually insulting ones. "The NGO mentality," he said, "it's colonialist." And with or without them, most of what did happen was planned only with the media in mind, with no goal further than the next week's headlines. He had been trying to push the other popular resistance leaders, he said, to a more confrontational strategy, one that would forget the cameras for a while and strive to immediately disrupt the normalcy of the occupation. "The settlers," he said, "they go to work in Tel Aviv and drive home to their swimming pools—they're not even inconvenienced." But no one had been willing to go along with his ideas. No one wanted to take the risk.

Yet you keep fighting, I said.

"I have no choice," he answered. "I cannot stop, but I cannot continue."

He did, though.

LATE IN APRIL, more than 100 Palestinian prisoners being held without trial under Israel's "administrative detention" policy had launched a hunger strike. By the end of May, another 140 had joined in, forswearing all nourishment save water and salt until they were released and Israel abandoned the practice of administrative detention altogether. After forty days, 70 prisoners had already been hospitalized. The words "salt and water" had begun appearing on walls around town. They were painted on the side of Fakher Zayed's building on the road outside of Ofer. Solidarity demonstrations were being held all over the West Bank. They were small, but Netanyahu was sufficiently concerned that he began pushing a

bill to legalize the force-feeding of prisoners.* (He cited Guantánamo as a
model.) If the prisoners should start dying, everyone knew there would be
trouble. The tension had been building for so long. It had to break. But
when? And how?

My friends and I talked about it a lot. They were mainly journalists and
activists, both Palestinians and foreigners, people who, due to the nature of
their vocations, tended to show up at everything. Every clash and every
funeral. *It* was coming, we all knew it. There was too much rage, too much
despair, and too much grief. So we thought. Every door seemed closed.
There was no obvious way out, no alternative but conflagration. We didn't
spend much time wondering what would come after It, if anything would.
More out of fear than a lack of curiosity. We just waited anxiously, expec-
tantly, for It to arrive.

Meanwhile, Fatah and Hamas were going through the motions. On
June 1, only half a week late, the new unity government was sworn in at
the *muqata'a*. It was far from clear what exactly was new or unifying about
it. Though they were technically not allied with either party, half of the
ministers were holdovers from the previous government. The key posts
went to loyalists of Abbas. But then Hamas had been negotiating from a
position of severe weakness. When the Muslim Brotherhood was pushed
from power in Egypt the previous July, Hamas lost its main ally in the
region. Worse, the new military government in Cairo closed the smuggling
tunnels that had allowed Gazans to bypass the Israeli blockade. Fuel
stopped flowing, and most necessities, and with them Hamas's primary
source of tax revenue. Hamas had not been so vulnerable in all the years
since the division began. Reconciliation had never held much attraction for
Abbas before, but he had seen an opportunity. If Hamas were to survive at
all, its leadership would have to accept his terms. So "reconciliation" was
probably not the right word. "Unity" certainly was not. In the West Bank,

----

*The bill would be voted into law the following summer.

the PA continued to arrest Hamas members, as it had been doing for years. And at the first sign of strain, the deal seemed ready to unravel. When salaries came due at the beginning of the month, the PA paid its own people but refused to issue checks to Hamas-allied civil servants in Gaza, though they were now technically all employees of the same government. Clashes broke out in front of banks in Gaza City as Hamas security forces tried to prevent Fatah-loyal PA employees from withdrawing their salaries. Hamas police smashed ATMs. The banks stayed closed all week.

If he had been a different sort of politician, Netanyahu could have waited it out. The heads of the Shabak and Israeli military intelligence both reportedly informed Netanyahu's security cabinet that the chances that the unity government would survive long enough to hold new elections—as the two factions had promised to do within five months—were "extremely low." His problem, if it was a problem, would almost certainly resolve itself. But then what advantage could he wring from it? "Today, Abu Mazen said yes to terrorism and no to peace," pronounced the prime minister the day the unity government was sworn in. He would repeat some variation of the same thing dozens if not hundreds of times before the summer ended. But in May and early June, he was still in a bit of a bind. The U.S. had without much enthusiasm recognized the unity government. So had the rest of the world, and no matter how Netanyahu tried to spin it, Israel had come out of the negotiations looking bad. So he relied—and would continue to rely—on the one tool that never failed him: fear. For the moment, it wasn't working. He could pronounce the Hamas = Terror equation all he wanted, but no one appeared to be listening.

He tried other tools too. Like punishment. In what was meant to be a blow to the Palestinian economy, Israel announced that its central bank would no longer accept surplus currency from Palestinian banks. It was, wrote Palestinian-American business analyst Sam Bahour, "an act that is unheard of in the world of banking. Israel is refusing to serve its own currency." It didn't work. The two economies were too closely linked—Israeli businesses complained, and the central bank was forced to back down.

The Israeli Electric Corporation tried too—the utility announced in May that, because the PA had amassed outstanding debts, it would begin cutting power to the West Bank and East Jerusalem. That wouldn't work either: Major General Yoav Mordechai, who oversaw the Civil Administration, dispatched a letter to Israel's national security adviser, warning that shutting off the lights for an entire population might open Israel to war crimes charges for collective punishment and, more immediately, would "undermine the stability of the security [situation] . . . and create difficulties on the part of the Palestinian security services to contain events." Once again, Israel could not punish the PA without hurting itself. The cuts were called off. The Civil Administration tried too. According to *Haaretz*, IDF and DCO officials convened a "brainstorming session" on June 5 at which staff officers "were asked to suggest ways to inflict harm on the Palestinians." Their proposals were to be passed on to Netanyahu for approval. The officers, to their credit, did not cooperate.

That week, the U.S. State Department briefly lost patience with the Netanyahu government's hectoring. Members of his security cabinet agreed, it had been leaked, that the American response to the unity deal had been "insufficient, weak, merely for show, and didn't include enough exclamation marks." A senior U.S. official who preferred to remain nameless reminded *Haaretz* that, however heated the Abu-Mazen-Said-Yes-to-Terrorism rhetoric had become, Israeli security forces remained in constant cooperation with their Palestinian counterparts. Israel needed the PA, and the PA needed Israel. On the very day the unity government took power, Israel had gone ahead with a scheduled transfer of 500 million shekels of tax revenue that it had collected on the PA's behalf. That action, the American official said, "reflects the Israeli establishment's clear interest in maintaining a functioning and stable PA that can effectively administer Palestinian areas." Despite Netanyahu's threats, the official went on, "It is against our interest—and Israel's interests—to cut ties with and funding to such a PA government. A functioning, stable PA serves our interests, Palestinian interests, and Israeli interests."

Abu Mazen, it seemed, agreed. A week earlier, the Palestinian president had told an audience of Israeli visitors to the *muqata'a* that he regarded his own security forces' policy of cooperation with the Israeli military as nothing less than "sacred." There was probably no single policy so hated by his own people as the PA's ongoing collaboration with the occupying army. Hamas and the PFLP had both urged him to end it, the latter group demanding that the PA behave like "a state in which security services act to protect Palestinians rather than the occupier." But Abbas was not shy. "I say it on the air," he said, "security coordination is sacred, is sacred. And we will continue it whether we disagree or agree."* In case anyone had any doubts, on June 9, when Hamas supporters demonstrated in Ramallah to show solidarity with the hunger strikers, PA security forces broke up the protest with force, beating demonstrators as well as journalists covering the event. Two days later they demonstrated again, and were again beaten by PA police. That was June 11.

WHAT I WILL remember of that long summer had nothing to do with Fatah or Hamas or the unity government or what appeared to be the real and final end of the peace process and the Two State Solution. I will remember it as the summer of children dying. I visited Nadeem Nawara's father with another journalist, a Texan. Nadeem had been buried in Mazra'a al-Qabilia, where his father was from, but the family lived in Ramallah, in an apartment building that was a quick drive from my own. The father, Siam Nawara, had a salon on the ground floor. He was very successful, and did hair and makeup for weddings. Everything, he said:

---

*Seven months later, in December, when PA minister Ziad Abu Ein died after being beaten by Israeli soldiers during a protest in the village of Turmus'ayya, high-ranking PA officials announced that security coordination would be halted or curtailed. It wasn't. The following March, the PLO's 110-member Central Council voted to suspend all security cooperation with Israel. The body's resolutions are not binding on the PA, but nonetheless represent the will of the Palestinian political establishment. Abbas chose not to implement the decision.

extensions, eyebrows, up-dos. Nadeem Salon, it was called. He had named it for his eldest son. We talked for a while about the allegations on the Israeli news—that the videos were forgeries, that Nadeem had not been killed. "My son is real," he said. "He's dead." He had photos that showed the wound, where the bullet entered and where it left Nadeem's body. Did we want to see them? he asked.

What could we say?

He led us to a small room with two twin beds, both stripped of sheets, a shelf lined with schoolbooks, and a desk with a computer. It was Nadeem's room. Siam Nawara loaded a disc into the PC and clicked through photos of his son's corpse wrapped in a pale blue sheet. There was the entry wound, in the center of his chest. A wide arc of flesh cut by the surgeons had been sutured crudely into place. And there was the exit wound, a little lower, a dark hole in his back leaking blood. "This is my son," Nawara said. He clicked open the CNN footage of the shooting and pointed to a soldier on the hillside in the gray-black uniform of the Border Police. "One hundred percent," he said, "that's the one who shot Nadeem."*

There was more. "Watch, that's Nadeem," he said. A dim, shaky cell phone video appeared on the monitor. In it, Nadeem was clowning as his mother tried to cook. She waved a ladle at him, but he caught it in the air and kissed her three times on the cheeks. She was laughing. Beside me his father was laughing too. He had watched these clips so many times that he

---

*Seven Border Police officers and one IDF soldier assigned to a communications unit had gathered on a driveway on the hill above the road. Media attention initially focused on the soldier, who could be clearly seen in the CNN video squatting and supporting his rifle on a low wall before firing. I hadn't noticed until Nawara's father pointed it out that a Border Policeman who was partially obscured by foliage fired seconds before the green-uniformed soldier did. In November, the Border Police officer, whose name was Ben Deri, would be arrested and charged with manslaughter. This was an anomaly: according to the Israeli human rights group Yesh Din, between 2010 and 2013 only 1.4 percent of all complaints regarding misconduct by soldiers against Palestinians resulted in indictments. In the months following Deri's arrest, legal proceedings against him were repeatedly postponed. In December 2015, more than a year after his indictment and three months after evidentiary hearings were scheduled to begin, they were again pushed back, this time for six months.

could recite every line his son said before it left the boy's mouth. There were others: Nadeem doing a backflip into a deep drift of snow the previous December; Nadeem laughing and screaming with two friends as they ran through the streets in the rain; Nadeem sitting in a car packed with other teenagers, music blasting and the boys all dancing in their seats; Nadeem and a friend goofing in class as a teacher droned on in the background; Nadeem riding a horse in Mazra'a al-Qabilia just a week before his death. He had shot that one himself, the reins in one hand, his phone in another. It was late in the day. The shadows were long, the sky a deep, dark blue.

10.

MY BROTHER'S KEEPER

Ramallah, Hebron, Balata, Nablus, Nabi Saleh

Night is always a giant but this one was especially terrible.

—Vladimir Nabokov

On June 12, 2014, three Israeli teenagers—Gilad Shaar and Naftali Frankel, both sixteen, and Eyal Yifrach, who was nineteen—disappeared while hitchhiking in the southern West Bank. It was a Thursday night and they were on their way home for the weekend. All three were students at West Bank yeshivas, Shaar and Frankel in Gush Etzion, Yifrach on Shuhada Street in Hebron. One of the boys, Israeli police spokesman Micky Rosenfeld told *The New York Times*, was able to make an emergency call to the police. He did not speak, Rosenfeld said, "but background noises indicated that he was in some kind of trouble." This, it would turn out, was not quite true, and far from complete. But the Israeli government was, and would remain, more interested in concealing the truth than in uncovering it. A gag order was swiftly placed over the case, forbidding the press from reporting on any details of the investigation, the existence of the investigation, and the existence of the gag order. This made things easier for Netanyahu, who, before the boys' names had even been made public, issued a statement declaring the kidnapping to be "the result of bringing a terrorist organization into the government." He did not specify the nature of this link, nor did anyone ask him to.

That night, a burned-out Hyundai with Israeli plates was found in a field outside the town of Dura, west of Hebron. Arrest raids began almost immediately. Checkpoints went up around Hebron, and thousands of additional troops were deployed to the West Bank. Netanyahu waited until the Sabbath had passed to voice his firm conviction that the kidnappers "were members of Hamas, the same Hamas that Abu Mazen made a unity government with." He offered no evidence. Neither the Israeli nor the American media demanded any. Later that day he said it again: "Hamas terrorists carried out Thursday's kidnapping of three Israeli teenagers. We know that for a fact." He didn't identify the "terrorists" or let on how he knew they were with Hamas. He didn't say anything at all that might count as fact, but he kept saying the same thing again and again and he would continue to do so throughout all the weeks that followed, allowing repetition to substitute for evidence. For Netanyahu, the abduction provided an easy solution to a problem that had been nagging him for weeks, a cudgel with which to crush Hamas and discipline Abbas. It didn't matter that Hamas denied the charge, and that it made so little sense: there was no point to political kidnappings if the kidnappers did not take credit for the act. In the past, Hamas had bragged whenever it managed to capture an Israeli. In the Shalit deal, one soldier had netted them 1,027 Palestinian prisoners. If they had three Israeli teenagers, why would they deny it? Even dead, the teens would have been worth something. A Hamas spokesman dismissed Netanyahu's claims as "stupid." Stupid or no, by the end of that day 150 Palestinians—mostly Hamas supporters—had been arrested. Among them were the elected speaker of the Palestinian Legislative Council and five other Hamas parliamentarians. All 700,000 inhabitants of the Hebron governorate had been sealed off from the rest of the West Bank. Hebronites were not allowed to pass through the Container checkpoint. Even if they had permits, they couldn't cross into Israel, or leave Palestine for Jordan. And it wasn't just Hebron: Israeli troops began conducting raids in every major city of the West Bank. Clashes followed nearly everywhere they went. In the Jalazoun camp, soldiers killed a twenty-year-old named Ahmad Sabarin. When the young men from the camp marched on the checkpoint at Qalandia, soldiers shot and wounded six of them.

By then the campaign had a name: Operation Brother's Keeper. No one seemed to notice that for all its scriptural weight and apparent good feeling, the verse to which the operation's name referred was not about fraternal devotion but disavowal, fratricide, and deceit.* By that Monday night, it was clear that Netanyahu had unleashed something enormous. More troops had flooded the West Bank than had been there at any point since the Second Intifada. Each day brought another forty or fifty or sixty arrests, and not just in or around Hebron, but in Nablus, Jenin, Tulkarem, Ramallah. Nearly everyone with a known link to Hamas was being pulled out of bed in the night. *Haaretz* quoted a "high-ranking military officer" who admitted that the government did not know "if the kidnapping was perpetrated by a local cell, or if it was directed by an outsider." In other words, the authorities knew next to nothing, and we had to take them at their word that Hamas had been responsible—not just individual members, but the entire organization. In the absence of sound evidence—which, thanks to the gag order, the press was not permitted to publish—the media whipped the Israeli public into a frenzy of anxiety and rage. The IDF did its part, with forty officers assigned to a social media desk, making sure the hashtag #BringBackOurBoys stayed viral. Those words appeared overnight in huge letters on the sides of public buses in Jerusalem—in English, not Hebrew, just an Israeli flag and the imperative "BRING BACK OUR BOYS" in blue and white block capitals. A Facebook page calling on citizens to "eliminate" a Palestinian every hour until the teens were found got more than seventeen thousand likes in its first three days online. IDF officials spoke openly and even giddily of collective punishment. "I think

---

*A jealous Cain had just slain his brother Abel, "And the LORD said unto Cain, Where is Abel thy brother? And he said, I know not: Am I my brother's keeper?"

Ramadan will be spoiled," one promised—the month of fasting was then still a fortnight away. The army was "cleansing the stables," he said. "If today it takes 40 minutes to get from Nablus to Jenin, next week it might take seven hours." The defense minister promised, "We will know how to exact a very heavy price from the leaders of Hamas, wherever and whenever we find it appropriate," which the local press, with no apparent misgivings, took to imply a return to the policy of open assassinations. Major General Nitzan Alon, the head of the army's Central Command, predicted that the operation, which he characterized not as a search but as "the campaign against Hamas," would be "complicated and prolonged." Hamas, he said, would "leave the fray . . . weakened both operationally and strategically."

The arrest raids continued—in Nablus and the villages and refugee camps around it, in Salfit, Jenin, Hebron, and throughout the south. More than three quarters of the sixty-five people arrested that Tuesday night had been released in the Gilad Shalit swap. Israel was taking them back. How, asked *The Jerusalem Post*, would the overloaded military court system deal with the mass influx of arrestees? It wouldn't: no extra prosecutors or judges would be assigned. They weren't charging anyone. They were just rounding people up. In Ramallah, there were clashes with the IDF on Irsal Street, blocks from the *muqata'a*. Abbas was in Saudi Arabia, and didn't hear a thing. From a comfortable distance he defended the PA's continuing security coordination with the Israeli military as "in our interest and for our protection," and went on to warn his people against the dangers of resistance. "We don't want to go back to chaos and destruction," the Palestinian president said. "I say it openly and frankly: we will not go back to an uprising that will destroy us." But then Abbas had no problem with the arrests. Reconciliation or no, Hamas's weakness was his strength. When the troops left their bases, all the veils that Oslo had draped over the occupation burned away. The real unity government was suddenly apparent, and it wasn't with Hamas. Abbas, the bloated regent, was reminded rudely of his station. He was there to keep things quiet, and to keep his vassals happy and fat. Whatever squabbles might divide them and whatever disagreements the PA and the Israelis might trot out before the world, when it came down to it, only one government ruled over the West Bank, whether in Area A or B or C, and it was doing as it wished.

THE BUBBLE OF SAFETY and comfort for which Ramallah was famous seemed finally to be bursting. At night at least. During the day the markets were full, the shops and cafés crowded, but everyone had stories. Most of the raids were in the camps and in middle- and working-class areas like al-Bireh and Umm al-Sharayit, but they were in al-Tireh too, where the wealthy lived. A friend had been at her mother's apartment there when she noticed tiny red lights dancing on the walls—the army had raided the building and soldiers outside were aiming the laser sights of their weapons through the windows. My Arabic teacher, whose home in al-Bireh was a twenty-minute walk from my apartment downtown, woke in the night to a dozen IDF jeeps parked outside a neighbor's house. Two of the family's sons, both Hamas militants, had been killed during the Second Intifada. No one was arrested, he said, but the soldiers trashed everything. The army visited Fakher Zayed in Beitunia too. The day the CNN video of Nadeem Nawara's shooter was released, soldiers had come and seized his computer and the recording equipment for his security cameras. After the kidnapping, they visited his neighbors and did the same, seizing DVR equipment from every shop with cameras outside. A few days later, Zayed told Human Rights Watch, four jeeps full of soldiers arrived at his door. They took him to Ofer, he said, and threatened him, telling him the video he had recorded had made the army look bad. One officer told him, Zayed said: "We will crush you, according to the law." They gave him twenty-four hours to take the now-useless cameras down.

Only the young men in the camps were fighting back. The streets at night were empty, but small groups of guys took shifts beside burning Dumpsters on the Jerusalem road outside the Qalandia camp and the al-'Amari camp and at the turnoff to al-Bireh. If they spotted soldiers or got a call that the army was coming, they would block the street, pelt the jeeps with stones, and alert their allies farther down the road. Sometimes they succeeded and prevented a raid, chasing the soldiers to their next target, somewhere else in town. One Wednesday night the tweets and calls and text messages began rolling in at a little after midnight. Troops were in Yatta and Bani Nai'm, outside of Hebron. They were in Jalazoun and in al-Ram, just past Qalandia. They were massing near the entrance to Ramallah. Dozens of soldiers had stormed the university in Birzeit. There were troops in the main square in Nablus. They had reached the edge of town already. They were in al-Tireh, and there was shooting in al-Bireh. In Birzeit they had arrested thirty students and raided the student union, hauling away a truckload of green Hamas flags. (The next day, *Haaretz* would describe this as "confiscating equipment.") The students somehow got away. There were clashes on the edges of the campus, and in Surda, to its south. It was late when I got home, after two. As I turned the key in the gate outside my building, I heard a blast. It was close, a few blocks away. I went upstairs and got in bed. Dogs were barking all across the city. I lay awake for another hour and listened to them howl.

I didn't sleep much that week, or any of the weeks that followed. I spent a lot of time in the hours before the dawn call to prayer listening to the dogs bark, wondering what urgent gossip they might be spreading, what they knew that hadn't made it onto Twitter yet. In the daytime they stayed silent and isolated from one another, locked in yards or chained on rooftops. An archipelago of dogs. Normally they were quiet at night, or maybe I was usually able to sleep through it all, but during those weeks they had a lot to say. A web of canine utterance stretched across the city, a different sort of map. They cried and yelped from yard to yard and roof to roof, calling out to one another, perhaps with taunts or confessions of their longings and their loneliness, or announcements of more concrete phenomena, of inexplicable noises and scents, a hostile presence in the city, an anxiety that would not let them rest.

THE NEXT MORNING, Netanyahu visited the West Bank. He went to the IDF base at Beit El, just outside Ramallah, to rouse the troops. His statement is worth quoting in full: "We're doing everything in our power to bring back our three kidnapped teenagers. They were kidnapped by Hamas. We had no doubt of that. It's absolutely certain. Hamas repeatedly has called for the kidnap and murder of Israeli citizens. It is an organization that is designated as a terror organization by many countries, and it is a terror organization that is committed to Israel's destruction. I expect President Abbas to dissolve the union with this murderous terrorist organization. I think that's important for our common future. Thank you."

He knew the teens were dead. He had known from the beginning. The recording wasn't leaked until later, but in the call made from Gilad Shaar's cell phone to the police emergency hotline shortly after the boys were last seen, one of the teens spoke. Shaar's parents confirmed it was their son's voice on the tape. "They've kidnapped me," he said. Then a voice in Arabic-accented Hebrew could be heard shouting, "Heads down!" Then a long volley of shots from an automatic weapon. Then a voice in Arabic, "Take the phone from him." Then silence. There were eight bullet holes in the burned-out Hyundai, and bloodstains. DNA samples taken from the car matched the teens' parents. The politicians knew all this. The higher echelons of the military and the police and the Shabak knew. Some journalists knew, but they honored the gag order and didn't say a word. Nonetheless, two days after the abduction, Defense Minister Ya'alon had told the press, "Our working assumption is that the missing boys are alive." No one challenged him. The massive propaganda effort—on TV and in the papers, on the Internet, on the sides of buses—had gone ahead. "Bring back our boys," they all said. The West Bank was on lockdown—Israeli troops had shut down the Container checkpoint and the two main checkpoints south of

Nablus, cleaving the West Bank into three discrete and isolated stumps. The "search" would go on.

THE OPERATION, as it was called, was still centered on Hebron, so I drove down with a friend. Merchants in the center of town told us that Israeli soldiers had been around, confiscating DVR equipment from every shop with security cameras. They had learned their lesson in Beitunia, it seemed. We walked to Tel Rumeida and climbed the hill to the center. Jawad was there. H2 had become the safest place in Hebron, he said, laughing. Everywhere else, soldiers were raiding houses one by one, almost every house in almost every neighborhood. As usual, the searches seemed aimed more at humiliation than anything like crime solving. The troops smashed furniture and poured the contents of people's pantries out on their kitchen floors. So many soldiers had flooded the city that they didn't fit in the bases, so they would push families out of their homes and bunk down for a night or two or three, leaving the places trashed when they finally left.

We took a taxi to the home of Akram Qawasmeh in the neighborhood of 'Ein Deir Bahaa. The first time the army came to the house, Qawasmeh told me, they used explosives to blow open the door. If the soldiers had knocked, he would have opened it, Qawasmeh said, but they hadn't. His eight-year-old son Mohammad was hit by shrapnel. He was in the hospital in Jerusalem, recovering from surgery "from his navel to his neck" to remove the shards of door. The soldiers locked the family in a neighbor's house, took their cell phones from them, and trashed the place. "They even took the meat from the refrigerator," Qawasmeh said, and trampled it. They arrested his nephew Zayd and had come back three times since, most recently at noon that day. Each time they brought a summons for another few family members, calling them in for Shabak interrogation. The soldiers hadn't said why they were taking Zayd, or where, and the family hadn't heard a word from him. They couldn't visit little Mohammad either—no one had permits to get into Jerusalem. The boy's mother was with him, Qawasmeh said, and had been there for six days. The authorities wouldn't let her leave the hospital.

AT A LITTLE after one o'clock on the morning of June 22, the IDF visited Ramallah. They went to al-Bireh first and raided a school run by a charity affiliated with Hamas. The neighborhood's young men came out to meet them. The soldiers hit Umm al-Sharayit next, but the guys they had been planning to arrest there heard they were coming and got away. The soldiers drove on to al-Manara, blocked the square with their jeeps, and rushed into the police station, posting snipers on the roof. They raided a building nearby that housed the offices of several media outfits, seizing files and computers from Al Jazeera and Russia Today. By then word had gotten around. Hundreds of young men converged in the blocks surrounding the police station. They spread out in small groups in the streets and on the rooftops, raining bottles and rocks on the soldiers below. I wasn't in Ramallah that night, but several of my friends were, and news of the battle spread quickly on social media—reports of injuries from both live and rubber-coated bullets, blurry cell phone photos of fires burning in the streets. At about three, the Israelis drove off. The crowd descended on the police station, attacking it with rocks and chunks of concrete, yelling, "Traitors!" and chanting, "The PA is a whore!" Palestinian police came out with Kalashnikovs and fired into the air above the crowd. Soon the Israelis returned—everyone I spoke to who was there assumed the PA had called them back. The soldiers began firing tear gas and both live and rubber-coated bullets from a few blocks away as the Palestinian police battled the crowd around the station. The streets were thick with smoke and gas, but for a few minutes before the jeeps sped off again, everything was perfectly clear. The Israelis were shooting from one direction and the PA from another, the two security forces acting in concert against the same opponent—the young men who had come out in defense of their city. Things didn't quiet down until just before dawn. Al-Manara and Clock Square and Rukab Street—the entire central commercial district of Ramallah—were left blanketed in stones, broken glass, and gas grenades, the fires guttering out in the streets. Hours later, the body of Mahmoud Ismail Atallah Tarifi was found on a rooftop. He had been shot in the head. As far as I know, it was never conclusively established if the bullet that killed him was fired by the IDF or the PA.*

By the time I got to town late that morning, the streets and the squares had been thoroughly swept. The rocks and the broken glass and the black-ened skeins of wire left by burning tires were gone. A couple of windows on Rukab Street had been boarded up, but otherwise no visible trace remained of the Battle of Ramallah. Everything, once again, was normal. The shops were open, and packed as always. Except that everyone knew what had happened. It was a brilliant move really. It's hard to imagine that the night's raids on media offices† had fulfilled any vital security function other than mild diplomatic insult, or that soldiers could not have found some other temporary post than the police station. This was the humilia-tion machine on overdrive, working in Abbas's front yard with an impres-sive degree of semiotic sophistication. By taking over the police station in the heart of Ramallah, the army had sent two messages at once. First, to the PA: You are ours and everyone knows it; you cannot even pretend to resist. And second, to the Palestinian people, the ones in the street that night and the ones who heard about it later: your leaders take their orders from us. Even their dogs are ours. You have nothing and no one and no options at all.

---

*Another Palestinian was killed in Nablus that day, a man named Ahmad Said Soud Khaled. He was on his way to the mosque for morning prayers and was shot repeatedly after ignoring a soldier's orders to stop.

†An IDF spokesperson told *Russia Today* that the target of the raid had been Al Aqsa TV, which is linked to Hamas, but the Al Aqsa offices were in fact in a different building entirely.

———

THE "SEARCH" CONTINUED. Irene and I went to the Balata refugee camp just outside Nablus, a labyrinth of bullet-pocked streets and alleys so narrow we had to walk down some of them sideways, nearly thirty thousand people squeezed into a square quarter kilometer of land. It was in Balata that the First Intifada arrived in the West Bank. During the Second Intifada too, the camp's name had been synonymous with fierce resistance. Its entrances had been barricaded, the streets mined with improvised explosives, doors and stairwells booby-trapped. When the IDF occupied Balata in 2002, soldiers avoided the alleys and moved from building to building by blasting straight through the walls. They had not, apparently, forgotten. We visited the home of the Abu Arab family. The metal doorframes had been freshly cemented in place. Four days earlier, at one-thirty in the morning, soldiers had blown both doors open. They rushed from room to room, overturning and smashing furniture until they came to the third floor, the construction of which had only recently been completed. Ra'ed Abu Arab had built an apartment atop the home in which he had been raised—the only place to build in Balata is up—and had just moved in with his new bride. When he opened the door for the soldiers, his cousin Khaled told me, they punched him in the face and dragged him down the stairs. "Tell the kids to cover their ears," one of the soldiers said. Something exploded. Only later did they learn that whatever device the soldiers had detonated had blown out all four walls of the corner room, leaving a crater in the tile floor, holes in the concrete ceiling and in the screens of the neighbors' windows, a hole in the new flat-screen TV mounted on the wall one room over. They arrested Ra'ed and his cousin Mohammad. The rest of the family—twenty people, most of them children—were confined for more than four hours in one small room on the first floor until the soldiers finished ransacking the house. No one ever told them why Ra'ed and Mohammad had been taken from them, or why their home had been destroyed.

Since that night, the Abu Arab family had been cleaning, stacking everything worth saving in the kitchen—a stereo, dishes, clothing stuffed in garbage bags. They had moved the ruined furniture and carpets down to the second floor and knocked out what little broken concrete still separated the room from the open air; where the exterior walls had once provided shelter and some illusory degree of security, there was now a precipitous drop to the alleys fifteen meters below. "It's not like the old days," Khaled said. The soldiers had parked their jeeps outside the camp and come in on foot. "No one threw a single stone," he said. "Not one shot, nothing."

THE HUNGER STRIKE ENDED. The kidnapping had pushed it from the headlines. Without publicity and the political pressure it generated, the prisoners would have quietly starved. The details of the deal they struck with the Israeli prison service were not made public, but at a press conference in Ramallah a spokesman for the prisoners warned, "This cannot be called a victory." The understatement was extreme. Israel had not only refused to meet any of the prisoners' demands, but the army had announced two days earlier that it planned to issue new administrative detention orders for half of the more than four hundred people it had arrested since the teens' abduction, doubling the number of Palestinians being held without trial. Resistance in the prisons had been effectively crushed. In the streets it wasn't doing much better. The popular resistance movement—all the activists in all the villages that had been holding weekly demonstrations for years, the ones who organized Bab al-Shams, al-Manatir, and 'Ein Hijleh—had done nothing. The same old ritual Friday protests dragged on. Barely. Beyond that, not a march or a sit-in or a vigil. Not a road or a checkpoint closed. Not even a press conference, just silence. The only organized resistance—the only resistance at all—was coming from the young men in the villages and the refugee camps, and the guys in the street who were blocking roads with burning tires and throwing stones at armored jeeps. They were the only ones fighting—and being injured and killed—on behalf of the values that everyone supposedly believed in.

I was downtown the afternoon the hunger strike was called off, running errands before meeting Bassem and Nariman, who were in Ramallah buying clothes for the kids. When I left the market on my way to the bank, al-Manara was half filled with PA police: a special unit in blue uniforms, white helmets, and body armor, plus the green-uniformed National Security Forces with their Kalashnikovs and bamboo clubs. A few days earlier I had seen the same cops stop a demonstration for the hunger strikers from marching to Beit El. Now dozens of them had formed a line in front of the Bank of Palestine. One of the young men from Qalandia who had been shot the week before had died after five days on life support in a Jerusalem hospital. His name was Mustafa Aslan. He was twenty-two, a taxi driver's son with a four-month-old child of his own. The police were there to prevent the guys from the camp from closing the shops. The PA was finally taking a stand over something, and it was commerce.

About half of the stores had already pulled their shutters. Some had closed up entirely. Others had left the shutters cracked and were discreetly doing business out of sight. The square was still packed, with *mukhabarat* as well as uniformed cops and the usual vendors—the money changers outside the Arab Bank with their fist-sized rolls of cash, the guys in pantaloons and fezzes selling coffee from giant hammered-metal carafes, others hawking boiled fava beans and plastic guns that shot soap bubbles in glistening, slippery streams. I watched two young women pause to snap photos of the riot squad with their cell phones and heard an officer order his men to get rid of them. Three cops walked over, and the girls hustled off. Eventually the guys arrived from Qalandia. There weren't many of them. Maybe thirty. I recognized a face or two from Nabi Saleh among them as they yelled at the merchants to close and the police pushed their way toward them through the crowd. The guys turned up the Nablus Road and cut back toward the market. The cops were running now and shouting. There was a brief confrontation, a few words exchanged, an officer with his arm heavy around the shoulders of a young kid from the camp. Hundreds were watching. The cop let him go. The shops stayed open.

Mustafa Aslan's body didn't make it back from the hospital until late that evening. Under normal circumstances, wherever those might be found, the funeral would have been held the following morning, but the PA didn't want to risk a daylight confrontation, so Aslan was buried in the dark, in the camp's cemetery, at nearly ten p.m.

OPERATION BROTHER'S KEEPER appeared to be winding down. Arrests fell to seventeen on Tuesday, and ten on Wednesday. The closures were being lifted, the extra checkpoints withdrawn. "A large part of the operation against Hamas has been exhausted," announced Ya'alon. "Most of the Hamas activists on the lists prepared by the IDF and Shin Bet security service for arrest have already been taken in," reported *Haaretz*. And the search for the boys? That too appeared to be ending. The Shabak had named two suspects, Marwan Qawasmeh and Amer Abu Aisha, both of Hebron.* In August, the army would bulldoze their family homes. In September soldiers would kill them both. No evidence would ever be presented against the two men.† But it was June still, and Lieutenant General Benny Gantz, the IDF's chief of staff, appeared to be preparing the public for bad news. The army, he said, was still operating on the assumption that the three teens were alive, "but with the passing of time, fears grow."

---

*The Qawasmehs and Abu Aishas are both large Hebronite families. Akram Qawasmeh and his brothers, whom I interviewed in 'Ein Deir Bahaa, were relatives of Marwan, but distant ones; Amer Abu Aisha was likewise only distantly related to Jawad Abu Aisha from YAS.
†A third suspect, Hussam Qawasmeh, later confessed to planning the abduction, and received three life sentences. His lawyer alleged that the confession was coerced under "heavy torture." This would be almost impossible to confirm, but in mid-June, the Israeli attorney general reportedly approved the application of "moderate physical pressure" in the Shabak's investigation of the kidnapping. This would include techniques such as shaking, which nearly killed Bassem, and stress positions such as the one that crippled Mufid Sharabati.

This too was a lie. No matter. It had worked out well for Netanyahu. If the collapse of the peace talks had left him feeling inadequate, he looked strong again. The hunger strike had died without a whimper. Abbas had been put firmly in his place. What little infrastructure Hamas had in the West Bank had been decimated, and Palestinians had been reminded of their powerlessness. Their faces had been shoved in it. A few of the more stubborn militant groups in Gaza had been firing rockets into Israel, but no one had been seriously injured, and the IDF was taking care of it, bombing the Strip every night.

11.

SATAN NEVER DREAMED

Ramallah, Jerusalem, Sderot, Nabi Saleh

Madness is like a hurricane, and its motion is circular.

—Etel Adnan

They found the bodies on the 30th of June. They were not even buried, just piled with rocks in a field near Halhul, north of Hebron in an area that thousands of soldiers had been searching for two and a half weeks. The gag order was lifted. The details of the emergency call came out. Outrage did not follow—at least not over the authorities' ongoing manipulation of the entire country via three murdered teenage boys. Once again, Netanyahu sniffed an opportunity. He released a statement aimed at stoking Israel's sadness into rage.* The teens, he said, "were abducted and murdered in cold blood by human animals." He quoted the poet Chaim Bialik: "Vengeance for the blood of a small child, Satan has not yet created."† The prime minister would not let Satan's lack of creativity stop him. "Hamas is responsible," he said—it was by now an incantation—"and Hamas will

---

*Elias Khoury again: "the only thing that can make one forget a massacre is an even bigger massacre."

†Netanyahu did not mention that the lines' source, Bialik's poem "On the Slaughter," was a lament over the futility of earthly revenge. Written after the pogroms of 1903, the poem concluded: "Blood will fill the dark abyss/and eat away in darkness and rot/all the dark foundations of the earth."

pay." Politician after politician joined him, calling out for blood, for "a war of annihilation," as one Knesset member put it.

The funeral for Gilad Shaar, Naftali Frankel, and Eyal Yifrach, held in the West Bank settlement of Talmon, would be staged as a massive national-ist spectacle. It was televised of course. *The New York Times* live-tweeted the event. The paper's Isabel Kershner observed that the funeral had "uplifted" Israelis "with a rare sense of commonality" and that the teens' deaths had "fulfilled a larger purpose of bringing together a fractious people." Indeed it had. I drove into Jerusalem that night. The streets around the old city, usu-ally mixed, were empty of Palestinians. Mobs had gathered downtown carry-ing signs emblazoned with the single word, "Revenge." Gangs of adolescents in skinny jeans and white yarmulkes marched through the streets, wearing Israeli flags as capes, chanting, "Death to Arabs," and looking for Palestin-ians to beat. In the West Bank, soldiers performed an analogous task. The raids resumed—there were arrests that night in Nablus, Salfit, Qalqilia, Ramallah, and Hebron, which was once again sealed off.

In the morning, more bad news. A Palestinian teen named Mohammad Abu Khdeir had been abducted in the East Jerusalem neighborhood of Shu'fat while waiting outside the mosque across the street from his home before the dawn prayer. He was sixteen, a small, thin boy with large and slightly mischievous eyes. Before the morning was over, the police had found his body in a forest outside Jerusalem. His corpse had been badly burned. There would be no state funeral for Abu Khdeir. By the time the Israeli authorities released his body to the family two days later, Shu'fat— normally a quiet, even affluent neighborhood—was in tatters, its streets littered with rocks and broken glass and tear gas canisters, here and there a melted traffic light or the burned and smashed remains of a ticket machine from the light rail station. Hundreds had been injured. Ramadan had begun and the sun was hot and more than a thousand people waited outside the mosque across from the Abu Khdeirs' home. When the prayer began all went silent save the buzz of police helicopters overhead. The boy's body, too disfigured to display, lay in a coffin, not a bier. It looked oddly light on the shoulders of his relatives. They barely made it a block toward the cemetery before the police started shooting. It was night when I left. Shots were still echoing through the burning streets.

It got worse. The autopsy report was leaked to the press. The medical examiners had found soot in Abu Khdeir's lungs, bronchi, and throat—he had been breathing when his kidnappers lit him on fire. They burned him alive.* The next day six suspects were arrested—Israeli youths from a Jerusalem suburb and from the settlement of Adam. Three were released. The clashes spread to almost every neighborhood in East Jerusalem that night. Inside Israel too, all over the Arab north—in Tireh, Taybeh, Sakhnin, Umm al-Fahm, Nazareth, and even Haifa—young Palestinians fought the police in the streets. And from Jerusalem to Tel Aviv to the north of Israel, Israeli civilians were assaulting Palestinians in buses, in shops, and on the street. Netanyahu had unleashed something that he could not control. The fear and rage that he and most of Israel's political class had been feeding and manipulating for years had slipped away from him. And so history is made—not by strategies or decisions carefully arrived at, but by chaos and improvisation. Something ugly was spilling everywhere.

It got much worse. Throughout the second half of June, while the IDF was flooding the West Bank with troops, rockets launched from Gaza had been landing inside Israel. The numbers were slightly higher than usual, but this was fairly normal. Since the end of the last brief war in November 2012, the smaller armed groups in Gaza, mainly Islamic Jihad and the

---

*From Netanyahu's eulogy for the three Israeli teens: "A deep and wide moral abyss separates us from our enemies. They sanctify death while we sanctify life. They sanctify cruelty while we sanctify compassion. This is the secret of our strength; it is the foundation of our unity." Thirteen months later, another Palestinian child would be burned alive, this time an eighteen-month-old infant, Ali Saad Dawabsha. Settlers threw a firebomb through the window of his home in the West Bank village of Duma as his family slept. The child's father, Saad Dawabsha, died soon after from burns sustained in the attack. The mother, Riham Dawabsha, died one month later.

Popular Resistance Committees,* had been firing occasional rockets into southern Israel. Hamas made efforts to repress them, but three or four got through most months, and sometimes as many as a dozen or more. IDF airstrikes usually followed, but little fuss. Fewer rockets were launched in 2013 than had been fired for a decade. And the rockets were primitive things, and rarely lethal. For all the many dozens that had been fired, according to the Shabak's online archive of "Terror Data," they had not managed to kill or even injure a single Israeli civilian since 2012. More rockets had been launched in March 2014 than fell in all of June, but in March the populace had not yet been spun into a vengeful frenzy, and the Israeli response—strikes that killed five Islamic Jihad fighters—had been relatively restrained. No one said anything then about rocket fire posing an existential threat, or pretended that Israel had no choice but to go to war.

On June 29, an IDF airstrike on Khan Younis, in the south of Gaza, killed one Hamas fighter and injured three others. Until then, Hamas had not been launching rockets, and Israel had not been targeting Hamas. That day, the group resumed firing into Israel for the first time since 2012. At the end of that week, Hamas announced that it would no longer attempt to prevent rocket attacks by the other armed factions. The PA and Hamas were still fighting over salaries, and Hamas was furious over Abbas's complicity in the Israeli campaign against its membership and infrastructure in the West Bank. "Hamas is not ruling the Gaza Strip," said Ahmad Yousef, a senior Hamas adviser—it was hard not to imagine him smirking—"so it's not responsible for protecting borders." Two days later the Israelis bombed a tunnel in the southern Gaza city of Rafah, killing seven Hamas fighters. A Hamas spokesman called the strike "a dangerous escalation for which the enemy will pay a toll." Before the day's end, eighty-five rockets had left Gaza, as many as had been fired in the previous three months. Two Israelis were "lightly wounded." By the end of the following night,

---

*Not to be confused with the unarmed popular resistance movement in the West Bank, the PRC was a coalition of armed groups composed mainly of former Fatah fighters.

Israel had dropped four hundred tons of explosives, killing more than sixty Palestinians, sixteen of them children.

And so It began. Israel was at war. The rhetoric shifted. The unity deal was forgotten, the kidnapped boys a memory. Later the threat would be the tunnels that Hamas had dug beneath the border fence, but for now Israel was fighting over rockets. "No country would accept such a threat," Netanyahu said, and kept saying it. The campaign had a name, or a brand rather, like a shaving gel or a ribbed condom: Operation Protective Edge, it was called. Even the official discourse had become frankly genocidal. "We will do more than mow the lawn in Gaza. We will scorch it," promised an IDF official in a briefing to reporters. This war, Knesset member Ayelet Shaked posted on Facebook, "is not a war against terror, and not a war against extremists, and not even a war against the Palestinian Authority. . . . Who is the enemy? The Palestinian people." Even "the mothers of the martyrs," the post went on, "should follow their sons." Their homes should be destroyed: "Otherwise, more little snakes will be raised there."*

A WORD ABOUT the rockets. They are highly effective weapons, but only for the creation of panic. I was in Jerusalem the first night the sirens sounded there. It was not a pleasant feeling. I went to Sderot, in the south, on the Gaza border, and a couple of times each hour I heard the sirens and the blasts. From the open doorways of Sderot's public bomb shelters— there was one at every bus stop—you could crane your exposed neck and search the sky for contrails: not only from the rockets fired from Gaza but from the missiles launched by Israel to knock them from the air. When the two collided, the white trails of the rockets terminated in delicate puffs of

---

*Shaked demurred that the words were not her own: she had simply shared an unpublished article by the settler leader and former Netanyahu adviser Uri Elitzur. Following elections held eight months later, Netanyahu would form a new coalition government and appoint Shaked as Israel's minister of justice.

smoke. A moment later you heard the impact: not a bang but a gentle, popping thud.

The rockets were unnerving, but they were not much more dangerous than very large stones. I'm not being glib. What little damage they were capable of inflicting was caused mainly by the momentum of their impact. Behind the police station in Sderot were metal shelves stacked with rockets the authorities had picked up in the streets and fields around the town. You wouldn't want them to land on you, or within a few yards of you, but they were more like something you might have learned to build in high school shop class than any sort of twenty-first-century artillery: thick metal pipes a meter or so long with fins welded on, an engine at the base, and room for a few pounds of explosive at the head. Most, even after detonating, were bent or torn but basically intact. In the thirteen years between 2001, when Hamas first employed the tactic, and the late summer of 2014—a period that includes most of the Second Intifada and three wars against Gaza—a total of thirty Israeli civilians were killed by rockets and mortars fired from the Strip, about as many as died in traffic accidents in any given month. Israel's vaunted "Iron Dome" missile defense system had little to do with this—the system was not deployed until 2011.

Two images should suffice to illustrate. First: I went to a kibbutz just across the border fence from Gaza. A rocket had landed there shortly before I arrived. It hit a small pottery studio in the center of the kibbutz. There was a hole in the roof, some scattered concrete, but no blast, and no sign of char or flames. The windows on the other side of the room remained intact. So did the ceramic pots on the shelves that lined the walls.

Second: On July 8, the official first day of the war, *Haaretz* held a "Conference on Peace" in Tel Aviv. The irony was not intentional—the event had been planned months in advance. The participants were mainly from Israel's liberal intelligentsia, but Naftali Bennett, the leader of the far-right Jewish Home Party, spoke, and so did the settler leader Dani Dayan. The newspaper later ran a photograph of a nearly empty auditorium. During the conference, the sirens had sounded. Rockets were headed for Tel Aviv and the audience had been instructed to evacuate. In the photo, one man remained, sitting calmly and checking his cell phone as the last stragglers rushed for the exits. It was Yuval Diskin, who had headed the Shabak for six years and, presumably, knew a few things that most people did not. Such as that there was no reason to leave his seat, incoming rockets or no.

RAMALLAH, AS ALWAYS, was a world away. There were daily clashes in the camps and on the city's periphery, at its few direct interfaces with the occupation: Qalandia and Beitunia, the area of al-Bireh just beneath the settlement of Psagot, and the road leading to the IDF base at Beit El. Crossing Qalandia in the middle of a clash had become a new routine, listening to the gunshots ahead while stuck in standstill traffic and crawling slowly toward them, keeping the windows open for as long as possible before they had to be jammed shut against the gas. Everyone was irritable, honking and racing through any brief opening between cars until finally we turned that last bend and were in the middle of it all, the soldiers taking aim a few meters off, the guys directing traffic with rocks in their hands, smoking and laughing before they returned to the fray.

The raids had resumed, and the explosions late at night, and the dogs barking coded messages from block to block. Arrests in the West Bank had reached one thousand since the kidnapping in June. It felt like years had passed. In the daytime, Ramallah seemed not only unruffled but ebullient. It was Ramadan, and the city's rhythms had adjusted. In the morning the streets were quiet, almost dead, slowly filling with traffic and shoppers as afternoon approached and the side streets clogged with carts piled high with cheap shoes and sneakers, underwear and bras; the streets outside the market with lychees, figs, mangos, peaches, grapes, and plums. The hawkers shouted, "Sweet red watermelons!" or sang of tomatoes at ten shekels for two kilos. The shops that usually sold kebab and falafel were blocked with long tables piled with plastic bins of pickled cucumber and cauliflower, baby eggplants stuffed with garlic, green and black olives, stuffed or spicy, oil cured or brined. All the bakeries were making *awamat*, little fried balls of dough soaked in sugary syrup, and pancakes for *qatayef.* Nearly everyone walked with both hands weighed down by shopping bags until about half an hour before the sunset, when the fast could be broken and the streets emptied out. At about nine o'clock the sidewalks began to slowly fill again, and the shops to reopen. The World Cup was on, and the coffee shops were packed with fans.

In Gaza, the death toll climbed to one hundred, then two hundred. Every morning the figure would jump a few dozen and every few days I would hear a new story from friends in Israel about Israelis attacking Palestinians in the streets and in shops. Almost none made the news. The clashes at Qalandia kept growing. The guys piled tires beneath the sniper tower and lit them aflame with Molotovs. It burned so hot that the concrete cracked. On the wall beside it, the mural of Arafat was almost invisible beneath the ash, and Marwan Barghouti's face was disappearing into blackness. There were clashes still in Jerusalem, and in the north of Israel, and even in the Bedouin communities and townships of the south. Leftists demonstrating against the war in Tel Aviv were beaten by right-wing gangs when the rocket sirens rang and the police ran for the shelters. There were a few protests in Ramallah, but they were small, and the PA police blocked them each time they tried to march to Beit El. "Something really ugly is going to happen," Irene said to me one evening, meaning that the ugliness that had occurred over the previous month was only the beginning. She was right. The war had its own momentum, with new horrors every day: whole families wiped out, children and more children, mosques and hospitals targeted, refugees running from the ruins of their houses to UN shelters, which the Israelis bombed in turn. Hamas offered Israel a ten-year truce in exchange for an end to the siege on Gaza, a seaport and airport under UN supervision, and a number of other quite reasonable demands. But Netanyahu was digging in, and not just in Gaza: "I think the Israeli people understand now," he said, "that there cannot be a situation, under any agreement, in which we relinquish security control of the territory west of the River Jordan." In other words, the Palestinians would get no state. Ever. The occupation would not end.

I was at home in Ramallah on the 16th of July when I read the news. Virtually every journalist in Gaza was tweeting at the same time. Israel had bombed the beach beside the port in Gaza City. Five days earlier they had hit the jetty, torching much of Gaza's small and bedraggled fleet of fishing boats. This time they shelled a fisherman's shack. Four young boys started running, screaming, up the beach. Most of the foreign journalists in Gaza were staying in the hotels and apartments right there on the shore, and most of them were watching from their windows and the terraces of their hotels, yelling at the kids to run, when a second shell blew the boys to pieces in front of them. Their names were Ismail, Ahed, Zakaria, and Moham-mad Bakr. They were all between seven and eleven years old. Two other boys from the same family, Hamad and Mo'atassim Bakr, and one adult, Mohammad Abu Watfah, were badly injured. No one else had been on the beach. "The target of this strike was Hamas terrorist operatives," said an IDF spokesperson. A photographer friend e-mailed images he had shot on the beach that afternoon. He wanted help getting them published. No edi-tor would touch them. The most disturbing of his photos was not one of the gory ones. It was simply confusing: rubble, rebar, concrete, and at the top of the frame, the sea. Beneath it was something that looked like a doll, or like parts of a doll, but which, on closer inspection, was a child's arm and torso partly buried in the sand.

I realized that evening, waiting to cross through Qalandia, that I had been wrong. I sat there idling in traffic for I don't know how long, listen-ing to the concussions of gunshots and stun grenades less than a mile away in al-Ram, breathing in the dust and the car exhaust among the squeegee kids with greasy rags, their eyes dead from inhalants or painkillers, and it occurred to me that perhaps the occupation was not the clever and highly sophisticated machine I had thought it was, that it was not a machine at all. No mechanistic explanation could account for what was happening. It wasn't calm calculation that had brought us to this point. Careful and pragmatic decisions had surely been made all along the way at multiple levels of Israel's political and security apparatus. But whatever force was pushing those bureaucratic processes forward was not rational at all. It was merely murderous, rooted in a fear and a rage that flowed beneath the ground in hidden channels, secret and unmentionable conduits that had been there all along and were only now erupting.

THE GROUND WAR BEGAN. Israel was no longer worried about rockets. Hamas's "terror tunnels" were the new threat, and it would take a full-scale invasion to destroy them. Two nights in, troops and tanks entered Shuja'iyya, a densely populated Gaza City neighborhood of about 100,000 people. Hamas fought back, hard. The IDF lost thirteen soldiers and fired seven thousand shells into the neighborhood, leveling wide swaths of it. I heard from friends in Gaza that the hospitals were full, corpses stacked on the floors of the morgue.* The next day was another one in which time seemed to bend and expand, to find hidden pockets within itself and hide inside them. Ramallah's streets and markets were as crowded as always, but people's brows seemed heavy, and there was less laughter, banter, joy. Everyone knew there had been a massacre. Photos and videos from Shuja'iyya were all over the Internet—people running in terror through the streets to flee the shelling, hurrying past the cadavers of children lying dusty in the gutters. The shops closed that afternoon. Abbas had declared three official days of mourning. (It barely lasted one—the next day everything would open again.) The PA allowed a tiny Hamas march to leave from Clock Square, and a larger group of perhaps two hundred Islamists demonstrated in al-Manara. Thousands were protesting Israel's massacres in New York, London, Paris, Athens, Seoul, Johannesburg—all over the

---

*One friend, the Italian journalist Michele Monni, came back to Ramallah a few days later. He had visited Shuja'iyya the morning after the first assault. It had been a beautiful neighborhood, he said, its streets lined with trees. He recalled one tree, still standing, that was missing all its leaves. They lay green on the ground beneath it, all shaken off at once.

world—but in the West Bank, none of the demonstrations against the war had attracted more than a few hundred people.

At a little before eleven that night, I heard honking in the streets. It sounded like every driver in Ramallah was hitting their horn at once. Groups of young men were driving around, leaning out windows and sunroofs, shouting. Hamas's military wing, the al-Qassam Brigades, announced that they had captured an Israeli soldier. They tweeted photos of his ID. Fireworks began to explode above the city. Finally, Gazans had something to bargain with, something other than their own lives. People were pouring through the streets toward al-Manara. They were chanting, "Qassam!" In the square, someone read the al-Qassam Brigades' announcement over a PA system to thunderous applause and someone else started lighting fireworks from the fountain, each rocket exploding in a different color until whoever it was lost control and the fireworks started shooting out into the crowd, smoke billowing from the stone lions around the fountain, everyone running in the frantic, mindless way that crowds do. It all calmed down after a minute or two and people were laughing with relief, but despite the excitement, the fireworks, the honking, the shouting, and the news of the captured soldier, no one seemed exactly happy. Most stood in silence, watching one another as if they were waiting for something, for someone to do something. Because something had to happen. The tension had broken, the suffocating sadness of the day had lifted for a moment, but who could say it wouldn't lead to fresh catastrophe?

A friend got a message saying that a larger group that had left the square to head for Beit El had been stopped by the PA, that the police were beating them and shooting gas. A bunch of us piled into a car and headed after them. On one poorly lit back street, we came upon a strange sight— the silhouettes of twenty or thirty men marching toward us in a line. They were wearing body armor and carrying clubs, the yellow lamplight glinting off their riot shields. It was the police. They were going home, back to the *muqata'a*. They had tried to halt the marchers—brutally, I learned later, beating them and firing gas canisters directly at them—but they had suddenly stopped. Perhaps they were overwhelmed, and said to hell with it. More likely they were ordered to stand down. Someone had decided that the PA could no longer afford to do Israel's bidding quite so openly.

We turned onto the main road leading to Beit El. It looked like Shu'fat had a few weeks earlier in the days that followed the abduction of Mohammad Abu Khdeir—the pavement was littered with rocks and blocked with burning Dumpsters. An unending stream of young men flowed toward the IDF base, hundreds of them in groups of three or four spread out across the long, wide road. They weren't all the usual kids from the camps. Some were well dressed, with soft cheeks and frightened eyes, middle-class boys unused to clashes. Some had covered their faces already. Some carried sticks and some were kicking tires in front of them. Most of them looked happy, or if not happy, at least excited and relieved, like people gulping hungrily at poisoned air. We parked the car and three guys hurried past us. One was lugging a heavy canister of petrol. The other two carried trays stacked with dozens of glass bottles, a scrap of white cloth protruding from the neck of each bottle. At the traffic circle nearest to Beit El, the guys had blocked the roads with enormous bonfires of tires. I walked up toward the base through the shifting orangey light, passing groups of youth taking shelter behind walls. "Where are the soldiers?" I would ask them. "Up there," they would say, "on the other side," but no one seemed to know exactly. We'd hear a shot and everyone would run for cover. Or more often we would hear nothing—the soldiers were using silencers. Bullets would bounce off the pavement and everyone would scatter as the ambulances screamed past. Dozens of wounded filled the ER that night. The honking didn't stop until after three.

THE CELEBRATION, if that's what it was, was short-lived. The captured soldier, whose name was Oron Shaul, was dead—or near-dead anyway—when the al-Qassam fighters pulled him from the wreckage of an armored personnel carrier in which six other Israeli soldiers had been killed. Hamas would not be able to exchange him for prisoners, or even for a pause in the assault. Five days later, the IDF's chief rabbi informed Shaul's parents that they could begin sitting shiva for their son. I was on my way back to the U.S. by then. I had delayed my trip twice already and didn't know how long the war would last, if it would be over in a week or never end. I should have stayed. The day I left Ramallah, a march had been called on Qalandia, this time with the open blessing of the PA. The imams were announcing it over loudspeakers from the mosques. That hadn't happened since the last intifada. Perhaps this was the beginning of something new.

I was sitting in the airport in Amman when it started. Thousands marched on the checkpoint. Counts varied, but none I saw put it lower than ten thousand. It wasn't just the usual young men, but women, children, families. The guys hurled rocks and Molotovs. The soldiers fired rubber-coated bullets at first, then live ones through silencers again. At some point, a small group began firing back with Kalashnikovs. The Al-Aqsa Brigades later took credit. The hospital was overwhelmed with the wounded. Patients were treated on the floor because there weren't enough beds. A woman I knew was shot in the foot. Two men, Mohammad al-Araj and Majd Sufyan, were killed. Over the next twenty-four hours, six more would die in clashes near Hebron, Nablus, Bethlehem, and Jenin.

By the time I had landed in the United States, taken a taxi to my sister's home, slept and showered and hugged my nieces, the death toll in Gaza had passed 1,000. In the West Bank, things would soon cool down. The march on Qalandia had not been the beginning of something, but the end, a *muqata'a*-approved release valve, nothing more. Security coordination would not cease. The war would go on for another month. Before it was over, 2,220 Palestinians would die, 551 of them children, two thirds of them civilians. More than 11,000 others would be injured, and half a million—more than a quarter of the population—would flee their homes. Much of Gaza's water and sewage infrastructure would be decimated. The one functioning electrical plant would be destroyed. Half of the Strip's hospitals would be damaged in the bombing, and six forced to close; 148

schools would be partially or entirely leveled, as would 278 mosques, including one that had been standing for 1,365 years. In the West Bank, another 25 people were killed from the beginning of the June incursions until the end of the war in late August. Israel would kill more Palestinians in the summer of 2014 than in any conflict since 1967. The war remained overwhelmingly popular with the Israeli public. According to one poll published at the end of July, 95 percent of Jewish Israelis considered the assault justified, and less than 4 percent thought excessive firepower had been used. In the end, 6 civilians would be killed by Palestinian rocket fire, and 66 Israeli soldiers would die. Like I said, something had come unplugged. This was not a rational machine.

A WEEK BEFORE I LEFT, I went to Nabi Saleh. It was a Friday. The road, when I arrived, was already littered with stones. The guys had been up early to eat *suhur*, the last predawn meal before the Ramadan fast. They went down to the tower at about 6:30 a.m., and the clashes had lasted until eight. Most of them were still asleep. The demo was tiny. It was over after barely an hour. I went back to Bilal's to rest. We watched the news for a while: the same footage again and again of morgue workers in Gaza struggling to lift a corpse into the only empty slot left in the freezer and opening another freezer door so weeping relatives could view the body of their child. Bilal's daughter Rand sat on the floor staring up at the TV. Her face was blank. Bilal changed the channel. The Hamas-affiliated network was airing a propaganda video showing al-Qassam soldiers fighting valiantly and Israeli soldiers looking exhausted and afraid. Four coffins draped in Israeli flags appeared on the screen and little Rand clapped her hands. "They have dead too!" she enthused.

Bilal fell asleep and Rand and her little brother Samer switched the channel. *Tom and Jerry* was on. I called some friends in Gaza whom I hadn't been able to reach all day. By default, I was fasting too, and hadn't slept much anyway. I drifted in and out, checking Twitter and reading the

latest bad news on my phone, dozing off and opening my eyes to see an
octopuslike alien Tom stalk a beaming astronaut Jerry. About an hour
before dusk, Bilal woke up. Or maybe Samer woke him. We hiked up the
hill on the other side of the road, climbing the old stone fences into the
orchards. The sun was low and the shadows of the trees and of the children as they jogged ahead of us were long. Bilal had brought a plastic bag
and he and I began to fill it with ripe figs as the kids scurried through the
branches, sticky handed, eating more than they picked. Samer was eight
but tiny, a squirming, giggly boy. Rand was maybe three years older, with
long and straight brown hair and a sideways smile. She and Samer were
laughing it up in the high branches of a low tree. "He's crazy," she said of
her brother, using the English adjective and the Arabic pronoun.

"The whole world is crazy," I responded.

"You're crazy!" she said, delighted with the direction the conversation
had taken.

"Of course," I agreed.

The orchard went on and on. Bilal talked about his childhood, when
every household had fig trees and you didn't have to walk this far to pick
them. We were somewhere behind Bassem's house now, far enough from
the road that there were no longer any tear gas canisters among the rocks at
our feet. I had only ever been on these hills and in these groves to seek shelter from the soldiers or the gas, I realized, never because they were beautiful,
or because the trees were heavy with fruit. The sky to the west had turned
a violent pink. I had seen Bilal in Jerusalem a few days earlier. Bassem had
asked me to accompany some kids from the village to the French consulate
to apply for visas for a trip to France, and Bilal ended up meeting us there.
Walking around the old city had made him very sad, he said. When he
had been there last, many years before, it had always been crowded but now
the streets and alleys were empty, the shopkeepers sleeping in front of the
few open stalls. The world seemed to be getting worse by the day, I observed.

"I think it always has been," said Bilal. "It is always difficult just to keep
what you have."

The kids had begun swinging at each other with fallen branches, play-ing at sword-fighting and gripping the wood with black, figgy hands, squealing with laughter as they dodged through the trees. "They will hit each other," Bilal said, but made no move to stop them. They didn't. They kept at it, banging stick against stick, howling and giggling until they were too tired to swing anymore. I don't remember if Rand tackled Samer or Samer tackled Rand but soon they were both lying on the rocky ground, exhausted, their arms around each other, panting and grinning, forgetting to fight.

EPILOGUE

Ramallah, Nabi Saleh, Wadi Fukin, Los Angeles

What else is there for any of us but courage?

—Doris Lessing

I went back in September 2014. Qalandia looked worse than ever, the wall and the sniper tower still blackened and a new array of blast walls up. I could imagine no landscape more human than that. Ramallah was the same as ever. I found it beautiful, the smells of it, its defiant, concrete ugliness, and all the shaky pleasures people were able to wrest from that stiff little island of relative calm. Construction had resumed on the Goodluck Houses, the long-abandoned building that the sunroom of my apartment looked out on, the concrete skeleton of which I had stared out at on so many nights, smoking before bed, listening to the dogs howl as the fog rolled in. The PA had erected billboards depicting the corpses of children killed in Gaza. "We Are All Gaza," they said. The shops in Clock Square sold T-shirts bearing the same message. It wasn't true. Zamn, the slick coffee shop in al-Tireh, had changed its Wi-Fi password to "freegaza." This counted as solidarity.

I visited Bassem and Nariman in Nabi Saleh. Waed was sleeping on the couch, Abu Yazan watching an Egyptian soap opera on TV. Salam came in later, strutting like a proud, miniature man. Nariman made him do his homework and sat beside him, her eyes mournful and lost above the coffee table. She had been hospitalized two days earlier after inhaling too much tear gas. She said she was fine, but it was hard to believe her. We talked about the Gaza war. It changed everything, Bassem said. "How can I talk about peaceful resistance now?" he asked. "They will laugh at me."

Two months later, Nariman and two others were shot with live bullets at a Friday demonstration in the village. She was hit in the left thigh. The bullet broke her bone. The march that week had been dedicated to the memory of her brother Rushdie, who had died almost precisely two years earlier.

THREE WEEKS AFTER Nariman was shot, on December 9, Brigadier General Tamir Yadai, the commander of all IDF troops in the West Bank, assured a meeting of settlers in Halamish that his soldiers had taken "a slightly tougher approach with people around here." Where they had previously fired tear gas and rubber-coated bullets, the general went on, they now fired live ammunition. "If I remember the figures correctly," he boasted, "we're at around twenty-five people hit here in the last three weeks. That's a relatively high figure on any scale." Nearly a year later, Nariman would still be unable to walk without a cane.

BILAL AND MANAL seemed well. "Nothing is new," Bilal said, and laughed. Manal had found a job in Ramallah and seemed happy for the opportunity to spend time outside the village. She was almost done with the master's program in which she had been enrolled, and was thinking of going on for a PhD. Five months later she too would be shot by an Israeli sniper, also on a Friday, also in the leg, also with live fire.

On my way to their house I ran into Bahaa's mother, who invited me in for a coffee. Maybe I caught him on a bad day, but Bahaa was doing poorly. He had been napping, and his hair, ungelled, was soft and blond and long over his small, thin face, which made him look more like a little boy than ever. He was fed up again with the situation in the village. The resistance had been going down one road, he said, with everyone together, and "they" took it down a different path. We both knew whom he meant. He wanted nothing more to do with it, he said. He was out of work too, and his engagement had broken off. I said I was sorry. Bahaa shook his head. He was tired of this place, he said. It was too closed off—not just Nabi Saleh, but Ramallah too, and all of Palestine. "The only words here are *forbidden*, *shameful*, *sinful*," he said. "That's all anyone knows how to say." He wanted to leave the country, to go somewhere where there was work, somewhere more open—maybe Canada, or Turkey. He wanted to live by the beach, he said, and to live a different kind of life.

WINTER IN THE South Hebron Hills is as cold as the summer there is hot, and the weather had just started to turn on October 27, 2014, when IDF bulldozers arrived in Umm al-Kheir. They destroyed six buildings which together had provided shelter for twenty-eight people. Among them were the homes of Bilal, Khaire, and Tariq's mother. They also demolished the oven. They did it all in just two hours. I was back in the U.S. by then, in Los Angeles. "It's like a dream," Eid told me on the phone. "It came quickly, and was gone."

In April, soldiers and Civil Administration officials returned to Umm al-Kheir to issue demolition orders for the tents and temporary structures in which the villagers whose homes had been destroyed spent the winter. Like the prime minister said, "Security comes before all else. Security is the foundation for everything."

IN HEBRON, everything was normal. Little Ahmad was arrested in November and accused of throwing stones. Mufid, who had finally gone to Jordan for an operation on his back, had to be hospitalized again at the end of March. YAS had organized a tree-planting ceremony beside the Qurtuba school and soldiers shoved Mufid until he lost consciousness and had to be taken away in an ambulance. A young German woman who had been filming the incident was arrested after Anat Cohen claimed she had attacked her.

The wheel continued to turn. What had felt like the end turned out to be no more than an episode, a station on the way to something else. Early in the morning of July 31, 2015, an eighteen-month-old infant named Ali Saad Dawabsha burned to death after a firebomb was thrown through the window of his parents' home in the village of Duma, southeast of Nablus. The words "Revenge"* and "Long Live the Messiah" were left painted in Hebrew on the walls. Within weeks, both of the child's parents died from burns sustained in the attack. But attention had already shifted to Jerusalem, where Israeli restrictions on prayer at the al-Aqsa were sparking clashes in the old city. By late September, there were clashes almost daily, not only around the holy site but in nearly every neighborhood of East Jerusalem again.

The clashes spread to the West Bank, to Hebron, Bethlehem, and the outskirts of Ramallah. On September 22, eighteen-year-old Hadeel al-Hashlamoun was killed by Israeli soldiers while waiting to cross through Checkpoint 56 onto Shuhada Street in Hebron. They shot her in the leg, which, according to one witness interviewed by Amnesty International, caused her to drop a knife she had concealed beneath her clothes. After that they shot her nine more times. Amnesty condemned the shooting as an "extrajudicial execution," a phrase that would grow in resonance in the months that followed. The first of October brought the deaths of two settlers, Eitam and Na'ama Henkin, shot in their car while driving home to the settlement of Neria. Their four children, in the backseat, survived.

That October, Israeli security forces and civilians would kill more than

---

*Amiram Ben-Uliel, the twenty-one-year-old settler later indicted for the Dawabsha murders, would tell investigators that he was acting to avenge the death of Malachi Moshe Rosenfeld, who was shot in June 2015 near the central West Bank settlement of Shilo.

two Palestinians a day, a rate not seen outside of Gaza since the Second Intifada. Many died at demonstrations, but more than half of the sixty-nine Palestinians who lost their lives that first month were shot while attacking Israeli soldiers or civilians, usually with knives. Ten Israelis died in such attacks and another eighty were injured. Or allegedly attacking: in several cases, video evidence and witness testimony revealed that Palestinians killed by security forces were unarmed at the time of their deaths. The panic was widespread: near Haifa, an Israeli man stabbed a dark-complected Jewish supermarket worker, mistaking him for a Palestinian; in Jerusalem, police killed a Russian Jew after he became belligerent when asked for ID and shouted "I am ISIS"; in Beersheba, an Eritrean immigrant was shot by a bus station security guard and then beaten to death by a mob.

Something new was happening. Fully half of the alleged attackers killed in October were under twenty years old. All but one were under thirty. Some of the attacks might have been imagined or fabricated, but many were not. Knowing that it would almost certainly mean their deaths, young Palestinians were acting alone or in pairs, striking out at Israeli soldiers, police, and civilians with the limited means available to them: kitchen knives, scissors, screwdrivers. Sometimes they tried to hit them with cars. The attacks were hardly strategic, but they were not irrational. There existed no movement for them to join, armed or unarmed, no viable collective response to a situation that they were no longer able to endure. Twenty-four-year-old Rasha Mohammad Oweisi, who was killed at a checkpoint near Qalqilya after soldiers spotted a knife in her hand, left a note in her bag apologizing to her family and insisting: "I'm doing this with a clear head. I can't bear what I see and I can't suffer anymore."

This was the uprising of the Oslo generation, born into the humiliation machine, determined to eject themselves from it on terms of their own choosing. Most of them had been children during the Second Intifada and grew up in its aftermath. They had no memory of the previous revolt and no experience of a unified resistance, or of any resistance at all that had not been immediately sold out or repressed by their leaders.* Netanyahu cried "incitement," but even Israeli intelligence services admitted that the attacks were spontaneous and uncoordinated, and that the traditional parties, factions, and armed groups were not involved. Shortly before boarding a Jerusalem bus and taking part in an attack that left two Israelis dead, Bahaa Allyan, twenty-two, posted on Facebook, "I ask that the political parties do not claim responsibility for my attack. My death was for my nation and not for you."

EARLY IN 2016, I returned to the West Bank. It had just started snowing in Ramallah when I left for Nabi Saleh, big heavy flakes that melted the moment they hit the street, but the skies above the village were clear. Bassem met me with a hug at the door. The yard had once again been transformed, terraced and divided with neat stone paths. Bassem walked me around the perimeter to show off the work. It wasn't done yet. The earth still needed leveling and he planned to plant more trees—apple, he said, and apricot and lemon. Nariman was walking without crutches—they leaned against the wall in the corner of the living room—but she did not seem well. She was pale and had been to the hospital that morning for stomach pains. Salam had grown enormously. So had Abu Yazan, who had endured his own brief burst of fame the previous August, when a masked Israeli soldier attempted to arrest him and was caught on camera with his arm clenched around Abu Yazan's neck, the barrel of his gun beside Abu Yazan's red and screaming face. Within three days, footage of the incident had been viewed 2.4 million times. Ahed, in a pink Tweety Bird T-shirt, had bitten the soldier's hand while Nariman and Nawal, Janna's mother, wrestled Abu Yazan free. Now Ahed, with a giant mop of curly hair that she shifted from shoulder to shoulder like a disobedient pet,

*In early January, *Haaretz* would report that security coordination between Israel and the PA was "exceptionally good."

sat beside her brothers, as lost in the video game on her smart phone as they were lost in theirs.

The phone rang a few minutes after I sat down. It was Waed. He was at Ofer but was about to be transferred to another prison in the Negev and didn't know when he would have a chance to call again. He had been arrested on October 19. Twenty-two of the guys—including Odai and Loai, Naji and Boshra's son Anan, and the entirety of Nabi Saleh's soccer team—had been arrested that fall. Seventeen were still in prison. Interrogators had pressured one boy into testifying against the others, whom they then charged with throwing stones or Molotov cocktails, or with some combination of the two. Waed had been sentenced to eight months, Anan to seven. Naji and Boshra and their daughters dropped by and we all ate together in the living room, staying close to the woodstove for warmth. I asked Naji how Anan was holding up. "He's okay," he said. "He's safer there." Bassem had said the same thing to me a few weeks earlier, when I had phoned to ask after Waed.*

I MET JAWAD in Bab al-Zawiya, just outside Checkpoint 56. It had been transformed since I had been there last from a single grubby shipping container into a baby Qalandia with high turnstiles, a caged wire passageway, a guard tower and bulletproof windows for the soldiers. I didn't bother to try to cross. On October 30, soldiers had informed residents that the area of H2 including Tel Rumeida and the short section of Shuhada Street still open to Palestinians would be declared a closed military zone. Residents were required to register with the army, then issued numbers and instructed to call them out each time they wished to pass through a checkpoint. Anyone without a number could not cross. Jawad showed me his, a handwritten 84 stuck onto the green plastic cover of his ID.

---

*At that point 151 Palestinians had been killed since the beginning of October, nearly one third of them at demonstrations. Twenty-five Israelis were killed in the same period.

I followed Jawad up to the second floor of a building perhaps a hundred meters from the checkpoint. He opened a door, switched on a small space heater, and sat beside it, hunching to warm his hands. On November 7, soldiers had raided the Youth Against Settlements center in Tel Rumeida. They locked Issa and an Italian activist in one small room overnight and trashed the office upstairs, confiscating the group's computer and camera equipment. Two weeks later they came back and arrested young Ahmad Azza,* and soon after returned with a closed military zone order for the center itself. Only Issa, who held the lease, would be allowed to enter the building. For now, YAS had rented this flat and erected a protest tent on the street outside, not far from the spot where Hadeel al-Hashlamoun had died.

Since her death, Hebron had been at the center of the new intifada, if that's what this was. More Palestinians had been killed in and around Hebron than anywhere else in Palestine. Even just in the small triangle of land marked out by Bab al-Zawiya, Tel Rumeida, and the Ibrahimi Mosque, Jawad couldn't keep track of them all. After al-Hashlamoun came Fadil al-Qawasmeh, he remembered. Qawasmeh was eighteen when he was shot by a settler just down the street from Beit Hadassah. Mufid's daughter saw the killing from her roof and Zidan had recorded video that he said depicted a soldier dropping a knife beside al-Qawasmeh's corpse. (It was too blurry to be sure.) That same day, Jawad said, a teenage boy from the Natsha family had tried to stab a soldier right here at Checkpoint 56. "They shot him," Jawad said.† "Later," he went on, at a checkpoint up the hill in Tel Rumeida, "they shot someone from the Sa'id family, and another from the 'Ebeido family."‡ Then there were the two in the al-

---

*Later the police produced a knife and claimed it had been Ahmad's. Issa and the others contacted everyone they could who might be able to pressure the authorities: diplomats, Israeli and foreign activists and NGO workers. In the end the court agreed to test the knife for DNA. Ahmad was cleared and released.
†His name was Tariq Ziad al-Natsha. He was sixteen.
‡Houmam Adnan Sa'id was twenty-three, as was Islam Rafiq 'Ebeido. They died on October 27 and 28. Witnesses of both shootings claimed the young men were unarmed.

Fanoun family. That was in December. They were cousins, Mustafa and Taher, age eighteen and twenty-two. "They shot them both," Jawad said. He couldn't remember all the rest. Among others, he left out Farouq 'Abd al-Qadr Sedr, nineteen, who was shot at the base of the staircase next to the Sharabati house on October 29, and Mahdi Mohammad Ramadan al-Muhtasib, twenty-three, whose death was caught on video that same day: he lay wounded and writhing on the ground when a soldier approached, circled, and fired into his body from a few feet away.

WHEN I ARRIVED in Umm al-Kheir, Mo'atassim came out to greet me. We found Bilal working near the foundation of what had been his house. The rubble had been cleared away and he had moved with his wife and children into a new white sheet-metal structure about twice the size of the storage sheds that you find in American backyards. There were a few others scattered throughout the village to replace the homes that had been bulldozed. The new homes were cold in the winter and hot in the summer, Mo'atassim told me, and the army had already issued demolition orders for all of them. Khaire, who had grown a long beard, walked over and he and Bilal teased me for still not being married and the three of them excused themselves and kneeled to pray on the concrete pad of the house, facing the mountains that rose in the desert to the southeast.

Later Eid arrived. The others seemed tense and depressed, but Eid was more cheerful than he had been when I had seen him last. He had been to the U.S., to New York and to Washington to meet with politicians, and he was eager to talk about everything he had seen. A gallery in Tel Aviv had put on a show of his work. Someone had bought one of his bulldozers, and someone had expressed interest in having him show work in Germany, and maybe in California too. We walked over to the edge of the village to see what was left of the oven. It had been bulldozed and rebuilt three times in the previous year. They were baking bread on the far side of the village now, hoping to avoid the attention of the army. Suleiman returned with his flock and hurried off to milk the sheep. It was at this time of year, Eid said, that the sheep and goats produced the most and the sweetest tasting milk because the hills and valleys were green with the winter's rains. As we walked, he said something about the importance of not losing hope. I asked him how to do that. "We only have this one life," Eid said. "And it is holy." He said it more than once, not preaching so much as marveling, as if he had discovered something and was hesitant to share it, afraid that he would be misunderstood. "It is holy," he said again. "We must not waste it."

A LITTLE MORE THAN one year earlier, late in September 2014, shortly before I had packed up my apartment in Ramallah and moved back to the United States, I had taken a shared taxi through Wadi Naar and the Container checkpoint to Bethlehem, where I hailed another taxi to the al-'Aida refugee camp and caught a ride with some activists there headed for a village called Wadi Fukin. It was a clear, windy Friday and the village was a pretty one, flush against the Green Line, with a gold-domed mosque and lush fields of winter wheat and cabbages. Atop the steep hill directly to the southeast of the village, like a castle on a cliff, was the Orthodox settlement of Beitar Illit, a crenellated wall of white stone apartment buildings seven stories high. More than 45,000 Israelis lived there already and it was growing fast, as settlements do. On the last day of that August, soldiers had entered Wadi Fukin and posted bright yellow signs in the hills and the fields. "No TRESPASSING," they said in Hebrew, "STATE LAND." The war in Gaza had just ended, and Netanyahu had marked the occasion by announcing the largest expropriation of Palestinian land in decades—nearly one thousand acres stretching between the Gush Etzion settlement bloc and the Green Line. More than one third of it belonged to Wadi Fukin and amounted, the head of the local council told me, to half the village's land, not counting the thousands of dunams that had already been lost. Unlike Nabi Saleh and most of the villages along the path of the wall, Wadi Fukin had no history of resistance. Even during the Second Intifada, things had stayed quiet here. But it was now a question of survival, and on each of the three preceding Fridays, the people of Wadi Fukin had demonstrated against the confiscation. Soldiers had come and behaved as soldiers do.

When I arrived, a crowd was already gathering at a bend in the road at the center of town. A woman came over and yelled at her son, ordering him to go home. He ignored her. I spotted Jonathan and his partner Ifat and another of the Israeli activists I knew from Nabi Saleh. The midday prayer let out and we marched together down a narrow street through orchards of olives and figs, the kids in matching T-shirts, waving flags. Soldiers were waiting at the end of the road and I could see settlers gathering to watch the show from their balconies high above the village. Things proceeded as they always did, but no one here knew it yet. It was all still new. As if by script, a soldier announced that the area had been declared a closed military zone, and the Border Police formed a line to block the marchers. There was a standoff for a while and then stun grenades and shoving, and later tear gas, and soon almost everyone was running. Ten or fifteen of the young men from the village turned out and threw a few rocks. They were prepared if not experienced: a couple of them wore gloves on their right hands so they could pick up the tear gas canisters and hurl them back at the soldiers without burning themselves. They tried to bury one, kicking dirt over it as the gas streamed out. It didn't work. The grenade kept smoking no matter how much earth they piled on.

In the end everyone retreated but two teenage girls. Seven soldiers stood on top of a hill. The girls stood alone at its base. The soldiers had a clear and easy shot, and the girls were too far away to hit them, but still, they reached down and picked up stones and hurled them up as hard as they were able. Each time their stones fell short, they reached down and grabbed two more.

ACKNOWLEDGMENTS

I would not have been able to write this book without the abundant help, generosity, hospitality, kindness, laughter, encouragement, insights, and wise counsel of Bassem Tamimi, Nariman Tamimi, Bilal Tamimi, Manal Tamimi, Asya, Zidan Sharabati, Jawad Abu Aisha, Issa Amro, Abed al-Salaima, Muhannad Qafesha, Badia Dweik, Ghassan Najjar, Basil Najjar, Eid Suleiman al-Hathalin, Tariq Salim al-Hathalin, Ezra Nawi, Abir Kopty, Jonathan Pollak, Joseph Dana, Jesse Rosenfeld, Hugh Naylor, Dalia Hatuqa, Charles Fromm, Allison Deger, Mariam Barghouti, Lema Nazeeh, Diana Alzeer, Razi Nabulsi, Ashira Ramadan, Lazar Simeonov, Dylan Collins, Michele Monni, Peter Lagerquist, Emilio Dabed, Nithya Nagarajan, Gaia Squarci, Riad Nasser, Jen Hofer, Mike Murashige, Tom Lutz, Greg Veis, Ilena Silverman, Ted Ross, Gloria Loomis, the Mesa Refuge, Blue Mountain Center, the Hofer-Ray Astral Sanctuary for Lost and Headstrong Artists, and Barbara Ehrenreich. Many thanks to Peter van Agtmael for his unflagging good company and his generosity with the photos included herein. Scott Moyers helped make this a far better book than it otherwise would have been. Without the laughter and love of my nieces—Anna and Clara Brooks and Olivia and Pearl Cuevas—I would surely have been lost. Without Irene Nasser, I could not have written a page.

NOTES

viii **"The dawn is breaking . . ."** Viktor Shklovsky, *A Hunt for Optimism*, trans. Shushan Avagyan (Champaign, IL: Dalkey Archive Press, 2012), 113.

INTRODUCTION
1 **"I'm scared of a history . . ."** Elias Khoury, *The Gate of the Sun*, trans. Humphrey Davies (New York: Picador, 2006), 291.

2 **"No spectators at chasm's door . . ."** Mahmoud Darwish, "I Have a Seat in the Abandoned Theater," in *The Butterfly's Burden,* trans. Fady Joudah (Port Townsend, WA: Copper Canyon Press, 2007).

2 **Insistence on objectivity is always . . .** Frantz Fanon, *The Wretched of the Earth*, trans. Constance Farrington (New York: Grove Press, 1963), 77.

PART ONE: NABI SALEH

PROLOGUE
7 **"And the nations' roads . . ."** Mahmoud Darwish, "The Hoopoe," in *If I Were Another*, trans. Fady Joudah (New York: Farrar, Straus & Giroux, 2009), 46.

7 **In Tunis, a fruit vendor . . .** Marc Fisher, "In Tunisia, Act of One Fruit Vendor Sparks Wave of Revolution Through Arab World," *Washington Post*, March 26, 2011, www.washingtonpost.com/world/in-tunisia-act-of-one-fruit-vendor-sparks-wave-of-revolution-through-arab-world/2011/03/16/AFjfsueB_story.html.

8 **Peace talks between Israel and the Palestinian Authority . . .** Chris McGreal and Harriet Sherwood, "US Middle East Peace Plan Flounders," *Guardian*, December 8, 2010, www.theguardian.com/world/2010/dec/08/us-middle-east-peace-talks.

8 **The number of Israeli settlers . . .** Batsheva Sobelman, "Israel's Settlement Building Up Sharply in 2013, Report Says," *Los Angeles Times*, October 17, 2013, http://articles.latimes.com/2013/oct/17/world/la-fg-wn-israel-settlements-20131017.

8 **Hamas had won, but Fatah . . .** David Rose, "The Gaza Bombshell," *Vanity Fair*, April 2008, www.vanityfair.com/news/2008/04/gaza200804.

9 **Hundreds died in factional fighting . . .** "Over 600 Palestinians Killed in Internal Clashes Since 2006," *Ynet News*, June 6, 2007, www.ynetnews.com/articles/0,7340,L-3409548,00.html.

9 Each faction persecuted and imprisoned . . . Fred Abrahams, *Internal Fight: Palestinian Abuses in Gaza and the West Bank* (New York: Human Rights Watch, 2008), www.hrw.org/report/2008/07/29/internal-fight/palestinian-abuses-gaza-and-west-bank#8a38d4.

9 The response in Gaza was direct . . . Fares Akram, "Hamas Forces Break Up Pro-Unity Protests in Gaza," *New York Times,* March 15, 2011, www.nytimes.com/2011/03/16/world/middleeast/16gaza.html.

10 They started at the house of Bassem's cousin . . . Joseph Dana, "Nabi Saleh Popular Committee Leader Arrested in a Night Raid," +972, March 6, 2011, http://972mag.com/nabi-saleh-popular-committee-leader-arrested-in-a-night-raid/11573/.

11 (Footnote) Mizrahi was abducted while on his way . . . "Rampage over West Bank Death," *New York Times*, October 30, 1993, www.nytimes.com/1993/10/31/world/rampage-over-west-bank-death.html; Michael Parks, "Prominent West Bank Palestinian Is Murdered as Violence Escalates," *Los Angeles Times*, October 31, 1993, http://articles.latimes.com/1993-10-31/news/mn-51807_1_west-bank; "List of Palestinian Terrorists Set to Be Freed by Israel," *Jerusalem Post*, December 29, 2013, www.jpost.com/Diplomacy-and-Politics/List-of-Palestinian-terrorists-set-to-be-freed-by-Israel-336440.

11 "I felt as if my brain . . ." James Ron and Eric Goldstein, *Torture and Ill-Treatment: Israel's Interrogation of Palestinians from the Occupied Territories* (New York: Human Rights Watch, June 1994), www.hrw.org/reports/1994/06/01/torture-and-ill-treatment.

12 (Footnote) In June 1994, eight months . . . Ibid.

12 (Footnote) During the brief period . . . Lisa Hajjar, *Courting Conflict: The Israeli Military Court System in the West Bank and Gaza* (Berkeley: University of California Press, 2005), 59–60; Sabri Jiryis, *The Arabs in Israel*, trans. Inea Bushnaq (New York: Monthly Review Press, 1976), 11.

13 Residents of Nabi Saleh . . . Hagar Shezaf, Yesh Din: Volunteers for Human Rights, e-mail to author, August 24, 2014.

13 The following year, the state seized . . . "How Dispossession Happens: The Humanitarian Impact of the Takeover of Palestinian Water Springs by Israeli Settlers," United Nations Office for the Coordination of Humanitarian Affairs, March 2012, http://reliefweb.int/sites/reliefweb.int/files/resources/Full%20Report_655.pdf.

13 It now has a population . . . "Statistics on Settlements and Settler Population," B'Tselem, May 11, 2015, www.btselem.org/settlements/statistics.

13 (Footnote) In March 2007, the Israeli NGO Peace Now . . . Dror Etkes and Hagit Ofran, "Guilty!: Construction of Settlements upon Private Land," Peace Now, March 2007, http://peacenow.org.il/eng/sites/default/files/Breaking_The_Law_formal%20data_March07Eng.pdf.

14 (Footnote) Years later, the settlers retroactively . . . "Dismantling of Illegal Construction on Nabi Salah Spring Begins," Yesh Din, January 3, 2013, www.yesh-din.org/postview.asp?catid=237.

18 (Footnote) The consequences for Israelis and Palestinians . . . For a detailed account of the military legal system in the West Bank, see Lisa Hajjar, *Courting Conflict*.

18 (Footnote) "But for all his arrests, he had only . . ." Yigai Sarna, "Back in Action," *Ynet News*, March 11, 2011, www.ynetnews.com/articles/0,7340,L-4035484,00.html.

19 Bassem would ultimately be charged . . . "West Bank Protest Organizer, Bassem Tamimi, to Judge: 'Your Military Laws Are Non-Legit. Our Peaceful Protest Is Just,'" Popular Struggle Coordination Committee, June 6, 2011, http://popularstruggle.org/content/west-bank-protest-organizer-bassem-tamimi-judge-%E2%80%9Cyour-military-laws-are-non-legit-our-peacef.

19 (Footnote) Israel's Military Order 101 . . . "Order No. 101 Regarding Prohibition of Incitement and Hostile Propaganda Actions," Israel Defense Forces, August 27, 1967, www.btselem.org/download/19670827_order_regarding_prohibition_of_incitement_and_hostile_propaganda.pdf.

19 **the bulk of the evidence** . . . Isabel Kershner, "Palestinian's Trial Shines Light on Military Justice," *New York Times*, February 28, 2012, www.nytimes.com/2012/02/19/world/middleeast/palestinians-trial-shines-light-on-justice-system.html; "Israel: Palestinian's Conviction Violates Freedom of Assembly," Human Rights Watch, May 30, 2012, www.hrw.org/news/2012/05/30/israel-palestinian-s-conviction-violates-freedom-assembly.

19 **He read from a prepared statement** . . . Popular Struggle Coordination Committee, June 6, 2011, http://popularstruggle.org/content/west-bank-protest-organizer-bassem-tamimi-judge-%E2%80%9Cyour-military-laws-are-non-legit-our-peacef#statement.

19 **(Footnote) The 1977 Geneva Protocol I** . . . "Protocol Additional to the Geneva Conventions of 12 August 1949, and relating to the Protection of Victims of International Armed Conflicts (Protocol I)," June 8, 1977, www.icrc.org/ihl/INTRO/470.

20 **in 2010, the last year** . . . Chaim Levinson, "Nearly 100% of All Military Court Cases in West Bank End in Conviction, Haaretz Learns," *Haaretz*, November 29, 2011, www.haaretz.com/print-edition/news/nearly-100-of-all-military-court-cases-in-west-bank-end-in-conviction-haaretz-learns-1.398369.

20 **Bassem would be found guilty** . . . Amira Hass, "Israel's Military Court Sentences Palestinian Protest Leader to 13 Months in Jail," *Haaretz,* May 29, 2012, www.haaretz.com/news/diplomacy-defense/israel-s-military-court-sentences-palestinian-protest-leader-to-13-months-in-jail-1.433191.

CHAPTER 1: LIFE IS BEAUTIFUL

21 **"One does so rejoice in a spring!"** Quoted in Raja Shehadeh, *A Rift in Time* (London: Profile Books, 2010) 189.

21 **On December 9, 2011, Mustafa Tamimi** . . . Haggai Mattar, "Mustafa Tamimi: A Murder Captured on Camera," *+972*, December 11, 2011, http://972mag.com/mustafa-tamimi-a-murder-captured-on-camera/29459/.

30 **(Footnote) An army spokesman demurred** . . . Eytan Buchman, e-mail to author, July 19, 2012.

32 **As the region was then** . . . *The Covenant of the League of Nations* (Boston: World Peace Foundation, 1920), ix.

32 **"In the case of Palestine," wrote** . . . **Lord Arthur Balfour** . . . Gudrun Krämer, *A History of Palestine: From the Ottoman Conquest to the Founding of the State of Israel* (Princeton, NJ: Princeton University Press, 2008), 167.

32 **To complicate matters, Balfour** . . . "Palestine for the Jews," *The Times,* November 9, 1917, 1.

32 **(Footnote) There were at the time** . . . Baylis Thomas, *How Israel Was Won: A Concise History of the Arab-Israeli Conflict* (Boston: Lexington Books, 1999), 27.

32 **By the mid-1930s, British policies** . . . Ilan Pappe, *A History of Modern Palestine: One Land, Two Peoples* (Cambridge, UK: Cambridge University Press, 2004), 98–102.

32 **(Footnote) By 1931, the Jewish population** . . . Krämer, *A History of Palestine*, 182, 264.

33 **Women led protests in Gaza** . . . Ibid., 271–72.

33 **The British responded to this early outbreak** . . . Ibid., 274.

33 **The following year, the British** . . . Anglo-American Committee of Inquiry, *Report to the United States Government and His Majesty's Government in the United Kingdom* (Washington, DC: United States Government Printing Office, 1946), http://avalon.law.yale.edu/20th_century/angap04.asp.

33 **more than one thousand Palestinians** . . . *The Peel Commission Report: Report of the Palestine Royal Commission Presented by the Secretary of State for the Colonies to the United Kingdom Parliament by Command of His Britannic Majesty* (London, 1937), 105.

33 **By early 1939, when the insurrection** . . . Rashid Khalidi, "The Palestinians and 1948," in *The War for Palestine: Rewriting the History of 1948*, ed. Eugene Rogan and Avi Shlaim (Cambridge, UK: Cambridge University Press, 2001), 27.

33 **the underground Zionist militia** . . . Krämer, *History of Palestine*, 291.

33 **In February 1947, Britain** . . . Winston Churchill, speech to the House of Commons, March 6, 1947, United Kingdom, Parliamentary Debates, Commons, 5th ser., vol. 434, 675.

34 nearly three quarters of a million Palestinians . . . United Nations Conciliation Commission for Palestine, "Final Report of the United Nations Economic Survey Mission for the Middle East," Jerusalem, December 28, 1949.

34 The Irgun was integrated . . . Uri Ben Eliezer, *The Making of Israeli Militarism* (Bloomington: Indiana University Press, 1998), 184.

34 killing seventeen-year-old Hatem al-Sisi . . . Neve Gordon, *Israel's Occupation* (Berkeley: University of California Press, 2008), 147.

35 the "children of the stones" celebrated . . . Nizar Qabbani, "Trilogy of the Children of the Stones," in Tariq Ali, *The Clash of Civilizations: Crusade, Jihads and Modernity* (London: Verso Books, 2002), 141.

35 After a month of purely local coordination . . . Penny Johnson, Lee O'Brien, and Joost Hilterman, "The West Bank Rises Up," in *Intifada: the Palestinian Uprising Against Israeli Occupation*, ed. Zachary Lockman and Joel Beinin (Boston: South End Press, 1989), 30. Most of the communiqués are reproduced as an appendix to Lockman and Beinin, *Intifada*, 327–94.

35 In the first year of the Intifada . . . Lockman and Beinin, *Intifada*, 317–25.

35 and not a single Israeli soldier . . . Mary Elizabeth King, *A Quiet Revolution: The First Palestinian Intifada and Nonviolent Resistance* (New York: Nation Books, 2007), 9.

35 Fatah and the three main left-wing Palestinian . . . Joost R. Hiltermann, *Behind the Intifada: Labor and Women's Movements in the Occupied Territories* (Princeton, NJ: Princeton University Press, 1991), 45, 51, 65, 173–76.

36 (Footnote) In February 1988, Israel shuttered . . . King, *Quiet Revolution,* 221.

36 The result was revolutionary . . . On the social transformations that accompanied the early years of the Intifada, see Edward Said, "Intifada and Independence," in Lockman and Beinin, *Intifada*, 20.

36 (Footnote) From Qabbani's *Trilogy of the Children of the Stones* . . . "The most important/thing about them is . . ." Ali, *Clash of Civilizations*, 141.

36 After 1990, power shifted . . . King, *Quiet Revolution*, 287.

37 By the end of the next day . . . Menachem Klein, *The Jerusalem Problem: the Struggle for Permanent Status,* trans. Haim Watzman (Gainesville: University Press of Florida, 2003), 97–98.

37 In the first five days, nearly 50 . . . Ibid., 97.

37 The first suicide bombing . . . King, *Quiet Revolution*, 330.

37 The next year brought two dozen . . . "Suicide and Other Bombing Attacks in Israel Since the Declaration of Principles (Sept. 1993)," Israel Ministry of Foreign Affairs, www.mfa.gov.il/mfa/foreignpolicy/terrorism/palestinian/pages/suicide%20and%20other%20bombing%20attacks%20in%20israel%20since.aspx.

37 In the beginning it was just . . . "Erased in a Moment: Suicide Bombing Attacks Against Israeli Civilians," Human Rights Watch, New York, October 2002, www.hrw.org/reports/2002/isrl-pa/index.htm#TopOfPage.

37 By 2002, Fatah's Al-Aqsa Martyrs Brigade . . . "Without Distinction: Attacks on Civilians by Palestinian Armed Groups," Amnesty International, July 10, 2002, 11, 15, www.amnesty.org/en/documents/MDE02/003/2002/en/.

37 More than half of the nearly 700 . . . "Israeli-Palestinian Fatalities Since 2000—Key Trends," United Nations Office for the Coordination of Humanitarian Affairs, August 2007, http://unispal.un.org/UNISPAL.NSF/0/BE07C80CDA4579468525734800500272.

37 In one early bombing . . . Frimet Roth, "Remembering the Sbarro Bombing Five Years On," *Haaretz,* August 11, 2006, www.haaretz.com/print-edition/features/remembering-the-sbarro-bombing-five-years-on-1.194921.

37 Ahlam was sentenced to sixteen . . . Nida Tuma, "Sbarro Bomber's Family Hopes She Will Lead Quiet Life," *Jerusalem Post*, October 17, 2011, www.jpost.com/National-News/Sbarro-bombers-family-hopes-she-will-lead-quiet-life.

37 when Israel traded 1,027 Palestinian prisoners . . . Ben Quinn, "Gilad Shalit Freed in Exchange for Palestinian Prisoners," *Guardian*, October 28, 2011, www.theguardian.com/world/2011/oct/18/gilad-shalit-palestine-prisoners-freed.

38 Sharon, who was soon elected . . . Eyal Weizman, *Hollow Land: Israel's Architecture of Occupation* (London: Verso Books, 2007), 196.

38 (Footnote) If we consider the Second Intifada . . . "Palestinians Killed by Israeli Security Forces in the Occupied Territories, Before Operation 'Cast Lead,'" B'Tselem, www.btselem.org/statistics/fatalities/before-cast-lead/by-date-of-event/wb-gaza/palestinians-killed-by-israeli-security-forces/by-month.

38 Hundreds of roadblocks and checkpoints . . . "Fragmented Lives: Humanitarian Overview 2012," United Nations Office for the Coordination of Humanitarian Affairs (East Jerusalem, May 2013), 38, www.ochaopt.org/documents/ocha_opt_fragmented_lives_annual_report_2013_english_web.pdf.

38 A barrier composed of eight-meter-high . . . Ray Dolphin, *The West Bank Wall: Unmaking Palestine* (London: Pluto Press, 2006), 38–39.

38 In 2002, residents of the village of Jayyous . . . Sharif Omar, "Israel's Wall Hems in Livelihoods— and Dreams," *USA Today*, August 17, 2003, http://usatoday30.usatoday.com/news/opinion/editorials/2003-08-17-omar_x.htm; Dolphin, *West Bank Wall*, 88–94; see also Nida Sinnokrot's excellent 2006 documentary about the popular resistance movement in Jayyous, *Palestine Blues*.

38 in this case, to make room . . . Yehezkel Lein and Alon Cohen-Lifshitz, *Under the Guise of Security: Routing the Separation Barrier to Enable the Expansion of Israeli Settlements in the West Bank* (Jerusalem: B'Tselem, December 2005), 5–6, www.btselem.org/download/200512_under_the_guise_of_security_eng.pdf.

38 The barrier . . . Idith Zertal and . . . Akiva Eldar wrote . . . Idith Zertal and Akiva Eldar, *Lords of the Land: The War over Israel's Settlements in the Occupied Territories, 1967–2007*, trans. Vivian Eden (New York: Nation Books, 2007), 424.

39 In Biddu, just west of Ramallah . . . "List of Demonstrators Killed During Protests Against the Wall," International Solidarity Movement, December 2010, http://palsolidarity.org/2010/12/list-of-demonstrators-killed-during-protests-against-the-wall/.

39 The wall went up . . . "Restricted Access to Land: Biddu Enclave," United Nations Relief and Works Agency, October 2014, http://reliefweb.int/sites/reliefweb.int/files/resources/biddu_enclave_infographic.pdf.

39 In Beit Liqya, soldiers shot and killed . . . Arnon Regular, "Security Guard Shoots Palestinian Teen in Family Vineyard," *Haaretz*, October 7, 2005, www.haaretz.com/print-edition/news/security-guard-shoots-palestinian-teen-in-family-vineyard-1.163435.

39 They lost in Beit Ijza . . . "Beit Ijza Village Profile," Applied Research Institute, Jerusalem, 2012, 16–17, http://vprofile.arij.org/jerusalem/pdfs/vprofile/Beit%20Ijza_EN.pdf.

39 In Budrus, though, about twenty minutes . . . Dolphin, *West Bank Wall*, 190–91; interview with Ayed Morrar, July 2012. See also Juliet Bacha's documentary, *Budrus*, Just Vision Films, 2010.

39 in 2006 to al-Ma'sara . . . "Five Shot as Israeli Forces Disperse Protests Across West Bank," *Palestine Chronicle*, January 18, 2014, www.palestinechronicle.com/five-shot-as-israeli-forces-disperse-protests-across-west-bank/.

40 In 2011, Wikileaks released . . . "IDF Plans Harsher Methods with West Bank Demonstrations," United States Embassy, Tel Aviv, February 16, 2010, https://cablegatesearch.wikileaks.org/cable.php?id=10TELAVIV344.

43 Mohammad, who maintained the Facebook page . . . "Tamimi Press," Facebook, www.facebook.com/Tamimipresspage?fref=nf. Accessed January 1, 2016.

44 (Footnote) While visiting Palestine in 1857 . . . Herman Melville, *Journal of a Visit to Europe and the Levant* (Westport, CT: Greenwood Press, 1955), 137.

44 (Footnote) the United States has supplied Israel with $3 billion . . . Jeremy M. Sharp, "U.S. Foreign Aid to Israel," Congressional Research Service, June 10, 2015, www.fas.org/sgp/crs/mideast/RL33222.pdf.

44 (Footnote) The tear gas used in Nabi Saleh . . . Ryan Rodrick Beiler, "This Tear Gas Brought to You by the U.S.A.," *+972*, December 3, 2013, http://972mag.com/photos-this-tear-gas-brought-to-you-by-the-u-s-a/82650/.

45 (Footnote) The IDF spokesperson's office . . . IDF Spokesperson's Office, North America Desk, e-mail to author, November 5, 2014.

50 Bilal caught it on video . . . www.youtube.com/watch?v=gW5Ce2CqT0I.

51 Ma'an, the official Palestinian news agency . . . "Witnesses: Settlers, Forces Expand Halamish Settlement," Ma'an News Agency, January 22, 2013, www.maannews.com/Content .aspx?id=558288.

52 "Memory," wrote the Lebanese novelist Elias Khoury . . . Khoury, *Gate of the Sun,* 161.

INTERLUDE: THE NATION OF HANI AMER

56 the infamous massacre of Kufr Qassem . . . For a comprehensive account of this incident, see chapter 6 of Sabri Jiryis's *The Arabs in Israel,* 140–53.

56 Yshishkar Shadmi, the officer who ordered . . . Jiryis, *Arabs in Israel,* 153.

56 Among them was a young officer . . . Mati Tuchfeld, "When Shaul Mofaz Was a Settler," *Israel Hayom,* April 12, 2012, www.israelhayom.com/site/newsletter_article.php?id=3927; Akiva Eldar, "The 'Road Map' Has Been Folded Up," *Haaretz,* November 14, 2002, www.remembershaden .org/articles/the_road_map_has_been_folded_up.htm.

CHAPTER 2: THE PEACE OF THE BRAVE

61 "Here you may witness . . ." Mariano Azuela, *The Underdogs,* trans. E. Munguía (New York: Signet Classics, 1996), 151.

63 Most Palestinians are exiles . . . "FAQs about Palestinian Refugees," al-Awda, http://al-awda .org/learn-more/faqs-about-palestinian-refugees.

65 The Oslo Accords had given Israel . . . "Discriminatory Water Supply," B'Tselem, March 10, 2014, www.btselem.org/water/discrimination_in_water_supply.

65 (Footnote) Palestinians were allotted just 20 percent . . . Ibid.

65 (Footnote) During the talks leading up . . . Uri Savir, *The Process: 1,100 Days That Changed the Middle East* (New York: Random House, 2010), 213.

65 (Footnote) In areas connected to the water grid . . . B'Tselem, "Discriminatory Water Supply."

65 (Footnote) Some West Bank settlements use nearly ten times . . . "Limited Availability of Water in the West Bank," United Nations Office for the Coordination of Humanitarian Affairs, www .ochaopt.org/annual/c7/3.html.

67 A few days earlier . . . "Hundreds Protest Negotiations in Ramallah," Ma'an News Agency, July 3, 2012, www.maannews.com/Content.aspx?id=501119.

67 In March 2002, forces under his command . . . Mary Curtius, "Israel Invades Ramallah in Show of Might," *Los Angeles Times,* March 13, 2002, http://articles.latimes.com/2002/mar/13/news/ mn-32564.

67 Yasser Arafat would effectively remain . . . John Kifner, "Israel Surrounds Arafat Compound in a Predawn Raid," *New York Times,* June 10, 2002, www.nytimes.com/2002/06/10/international/ middleeast/10ISRA.html; "Inside Arafat's Compound of Rubble," BBC, September 22, 2002, http://news.bbc.co.uk/2/hi/middle_east/1902566.stm; Linda Tabar, "The Muqata: Facade of a Palestinian State," *al-Akhbar English,* December 26, 2011, http://english.al-akhbar.com/node/2821.

67 (Footnote) Later that year, Mofaz was forced . . . Justin Juggler, "General Linked to Jenin Atrocities Named Defense Chief," *Independent,* November 1, 2002, www.independent.co.uk/news/ world/middle-east/general-linked-to-jenin-atrocities-named-defence-chief-133069.html.

67 PA police and *mukhabarat* attacked . . . Linah Alsaafin, "First Hand: Ramallah Protests Against Mofaz Meeting Attacked by PA Police, Thugs," *Electronic Intifada,* July 3, 2012, https://electronicintifada.net/blogs/linah-alsaafin/first-hand-ramallah-protests-against-mofaz -meeting-attacked-pa-police-thugs.

68 In September 1993, after months . . . Savir, *Process;* Edward Said, "The Morning After," *London Review of Books,* October 20, 1993, www.lrb.co.uk/v15/n20/edward-said-the-morning-after.

68 "A peace of the brave . . ." "Statements by Leaders at the Signing of the Middle East Pact," *New York Times*, September 14, 1993, www.nytimes.com/1993/09/14/world/mideast-accord-statements-by -leaders-at-the-signing-of-the-middle-east-pact.html.

68 "the truly astonishing proportions . . ." Said, "The Morning After."

68 Oslo carved the West Bank . . . Adam Hanieh, *Lineages of Revolt: Issues of Contemporary Capitalism in the Middle East* (Chicago: Haymarket Books, 2013), electronic edition, 439–44; Heinrich Böll Stiftung, *Perspectives* 5 (December 2013): 6.

69 (Footnote) The boundaries have since shifted . . . Amira Hass, "UN Report: 300,000 Palestinians Live in Area C of West Bank," *Haaretz*, March 5, 2014, www.haaretz.com/news /diplomacy-defense/.premium-1.577997; *Perspectives* 5, 6.

69 in the words of scholar Adam Hanieh . . . Hanieh, *Lineages of Revolt*, 439.

69 Between 2000 and 2012, less than 6 percent . . . Noga Kadman, "Acting the Landlord: Israel's Policy in Area C, West Bank," B'Tselem, June 2013, 19–20.

69 "The fact is," Said wrote . . . Said, "The Morning After."

70 Israel was, to use Israeli political scientist . . . Gordon, *Israel's Occupation*, 169.

70 those living in Areas A and B—would be confined . . . Hanieh, *Lineages of Revolt*, 405–6; Nasser Abourahme, "The Bantustan Sublime: Reframing the Colonial in Ramallah," *City* 12(3) (December 2008); Rashid Khalidi, *The Iron Cage: The Story of the Palestinian Struggle for Statehood* (Boston: Beacon Press, 2006) 199.

70 The Paris Protocol allowed Israel . . . Hanieh, *Lineages of Revolt*, 449–53.

70 one third of the PA's budget . . . Gordon, *Israel's Occupation*, 186.

71 Before the Intifada began . . . Hiltermann, *Behind the Intifada*, 32; Hanieh, *Lineages of Revolt*, 444–46.

71 Some 150,000 Palestinians found jobs . . . Gordon, *Israel's Occupation*, 186.

71 Another large slice of the Palestinian population . . . Hanieh, *Lineages of Revolt*, 1033.

72 "It is most dangerous," wrote the poet Mahmoud Darwish . . . Mahmoud Darwish, *Journal of an Ordinary Grief*, trans. Ibrahim Muhawi (New York: Archipelago Books: 2010), 47.

72 the same one Victor Serge had raised . . . Victor Serge, *Unforgiving Years*, trans. Richard Greenman (New York: New York Review Books, 2008), 326.

72 He had lost the backing of the Gulf states . . . Khalidi, *Iron Cage*, 157.

72 Talks collapsed in early 2001 . . . Ibid., 158.

73 "Our people will continue their popular . . ." "Full Transcript of Abbas Speech at UN General Assembly," *Haaretz*, September 23, 2011, www.haaretz.com/news/diplomacy-defense/full -transcript-of-abbas-speech-at-un-general-assembly-1.386385.

75 The Mofaz visit, in the end . . . "Official: Abbas-Mofaz Meeting Postponed Indefinitely," Ma'an News Agency, June 30, 2012, www.maannews.com/Content.aspx?id=499870; "Hundreds Protest Against Abbas in Ramallah," *Al-Akhbar English*, July 3, 2102, http://english.al-akhbar.com /node/9207.

75 (Footnote) earlier that week, defying the rulings . . . Chaim Levinson, "Israel's Immigration Police Granted Power to Deport Foreign Activists from West Bank," *Haaretz*, July 13, 2012, www.haaretz.com/news/diplomacy-defense/israel-s-immigration-police-granted-power-to -deport-foreign-activists-from-west-bank-1.450794.

INTERLUDE: EVERY BEGINNING IS DIFFERENT

83 Eyal Weizman observed in 2007 . . . Weizman, *Hollow Land*, 177–78.

84 Gershom Gorenberg has described . . . Gershom Gorenberg, "Road 443: More Evidence of a Long Deception," *The Daily Beast*, October 7, 2013, www.thedailybeast.com/articles/2013/10/07/ road-443-more-evidence-of-a-long-deception.html.

84 Five men had been killed in Biddu . . . "List of Demonstrators Killed During Protests Against the Wall," International Solidarity Movement.

84 Biddu and the seven villages . . . "Restricted Access to Land: Biddu Enclave," UNRWA.

87 (Footnote) "In the occupied territories," observed the French writer Christian Salmon . . . Christian Salmon, "The Bulldozer War," *Le Monde Diplomatique*, May 2002, https://mondediplo .com/2002/05/08bulldozer.

87 "Man is a creature that can get used . . ." Fyodor Dostoevsky, *The House of the Dead*, David McDuff, tr. (New York: Penguin Classics, 1985), 29.

CHAPTER 3: ABOVE THE CAROB TREE

89 "And if the dead by displacement . . ." Mourid Barghouti, *I Saw Ramallah* (New York: Anchor Books, 2003), 161.

90 In mid-October, they blocked a settler road . . . "Palestinians Block Road to Protest Settler Attacks," *Al-Akhbar English*, October 16, 2012, http://english.al-akhbar.com/node/12980.

90 Twelve days later, they staged a protest . . . Tovah Lazaroff, "Palestinian Activists Raise Their Flags in Rami Levy," *The Jerusalem Post*, October 24, 2012, www.jpost.com/Features/ In-Thespotlight/Palestinian-activists-raise-their-flags-in-Rami-Levy.

90 They blocked more roads . . . "Palestinians Protest Occupation, Block Roads Throughout West Bank," *+972*, November 14, 2012, http://972mag.com/photos-palestinians-protest-occupation -block-roads-throughout-west-bank/59795/.

90 activists built a "village" . . . Patrick Strickland, "Israel, E1, and the Meaning of Bab al-Shams," *Middle East Monitor*, January 15, 2013, www.middleeastmonitor.com/articles/middle-east/ 4999-israel-e1-and-the-meaning-of-bab-al-shams.

90 A month and a half earlier . . . Barak Ravid, "In Response to UN Vote, Israel to Build 3,000 New Homes in Settlements," *Haaretz*, November 30, 2012, www.haaretz.com/news/diplomacy -defense/in-response-to-un-vote-israel-to-build-3-000-new-homes-in-settlements .premium-1.481695.

90 "We the people," the press release read . . . "Palestinians Establish a New Village, Bab Alshams, in Area E1," Popular Struggle Coordination Committee, January 11, 2013, http://popularstruggle .org/content/palestinians-establish-new-village-bab-alshams-area-e1.

90 It was, in Khoury's words . . . Khoury, *Gate of the Sun*, 514.

91 Netanyahu personally gave the order . . . Karl Vick, "When Palestinians Use Settler Tactics: A Beleaguered Netanyahu Responds," *Time*, January 14, 2013, http://world.time.com/2013/01/14/ when-palestinians-use-settler-tactics-a-beleaguered-netanyahu-responds/.

91 two copycat protest villages . . . "Clashes Break Out at New Protest Village in Jenin," Ma'an News Agency, January 26, 2013, www.maannews.com/Content.aspx?id=559390; "Israeli Army Removes Activists from Bab al-Karameh," *WAFA*, January 21, 2013, http://english.wafa.ps/index .php?action=detail&id=21531.

91 In 2011, when the UN's Office . . . "Palestinian Villages Affected by Violence from Yitzhar Settlement and Outposts," United Nations Office for the Coordination of Humanitarian Affairs, February 2012, http://unispal.un.org/unispal.nsf/634ea0efe460133c852570c0006 d53f2/b058917b40 f82bed85257dff00616387?OpenDocument.

91 Another UN agency found . . . "Olive Harvest: Continued Settler Attacks Against Refugee Livelihoods," United Nations Relief and Works Agency, October 2013, www.unrwa.org/sites/ default/files/olive_harvest_continued_settler_attacks_against_refugee_livelihoods.pdf.

94 (Footnote) IDF regulations forbid soldiers from . . . Sarit Michaeli, *Crowd Control: Israel's Use of Crowd Control Weapons in the West Bank*, B'Tselem, January 2013, 21, www.btselem.org/ download/201212_crowd_control_eng.pdf.

96 sixteen-year-old Samir 'Awad . . . Harriet Sherwood, "Israeli Forces Shot Youth in the Back as He Ran Away, Say Palestinians," *Guardian*, January 15, 2013, www.theguardian.com/world/2013/ jan/15/israeli-shot-youth-in-back-palestinians; "B'Tselem Inquiry: No Justification for Shooting and Killing Samir 'Awad, 16," B'Tselem, February 21, 2013, www.btselem.org/firearm/20130221 _killing_of_samir_awad_budrus.

96 They beat him pretty badly ... "Palestinians Beaten After Protesting at Settlement Supermarket," *Al-Akhbar English*, October 24, 2012, http://english.al-akhbar.com/node/13095.

97 I had seen video of the protest ... "Palestinian Activists Protest at Rami Levi Settlement's Supermarket," YouTube, www.youtube.com/watch?v=wt4x1WIzcYw.

97 The full video was excruciating ... "Ahed Tamimi, a Brave Palestinian Girl," YouTube, www.youtube.com/watch?v=u3783A3HOkw.

98 Recep Erdogan, the president of Turkey ... "Turkish PM Eats Breakfast with Palestinian Girl Who Challenged Israeli Troops," *Hurriyet Daily News*, December 30, 2012, www.hurriyetdailynews.com/turkish-pm-eats-breakfast-with-palestinian-girl-who-challenged-israeli-troops.aspx?pageID=238&nID=37955&NewsCatID=338.

98 Six Israelis and 167 Palestinians ... "Harm to Civilians Significantly Higher in Second Half of Operation Pillar of Defense," B'Tselem, May 8, 2013, www.btselem.org/press_releases/20130509_pillar_of_defense_report.

99 Two weeks earlier, an IDF inquiry ... Chaim Levinson and Jack Khoury, "IDF Probe: 80 Bullets Fired Without Justification in Death of West Bank Palestinian," *Haaretz,* January 16, 2013, www.haaretz.com/news/diplomacy-defense/idf-probe-80-bullets-fired-without-justification-in-death-of-west-bank-palestinian.premium-1.494352.

INTERLUDE: STAGECRAFT

111 They were equipped and specially trained ... Jim Zanotti, "U.S. Foreign Aid to the Palestinians"; Jim Zanotti, "U.S. Security Assistance to the Palestinian Authority," Congressional Research Service, January 8, 2010, www.fas.org/sgp/crs/mideast/R40664.pdf.

111 the U.S., with the approval ... Steven Erlanger, "U.S. Urging Bigger Force for Abbas," *New York Times*, October 4, 2006, www.nytimes.com/2006/10/04/world/middleeast/05mideastcnd.html?pagewanted=print&_r=0; "US Embassy Cables: Israel Discusses Gaza and West Bank with US," *Guardian*, January 23, 2011, www.theguardian.com/world/us-embassy-cables-documents/81613.

112 "One authority, one gun ..." "Meeting Summary: Saeb Erekat and Keith Dayton," The Palestine Papers, June 24, 2009, http://transparency.aljazeera.net/en/projects/thepalestinepapers/201218205912859354.html.

112 specifically by an Irish Protestant policeman ... Kevin Connolly, "Charles Tegart and the Forts That Tower over Israel," BBC News, September 10, 2012, www.bbc.com/news/magazine-19019949; Seth J. Frantzman, "Tegart's Shadow," *The Jerusalem Post Magazine*, October 21, 2011, www.jpost.com/Magazine/Features/Tegarts-shadow; Matthew Hughes, "From Law and Order to Pacification: Britain's Suppression of the Arab Revolt in Palestine, 1936–39," *Journal of Palestine Studies* 39(2) (Winter 2010): 6–22, www.palestine-studies.org/sites/default/files/jps-articles/From%20Law%20and%20Order%20to%20Pacification-%20Britain's%20Suppression%20of%20the%20Arab%20Revolt%20in%20Palestine,.pdf.

113 One became a secret IDF prison ... Chris McGreal, "Facility 1391: Israel's Secret Prison," *Guardian*, November 13, 2003, www.theguardian.com/world/2003/nov/14/israel2; Aviv Lavie, "Inside Israel's Secret Prison," *Haaretz*, August 20, 2003, www.haaretz.com/inside-israel-s-secret-prison-1.97813; "Secrets of Unit 1391," *Newsweek*, June 27, 2004, www.newsweek.com/secrets-unit-1391-128665.

113 (Footnote) Prisoners held at the site ... McGreal, "Facility 1391"; Lavie, "Inside Israel's Secret Prison."

113 Tegart, who had imported waterboarding ... Hughes, "From Law and Order to Pacification."

113 The forts that fell in the West Bank ... Eyal Weizman, "Short Cuts," *London Review of Books*, January 9, 2014, www.lrb.co.uk/v36/n01/eyal-weizman/short-cuts.

113 "There was such euphoria then ..." Raja Shehadeh, *Occupation Diaries* (New York: OR Books, 2012), 135–36.

113 **On a later visit to the *muqata'a* . . .** Raja Shehadeh, *When the Birds Stopped Singing: Life in Ramallah Under Siege* (Hanover, NH: Steerforth Press, 2013), 130.

113 **After Arafat's death in 2004 . . .** Linda Tabar, "The Muqata: Façade of a Palestinian State."

114 **Appropriately, the refurbished *muqata'a* . . .** "Japan to Finance Renovation of PA's Muqata Headquarters in Ramallah," *Haaretz*, October 25, 2005, www.haaretz.com/news/japan-to-finance -renovation-of-pa-s-muqata-headquarters-in-ramallah-1.172482.

114 **(Footnote) I might have quoted Elias Khoury here . . .** Khoury, *Gate of the Sun*, 143.

CHAPTER 4: THE ANT AND THE SWEET

115 **"There is a point at which methods . . ."** Frantz Fanon, *Black Skin, White Masks*, trans. C. L. Markham (London: Pluto Press,1986), 5.

115 **The story went that it had taken Assaf . . .** Leona Vicario, "Mohammad Assaf 'Cheers Up' Palestine," *Palestine Monitor*, June 20, 2013, www.palestinemonitor.org/details.php?id =vish8va4427yt0bkh3pui.

124 **More than ten million people . . .** Shaimaa Fayed and Yasmine Saleh, "Millions Flood Egypt's Streets to Demand Mursi Quit," Reuters, June 30, 2013, www.reuters.com/article/2013/06/30/ cnews-us-egypt-protests-idCABRE95Q0NO20130630.

124 **the Egyptian military deposed Morsi . . .** "President Morsi Overthrown in Egypt," Al Jazeera, July 4, 2013, www.aljazeera.com/news/middleeast/2013/07/20137319828176718.html.

124 **Five days later, soldiers mowed down . . .** Kim Sengupta and Alistair Beach, "Cairo Massacre Eyewitness Report," *Independent*, July 9, 2013, www.independent.co.uk/news/world/africa/cairo -massacre-eyewitness-report-at-least-51-dead-and-more-than-440-injured-as-army-hits-back-at -muslim-brotherhood-supporters-8694785.html.

124 **At the end of the month, they slaughtered . . .** Patrick Kingsley, "At Least 120 Morsi Supporters Reported Killed in Egypt Clashes," *Guardian*, July 27, 2013, www.theguardian.com/world/2013/ jul/27/morsi-supporters-killed-egypt-cairo.

124 **and two weeks later killed more . . .** Omar Shakir, *All According to Plan: The Rab'a Massacre and Mass Killings of Protesters in Egypt* (New York: Human Rights Watch, August 12, 2014), www .hrw.org/node/127942.

124 **Meanwhile the death toll in Syria . . .** "Syrian Civil War Death Toll Rises to More Than 191,300, According to UN," *The Guardian*, August 22, 2014, www.theguardian.com/world/2014/aug/22/ syria-civil-war-death-toll-191300-un.

124 *The Washington Post*'s **editorial board . . .** "John Kerry Pursues a Narrow Peace," *Washington Post*, July 7, 2013, www.washingtonpost.com/opinions/john-kerry-pursues-a-narrow-peace/2013/ 07/07/66934ef8-e405-11e2-a11e-c2ea876a8f30_story.html.

124 **Netanyahu's deputy defense minister Danny Danon . . .** Raphael Ahren, "Deputy Defense Minister: This Government Will Block Any Two-State Deal," *Times of Israel*, June 6, 2013, www .timesofisrael.com/deputy-defense-minister-this-government-will-block-any-peace-deal/.

125 **Sarit Michaeli, a researcher for . . .** Michaeli, *Crowd Control*.

126 **Netanyahu had agreed to the release of 104 . . .** William Booth, "Mideast Peace Talks Set to Begin After Israel Agrees to Free 104 Palestinian Prisoners," *Washington Post*, July 28, 2013, www .washingtonpost.com/world/middle_east/israel-to-free-104-palestinian-prisoners/2013/07/28/ 390ad8d2-f7a3-11e2-a954-358d90d5d72d_story.html.

128 **the prisoners were to be let out in batches . . .** Ben Birnbaum and Amir Tibon, "The Explosive, Inside Story of How John Kerry Built an Israel-Palestine Peace Plan—and Watched It Crumble," *New Republic*, July 20, 2014, www.newrepublic.com/article/118751/how-israel-palestine -peace-deal-died.

128 **On July 30, Saeb Erekat and Tzipi Livni . . .** "After 'Productive' Start, Second Day of Mideast Talks," Agence France-Press, July 30, 2013.

128 **Martin Indyk, the former ambassador . . .** Grace Halsell, "Clinton's Indyk Appointment One of Many from Pro-Israel Think Tank," *Washington Report on Middle East Affairs*, March 1993, 9,

www.wrmea.org/1993-march/clinton-s-indyk-appointment-one-of-many-from-pro-israel-think
-tank.html.

128 **It was, Kerry said . . .** Arshad Mohammed and Lesley Wroughton, "Israeli-Palestinian Talks
Begin amid Deep Divisions," Reuters, July 30, 2013, www.reuters.com/article/2013/07/30/
us-palestinians-israel-idUSBRE96S0SY20130730.

128 **(Footnote) Two nights earlier, the leftist Popular Front . . .** "Palestinian Authority Police Beat
Protesters," Human Rights Watch, July 30, 2013, www.hrw.org/news/2013/07/30/palestine
-palestinian-authority-police-beat-protesters.

129 **it was Ramadan, and every Friday . . .** "Police: 75,000 Perform Ramadan Prayers at Al-Aqsa,"
Ma'an News Agency, July 12, 2013, www.maannews.com/Content.aspx?id=613361.

129 **(Footnote) In 1946, only 50 of Acre's 13,560 inhabitants . . .** Mustafa Abbasi, "The Fall of Acre
in the 1948 Palestine War," *Journal of Palestine Studies* 39(4) (Summer 2010): 6–27.

PART TWO: HEBRON

PROLOGUE

135 **"And on the whole, nothing . . ."** Shklovsky, *Hunt for Optimism*, 23.

137 **We passed the Gush Etzion roundabout . . .** Peter Beaumont and Orlando Crowcroft, "Bodies
of Three Missing Israeli Teenagers Found in West Bank," *Guardian*, June 30, 2014, www
.theguardian.com/world/2014/jun/30/bodies-missing-israeli-teenagers-found-west-bank.

137 **where seven months earlier a twenty-one-year-old woman . . .** Harriet Sherwood, "Palestinian
Deaths Raise Concern over Israeli Army Use of Live Fire," *Guardian*, January 27, 2013, www
.theguardian.com/world/2013/jan/28/palestinian-deaths-israel-army-live-fire; "MAG Corps
Closes Investigation into Killing of Lubna al-Hanash Without Indicting Soldier Who Fired or
His Commander," B'Tselem, June 29, 2014, www.btselem.org/accountability/20140629_lubna_al
_hanash_appeal_rejected.

138 **Tel Rumeida, the oldest neighborhood . . .** "Old Town of Hebron al-Khalil & Its Environs,"
United Nations Educational, Scientific, and Cultural Organization, http://whc.unesco.org/en/
tentativelists/5705/; Jeffrey R. Chadwick, "Discovering Hebron," *Biblical Archaeology Review* 31(5)
(September/October 2005).

139 **They beat him so severely . . .** "UN Experts Urge Israel to Stop Harassment of Human Rights
Activist Issa Amro," UN News Centre, August 2013, www.un.org/apps/news/story.asp?NewsID
=45615#.Veiyvbx3m2w.

CHAPTER 5: A MATTER OF HOPE

143 **"Normality is the essence . . ."** Quoted in the documentary *Inside God's Bunker*, directed by
Micha Peled (Mill Valley, CA: MXP Productions, 1994).

144 **Soldiers had come for her . . .** "UPDATE: Woman Arrested in Hebron Is Accused of Stone
Throwing by a Settler," International Solidarity Movement, May 19, 2013, http://palsolidarity.org/
2013/05/update-woman-arrested-in-hebron-is-accused-of-stone-throwing-by-a-settler/.

146 **(Footnote) "As kids we would assiduously . . ."** China Miéville, *The City & the City* (New York:
Del Rey, 2010), 70–71.

147 **Another sci-fi hero, Philip K. Dick . . .** Philip K. Dick, *The Transmigration of Timothy Archer*
(New York: Mariner Books, 2011), 63–64.

148 **H1—the part of the city governed . . .** "The Humanitarian Impact of Israeli Settlements
in Hebron City," United Nations Office for the Coordination of Humanitarian Affairs,
November 29, 2013, http://unispal.un.org/unispal.nsf/47d4e277b48d9d3685256ddc
00612265/3f1282254b7d083a85257c320056b46e?OpenDocument; "Hebron Settlements,"
Temporary International Presence in Hebron, www.tiph.org/en/About_Hebron/Hebron
_today/Settlements/.

148 (Footnote) About five hundred Jews reside permanently . . . Patrick Muller, "Occupation in Hebron," Alternative Information Center, 2004, 6, 30, www.ochaopt.org/documents/opt _prot_aic_hebron_dec_2004.pdf.

148 The Israeli military refers to such thoroughfares . . . *Soldiers' Testimonies from Hebron 2008– 2010,* Breaking the Silence, 40, www.breakingthesilence.org.il/wp-content/uploads/2011/09/ Soldiers_Testimonies_from_Hebron_2008_2010_Eng.pdf.

148 Kiryat Arba, which, with a population . . . "Localities, Their Population and Additional Information," Israel Central Bureau of Statistics, www.cbs.gov.il/reader/?MIval=%2Fpop_in _locs%2Fpop_in_locs_e.html&Name_e=QIRYAT+ARBA.

149 Noam Federman, who was arrested in 2002 . . . John Kifner, "Israel Arrests Settlers It Says Tried to Bomb Palestinians," *New York Times,* May 19, 2002, www.nytimes.com/2002/05/19/world/ israel-arrests-settlers-it-says-tried-to-bomb-palestinians.html.

149 The incident had been recorded . . . www.youtube.com/watch?v=PQSQg99r55A&feature =youtu.be.

151 on the Jewish holiday of Sukkot . . . Adiv Sterman, "Soldier Killed by Sniper's Bullet in Hebron," *Times of Israel,* September 22, 2013, www.timesofisrael.com/israeli-seriously-wounded -in-hebron-sniper-shooting/.

151 During the same period, sixteen Palestinians . . . "Fatalities Before Operation 'Cast Lead,'" B'Tselem, www.btselem.org/statistics/fatalities/before-cast-lead/by-date-of-event; "Israeli Security Force Personnel Killed by Palestinians in the West Bank, After Operation Cast Lead," B'Tselem, www.btselem.org/statistics/fatalities/after-cast-lead/by-date-of-event /westbank/israeli-security-force-personnel-killed-by-palestinians.

153 A Jew named Jacob Ezra . . . Michelle Campos, "Remembering Jewish-Arab Contact and Conflict," in *Reapproaching Borders: New Perspectives on the Study of Israel-Palestine,* ed. Sandy Sufian and Mark LeVine (Plymouth, UK: Rowman and Littlefield, 2007), 56–57.

153 the 1929 massacre, in which . . . Zertal and Eldar, *Lords of the Land,* 246.

153 (Footnote) The unrest that shook the region . . . Tom Segev, *One Palestine, Complete: Jews and Arabs Under the British Mandate,* trans. Haim Watzman (New York: Henry Holt, 2000), 327.

154 (Footnote) The plan, which was rejected . . . Phillip Mattar, ed., *Encyclopedia of the Palestinians* (New York: Facts on File, 2005), 387–89.

154 Rabbi Zvi Yehuda Kook, who would . . . Ian S. Lustick, *For the Land and the Lord: Jewish Fundamentalism in Israel* (New York: Council on Foreign Relations), 36, 91.

154 a group of Kook's former students . . . Ibid., 34; Zertal and Eldar, *Lords of the Land,* 17–21.

154 The generally accepted Israeli narrative . . . Lustick, *For the Land and the Lord,* 42.

154 Idith Zertal and . . . **Akiva Eldar, though** . . . Zertal and Eldar, *Lords of the Land,* 17–26.

155 In a Knesset hearing that summer . . . Ibid., 280, 485.

155 the Israeli government confiscated . . . Ibid., 25.

155 (Footnote) When in 1988 Levinger shot . . . Sabra Chartrand, "A Rabbi, a Slain Arab and an Inquiry," *New York Times,* January 22, 1989, www.nytimes.com/1989/01/22/world/a-rabbi-a -slain-arab-and-an-inquiry.html; "Rabbi Settler Jailed in Arab's Killing Freed," *Los Angeles Times,* August 14, 1990, http://articles.latimes.com/1990-08-14/news/mn-857_1_rabbi-moshe -levinger.

155 late one night in the spring of 1979 . . . Lara Friedman, "Hebron—Settlements in Focus," Peace Now, October 2005, http://peacenow.org.il/eng/content/hebron-settlements-focus; Khalid Amayreh, "Shuhada Street," *The Link,* Americans for Middle East Understanding, September 2010, www.ameu.org/getattachment/b8f6b14b-2be7-4b80-ab93-b643f22cfc82/ Shuhada-Street.aspx.

155 in January 1980, after a yeshiva student . . . Zertal and Eldar, *Lords of the Land,* 262–66.

155 Years later, the spokesman . . . Ibid., 260.

155 (Footnote) Hours after the shooting . . . "In Wake of Soldier's Killing, PM Orders Resettlement of Hebron House," *Times of Israel,* September 23, 2013, www.timesofisrael.com/in-wake-of -soldiers-killing-pm-orders-resettlement-of-hebron-house/.

155 In May 1980, Palestinian gunmen retaliated . . . Zertal and Eldar, *Lords of the Land*, 264–65.

156 Baruch Goldstein, another ex-Brooklynite . . . Ibid., 119–20.

157 Prime Minister Yitzhak Rabin considered uprooting . . . Ibid., 123–26.

157 sixty shops were ordered closed . . . "Ghost Town: Israel's Separation Policy and Forced Evacuation of Palestinians from the Center of Hebron," B'Tselem, May 2007, 34, www.btselem .org/download/200705_hebron_eng.pdf.

158 the use of torture at the Russian Compound . . . "Israel and Torture," *Journal of Palestine Studies* 6(4) (Summer 1977): 191–219; Serge Schmemann, "In Israel, Coercing Prisoners Is Becoming Law of the Land," *The New York Times*, May 8, 1997, www.nytimes.com/1997/05/08/world/in-israel -coercing-prisoners-is-becoming-law-of-the-land.html; Stanley Cohen and Daphna Golan, *The Interrogation of Palestinians During the Intifada: Ill-treatment, "Moderate Physical Pressure" or Torture?* (Jerusalem: B'Tselem, March 1991), www.btselem.org/download/199103_torture_eng .doc; *Torture and Ill-Treatment: Israel's Interrogation of Palestinians from the Occupied Territories*, Human Rights Watch, June 1994, www.hrw.org/reports/1994/06/01/torture-and-ill-treatment; "Ticking Bombs: Testimonies of Torture Victims in Israel," Public Committee Against Torture in Israel, May 2007, www.stoptorture.org.il/files/pcat%20new%20web%20file%20eng%20light .pdf; "Shackling as a Form of Torture and Abuse," Public Committee Against Torture in Israel, June 2009, www.stoptorture.org.il/files/eng_report.pdf.

158 Other prisoners have described similar treatment . . . Cohen and Golan, *Interrogation of Palestinians*, 29, 31, 36.

158 The position Mufid described . . . Joseph Lelyveld, "Interrogating Ourselves," *New York Times Magazine*, June 12, 2005, www.nytimes.com/2005/06/12/magazine/interrogating-ourselves.html ; "Torture & Abuse Under Interrogation," B'Tselem, January 1, 2011, www.btselem.org/torture/ special_interrogation_methods.

158 All of these practices have been legal . . . Cohen and Golan, *Interrogation of Palestinians*, 20–22; Amany Dayif, Katie Hesketh, and Jane Rice, eds., *On Torture* (Haifa: Adalah, June 2012), 41–53, www.adalah.org/uploads/oldfiles/Public/files/English/Publications/On%20Torture% 20(English).pdf.

158 (Footnote) A 1999 High Court ruling . . . Irit Ballas, "Regimes of Impunity," in *On Torture*, 42.

158 More than 1,800 businesses closed . . . "Ghost Town," B'Tselem, 14, 33.

158 By the end of 2006 . . . Ibid., 14.

160 (Footnote) The ability of local military commanders . . . Jiryis, *Arabs in Israel*, 17–18, 23–26, 53, 110.

161 the Israeli government announced . . . Barak Ravid, "Israel Advancing Plan for Some 5,000 New Homes in West Bank and East Jerusalem," *Haaretz*, October 30, 2013, www.haaretz.com/news/ diplomacy-defense/.premium-1.555373.

161 settlement construction in the West Bank . . . "Israel to Build 1,500 New Settlement Homes in East Jerusalem," *Al Jazeera America*, October 30, 2013, http://america.aljazeera.com/articles/2013/ 10/30/israel-to-build-1500newsettlementhomesineastjerusalem.html.

161 Saeb Erekat and Mohammed Shtayyeh, had . . . "PLO Negotiators Present Resignation to Abbas, Meeting to Follow," Ma'an News Agency, October 31, 2013, www.maannews.com/Content.aspx ?id=643258.

161 The next day Erekat denied . . . Elior Levy, "PA's Erekat: I Didn't Resign," *Ynet News*, November 1, 2013, www.ynetnews.com/articles/0,7340,L-4448182,00.html.

162 (Footnote) The official unemployment rate . . . "The Labour Force Survey Results Fourth Quarter," Palestine Central Bureau of Statistics, December 2, 2014, www.pcbs.gov.ps/site/512/ default.aspx?tabID=512&lang=en&ItemID=1022&mid=3171&wversion=Staging.

163 "How can one emerge unharmed . . ." Juan Goytisolo, *Landscapes of War: From Sarajevo to Chechnya*, trans. Peter Bush (San Francisco: City Lights Books, 2000), 142.

165 During the first three years . . . "Ghost Town," B'Tselem, 18.

166 After the Goldstein massacre . . . Amy Wilentz, "Battling over Abraham," *New Yorker*, September 16, 1996, www.newyorker.com/magazine/1996/09/16/battling-over-abraham.

167 I found a link to a video . . . "Video: Settler Tries to Take Down Palestinian Flag from Roof of Hebron Man," B'Tselem, March 12, 2014, www.btselem.org/press_releases/20140312_soldiers _demand_removal_of_flag_in_hebron.

169 (Footnote) Transportation to West Bank settlements . . . Anna Lekas Miller, "West Bank Buses Only the Latest in Israel's Segregated Public Transport," *Daily Beast*, March 4, 2013, www.thedailybeast.com/articles/2013/03/04/buses-only-the-latest-in-israel-s-segretated-public -transport.html.

169 In 1983, the IDF seized the compound . . . Dan Izenberg, "Peace Now Petitions Against Civilians in Hebron Army Base," *Jerusalem Post,* July 30, 2008, www.jpost.com/Israel/Peace-Now -petitions-against-civilians-at-Hebron-army-base.

169 that there is no archaeological evidence . . . Israel Finkelstein and Neil Asher Silberman, *The Bible Unearthed: Archaeology's New Vision of Ancient Israel and the Origin of Its Sacred Texts* (New York: Simon and Schuster, 2002), 23, 35–46, 124, 128, 132–33, 140–43, 321, 323.

172 It was new then . . . Charles Levinson, "Israel Allows Journalists to Tour Ofer Prison," *Wall Street Journal*, April 16, 2013, http://blogs.wsj.com/middleeast/2013/04/16/israel-allows -journalists-to-tour-ofer-prison/.

173 The chief military prosecutor . . . Amira Hass, "The Unbearable Burden of Checking Data," *Haaretz*, December 23, 2013, www.haaretz.com/news/features/.premium-1.564880.

174 Rabbi Shlomo Shapira, shot . . . James Bennet, "A Holiday in Hebron, Just for Jews, but Death Attends," *New York Times,* September 28, 2002, www.nytimes.com/2002/09/28/world/a-holiday -in-hebron-just-for-jews-but-death-attends.html.

174 (Footnote) Over the course of the Second Intifada . . . "Ghost Town," B'Tselem, 11.

175 In January 2003, the army closed . . . Joel Greenberg, "Two Hebron Colleges Closed," *Chicago Tribune*, January 16, 2003, http://articles.chicagotribune.com/2003-01-16/news/0301160428 _1_hebron-university-israeli-soldiers-shot-west-bank.

177 The previous September, the PA . . . "Anti-Fayyad Protests Spread Across West Bank," *Al-Akhbar English*, September 11, 2012, http://english.al-akhbar.com/node/11975.

178 *The New York Times's* Thomas Friedman . . . Thomas L. Friedman, "Goodbye to All That," *New York Times*, April 23, 2013, www.nytimes.com/2013/04/24/opinion/friedman-goodbye -to-all-that.html.

178 On September 6, demonstrators in Hebron . . . "Fayyad 'Ready to Resign,'" Ma'an News Agency, September 6, 2012, www.maannews.com/Content.aspx?id=517945.

178 The march ended with protesters . . . "Anti-Fayyad Protests Spread Across West Bank," *Al-Akhbar English.*

178 he called off the price hike . . . Harriet Sherwood, "Protests Force Palestinian PM to Declare Emergency Economic Package," *Guardian*, September 11, 2012, www.theguardian .com/world/2012/sep/11/west-bank-protests-escalate-violence.

180 nine Israeli soldiers and three members . . . Christine Spolar, "Gunmen Targeted Troops, Not Settlers," *Chicago Tribune*, November 17, 2002, http://articles.chicagotribune.com/2002-11-17/ news/0211170293_1_israeli-soldiers-and-police-settlers-kiryat-arba; Amos Harel, "Analysis: The Attack in Hebron Was Not a 'Massacre,'" *Haaretz*, November 17, 2002, www.haaretz.com/ news/analysis-the-attack-in-hebron-was-not-a-massacre-1.28114.

180 Immediately after the skirmish . . . Spolar, "Gunmen Targeted Troops"; "Ghost Town," B'Tselem, 18.

180 and announced plans to demolish . . . Esther Zandberg, "Pernicious Promenade," *Haaretz*, December 12, 2002, www.haaretz.com/life/arts-leisure/pernicious-promenade-1.25658.

180 (Footnote) The Israeli High Court ultimately approved . . . Yuval Yoaz, "High Court Gives IDF Go-Ahead to Demolish Two Hebron Houses," *Haaretz,* March 5, 2004, www.haaretz.com/ print-edition/news/high-court-gives-idf-go-ahead-to-demolish-two-hebron-houses-1.115905.

180 (Footnote) In the end, three were leveled . . . "Progress Report on the Protection of the Palestinian Cultural and Natural Heritage," UNESCO World Heritage Committee, Durban, South Africa, July 2005, 5, http://whc.unesco.org/archive/2005/whc05-29com-11De.pdf.

181 **talked to a man named Jamal Abu Seifan** . . . Abu Seifan's account of the events of that day was also recorded in a sworn statement taken by the human rights organization Al-Haq and published in the report "Israel's Implementation of the International Covenant on Civil and Political Rights in Occupied Palestinian Territory," Al-Haq, August 9, 2009, 40–43, www.alhaq .org/attachments/article/251/Al-HaqAlternative-11-8-09.pdf.

181 **(Footnote) Israeli authorities initially found** . . . Tovah Lazaroff, "HJC Authenticates Jewish Purchase of Beit HaShalom in Hebron," *Jerusalem Post*, March 11, 2014, www.jpost.com/ National-News/HJC-authenticates-Jewish-purchase-of-Beit-HaShalom-in-Hebron-345049; Chaim Levinson, "Settlers Return to Disputed Hebron Building," *Haaretz*, April 13, 2014, www.haaretz.com/news/diplomacy-defense/.premium-1.585446.

182 **a young man named Anas Fouad al-Atrash** . . . "Israeli Forces Kill 2nd Palestinian," Ma'an News Agency, November 8, 2013, www.maannews.com/Content.aspx?id=645388.

182 **Earlier that same evening, another** . . . Michael Schaeffer Omer-Man, "2013 Was a Deadly Year in Israel-Palestine," +972, December 31, 2013, http://972mag.com/2013-was-a-deadly-year-in-israel -palestine/84728/.

182 **(Footnote) Haaretz, the newspaper of the Israeli liberal left** . . . Chaim Levinson and Gili Cohen, "Palestinian Firebomb Attack Wounds Israeli Mother, Daughter," *Haaretz*, November 8, 2013, www.haaretz.com/news/diplomacy-defense/.premium-1.556996.

182 **He had been on his way home** . . . Jessica Purkiss, "Israel Steps Up Its Assassination Policy in West Bank," *Middle East Monitor Memo*, December 19, 2013, www.middleeastmonitor.com/articles/ middle-east/8901-israel-steps-up-its-assassination-policy-in-west-bank.

183 **(Footnote) Representatives of the Israeli Military Advocate General Corps** . . . "Follow-up: Military Police and MAG Corps Investigations of Civilian Palestinian Fatalities in West Bank Since New Policy Imposed," B'Tselem, May 26, 2014, www.btselem.org/accountability/military _police_investigations_followup.

CHAPTER 6: MUCH LESS A COUNTRY

185 **"Still, that was just the city . . ."** Miéville, *The City & the City*, 22.

190 **By morning, Israeli newspapers had published** . . . Yaakov Lappin, "Border Police Shoot Dead Palestinian Who Attempted Knife Attack," *Jerusalem Post*, November 8, 2013, www.jpost.com/ Defense/Border-Police-shoot-kill-knife-brandishing-Palestinian-at-checkpoint-near -Jerusalem-330979.

191 **Kook was the first Ashkenazi** . . . Lustick, *For the Land and the Lord*, 25–37; Zertal and Eldar, *Lords of the Land*, 190–202.

191 **(Footnote) As early as 1920, he envisioned Israel** . . . Zertal and Eldar, *Lords of the Land,* 193.

191 **sacralizing every act of the Israeli state** . . . Ibid., 200.

191 **He was killed six years later** . . . "Tensions in Hebron Escalate After Murder of Settler Rabbi," Jewish Telegraphic Agency, August 24, 1998, www.jta.org/1998/08/24/life-religion/features/ tensions-in-hebron-escalate-after-murder-of-settler-rabbi.

192 **the old vegetable market on Shuhada Street** . . . Rebecca Stoil, "Hebron Eviction Orders Spur Unrest," *Jerusalem Post*, January 3, 2006, www.jpost.com/Israel/Hebron-eviction-orders -spur-unrest.

192 **The police dragged her out** . . . Rebecca Stoil, "In the Schlissels' Living Room," *Jerusalem Post*, January 4, 2006, www.jpost.com/Israel/In-the-Schlissels-living-room.

192 **The eviction, she told Haaretz at the time** . . . Nadav Shragai, "In Hebron, a Decision Made for the Greater Good," *Haaretz*, January 31, 2006, www.haaretz.com/print-edition/news/in-hebron -a-decision-made-for-the-greater-good-1.178872.

192 **a house a few blocks away** . . . Yaakov Katz and Tovah Lazaroff, "Only Token Resistance Offered as Police Evict Beit Shapira Families," *Jerusalem Post*, May 7, 2006, www.jpost.com/ Israel/Only-token-resistance-offered-as-police-evict-Beit-Shapira-families.

192 **The state ruled that the documents** . . . Dan Izenberg, "Hearing on Hebron's Disputed 'Beit Hashalom' to Take Place in Court Today," *Jerusalem Post*, October 29, 2008, www.jpost.com/

Israel/Hearing-on-Hebrons-disputed-Beit-Hashalom-to-take-place-in-court-today; Amos
Harel, "Company That Bought Hebron House Already in Fraud Probe," *Haaretz,* April 17, 2008,
www.haaretz.com/print-edition/news/company-that-bought-hebron-house-already-in-fraud
-probe-1.218282.

192 **that May Schlissel was again dragged off** . . . Efrat Weiss, "Forces Clear Hebron Home," *Ynet
News,* May 7, 2006, www.ynetnews.com/articles/0,7340,L-3247788,00.html.

192 **settler youth threw rocks and Molotov cocktails** . . . Katz and Lazaroff, "Only Token Resistance
Offered as Police Evict Beit Shapira Families."

192 **an "absent-present, not a past event"** . . . Zertal and Eldar, *Lords of the Land,* 253.

193 **Jews and Arabs lived in relative harmony** . . . Avigdor Levy, ed., *Jews, Turks, Ottomans: A Shared
History, Fifteenth Through the Twentieth Century* (Syracuse, NY: Syracuse University Press, 2002);
Michelle Campos, *Ottoman Brothers: Muslims, Christians, and Jews in Early-Twentieth Century
Palestine* (Palo Alto, CA: Stanford University Press, 2011).

193 **In his official report to the British Parliament** . . . Sir Walter Shaw, *Report of the Commission on
the Palestine Disturbances of August, 1929* (London: H. M. Stationery Office, 1930), 150–51.

193 **Such empirical subtleties** . . . Zertal and Eldar, *Lords of the Land,* 249.

193 **(Footnote) most of the Jews who survived** . . . David T. Zabecki, "Hebron Massacre," in Spencer
C. Tucker, ed., *Encyclopedia of the Arab-Israeli Conflict: A Political, Social, and Military History*
(Santa Barbara, CA: ABC-CLIO, 2008), 437; Segev, *One Palestine,* 325–26.

194 **the "beloved and also rejected"** . . . Zertal and Eldar, *Lords of the Land,* 248.

195 **the ancient stone walls unearthed** . . . Yonathan Mizrachi, "Tel Rumeida: Hebron's Archaeological
Park," *Emek Shaveh,* November 2014, http://alt-arch.org/en/wp-content/uploads/2014/11/12-Tel
-Rumeida-Eng-Web.pdf.

195 **(Footnote) The artifacts have been dated** . . . Israel Finkelstein and Neil Asher Silberman, *David
and Solomon: In Search of the Bible's Sacred Kings and the Roots of the Western Tradition* (New
York: Free Press, 2006), 58, 94–98, 267–74.

197 **Hammond was forced to abandon his project** . . . Jeffrey R. Chadwick, "Discovering Hebron,"
Biblical Archaeology Review 31(5) (September/October 2005).

197 **(Footnote) I am thinking of Aimé Césaire's consideration** . . . Aimé Césaire, *Discourse on
Colonialism,* trans. Joan Pinkham (New York: Monthly Review Press, 2000), 35.

198 **Marzel, who was quite well known** . . . "Cabinet Communique," Israel Ministry of Foreign
Affairs, March 13, 1994, http://mfa.gov.il/MFA/AboutIsrael/State/Law/Pages/Cabinet
%20Communique%20-%20March%2013-%201994.aspx; "Israel: Article Profiles Kakh Activist,
Knesset Election Candidate Barukh Marzel," Foreign Broadcast Information Service Report,
American Consulate, Jerusalem, March 6, 2003, http://dc.indymedia.org/media/all/display/31322/
index.php?limit_start=81.

198 **and was a frequent and vocal presence** . . . Shira Rubin, "Residents, Right-Wing Activists, Protest
Tel Aviv Presence of Migrant Workers," *Haaretz,* May 23, 2012, www.haaretz.com/news/israel/
residents-right-wing-activists-protest-tel-aviv-presence-of-migrant-workers.premium-1.432015;
"Marzel Declares 'Holy War' Against Gay Parade," *Ynet News,* September 18, 2006, www
.ynetnews.com/articles/0,7340,L-3305417,00.html.

198 **He once brought three donkeys** . . . Hezki Ezra and Gil Ronen, "Hareidi Protest Against 'Gay'
Parade," *Arutz Sheva,* August 2, 2012, www.israelnationalnews.com/News/News.aspx/158544#
.Ves84Lx3m2w.

199 **(Footnote) In 2011, Marzel was spotted** . . . Brendan Work, "Israeli Settlers Harass
Released Prisoners, Threaten Them with Death," *Electronic Intifada,* December 1, 2011,
https://electronicintifada.net/content/israeli-settlers-harass-released-prisoners-threaten-them
-death/10645.

203 **(Footnote) During the Arab Revolt** . . . Segev, *One Palestine,* 421.

208 **The Internet overflows with accounts** . . . "Anat Cohen Attacks ISM Volunteers," YouTube,
March 30, 2012, www.youtube.com/watch?v=FF3WC663LpE; "Israeli Settler Anat Cohen

Attacks Human Rights Observer in Hebron," YouTube, September 13, 2013, www.youtube.com/
watch?v=Xid0Q6H1OFY; "Woman Settler Attacks Two Female International Activists in
Hebron," Alternative Information Center, March 30, 2013; "Settlers Attack Internationals
Accompanying School Children on Shuhada Street," International Solidary Movement, March
28, 2012, http://palsolidarity.org/2012/03/settlers-attack-internationals-accompanying-school
-children-on-shuhada-street/; "Caught on Tape: Drunk Settlers in Al Khalil Assault Two
International Women," International Solidarity Movement, March 11, 2012, http://palsolidarity
.org/2012/03/caught-on-tape-drunk-settlers-in-al-khalil-assault-two-international-women-israeli
-military-admits-special-relationship-with-violent-settlers; "Complaint Filed with US Consulate
by Cliff Kindy, 22 March, 1997," Christian Peacemaker Teams, www.al-bushra.org/peaceteam/
consul.htm.

208 Her father, Moshe Zar . . . Samantha M. Shapiro, "The Unsettlers," *The New York Times
Magazine*, February 16, 2003, www.nytimes.com/2003/02/16/magazine/the-unsettlers.html.

208 (Footnote) Zar disowned Sharon after . . . Nadav Shragai, "Ramat Gilad Residents Prefer Their
Mobile Homes to Luxury Homes," *Haaretz*, July 6, 2006, www.haaretz.com/print-edition/news/
ramat-gilad-residents-prefer-their-mobile-homes-to-luxury-homes-1.189612. Nadav Shragai and
Amnon Barzilai, "Three Killed; Settlers Demand Revenge," *Haaretz,* May 30, 2001, www
.unitedjerusalem.org/index2.asp?id=47444&Date=5/31/2001.

209 (Footnote) One put an ax through his skull . . . Nadav Shragai, "Zar Patriach Has Had Brushes
with Death," *Haaretz,* October 21, 2002, www.haaretz.com/print-edition/news/zar-patriach-has
-had-brushes-with-death-1.30821.

209 the Jewish Underground, a right-wing terrorist group . . . Zertal and Eldar, *Lords of the
Land,* 76–95.

209 (Footnote) "Nearly all" of the twenty-six men . . . "Report of the Special Committee to
Investigate Israeli Practices Affecting the Human Rights of the Population of the Occupied
Territories," United Nations, July 17, 1985, http://unispal.un.org/UNISPAL.NSF/0/
B7A72309FFEA6F1485256A68004F0024.

209 He was convicted for his role . . . Nadav Shragai and Amnon Barzilai, "Three Killed: Settlers
Demand Revenge," *Haaretz*, May 30, 2001.

209 Zar served just four months . . . "Three Jewish Terrorists Get Life, 12 Others Receive Light
Terms," *Los Angeles Times*, July 22, 1985, http://articles.latimes.com/1985-07-22/news/mn-6076
_1_life-sentences.

209 Moshe Zar's son Gilad . . . Shragai and Barzilai, "Three Killed."

209 Three years later, when the American . . . Jeffrey Goldberg, "Among the Settlers," *New Yorker*,
May 31, 2004, www.newyorker.com/magazine/2004/05/31/among-the-settlers.

216 David Wilder had protested . . . Tovah Lazaroff, "Police to Three Hebron Families: Leave
Newly Bought Building," *Jerusalem Post*, May 1, 2006, www.jpost.com/Israel/Police-to-3-Hebron
-families-Leave-newly-bought-building.

216 They had a bill of sale . . . David Wilder, "The Eternal Flame of Hebron," *The Hebron Blog*,
August 8, 2007, http://davidwilder.blogspot.com/2007/08/eternal-flame-of-hebron.html.

217 The Bajayos were one of the oldest . . . Haya Gavish, *Unwitting Zionists: The Jewish Community
of Zakho in Iraqi Kurdistan* (Detroit: Wayne State University Press, 2010), 98.

218 "Where is the homeland" . . . **"and where the exile?"** . . . Edward Platt, *City of Abraham: History,
Myth and Memory: A Journey Through Hebron* (New York: Pan Macmillan, 2012).

218 "This hatred isn't a fateful decree . . ." *Matzpen*, directed by Eran Torbiner (Tel Aviv: Alma
Films, 2003).

220 "The permit was revoked," he wrote . . . Guy Inbar, Coordination of Government Activities in
the Territories spokesman, e-mail to author, November 20, 2013.

222 Twice in the year that followed . . . Khaled Abu Toameh and Tovah Lazaroff, "Palestinians
Throw Molotov Cocktail at IDF Checkpoint in Hebron," *Jerusalem Post,* August 22, 2014, www
.jpost.com/Defense/Palestinians-thrown-Molotov-cocktail-lands-on-Hebron-checkpoint-371970;

"Israeli Military Post in Central Hebron Attacked, Destroyed," Ma'an News Agency, November 21, 2014, www.maannews.com/Content.aspx?id=741641.

PART THREE: LOW CLOUDS

CHAPTER 7: SNOW

225 **"And yet joy was all around me"** . . . Jean Genet, *Prisoner of Love*, trans. Barbara Bray (New York: New York Review Books, 2003), 242.

227 **In 2006, after PA police killed** . . . Silvia Pasquetti, "The Reconfiguration of the Palestinian National Question," in *Political Power and Social Theory,* Volume 23, ed. Julian Go (Bingley, UK: Emerald Group Publishing, 2012), 119.

228 **shot in the back** . . . "Teen Killed by Israeli Sniper Posed 'No Threat' to Soldiers," Ma'an News Agency, January 6, 2014, www.maannews.com/Content.aspx?id=662990.

229 **In some respects at least, the circumstances** . . . "Israel: No Evidence That Boy Killed by Soldiers Posed Any Threat," Human Rights Watch, January 5, 2014, www.hrw.org/news/2014/01/04/ israel-no-evidence-boy-killed-soldiers-posed-any-threat; "Israeli Soldiers Kill Palestinian Boy from Jalazoun Refugee Camp," Defense for Children International, Palestine, December 12, 2013, www.dci-palestine.org/israeli_soldiers_kill_palestinian_boy_from_jalazoun_refugee_camp.

229 **The boy's friends said they had been playing** . . . Amira Hass, "Accounts of Palestinian Teen's Death Differ," *Haaretz*, December 8, 2013, www.haaretz.com/news/israel/.premium-1.562422.

229 **The soldiers shot him down** . . . Jack Khoury and Gili Cohen, "Palestinians Say Teen Killed by Israeli Army in West Bank," *Haaretz*, December 7, 2013, www.haaretz.com/news/diplomacy -defense/.premium-1.562258.

229 **Another witness claimed to have seen** . . . Amira Hass, "Accounts of Palestinian Teen's Death Differ."

233 **Kerry delivered a speech at the Saban Forum** . . . "Remarks at the Saban Forum," U.S. Department of State, December 7, 2013; www.state.gov/secretary/remarks/2013/12/218506.htm.

233 **At the same conference, Avigdor Lieberman** . . . "Liberman: Kerry Won't Achieve Deal in Current Peace Talks, Must Temper Expectations," *Jerusalem Post*, December 7, 2013, www.jpost .com/Diplomacy-and-Politics/Liberman-Kerry-wont-achieve-deal-in-current-peace-talks-must -temper-expectations-334245.

233 **He wouldn't admit it for another** . . . Birnbaum and Tibon, "The Explosive, Inside Story"; Michael R. Gordon and Jodi Rudoren, "Kerry to Press for 'Framework' Accord to Keep Mideast Peace Effort Moving," *New York Times*, December 31, 2013.

233 **Over the next few weeks, Netanyahu** . . . Michal Shmulovich, "Netanyahu Won't Back Down on Demand That IDF Stay in Jordan Valley," *Times of Israel,* February 8, 2014, www.timesofisrael .com/netanyahu-wont-back-down-on-demand-that-idf-stay-in-jordan-valley/; Barak Ravid, "Netanyahu: Israel Will Not Evacuate Hebron, Beit El as Part of Peace Deal," *Haaretz*, January 6, 2014, www.haaretz.com/news/diplomacy-defense/.premium-1.567343; Barak Ravid, "Netanyahu Rejects Inclusion of Jerusalem in Kerry's Framework Deal," *Haaretz*, January 10, 2014, www .haaretz.com/news/diplomacy-defense/.premium-1.567877.

234 **Kerry had enlisted General John Allen** . . . Birnbaum and Tibon, "The Explosive, Inside Story"; Barak Ravid, "U.S. Security Proposal Includes Israeli Military Presence in Jordan Valley," *Haaretz,* December 7, 2013, www.haaretz.com/news/diplomacy-defense/.premium-1.562242.

234 **Abbas, reportedly, was "boiling mad"** . . . Barak Ravid and Jack Khoury, "Abbas Raises Concerns to Obama on Kerry's Security Proposal," *Haaretz,* December 18, 2013, www.haaretz .com/news/diplomacy-defense/.premium-1.564290.

234 **The secretary, journalist Allison Deger observed** . . . Allison Deger, "Obama and Kerry Drop Talk of Palestinian State for 'State Institutions' and 'Transition,'" *Mondoweiss*, December 9, 2013, http://mondoweiss.net/2013/12/palestinian-institutions-transition.

234 Defense Minister Moshe Ya'alon would complain . . . Simon Shiffer, "Ya'alon: Kerry Should Win His Nobel and Leave Us Alone," *Ynet News*, January 14, 2014, www.ynetnews.com/articles/ 0,7340,L-4476582,00.html; Birnbaum and Tibon, "The Explosive, Inside Story."

235 an elite squad of Israeli paratroopers . . . "Israeli Soldiers Raid Qalqiliya, Kill Palestinian 'in Cold Blood,'" Ma'an News Agency, December 19, 2013, www.maannews.com/Content .aspx?id=658296; "Palestinians Killed in Israeli Arrest Raids," Al Jazeera, December 19, 2013, www.aljazeera.com/news/middleeast/2013/12/palestinians-killed-israeli-arrest-raids -20131219614950434.html; Gili Cohen and Jack Khoury, "Israeli Force Kills Palestinian During Military Operation in West Bank," *Haaretz*, December 19, 2013, www.haaretz.com/news/ diplomacy-defense/.premium-1.564334.

235 Two months earlier, the army had killed . . . "Israeli Forces Kill Palestinian Bomb Suspect in West Bank Shoot-Out," Al Jazeera, October 22, 2013, http://america.aljazeera.com/articles/2013/ 10/22/israeli-forces-killpalestinianmanaftershootout.html; Yoav Zitun and Elior Levy, "IDF Says Terrorist Killed in Cave 'Threatened Forces for Months,'" *Ynet News*, October 22, 2013, www .ynetnews.com/articles/0,7340,L-4444100,00.html.

235 The following month, Israeli special forces . . . Tzvi Ben-Gedalyahu, "IDF Kills Three Salafist Terrorists in Heart of Judea and Samaria," *Jewish Press*, November 26, 2013, www.jewishpress .com/news/idf-kills-two-pa-salafist-terrorists-in-heart-of-judea-and-samaria/2013/11/26/.

235 According to Palestinian witnesses . . . "In 2 Crimes of Extra-Judicial Execution and Excessive Use of Force, Israeli Forces Kill 3 Palestinian Civilians in Yatta, South of Hebron," Palestinian Centre for Human Rights, November 28, 2013, www.pchrgaza.org/portal/en/index.php?option =com_content&id=9955:in-2-crimes-of-extra-judicial-execution-and-excessive-use-of-force-israeli -forces-kill-3-palestinian-civilians-in-yatta-south-of-hebron; "Five Palestinians Killed in the West Bank in Three Days," *Palestine Monitor*, November 30, 2013, www.palestinemonitor.org/details .php?id=x2lvh5a5714y2umb9r8t6.

236 Targeted killings—by missiles fired . . . "Palestinians Who Were the Object of a Targeted Killing in the Gaza Strip, After Operation Cast Lead," B'Tselem, www.btselem.org/statistics/ fatalities/after-cast-lead/by-date-of-event/gaza/palestinians-who-were-the-object-of-a-targeted -killing; "Palestinians Who Were the Object of a Targeted Killing in the Gaza Strip, Before Operation 'Cast Lead,'" B'Tselem, www.btselem.org/statistics/fatalities/before-cast-lead/ by-date-of-event/gaza/palestinians-who-were-the-object-of-a-targeted-killing; "Palestinians Killed During the Course of a Targeted Killing in the West Bank, Before Operation 'Cast Lead,'" B'Tselem, www.btselem.org/statistics/fatalities/before-cast-lead/by-date-of-event/ westbank/palestinians-killed-during-the-course-of-a-targeted-killing; "Palestinians Killed During the Course of a Targeted Killing in the West Bank, During Operation Cast Lead," B'Tselem, www.btselem.org/statistics/fatalities/during-cast-lead/by-date-of-event/westbank/ palestinians-killed-during-the-course-of-a-targeted-killing; "Palestinians Who Were the Object of a Targeted Killing in the West Bank, After Operation Cast Lead," B'Tselem, www.btselem .org/statistics/fatalities/after-cast-lead/by-date-of-event/westbank/palestinians-who-were -the-object-of-a-targeted-killing.

236 During the Second Intifada, Israeli special units . . . "Palestinians Killed During the Course of a Targeted Killing in the West Bank, Before Operation 'Cast Lead,'" B'Tselem; Mustafa Barghouti, "Targeted Killing Won't Bring Peace," *New York Times*, June 8, 2007, www.nytimes .com/2007/06/08/opinion/08iht-edbarghouti.1.6056658.html?_r=0.

236 The hummus shop closest to the apartment . . . Sam Bahour, "Another Assassination in Ramallah's City Center," *Electronic Intifada*, May 29, 2007, https://electronicintifada.net /content/another-assassination-ramallahs-city-center/6963.

236 Early in January Netanyahu revealed . . . Cabinet Communiqué, Israel Ministry of Foreign Affairs, January 5, 2014, http://mfa.gov.il/MFA/PressRoom/2014/Pages/Cabinet-communique -5-Jan-2014.aspx.

237 It was a drum he had been beating . . . Tovah Lazaroff, "Netanyahu to Kerry: Palestinian Incitement Undermines Peace," *Jerusalem Post*, August 10, 2013, www.jpost.com/Diplomacy

-and-Politics/Netanyahu-tells-Kerry-Palestinians-incitement-undermines-peace-322647; Stuart Winer, "Israel Blames Terror Surge on Palestinian Incitement," *Times of Israel*, December 25, 2013, www.timesofisrael.com/israel-blames-violence-on-palestinian-incitement/.

237 **When Netanyahu's office . . .** "Israelis Document Incitement by the Palestinian Authority," *New York Times*, January 6, 2014.

237 **an accompanying article repeated . . .** Jodi Rudoren, "Israeli Official Points to 'Incitement' by Palestinians," *New York Times*, January 6, 2014, www.nytimes.com/interactive/2014/01/06/world/middleeast/07israel-doc.html.

238 **(Footnote) "And in its wedge of shadow . . ."** China Miéville, "Exit Strategy," *Guernica*, November 1, 2013, www.guernicamag.com/features/exit-strategy/.

238 **earlier that day, Israeli warplanes . . .** "Israel Airstrikes in Gaza Kill Toddler amid Escalating Violence," Al Jazeera, December 24, 2013, http://america.aljazeera.com/articles/2013/12/24/israel-launches-assaultongazafollowingdeathofisraelinearborder.html.

238 **(Footnote) Five days later, in apparent retaliation . . .** Shirly Seidler, "Family of Slain Defense Ministry Employee: Israel Doesn't Care About a Bedouin Boy," *Haaretz*, December 24, 2014, www.haaretz.com/news/israel/.premium-1.565236.

238 **(Footnote) The girl was playing in the courtyard . . .** "Gaza Lays to Rest 3-Year-Old Palestinian Girl Killed by Israeli Strike," Ma'an News Agency, December 25, 2013, www.maannews.com/Content.aspx?id=660172.

238 **And IDF bulldozers, accompanied . . .** "UNRWA Condemns Christmas Eve Demolitions in the West Bank and Calls on Israel to Respect International Law," Official Statement, United Nations Relief and Works Agency, December 26, 2013, www.unrwa.org/newsroom/official-statements/unrwa-condemns-christmas-eve-demolitions-west-bank-and-calls-israel; "Christmas Eve Demolitions Leave More than 60 Homeless," *Palestine Monitor*, December 31, 2013, http://palestinemonitor.org/details.php?id=s69zwca6013y2n1o5qoo8.

240 **"Those who enter jail in our country" . . .** Emile Habiby, *The Secret Life of Saeed the Pessoptimist*, trans. Salma K. Jayyusi and Trevor LeGassick (Northampton, MA: Interlink Books, 2003), 134.

240 **Forty percent of Palestinian males . . .** "General Briefing: Palestinian Political Prisoners in Israeli Prisons," Addameer Prisoner Support and Human Rights Association, January 2014, 4, www.addameer.org/userfiles/file/Palestinian%20Political%20Prisoners%20in%20Israeli%20Prisons%20(General%20Briefing%20January%202014).pdf.

244–45 **one of Ofra's founders had gone . . .** Zertal and Eldar, *Lords of the Land*, 33, 81–87.

245 **(Footnote) "It was my right to participate . . ."** Ibid., 82.

245 **(Footnote) He was sentenced to seven years . . .** Chaim Levinson, "Building a Palestinian-Free Kingdom," *Haaretz*, September 28, 2011, www.haaretz.com/weekend/week-s-end/building-a-palestinian-free-kingdom-1.387179.

245 **Eli alone covered six adjacent peaks . . .** Jodi Rudoren and Jeremy Ashkenas, "Netanyahu and the Settlements," *New York Times,* March 12, 2015, www.nytimes.com/interactive/2015/03/12/world/middleeast/netanyahu-west-bank-settlements-israel-election.html.

245 **"No one today doubts . . ."** David Grossman, *The Yellow Wind*, trans. Haim Watzman (New York: Picador, 2002), 43.

INTERLUDE: THE HUMILIATION MACHINE

250 **Until 2000, there was no checkpoint . . .** Helga Tawil-Souri, "Qalandia Checkpoint: The Historical Geography of a Non-Place," *Jerusalem Quarterly* 42 (summer 2010): 30.

251 **the constant reinforcement of "the radical contingency" . . .** "Spatial Collisions and Discordant Temporalities: Everyday Life Between Camp and Checkpoint," *International Journal of Urban and Regional Research* 35(2) (March 2011): 453–61.

251 **Except that military engineers . . .** Weizman, *Hollow Land*, 151.

252 **(Footnote) "What checkpoints reinforce," the scholar Helga Tawil-Souri writes** . . . Helga Tawil-Souri, "Qalandia Checkpoint," 41.

253 **(Footnote) Qalandia was once primarily associated** . . . Ibid., 26.

253 **(Footnote) which would become the scene** . . . Ilan Pappe, *The Ethnic Cleansing of Palestine* (Oxford, UK: One World Publications, 2006), 166–69.

CHAPTER 8: POKER

255 **"Oh, there is so much less truth . . ."** Samuel R. Delany, *Dhalgren* (Middletown, CT: Wesleyan University Press, 1996), 470.

255 **This one was called 'Ein Hijleh** . . . Jessica Purkiss, "Ein Hijleh: A Symbol of Resistance and Hope," *Middle East Monitor*, February 11, 2014, www.middleeastmonitor.com/articles/middle-east/9693-ein-hiljeh-a-symbol-of-resistance-and-hope.

256 **They surrounded the home** . . . Amira Hass, "Israeli Soldier's Needless Killing of Palestinian Activist," *Haaretz*, March 3, 2014, www.haaretz.com/news/diplomacy-defense/.premium-1.577477; Adam Wolf, "Autopsy of a State Crime," *Free Arabs*, March 1, 2014, www.freearabs.com/index.php/politics/69-stories/1153-jb-span-israel-jb-span-autopsy-of-a-state-crime.

256 **A week and a half later, six Palestinians** . . . Allison Deger, "Six Palestinians Killed in 24 Hours by Israeli Forces," *Mondoweiss*, March 11, 2014, http://mondoweiss.net/2014/03/palestinians-israeli-forces.

256 **an eighteen-year-old university student** . . . Jessica Purkiss, "A Whole System of Deception," *Middle East Monitor*, April 1, 2014, www.middleeastmonitor.com/articles/middle-east/10647-a-whole-system-of-deception; Yaakov Lappin, "IDF Soldier Shoots Dead Palestinian Rock Thrower," *Jerusalem Post*, March 10, 2014, www.jpost.com/Diplomacy-and-Politics/IDF-soldier-shoots-dead-Palestinian-rock-thrower-344943.

256 **Raed Zeiter, a Palestinian with** . . . Gili Cohen and Jack Khoury, "Jordanian Judge Ran Toward Soldier Screaming 'Allah Hu Akbar,' Israeli Probe Reveals," *Haaretz*, March 11, 2014, www.haaretz.com/news/diplomacy-defense/.premium-1.579084; Omar Obeidat, "Eyewitness Says Israeli Army Lying, Judge Did Not Try to Seize Soldier's Gun," *Jordan Times*, March 11, 2014, www.jordantimes.com/news/local/eyewitness-says-israeli-army-lying-judge-did-not-try-to-seize-soldier%E2%80%99s-gun; "Al-Haq Announces Investigation Results Regarding the Killing of Judge Zuaiter," Al-Haq, April 10, 2014, www.alhaq.org/advocacy/topics/right-to-life-and-body-integrity/795-al-haq-announces-investigation-results-regarding-the-killing-of-judge-zuaiter.

256 **No official explanation was given** . . . Purkiss, "A Whole System of Deception"; Saed Bannoura, "Palestinian Killed by Army Fire Near Tulkarem," International Middle East Media Center, March 11, 2014, www.imemc.org/article/67220.

256 **Nine days went by without a killing** . . . Amira Hass, "Otherwise Occupied: An Open Letter to Soldier X, Who Shot and Killed a 14-Year-Old," *Haaretz*, March 23, 2014, www.haaretz.com/opinion/.premium-1.581532; Gideon Levy and Alex Levac, "'It Was Nothing Personal,' Bereaved Palestinian Father Told," *Haaretz*, April 4, 2014, www.haaretz.com/weekend/twilight-zone/.premium-1.583667; "Update: Israeli Forces Kill Palestinian Teen in Southern West Bank," Defense for Children International Palestine, July 11, 2014, www.dci-palestine.org/update_israeli_forces_kill_palestinian_teen_in_southern_west_bank.

257 **Three more days passed** . . . "Israeli Forces Shoot Dead 3 Palestinians in Jenin Refugee Camp," Ma'an News Agency, March 22, 2014, www.maannews.com/Content.aspx?id=683555; Gideon Levy, "The Story Behind the Wanted Hamas Man in Jenin," *Haaretz*, March 23, 2014, www.haaretz.com/news/diplomacy-defense/1.581425.

257 **New numbers came out** . . . "Israel Doubles West Bank Outpost Construction," Al Jazeera, March 3, 2014, www.aljazeera.com/news/middleeast/2014/03/israel-doubles-west-bank-outpost-construction-201433143850913282.html.

257 **In 2014 it would jump** . . . "40 Percent Rise in New West Bank Settlement Homes in 2014," Ma'an News Agency, February 24, 2015, www.maannews.com/Content.aspx?id=759583.

261 **Two weeks earlier, on March 29 . . .** "Netanyahu: No Deal to Release Prisoners Without Clear Benefit for Israel," *Jerusalem Post*, March 30, 2014, www.jpost.com/Diplomacy-and-Politics/ Netanyahu-No-deal-to-release-prisoners-without-clear-benefit-for-Israel-346906.

261 **Of course a deal had been made . . .** Herb Keinon, "Palestinian Prisoner Release Passes Cabinet by Wide 13–7 Margin," *Jerusalem Post*, July 28, 2013, www.jpost.com/Diplomacy-and-Politics/ Palestinian-prisoner-release-passes-cabinet-by-wide-13-7-margin-321296.

261 **two days after the prisoner release deadline passed . . .** Birnbaum and Tibon, "The Explosive, Inside Story"; Nir Hasson and Barak Ravid, "While Kerry Tries to Clinch Deal, Israel Issues 700 Tenders Beyond Green Line," *Haaretz*, April 1, 2014, www.haaretz.com/news/diplomacy -defense/1.583200.

261 **Taken by surprise, Kerry canceled . . .** "Kerry Cancels Trip to Ramallah," Agence France-Presse, April 1, 2014, www.dailystar.com.lb/News/Middle-East/2014/Apr-01/251975-kerry-no-longer -travelling-to-ramallah-wednesday-us-official.ashx.

261 **Only three days later . . .** Barak Ravid, "Critical Israeli-Palestinian Meeting Ends in Stormy Failure, Sources Say," *Haaretz*, April 3, 2014, www.haaretz.com/news/diplomacy -defense/1.583595.

261 **It was, he suggested, about nine months . . .** Paul Richter, "Kerry: Mideast Talks May Be Scaled Back," *Los Angeles Times*, April 4, 2014, http://articles.latimes.com/2014/apr/04/world/la-fg-wn -john-kerry-mideast-talks-20140404.

261 **Before the week was out . . .** Moshe Arens, "Kerry Finally Got It: Peace Process Was a Farce," *Haaretz*, April 7, 2014, www.haaretz.com/opinion/.premium-1.584021.

262 **(Footnote) Unfortunately, prisoners were not released . . .** Barak Ravid, "Kerry Places Blame on Israel for Crisis in Peace Talks," *Haaretz*, April 4, 2014, www.haaretz.com/misc/iphone-article /.premium-1.584518; John B. Judis, "John Kerry Could Revive Peace Talks, but Don't Count on It," *New Republic*, April 9, 2014, www.newrepublic.com/article/117316/john-kerry-could-revive -peace-process-supporting-un.

262 **In May, the Israeli daily *Yedioth Ahronoth*'s Nahum Barnea . . .** Nahum Barnea, "Inside the Talks' Failure: US Officials Open Up," *Ynet News*, May 2, 2014, www.ynetnews.com/articles/ 0,7340,L-4515821,00.html.

263 **(Footnote) In 2010, basing their calculations . . .** Eyal Hareuveni, "By Hook and by Crook: Israeli Settlement Policy in the West Bank," B'Tselem, July 2010, 11, www.btselem.org/download /201007_by_hook_and_by_crook_eng.pdf; Amira Hass, "IDF Uses Live-Fire Zones to Expel Palestinians from Areas of West Bank, Officer Admits," *Haaretz*, May 21, 2014, www.haaretz .com/news/diplomacy-defense/.premium-1.591881.

264 **"Nothing speaks more clearly," said Hagel . . .** "Joint Press Conference with Secretary Hagel and Israeli Minister of Defense Moshe Ya'alon," U.S. Department of Defense, May 15, 2014, http://archive.defense.gov/transcripts/transcript.aspx?transcriptid=5433.

265 **(Footnote) In one, she wrote, "I saw friends . . ."** Mariam Barghouti, e-mail to author, May 22, 2014.

269 **On April 23, 2014, the day before Waed . . .** Kareem Khader and Jason Hanna, "Hamas, Fatah Announce Talks to Form Palestinian Unity Government," CNN, April 23, 2014, www.cnn.com/ 2014/04/23/world/meast/gaza-west-bank-palestinian-reconciliation/.

269 **"This is the good news . . ."** Nidal al-Mughrabi and Noah Browning, "Hamas, Abbas's PLO Announce Reconciliation Agreement," Reuters, April 23, 2014, http://mobile.reuters.com/article/ idUSBREA3M14420140423?irpc=932.

270 **Calling the announcement "a great reverse . . ."** Ian Black, Peter Beaumont, and Dan Roberts, "Israel Suspends Peace Talks with Palestinians After Fatah-Hamas Deal," *Guardian*, April 24, 2014, www.theguardian.com/world/2014/apr/24/middle-east-israel-halts -peace-talks-palestinians.

270 **"Whoever chooses Hamas does not want . . ."** al-Mughrabi and Browning, "Hamas, Abbas's PLO Announce Reconciliation Agreement."

270 **That same day, just after Haniyeh's announcement . . .** "Israeli Jets Hit Gaza During Unity Deal Celebrations," *Times of Israel*, April 23, 2014, www.timesofisrael.com/israeli-jets-hit-gaza

-during-unity-deal-celebrations/; "Protection of Civilians, Weekly Report 15–28 April 2014," United Nations Office for the Coordination of Humanitarian Affairs, April 28, 2014, http://unispal.un.org/UNISPAL.NSF/0/764C77EC470C62 A385257CCB00534AF1.

270 **99.74 percent of Palestinians tried** . . . Chaim Levinson, "Nearly 100% of All Military Court Cases in West Bank End in Conviction."

INTERLUDE: WHAT YOU SEE

276 **the average wage in the West Bank** . . . "2014 Investment Climate Statement—West Bank and Gaza," U.S. Department of State, June 2014, www.state.gov/e/eb/rls/othr/ics/2014/229097.htm; "UNSCO Socio-Economic Report: Overview of the Palestinian Economy in Q2/2013," Office of the United Nations Special Coordinator for the Middle East Peace Process, September 2013, www.unsco.org/Documents/Special/UNSCO%20Socio-Economic%20Report%20-%20Q2%202013.pdf.

277 **By the summer of 2013, Rawabi's developer** . . . Isabel Kershner, "Birth of a Palestinian City Is Punctuated by Struggles," *New York Times*, August 10, 2013, www.nytimes.com/2013/08/11/world/middleeast/birth-of-a-palestinian-city-is-punctuated-by-struggles.html?_r=0.

277 **the project's developer, Bashar al-Masri** . . . Ali Abunimah, *The Battle for Justice in Palestine* (Chicago: Haymarket Books, 2014), 88; Elhanan Miller, "In Rawabi, the Brand-New Palestinian City, Both Sides Win," *Times of Israel*, February 19, 2014, www.timesofisrael.com/in-rawabi-the-brand-new-palestinian-city-both-sides-win/.

277 **Al-Masri had secured a giant investment** . . . Armin Rosen, "A Middle-Class Paradise in Palestine?," *Atlantic*, February 11, 2013, www.theatlantic.com/international/archive/2013/02/a-middle-class-paradise-in-palestine/273004/.

277 **In 2009 Abbas had at al-Masri's** . . . Abunimah, *Battle for Justice*, 88–91.

277 **It was all legal, said a PA spokesman** . . . Ibid., 90.

277 *Time* **magazine called Rawabi** . . . "A Shining City on a Hill," *Time*, March 21, 2011, http://content.time.com/time/specials/packages/article/0,28804,2026474_2055581_2062499,00.html.

277 **The** *Financial Times* **went with** . . . John Reed, "City of Hope for Palestinians," *Financial Times*, April 8, 2013, www.ft.com/cms/s/0/9fdc4c7a-9c55-11e2-9a4b-00144feabdc0.html.

277 **(Footnote)** *The New York Times*'s **Tom Friedman** . . . Thomas L. Friedman, "Green Shoots in Palestine," *New York Times*, August 4, 2009, www.nytimes.com/2009/08/05/opinion/05friedman.html.

277 **(Footnote) The journalist Ali Abunimah, to whose** . . . Abunimah, *Battle for Justice*, 75.

278 **"It's crucial that you augment . . ."** Daisy Carrington, "New City Offers Vision of Better Life in West Bank," CNN, July 5, 2013, www.cnn.com/2013/07/04/world/meast/rawabi-palestinian-project/.

278 **(Footnote) Rawabi's official opening was delayed** . . . Tovah Lazaroff, "Rawabi, the First New Palestinian City, Can Finally Open Its Doors," *Jerusalem Post*, February 27, 2015, www.jpost.com/Middle-East/Rawabi-the-first-new-Palestinian-city-can-finally-open-its-doors-392402.

278 **But none of it had been possible** . . . Abunimah, *Battle for Justice*, 93–94; Ethan Bronner, "New Home-Buying Plan May Bolster Abbas," *New York Times*, April 15, 2008, www.nytimes.com/2008/04/15/world/middleeast/15mideast.html; Howard Schneider, "Palestinians Looking to American-Style Housing Developments, Financing," *Washington Post*, November 23, 2009, www.washingtonpost.com/wp-dyn/content/article/2009/11/22/AR2009112202106.html.

278 **the American government's quasi-public** . . . www.opic.gov.

278 **In 1990, the anthropologist James Ferguson published** . . . James Ferguson, *The Anti-Politics Machine: Development, Depoliticization, and Bureaucratic Power in Lesotho* (Minneapolis: University of Minnesota Press, 1994), 256.

279 **The investment giant Bear Stearns** . . . Bryan Burrough, "Bringing Down Bear Stearns," *Vanity Fair*, August 2008, www.vanityfair.com/news/2008/08/bear_stearns200808-2.

279 **Specifically, from a group called** . . . Schneider, "Palestinians Looking to American-Style Housing."

279 **Its president, chairman, and several of its board** . . . "Board of Directors," Middle East Investment Initiative, www.meiinitiative.org/index.php?TemplateId=staff&catId=1&MenuId=7&Lang=1.

279 **DLA Piper, one of the largest** . . . Ashby Jones, "DLA Piper: Soon to Be the Largest Law Firm in the World," *Wall Street Journal*, January 27, 2011, http://blogs.wsj.com/law/2011/01/27/dla-piper-soon-to-be-the-largest-law-firm-in-the-world/.

279 **Former secretary of state Madeleine Albright** . . . "Board of Directors," Middle East Investment Initiative.

279 **former Reagan administration labor secretary** . . . Sheryl Gay Stolberg, "Washington Talk," *New York Times,* October 22, 2003, www.nytimes.com/2003/10/22/us/washington-talk-some-wholly-new-work-for-old-washington-hand.html.

279 **The Islamist party had won the 2006** . . . Abunimah, *Battle for Justice*, 79–83; Rose, "Gaza Bombshell."

280 **OPIC's president, Robert Mosbacher** . . . Ethan Bronner, "New Home-Buying Plan May Bolster Abbas," *New York Times*, April 15, 2008, www.nytimes.com/2008/04/15/world/middleeast/15mideast.html.

280 **Korologos, Albright, and MEII director Jim Pickup** . . . "Board of Directors," Middle East Investment Initiative; Schneider, "Palestinians Looking to American-Style Housing."

280 **Between 2008 and 2014, consumer credit** . . . Abunimah, *Battle for Justice*, 85; "Table 23: Distribution of Credit Facilities by Economic Sector," Palestinian Monetary Fund, www.pma.ps/Portals/1/Users/002/02/2/Monthly%20Statistical%20Bulletin/Banking%20Data/table_23_facilities_by_economic_sectors.xls.

280 **Both Tom Korologos and MEII board member George Salem** . . . Dave Levinthal, "Al Jazeera Adds More Lobbying Heft," Center for Public Integrity, February 25, 2013, www.publicintegrity.org/2013/02/25/12234/al-jazeera-adds-more-lobbying-heft.

280 **Qatar, one of Hamas's only** . . . Asher Schechter, "A Finger in Every Pie: How Qatar Became an International Power," *Haaretz*, August 9, 2014, www.haaretz.com/news/features/.premium-1.609667.

280 **DLA Piper also did lobbying work** . . . "Raytheon Co," OpenSecrets.org, www.opensecrets.org/lobby/clientsum.php?id=D000000175.

280 **Raytheon, which produced the "Iron Dome"** . . . Bryan Bender, "Raytheon a Key in Israeli Defense Plan," *Boston Globe*, July 17, 2014, www.bostonglobe.com/news/nation/2014/07/17/under-rocket-fire-israel-looks-raytheon-build-more-anti-missile-systems/KziQB3E7zhRqkd6Zq W0R6N/story.html.

281 **And the Qatar Investment Authority** . . . Caroline Binham, "Stakes Are High for Barclays and SFO over Qatar Investors Probe," *Financial Times,* September 24, 2014, www.ft.com/intl/cms/s/0/a94cdea4-4407-11e4-8abd-00144feabdc0.html#axzz3lABKaYyZ.

281 **which in turn owned a substantial chunk** . . . Marcus Dysch, "Barclays Bank Branch Forced to Shut by Anti-Israel Protesters," *Jewish Chronicle*, December 1, 2014, www.thejc.com/news/uk-news/126252/barclays-bank-branch-forced-shut-anti-israel-protesters.

281 **which manufactured the drones that the IDF** . . . Barbara Opall-Rome, "Israeli Forces Praise Elbit UAVs in Gaza Op," *Defense News*, August 12, 2014, http://archive.defensenews.com/article/20140812/DEFREG04/308120026/Israeli-Forces-Praise-Elbit-UAVs-Gaza-Op.

281 **Qatari Diar, Rawabi's main outside investor.** . . . Abunimah, *Battle for Justice*, 88; "Qatari Diar and Massar International Partner to Build the New Palestinian Planned City of Rawabi," Rawabi, May 21, 2008, www.rawabi.ps/mobile/press_show.php?id=6.

281 **(Footnote) Qatari Diar had also acquired a stake** . . . Tara Patel, "Qatari Diar Acquires 5% Stake in Veolia, Gets Seat on Board," *Bloomberg*, April 16, 2010, www.bloomberg.com/apps/news?pid=newsarchive&sid=aoiOhu_RWSuI; "Veolia," WeDivest.org, https://wedivest.org/c/56/veolia#.VR8ykLq4m2w.

281 **Bashar al-Masri, Rawabi's developer** . . . Miller, "In Rawabi, the Brand-New Palestinian City";
Abunimah, *Battle for Justice*, 97.

281 **Weisglass, who had done business with al-Masri** . . . Danny Rubinstein, "It's Not Politics, It's
Just Business," *Ynet News*, January 6, 2011, www.ynetnews.com/articles/0,7340,L -4010020,00
.html; Conal Urquhart, "Gaza on Brink of Implosion as Aid Cut-Off Starts to Bite," *Guardian*,
April 15, 2006, www.theguardian.com/world/2006/apr/16/israel.

281 **Al-Masri, who faced no such danger** . . . Avi Nudelman, "Israeli-Palestinian Chamber of
Commerce and Industry December 2010 Newsletter," Israeli-Palestinian Chamber of Commerce
and Industry, December 2010, www.ipcc.org.il/webfiles/fck/files/newsletter_dec2010_eng.pdf;
Ali Abunimah, "Rawabi Developer Masri Helps Deepen Israel's Grip on West Bank," *Electronic
Intifada*, January 6, 2011, https://electronicintifada.net/content/rawabi-developer-masri-helps
-deepen-israels-grip-west-bank/9170; Phillip Weiss, "Palestinian Real Estate Developer
Participates in Conference Promoting Israel as 'High-Tech Haven,'" *Mondoweiss*, September 11,
2012, http://mondoweiss.net/2012/09/palestinian-real-estate-developer-participates-in-conference
-promoting-israel-as-high-tech-haven.

281 **the Israeli-Palestinian Chamber of Commerce, which was** . . . Israeli-Palestinian Chamber of
Commerce, www.ipcc.org.il/.

281 **On its board was a man named Gadi Zohar** . . . "Mr. Gadi Zohar," Israeli-Palestinian Chamber
of Commerce, www.ipcc.org.il/gadi_zohar; Peter Lagerquist, "Privatizing the Occupation: The
Political Economy of an Oslo Development Project," *Journal of Palestine Studies* 32(2) (Winter
2003): 14.

281 **Among Netacs's clients was PADICO** . . . Ali Abunimah, "Palestinian Firms Listed as Clients
of Israeli General Who Fled War Crimes Arrest," *Electronic Intifada*, September 10, 2013, https://
electronicintifada.net/blogs/ali-abunimah/palestinian-firms-listed-clients-israeli-general-who
-fled-war-crimes-arrest.

281 **PADICO, which was incorporated and registered** . . . Abunimah, *Battle for Justice*, 106–7;
"Articles of Incorporation of Palestine Development & Investment Inc.," October 14, 1993, www
.padico.com/library/635247558312107150.pdf; Omar Shaban, "Palestinian Stock Exchange Lacks
Public Regulation," *Al Monitor*, May 28, 2013, www.al-monitor.com/pulse/originals/2013/05/
palestinian-stock-exchange.html; "Investments: Financial & Services," PADICO, www.padico
.com/public/English.aspx?Lang=2&Page_Id=2713&PMID=30&Menu_ID=50&Site_ID=1.

282 **Nabil Sarraf, the chair of PADICO's real estate subsidiary** . . . "Eng. Nabil al-Sarraf," Palestine
Investment Fund, www.pif.ps/index.php?lang=en&page=124990472092.

282 **And PADICO's chief executive, Samir Hulileh** . . . "Samir Hulileh," Portland Trust, www
.portlandtrust.org/management/samir-hulileh; Abunimah, *Battle for Justice*, 107.

282 **the Portland Trust, a British NGO** . . . Portland Trust, www.portlandtrust.org/.

282 **which had helped design Rawabi's financing strategy** . . . "Affordable Housing Programme,"
Portland Trust, www.portlandtrust.org/projects/economic-infrastructure/affordable-housing
-programme.

282 **Until 2011, the Portland Trust's chief executive** . . . "About Us," Portland Trust, www
.portlandtrust.org/about-us; "Eival Gilady," Israeli-Palestinian Chamber of Commerce,
www.ipcc.org.il/eival-gilady.

282 **and which had previously been directed** . . . Abunimah, *Battle for Justice*, 97; Jason Gewirtz,
"Head of Israeli-Palestinian Business Group to Leave Role," CNBC, March 10, 2010, www.cnbc
.com/id/35798559.

282 **Another of Netacs's cofounders was** . . . Abunimah, "Palestinian Firms Listed as Clients of
Israeli General"; "Owners and Management," Netacs, http://netacs.biz/founders/.

282 **In 2011, Rothschild was forced to flee** . . . Danna Harman, "Arrest Warning Prompts Retired
Israeli General to Cut Short London Visit," *Haaretz*, July 6, 2011, www.haaretz.com/news/
diplomacy-defense/arrest-warning-prompts-retired-israeli-general-to-cut-short-london-visit
-1.371814.

283 **"What you see is not what is actually happening** . . ." Lagerquist, "Privatizing the Occupation," 15.

283 **private-sector wages in the West Bank** . . . Dr. Udo Kock, "Between a Rock and a Hard Place— Recent Developments in the Palestinian Economy," International Monetary Fund, February 19, 2014, www.imf.org/external/country/WBG/RR/2014/021914.pdf; "West Bank and Gaza: Labor Market Trends, Growth and Unemployment," International Monetary Fund, www.imf.org/external/country/WBG/RR/2012/121312.pdf; "Labour Force Participation, Employment, Unemployment and Average Daily Wage in NIS for Wage Employees in the Palestinian Territory by Governorate, January—March, 2012," Palestine Central Bureau of Statistics, www.pcbs.gov.ps/Portals/_Rainbow/Documents/Labor%20Force%20Annual.htm.

283 **poverty and food insecurity afflicted** . . . "Emergency Appeal—2013," United Nations Relief Works Agency, 14, 23, www.unrwa.org/userfiles/2013012971846.pdf; "Human Deprivation Under Occupation: Arab Development Challenges Report Background Paper 2011/12," United Nations Development Programme, 2–3, www.undp.org/content/dam/rbas/doc/poverty/BG_12_Human%20Deprivation%20Under%20Occupation.pdf.

283 **(Footnote) As one UN report put it** . . . "Report on UNCTAD Assistance to the Palestinian People: Developments in the Economy of the Occupied Palestinian Territory," United Nations Conference on Trade and Development, July 7, 2014, http://unctad.org/meetings/en/SessionalDocuments/tdb61d3_en.pdf.

284 **There was al-Reehan, a two-thousand-unit planned community** . . . "al-Reehan: Palestine's Landmark Neighborhood," Palestine Investment Fund, www.pif.ps/resources/file/booklets/ENAlReehanDraft006.pdf; "Amaar Real Estate Group," Palestine Investment Fund, www.pif.ps/index.php?lang=en&page=1245234449365; "Mohammad Mustafa," World Economic Forum, www.weforum.org/contributors/mohammad-mustafa; Abunimah, *Battle for Justice*, 94.

284 **Zamn's owner, Ahmad Aweidah, was also the CEO** . . . Patrick Martin, "The Ramallah Miracle: Is Palestine Ready for Independence?," *Globe and Mail*, April 15, 2011, www.theglobeandmail.com/news/world/the-ramallah-miracle-is-palestine-ready-for-independence/article576709/?page=all.

CHAPTER 9: SO EASY, SO HARD

287 **"well, let it be only a dream!"** Fyodor Dostoevsky, *The Eternal Husband and Other Stories*, trans. Richard Pevear and Larissa Volokhonsky (New York: Modern Library, 2012), 332.

292 **After the 1948 war, tens of thousands** . . . Isma'el Abu-Sa'ad, "Forced Sedentarisation, Land Rights and Indigenous Resistance: The Palestinian Bedouin in the Negev," in *Catastrophe Remembered: Palestine, Israel and the Internal Refugees*, ed. Nur Masalha (London: Zed Books, 2005) 115–20.

292 **(Footnote) In the mid-1940s, between 65,000** . . . Jiryis, *Arabs in Israel*, 19; Emanuel Marx, *Bedouin of the Negev* (Manchester, UK: University of Manchester Press, 1967), 11–12.

292 **(Footnote) "More than any other group"** . . . Jiryis, *Arabs in Israel*, 122.

292 **they began to selectively apply certain Jordanian laws** . . . Gordon, *Israel's Occupation*, 129; Weizman, *Hollow Land*, 116–18.

294 **the DCO had come** . . . Amira Hass, "Settlers Sue Bedouin over Outdoor Oven Fueled by Livestock Manure," *Haaretz*, January 20, 2014, www.haaretz.com/news/israel/.premium-1.569453.

301 **The previous June, officials from the Civil Administration** . . . Chaim Levinson, "Israel Seizes Bedouin Man's Toilet in West Bank After Deeming It Illegal," *Haaretz*, June 23, 2013, www.haaretz.com/news/diplomacy-defense/.premium-1.531502; "Toilet for Handicapped Person in Umm El Hair? Occupation Say NO!," YouTube, www.youtube.com/watch?v=1VQLHpLOq_U.

302 **"They wait," wrote Mahmoud Darwish** . . . Mahmoud Darwish, *Journal of an Ordinary Grief*, trans. Ibrahim Muhawi (New York: Archipelago Books, 2010), 172.

306–7 **activists had called for a boycott of Caterpillar** . . . "Global Movement to Boycott Caterpillar Gathers Momentum," Palestinian Grassroots Anti-Apartheid Wall Campaign, April 19, 2005, http://stopthewall.org/2005/04/19/global-movement-boycott-caterpillar-gathers-momentum.

307 It was a Caterpillar that had crushed . . . Harriet Sherwood, "Rachel Corrie Ruling 'Deeply Troubling,' Says Her Family," *Haaretz*, August 28, 2012, www.theguardian.com/world/2012/aug/28/rachel-corrie-ruling-deeply-troubling.

307 I remembered a Dostoevsky story . . . I have drawn freely here from two translations, David Magarshack's in *Great Short Works of Fyodor Dostoevsky* (New York: Harper & Row, 1968), 717–38; and Richard Pevear and Larissa Volokhonsky's in *The Eternal Husband and Other Stories*, 299–342.

309 (Footnote) Two weeks earlier, an Israeli police intelligence officer . . . Yifa Yaakov, "West Bank Shooting Victim Named as Baruch Mizrahi, 47," *Times of Israel*, April 15, 2014, www.timesofisrael.com/west-bank-shooting-victim-named-as-baruch-mizrahi/; Ilene Prusher, "Where One Man's Incitement Is Another Man's Fact," *Haaretz*, May 2, 2014, www.haaretz.com/blogs/jerusalem-vivendi/.premium-1.588660.

PART FOUR: A DEEP DARK BLUE

PROLOGUE: IF ONLY

315 "Afterwards, everything happened." David Grossman, *Yellow Wind*, 212.

317 Before the day was over . . . "2 Palestinian Teens Killed in Nakba Day Clashes," *Times of Israel*, May 15, 2014, www.timesofisrael.com/2-palestinian-teens-said-killed-in-nakba-day-clashes/; Jodi Rudoren, "Two Palestinians Killed in Clashes with Israeli Forces," *New York Times*, May 15, 2014, www.nytimes.com/2014/05/16/world/middleeast/two-palestinians-killed-in-clashes-with-israeli-forces.html.

318 The building's owner, a man named Fakher Zayed . . . "Israeli Forces Shoot and Kill Two Palestinian Teens Near Ramallah," Defense for Children International, Palestine, May 17, 2014, www.dci-palestine.org/documents/israeli-forces-shoot-and-kill-two-palestinian-teens-near-ramallah.

318–19 The U.S. State Department announced that it expected . . . Yitzhak Benhorin, "US to Israel: Investigate Killing of Palestinian Teens," *Ynet News*, May 21, 2014, www.ynetnews.com/articles/0,7340,L-4521979,00.html.

319 The UN called for an independent probe . . . "UN Calls for Probe into Shooting of Palestinian Youths," *Haaretz*, May 20, 2014, www.haaretz.com/news/diplomacy-defense/1.591855.

319 no live fire had been used . . . Peter Beaumont, "Video Footage Indicates Killed Palestinian Youths Posed No Threat," *Guardian*, May 20, 2014, www.theguardian.com/world/2014/may/20/video-indicates-killed-palestinian-youths-no-threat-israeli-forces.

319 B'Tselem released the full, unedited video . . . "The Killing of the Two Teens in Bitunya: Uncut Footage," B'Tselem, May 26, 2014, www.btselem.org/firearms/20140526_bitunya_killings_full_video_documentation.

319 An analyst for Israeli television's Channel Two . . . "Ya'alon Says Troops in Nakba Day Killings Were in Danger, Acted as Needed," *Times of Israel*, May 20, 2014, www.timesofisrael.com/yaalon-says-troops-in-nakba-day-killings-were-in-danger-acted-as-needed/.

319 The IDF liked that line, and went with it . . . Jack Khoury and Chaim Levinson, "IDF Says Forgery Likely in Video Showing Palestinian Teens' Deaths," *Haaretz*, May 22, 2014, www.haaretz.com/news/diplomacy-defense/.premium-1.592000.

319 Former Israeli ambassador Michael Oren . . . Raphael Ahren, "Michael Oren Says He Left CNN of His Own Accord," *Times of Israel*, August 12, 2014, www.timesofisrael.com/michael-oren-says-he-left-cnn-of-his-own-accord/; Transcript, CNN, May 22, 2014, http://transcripts.cnn.com/TRANSCRIPTS/1405/22/wolf.02.html.

320 Late in April, more than 100 . . . "Four More Palestinian Prisoners in Israeli Jail on Hunger Strike," Ma'an News Agency, April 27, 2014, www.maannews.com/Content.aspx?id=693169.

320 **By the end of May, another 140 . . .** Ido Efrati, "Israeli Hospitals Bracing for Wave of Hunger
-Striking Palestinian Prisoners," *Haaretz,* May 29, 2014, www.haaretz.com/news/diplomacy
-defense/.premium-1.595974; Batsheva Sobelman, "Palestinian Prisoners on Hunger Strike; Israel
Debates Force-feeding," *Los Angeles Times*, May 28, 2014, www.latimes.com/world/middleeast/
la-fg-palestinian-prisoners-hunger-strike-20140528-story.html.

320 **After forty days, 70 prisoners . . .** Barak Ravid, Ido Efrati, and Jack Khoury, "PM Pushes to
Force-feed Palestinian Hunger-strikers," *Haaretz*, June 3, 2014, www.haaretz.com/news/israel/
.premium-1.596901.

321 **(Footnote) The bill would be voted into law . . .** Judah Ari Gross, "Knesset Passes Controversial
'Force-Feeding' Bill for Prisoners," *Times of Israel*, July 30, 2015, www.timesofisrael.com/knesset
-passes-controversial-force-feeding-bill-for-prisoners/.

321 **On June 1, only half a week late . . .** Peter Beaumont, "Palestinian Unity Government of Fatah
and Hamas Sworn In," *Guardian*, June 2, 2014, www.theguardian.com/world/2014/jun/02/
palestinian-unity-government-sworn-in-fatah-hamas.

321 **Though they were technically not allied . . .** Jodi Rudoren and Isabel Kershner, "With Hope for
Unity, Abbas Swears In a New Palestinian Government," *New York Times,* June 2, 2014, www
.nytimes.com/2014/06/03/world/middleeast/abbas-swears-in-a-new-palestinian-government.html;
"New Members of Unity Govt Named," Ma'an News Agency, June 1, 2014, www.maannews
.com/Content.aspx?id=701510.

321–22 **In the West Bank, the PA continued . . .** "Political Arrests Continue in the West Bank, Despite
Unity Agreement," Ma'an News Agency, May 19, 2014, www.maannews.com/Content.aspx?id
=698105; "PA Forces Detain 16 Hamas Supporters in West Bank," Ma'an News Agency, June 8,
2014, www.maannews.com/Content.aspx?id=703128.

322 **When salaries came due . . .** "Clashes in Gaza as PA Employees Try to Withdraw Wages," Ma'an
News Agency, June 5, 2014, www.maannews.com/Content.aspx?id=702462.

322 **The banks stayed closed . . .** "Gaza Banks Still Closed as Unity Govt Financial Dispute Deepens,"
Ma'an News Agency, June 8, 2014, www.maannews.com/Content.aspx?id=703013; "Fatah Official
Plays Down Unity Disputes," Ma'an News Agency, June 11, 2014, www.maannews.com/Content
.aspx?id=703914.

322 **The heads of the Shabak . . .** Barak Ravid, "Israel Slams 'Weak' U.S. Response to Fatah
-Hamas Unity Deal,"*Haaretz*, April 24, 2014, www.haaretz.com/news/diplomacy-defense/
.premium-1.587291.

322 **"Today, Abu Mazen said yes to terrorism . . ."** Rudoren and Kershner, "With Hope for Unity."

322 **Israel announced that its central bank . . .** Sam Bahour, "Israel Declares War on Palestinian
Banks," *Talking Points Memo*, May 24, 2014, http://talkingpointsmemo.com/cafe/israel-declares
-war-on-palestinian-banks.

323 **The Israeli Electric Corporation tried too . . .** Barak Ravid, "Israel's Top General in West Bank
Warns: Power Blackouts Will Lead to Violence," *Haaretz*, May 26, 2014, www.haaretz.com/news/
diplomacy-defense/.premium-1.592778.

323 **According to *Haaretz*, IDF and DCO officials . . .** Chaim Levinson, "Civil Administration
Officials Refuse to Punish Palestinians for Unity Government," *Haaretz*, June 8, 2014, www
.haaretz.com/news/middle-east/.premium-1.597452.

323 **Members of his security cabinet . . .** Ravid, "Israel Slams 'Weak' U.S. Response to Fatah-Hamas
Unity Deal."

323 **A senior U.S. official who preferred to remain nameless . . .** Chemi Shalev, "White House:
Israel's 'Hard Line Public Position' on New PA Cabinet Belies Its Own Actions," *Haaretz*, June 5,
2014, www.haaretz.com/news/diplomacy-defense/.premium-1.597078.

324 **A week earlier, the Palestinian president . . .** Ali Abunimah, "Mahmoud Abbas: Collaboration
with Israeli Army, Secret Police Is 'Sacred,'" *Electronic Intifada*, May 30, 2014, https://electron
icintifada.net/blogs/ali-abunimah/mahmoud-abbas-collaboration-israeli-army-secret-police
-sacred.

324 (Footnote) Seven months later, in December . . . "PA to 'Halt Security Coordination' in Response to Abu Ein's Death," Ma'an News Agency, December 10, 2014, www.maannews.com/Content .aspx?id=746278; Ahmad Melhem, "PA All Talk, No Action on Abu Ein's Death," *Al-Monitor*, December 16, 2014, www.al-monitor.com/pulse/originals/2014/12/palestinian-authority-silence -abu-ein.html#ixzz3lGd27nsw.

324 (Footnote) The following March, the PLO's . . . Peter Beaumont, "PLO Leadership Votes to Suspend Security Cooperation with Israel," *Guardian*, March 5, 2015, www.theguardian .com/world/2015/mar/05/plo-leadership-votes-to-suspend-security-cooperation-with-israel; "PLO Calls for End to Security Coordination with Israel," Al Jazeera, March 6, 2015, www.aljazeera .com/news/middleeast/2015/03/plo-security-coordination-israel-150305201025380.html.

324 on June 9, when Hamas supporters . . . "Hamas: PA Forces Assault Protesters in Ramallah," Ma'an News Agency, June 10, 2014, www.maannews.com/Content.aspx?id=703651; "Security Forces Assault Journalists During Hamas March," Ma'an News Agency, June 11, 2014, www .maannews.com/Content.aspx?id=704102.

325 (Footnote) Media attention initially focused on the soldier . . . "Soldier Suspended for Nakba Day Shooting," *Times of Israel*, May 28, 2014, www.timesofisrael.com/soldier-suspended-for-nakba -day-shooting/.

325 (Footnote) a Border Policeman who was partially obscured . . . "Report: Nakba Day Killings," Forensic Architecture, http://beitunia.forensic-architecture.org/; Robert Mackey, "Video Analysis of Fatal West Bank Shooting Said to Implicate Israeli Officer," *New York Times*, November 24, 2014, www.nytimes.com/2014/11/25/world/middleeast/video-analysis-of-fatal-west-bank -shooting-said-to-implicate-israeli-officer.html.

325 (Footnote) In November, the Border Police officer . . . Stuart Winer, "Border Cop Charged in Palestinian Teen's Killing," *Times of Israel*, November 23, 2014, www.timesofisrael.com/border -policeman-charged-with-manslaughter-in-may-shooting/; "Law Enforcement upon IDF Soldiers in the Occupied Palestinian Territory," Yesh Din, September 2014, http://yesh-din.org/userfiles/ file/fix%20YeshDin%20-%20DataSheet %20Metzach%2010%2029%20-%20Eng.pdf; "Delays Preventing the Progress of Criminal Proceedings Against the Murderer of the Martyr Nadeem Nowarah," Palestinian News Network, December 18, 2015, http://english.pnn.ps/2015/12/18/delays-preventing-the-progress -of-criminal-proceedings-against-the-murderer-of-the-martyr-nadeem-nowarah/.

CHAPTER 10: MY BROTHER'S KEEPER

327 "Night is always a giant . . ." Vladimir Nabokov, *Transparent Things* (New York: McGraw Hill, 1972), 9.

327 On June 12, 2014, three Israeli teenagers . . . Itamar Sharon, "Officials Release Identities of Teens Who Disappeared Near Hebron," *Times of Israel*, June 15, 2014, www.timesofisrael.com/ yaalon-our-working-assumption-is-boys-still-alive/.

327 Yifrach on Shuhada Street in Hebron . . . Mitch Ginsburg, "Pain and Brotherhood at Kidnap Victim's Hebron Yeshiva," *Times of Israel*, June 19, 2014, www.timesofisrael.com /yeshiva-of-missing-teen-eyal-yifrach-opens-its-doors/.

327 One of the boys, Israeli police spokesman . . . Isabel Kershner, "Israeli Teenagers Said to Be Kidnapped in West Bank," *New York Times*, June 13, 2014, www.nytimes.com/2014/06/14 /world/middleeast/3-israeli-teenagers-said-to-be-kidnapped-in-west-bank.html.

327 A gag order was swiftly placed . . . Mitch Ginsburg, "Gagged! Are the Police and Courts Untenably Handcuffing the Media?," *Times of Israel*, July 11, 2014, www.timesofisrael.com /gagged are the police-and-courts-untenably-handcuffing-the-media/; Adam Horowitz, Scott Ross, and Phillip Weiss, "Israel Maintains Gag Order in Missing Teens' Case, Leading to Charge of Media 'Manipulation,'" *Mondoweiss*, June 23, 2014, http://mondoweiss.net/2014/06/ maintains-missing-manipulation.

327 Netanyahu, who, before the boys' names . . . Isabel Kershner, "Israeli Teenagers Said to Be Kidnapped."

328 That night, a burned-out Hyundai . . . Yoav Zitun, "Israel Fears Kidnappers Fled Hebron After Teens' Bodies Found," *Ynet News*, July 1, 2014, www.ynetnews.com/articles/0,7340,L -4536636,00.html.

328 Arrest raids began almost immediately . . . "Israel Deploys Heavily Near Hebron After Disappearance of Settlers," Ma'an News Agency, June 13, 2014, www.maannews.com/Content .aspx?id=704478.

328 Netanyahu waited until the Sabbath . . . Peter Beaumont, "Israeli Forces Tighten Grip on West Bank in Search for Three Abducted Teenagers," *Guardian*, June 16, 2014, www.theguardian .com/world/2014/jun/15/israeli-forces-west-bank-abducted-teenagers; Jodi Rudoren, "Netanyahu Says Three Were Taken by Hamas," *New York Times*, June 15, 2014, www.nytimes.com/2014/06/ 16/world/middleeast/netanyahu-blames-hamas-in-kidnapping-of-israeli-youths.html.

328 In the past, Hamas had bragged . . . Shlomi Eldar, "Hamas Military Wing Boasts About Israeli Kidnapped Soldiers," *Al-Monitor*, June 30, 2013, www.al-monitor.com/pulse/originals/2013/06/ hamas-kidnapped-army-branch.html.

328 by the end of that day 150 Palestinians . . . Peter Beaumont, "Palestinian Parliamentary Speaker Arrested in Search for Kidnapped Teens," *Guardian*, June 16, 2014, www.theguardian .com/world/2014/jun/16/palestinian-parliamentary-speaker-arrested-kidnapped-teenagers-aziz -dweik.

328 All 700,000 inhabitants of the Hebron governorate . . . "Localities in Hebron Governorate by Type of Locality and Population Estimates, 2007–2016," Palestine Central Bureau of Statistics, www.pcbs.gov.ps/Portals/_Rainbow/Documents/hebrn.htm; Beaumont, "Israeli Forces Tighten Grip"; "Hebron District and Its 680,000 Residents Under Third Day of Closure: Increasing Reports of Property Damage in Arrest Raids," B'Tselem, June 17, 2014, www.btselem.org/press _releases/20140617_collective_punishment_in_hebron_district; "Israel Imposes Indefinite Closure of Checkpoints in Southern West Bank," Ma'an News Agency, June 15, 2014, www .maannews.com/Content.aspx?id=704791.

329 In the Jalazoun camp, soldiers . . . "Israeli Forces Kill Palestinian During Arrest Raid," Ma'an News Agency, June 16, 2014, www.maannews.com/Content.aspx?id=766667; "Palestinian Critically Injured in Clashes Near Ramallah," Ma'an News Agency, June 16, 2014, www.maannews.com/ Content.aspx?id=705326.

329 (Footnote) "And the LORD said unto Cain . . ." Holy Bible, King James Version, Genesis 4:9.

329 More troops had flooded the West Bank . . . Alice Speri, "Search for Missing Teens Leads to Largest Israeli Military Escalation Since the Second Intifada," *Vice News*, June 18, 2014, https:// news.vice.com/article/search-for-missing-teens-leads-to-largest-israeli-military-escalation -since-the-second-intifada.

329 Each day brought another forty . . . "Israel Detains Over 40 Hamas Members Across West Bank," Ma'an News Agency, June 16, 2014, www.maannews.com/Content.aspx?id=705083; Gili Cohen, "Israeli Army Arrests 41 Palestinians in Overnight West Bank Raids," *Haaretz*, June 17, 2014, www.haaretz.com/news/diplomacy-defense/1.599264; "LIVE UPDATES: Israel Searches for Teens Kidnapped in West Bank, Day 5," *Haaretz*, June 17, 2014, www.haaretz.com/news/ diplomacy-defense/1.599302; "Israeli Forces Detain 300, Raid Over 750 Homes in Last Week," Ma'an News Agency, June 18, 2014, www.maannews.com/Content.aspx?id=705981; "Ongoing Arrest Campaign Brings Total Palestinians in Jail to 5,700," Ma'an News Agency, June 21, 2014.

329 *Haaretz* quoted a "high-ranking military officer" . . . "Israel Searches for Teens Kidnapped in West Bank, Day 5."

329 The IDF did its part, with forty officers . . . Daniel Estrin, "Bring Back Our Boys, Whoever They Are," Public Radio International, June 20, 2014, www.pri.org/stories/2014-06-20/bring-back -our-boys-whoever-they-are.

329 A Facebook page calling on citizens . . . Lizzie Dearden, "Facebook Campaign Calls on Israelis to Kill a Palestinian 'Terrorist' Every Hour Until Missing Teenagers Found," *Independent*, June 16, 2014, www.independent.co.uk/news/world/middle-east/online-campaign-calling-on-israelis -to-kill-a-palestinian-terrorist-every-hour-until-missing-teenagers-found-9540604.html.

329–30 "I think Ramadan will be spoiled" . . . "Israel Searches for Teens Kidnapped in West Bank, Day 5."

330 The defense minister promised . . . Mitch Ginsburg, "Israel Could Kill Hamas Leaders, Defense Minister Hints," *Times of Israel*, June 15, 2014, www.timesofisrael.com/israel-could-kill-hamas-leaders-defense-minister-hints/.

330 Major General Nitzan Alon, the head . . . "Israel Searches for Teens Kidnapped in West Bank, Day 5."

330 The arrest raids continued—in Nablus . . . "Israel Arrests Over 50 Palestinians Released in Shalit Deal," Ma'an News Agency, June 18, 2014, www.maannews.com/Content.aspx?id =705707.

330 How, asked *The Jerusalem Post* . . . Yonah Jeremy Bob, "How Will IDF Prosecutors Deal with 240 Palestinians Arrested All at Once?," *Jerusalem Post*, June 19, 2014, www.jpost.com/Operation-Brothers-Keeper/How-will-IDF-prosecutors-deal-with-240-Palestinians-arrested-all-at-once-359835; "Update on Hunger Strikes, Force Feeding & Arrest Campaign—June 2014," Addameer: Prisoner Support and Human Rights Association, June 2014, www.addameer.org/etemplate .php?id=701.

330 Abbas was in Saudi Arabia . . . Isabel Kershner, "Palestinian Leader Pledges to Hold Abductors of Israeli Teenagers to Account," *New York Times*, June 18, 2014, www.nytimes .com/2014/06/19/world/middleeast/palestinian-leader-condemns-kidnapping-of-israeli-teenagers .html?_r=0.

330 From a comfortable distance he defended . . . "Palestinian Leader Defends Cooperation with Israel," *New York Times*, June 19, 2014, www.nytimes.com/aponline/2014/06/18/world /middleeast/ap-ml-israel-palestinians.html.

331 The army visited Fakher Zayed . . . "Israel: Stop Threatening Witness to Killings," Human Rights Watch, June 19, 2014, www.hrw.org/news/2014/06/19/israel-stop-threatening -witness-killings.

332 The next day, *Haaretz* would describe . . . "LIVE UPDATES: Israel Searches for Teens Kidnapped in West Bank, Day 7," *Haaretz*, June 19, 2014, www.haaretz.com/news /diplomacy-defense/1.599757.

333 The next morning, Netanyahu visited . . . "PM Netanyahu Visits IDF Judea Brigade HQ," Government Press Office, e-mail to author, June 19, 2014.

333 The recording wasn't leaked until later . . . Ben Hartmann, "Recording of Kidnapped Teen's Distress Call to Police Released," *Jerusalem Post*, July 1, 2014, www.jpost.com/Operation -Brothers-Keeper/Recording-of-distress-call-to-police-by-kidnapped-teen-released-361169; Lazar Berman, "Recording of Teen's Emergency Call Released: 'They've Kidnapped Me,'" *Times of Israel*, July 1, 2014, www.timesofisrael.com/recording-of-teens-emergency-call-released-theyve -kidnapped-me/.

333 There were eight bullet holes . . . J. J. Goldberg, "How Politics and Lies Triggered an Unintended War in Gaza," *Forward*, July 10, 2014, http://forward.com/opinion/israel/201764/how -politics-and-lies-triggered-an-unintended-war/#ixzz3lMjiXbEa; Jodi Rudoren and Said Ghazali, "A Trail of Clues Leading to Victims and Heartbreak," *New York Times*, July 1, 2014, www .nytimes.com/2014/07/02/world/middleeast/details-emerge-in-deaths-of-israeli-teenagers.html; Danya Cohen, "Netanyahu Provoked an Unintended War—Public Deception of the Kidnapped Boys' Murder Led to a War of Revenge," *Times of Israel*, July 13, 2014, http://blogs.timesofisrael .com/netanyahu-provoked-an-unintended-war-public-deception-of-the-kidnapped-boys-murder -led-to-a-war-of-revenge/.

333 Some journalists knew, but they honored . . . Shlomi Eldar, "Was Israeli Public Misled on Abductions?," *Al-Monitor*, July 3, 2014, www.al-monitor.com/pulse/originals/2014/07/misleading -kidnapping-almoz-hamas-vengence-hatred.html#.

333 Nonetheless, two days after the abduction . . . Yoav Zitun, "Police Name Teens Missing in West Bank Since Thursday," *Ynet News*, June 13, 2014, www.ynetnews.com/articles/0,7340, L-4530177,00.html.

336 Hours later, the body of Mahmoud . . . "Two Palestinians Killed in Overnight Raids in Ramallah and Nablus," Ma'an News Agency, June 22, 2014, www.maannews.com/Content .aspx?id=706668.

336 (Footnote) Another Palestinian was killed in Nablus . . . Ibid.

336 (Footnote) An IDF spokesperson told *Russia Today* . . . "RT Office in Ramallah Raided by the IDF," *Russia Today*, June 22, 2014, www.rt.com/news/167628-israel-raid-rt -office/.

337 nearly thirty thousand people squeezed . . . "A New Type of Settlement," *Economist*, October 12, 2013, www.economist.com/news/middle-east-and-africa/21587846-some-palestinians-want-their -people-abandon-refugee-camps-without-demanding.

337 It was in Balata that the First Intifada . . . Lockman and Beinin, 70.

337 Its entrances had been barricaded . . . Weizman, *Hollow Land*, 193–94.

338 The hunger strike ended . . . Jack Khoury, "Palestinian official: Deal to End Prisoners' Hunger Strike Not a Victory," *Haaretz*, June 25, 2014, www.haaretz.com/news/diplomacy-defense /.premium-1.601079.

338 the army had announced two days earlier . . . Chaim Levinson, "Israel Set to Double Number of Palestinian Administrative Detainees," *Haaretz*, June 23, 2014, www.haaretz.com/news/ diplomacy-defense/.premium-1.600480.

339 One of the young men from Qalandia . . . "Palestinian Shot Friday Succumbs to Wounds," Ma'an News Agency, June 25, 2014, www.maannews.com/Content.aspx?id=707843; Ashira Husari, "Qalandia Bids Its Champion Farewell," *Oximity*, June 26, 2014, www.oximity.com /article/Qalandia-bids-its-champion-farewell-1.

340 Arrests fell to seventeen on Tuesday . . . "Israeli Forces Detain Palestinian Lawmakers, Hamas Leaders Overnight," Ma'an News Agency, June 25, 2014, www.maannews.com/Content.aspx?id= 707640; "IDF Arrests 10 Palestinians in West Bank Crackdown," *Times of Israel*, June 26, 2014, www.timesofisrael.com/idf-arrests-10-palestinians-in-west-bank/.

340 "A large part of the operation . . ." Gili Cohen and Amos Harel, "IDF Scales Back West Bank Operation Against Hamas, Shifts Focus to Intelligence," *Haaretz*, June 24, 2014, www.haaretz .com/news/diplomacy-defense/.premium-1.600940.

340 The Shabak had named two suspects . . . Gili Cohen, "Shin Bet Names Two Hamas Militants as West Bank Kidnappers," *Haaretz*, June 27, 2014, www.haaretz.com/news/diplomacy-defense/ .premium-1.601560.

340 In August, the army would bulldoze . . . Gili Cohen, "Israeli Army Demolishes Homes of West Bank Kidnapping Suspects," *Haaretz*, August 18, 2014, www.haaretz.com/news/diplomacy -defense/.premium-1.611046.

340 In September soldiers would kill . . . Gili Cohen, "Suspects in Kidnap of West Bank Teens Killed in IDF Firefight," *Haaretz*, September 23, 2014, www.haaretz.com/news/diplomacy -defense/.premium-1.617319.

340 (Footnote) A third suspect, Hussam Qawasmeh . . . Gili Cohen, "Israel Indicts Mastermind Behind West Bank Kidnapping," *Haaretz*, September 4, 2014; www.haaretz.com/news/ diplomacy-defense/.premium-1.614064; Chaim Levinson, "Palestinian Behind Kidnap, Murder of Three Israeli Teens Gets Three Life Sentences," *Haaretz*, January 6, 2015, www.haaretz.com/ news/diplomacy-defense/.premium-1.635625.

340 (Footnote) His lawyer alleged that the confession . . . Sheera Frenkel, "Israel Releases Details of Hamas Cell Accused of Kidnapping and Killing Three Israeli Teens," *BuzzFeed*, August 6, 2014, www.buzzfeed.com/sheerafrenkel/israel-releases-details-of-hamas-cell -accused-of-kidnapping.

340 (Footnote) in mid-June, the Israeli attorney general . . . Yonah Jeremy Bob, "Shin Bet, NGO Trade Barbs over Enhanced Interrogation During Kidnapping Crisis," *Jerusalem Post*, June 20, 2014, www.jpost.com/Operation-Brothers-Keeper/Shin-Bet-NGO-trade-barbs-over-enhanced -interrogation-during-kidnapping-crisis-359995.

340 (Footnote) This would include techniques such as shaking . . . "Public Committee Against Torture in Israel v. the State of Israel and the General Security Service,"

High Court of Justice, September 6, 1999: www.law.yale.edu/documents/pdf/Public
_Committee_Against_Torture.pdf; Glenn Frankel, "Prison Tactics a Longtime Dilemma for
Israel," *Washington Post*, June 14, 2004, www.washingtonpost.com/wp-dyn/articles/A44664
-2004Jun15.html; "Torture and Ill-treatment in Interrogations," B'Tselem, January 1, 2011,
www.btselem.org/torture.

340 Lieutenant General Benny Gantz, the IDF's . . . "Army Chief on Kidnapped Teens: As Time
Passes, the Fear Grows," *Times of Israel*, June 24, 2014, www.timesofisrael.com/army-chief-on
-kidnapped-teens-as-time-passes-the-fear-grows/.

341 A few of the more stubborn militant . . . Isabel Kershner and Fares Akram, "Tensions Continue
to Simmer as Attacks in Gaza Escalate," *New York Times*, June 27, 2014, www.nytimes.com/2014/
06/28/world/middleeast/tensions-continue-to-simmer-as-attacks-in-gaza-escalate.html; "Rocket
Fired from Gaza Sets Israeli Factory Aflame," i24 News, June 29, 2014, www.i24news.tv/en/news/
israel/diplomacy-defense/35744-140628-rocket-fired-from-gaza-sets-sderot-factory-aflame;
"Hamas Warns It Will Retaliate Against Any Offensive on Gaza," Ma'an News Agency,
June 25, 2014, www.maannews.com/Content.aspx?id=707872.

CHAPTER 11: SATAN NEVER DREAMED

343 "Madness is like a hurricane . . ." Etel Adnan, *Sitt Marie Rose* (Sausalito, CA: Post-Apollo Press,
1982), 70.

343 They found the bodies on . . . Jodi Rudoren and Isabel Kershner, "Israel's Search for Three
Teenagers Ends in Grief," *New York Times*, June 30, 2014, www.nytimes.com/2014/07/01/world/
middleeast/Israel-missing-teenagers.html?_r=0.

343 (Footnote) Elias Khoury again: "the only thing . . ." Elias Khoury, *Gate of the Sun*, 275.

343 The teens, he said, "were abducted . . ." "PM Netanyahu's Remarks at the Start of the Security
Cabinet Meeting," Prime Minister's Office, June 30, 2014, www.pmo.gov.il/English/MediaCenter/
Spokesman/Pages/spokecabinet300614.aspx.

343 (Footnote) Written after the pogroms of 1903 . . . Hayim Nahman Bialik, "On the Slaughter," in
Songs from Bialik, trans. Atar Hadari (Syracuse, NY: Syracuse University Press, 2000), 11.

344 Politician after politician joined him . . . Ali Abunimah, "Israelis Demand Blood After Youths'
Bodies Found," *Electronic Intifada*, July 1, 2014, https://electronicintifada.net/blogs/ali-abunimah/
israelis-demand-blood-after-youths-bodies-found.

344 *The New York Times* live-tweeted . . . Jodi Rudoren, Twitter, https://twitter.com/search
?q=funeral%20from%3Arudoren%20since%3A2014-06-30%20until%3A2014-07-02&src
=typd&lang=en.

344 The paper's Isabel Kershner observed . . . Isabel Kershner, "Deeply Divided Israel
Unites in Grief and Sees a Larger Purpose," *New York Times*, July 1, 2014, www.nytimes
.com/2014/07/02/world/middleeast/deeply-divided-israel-unites-in-grief-and-sees-a-larger
-purpose.html.

344 The raids resumed—there were arrests . . . "42 Palestinians Arrested Across West Bank as
Campaign Continues," Ma'an News Agency, July 2, 2014, www.maannews.com/Content
.aspx?id=709303; Yoav Zitun, "Israel Fears Kidnappers Fled Hebron After Teens' Bodies Found,"
Ynet News, July 1, 2014, http://www.ynetnews.com/articles/0,7340,L-4536636,00.html.

344 A Palestinian teen named Mohammad . . . Orlando Crowcroft, "Palestinian Family Mourns
Their 'Baby' amid Revenge Attack Claims," *National*, July 2, 2014, www.thenational.ae/world/
middle-east/palestinian-family-mourns-their-baby-amid-revenge -attack-claims.

344 Hundreds had been injured . . . "170 Palestinians Injured in East Jerusalem Clashes," Ma'an
News Agency, July 2, 2014, www.maannews.com/Content.aspx?id=709498.

345 The autopsy report was leaked to the press . . . Peter Beaumont, "Palestinian Boy Mohammed
Abu Khdeir Was Burned Alive, Says Official," *Guardian*, July 5, 2014, www.theguardian.com/
world/2014/jul/05/palestinian-boy-mohammed-abu-khdeir-burned-alive.

345 (Footnote) From Netanyahu's eulogy for the three . . . "Eulogy by PM Netanyahu for Eyal
Yifrah, Gilad Sha'er and Naftali Frenkel," Israeli Ministry of Foreign Affairs, July 1, 2014, http://

mfa.gov.il/MFA/PressRoom/2014/Pages/Eulogy-by-PM-Netanyahu-for-Eyal-Yifrah-Gilad-Shaer
-Naftali-Frenkel-1-July-2014.aspx.

345 **(Footnote) Thirteen months later, another Palestinian child** . . . Kate Shuttleworth and Mairav
Zonszein, "Palestinian Child Dead in Suspected Jewish Extremist Arson Attack on Home,"
Guardian, July 31, 2015, www.theguardian.com/world/2015/jul/31/child-dies-after
-suspected-jewish-extremist-attack-on-palestinian-home.

345 **(Footnote) The child's father, Saad Dawabsha** . . . "West Bank Arson: Dead Palestinian Child's
Father Dies of Wounds," BBC, August 8, 2015, www.bbc.com/news/world-middle-east-33833400.

345 **(Footnote) The mother, Riham Dawabsha, died** . . . Diaa Hadid, "Palestinians Pay Homage to a
3rd Firebomb Victim," *New York Times*, September 7, 2015, www.nytimes.com
/2015/09/08/world/middleeast/palestinians-pay-homage-to-a-3rd-firebomb-victim.html.

345 **The next day six suspects were arrested** . . . Peter Beaumont, "Israeli Police Arrest Six over
Mohamed Abu Khdeir Killing," *Guardian*, July 6, 2014, www.theguardian.com/world/2014
/jul/06/israel-arrests-abu-khdeir-killing.

345 **Three were released. The clashes spread** . . . Nir Hasson, "Court Orders Release of Three
Suspects in Palestinian Teen's Murder," *Haaretz*, July 10, 2014, www.haaretz.com/news
/diplomacy-defense/.premium-1.604141.

345 **to almost every neighborhood in East Jerusalem** . . . Nir Hasson and Jack Khoury, "Tense Quiet
in Jerusalem and Israel's North After Friday Rioting," *Haaretz*, July 5, 2014, www.haaretz.com/
news/diplomacy-defense/.premium-1.603163; "Live Updates, July 5: Riots Grip E. Jerusalem, Arab
Towns," *Haaretz*, July 5, 2014, www.haaretz.com/news/diplomacy-defense/1.603150.

345 **And from Jerusalem to Tel Aviv** . . . "Israelis Attack 2 Palestinians in Jerusalem Area," Ma'an
News Agency, July 1, 2014, www.maannews.com/Content.aspx?id=709149; Lisa Goldman,
"Israeli Jews Attack Palestinian on Public Bus," *+972*, July 4, 2014, http://972mag.com/watch
-israeli-jews-attack-palestinian-on-public-bus/93003/; Patrick Strickland, "'I Saw Blood All Over
Me': Gangs of Israeli Vigilantes Roam Streets Attacking Palestinians," Alternet, July 4, 2014,
www.alternet.org/world/i-saw-blood-all-over-me-gangs-israeli -vigilantes-roam-streets
-attacking-palestinians.

345 **Throughout the second half of June** . . . Ben Hartman and Yaakov Lappin, "Gaza Rocket
Ignites Sderot Plastics Factory," *Jerusalem Post*, June 28, 2014, www.jpost.com/Defense/Gaza
-rocket-strikes-factory-in-Sderot-360859; "Israel Bombs Gaza After Rocket Attacks, Hamas
Gunman Killed," Reuters, June 29, 2014, http://uk.reuters.com/article/2014/06/29/uk-israel
-palestinians-idUKKBN0F40F220140629; Yonah Jeremy Bob, "At Least 15 Rockets Explode in
Southern Israel as Tensions Escalate," *Jerusalem Post*, June 30, 2014, www.jpost.com/Defense/
In-sign-of-rising-tensions-8-more-rockets-explode-in-southern-Israel-360988.

345 **the smaller armed groups in Gaza** . . . "The Next Round in Gaza," International Crisis Group,
March 25, 2014, www.crisisgroup.org/~/media/Files/Middle%20East%20North%20Africa/Israel%
20Palestine/149-the-next-round-in-gaza.pdf.

346 **three or four got through most months** . . . "Rocket Fire from Gaza and Palestinian Ceasefire
Violations After Operation Cast Lead (Jan. 2009)," Israel Ministry of Foreign Affairs, August 19,
2015, http://mfa.gov.il/MFA/ForeignPolicy/Terrorism/Pages/Palestinian_ceasefire_violations
_since_end_Operation_Cast_Lead.aspx; "Reports," Israel Security Agency, www.shabak.gov.il/
English/EnTerrorData/Reports/Pages/default.aspx.

346 **Fewer rockets were launched in 2013** . . . Nathan Thrall, "Hamas's Chances," *London Review of
Books*, August 21, 2014, www.lrb.co.uk/v36/n16/nathan-thrall/hamass-chances.

346 **For all the many dozens** . . . Phan Nguyen, "How Many People Have Died from Gaza Rockets
into Israel?," *Mondoweiss*, July 14, 2014, http://mondoweiss.net/2014/07/rocket-deaths-israel;
"Reports," Israel Security Agency.

346 **More rockets had been launched** . . . "Monthly Summary—March 2014," Israel Security Agency,
www.shabak.gov.il/SiteCollectionDocuments/Monthly%20summary-%20March%202014.pdf;
"Monthly Summary—June 2014," Israel Security Agency, www.shabak.gov.il
/SiteCollectionDocuments/Monthly%20summary%20%E2%80%93%20June%202014.pdf.

346 **the Israeli response—strikes that killed . . .** Gili Cohen and Shirley Seidler, "Gaza Rockets Strike Israel Despite Talk of Cease-Fire," *Haaretz*, March 14, 2014, www.haaretz.com/news /diplomacy-defense/1.579573.

346 **On June 29, an IDF airstrike . . .** Avi Issacharoff, "Hamas Fires Rockets for First Time Since 2012, Israeli Officials Say," *Times of Israel*, June 30, 2014, www.timesofisrael.com/hamas-fired -rockets-for-first-time-since-2012-israeli-officials-say/.

346 **At the end of that week, Hamas . . .** "Hamas 'Considering Alternatives' to Unity Govt in Gaza," Ma'an News Agency, July 5, 2014, www.maannews.com/Content.aspx?id=710117.

346 **Two days later the Israeli bombed . . .** "IDF Strikes Hamas Tunnel While Terrorists Plan Attack," Israel Defense Forces, July 7, 2014, www.idfblog.com/blog/2014/07/07/idf-strikes-hamas -tunnel-terrorists-plan-attack/; Yaakov Lappin, "IAF Strikes Gaza Underground Rocket Launchers, Terror Tunnel amid Heavy Rocket Fire," *Jerusalem Post*, July 7, 2014, www.jpost.com/ Defense/IAF-strikes-Gaza-in-response-to-continuous-rocket-fire-361586; "'Nine Palestinians Killed' in Israeli Airstrikes on Gaza," Ma'an News Agency, July 7, 2014, www.maannews.com/ Content.aspx?id=710533.

346 **Before the day's end, eighty-five rockets . . .** "Israel on High Alert After More Than 85 Rockets Fired in 24 Hours," *Haaretz*, July 7, 2014, www.haaretz.com/news/diplomacy-defense/.premium -1.603653.

346 **By the end of the following night . . .** "Death Toll Climbs as Hamas, Israel Trade Blows," NBC News, July 9, 2014, www.nbcnews.com/news/world/death-toll-climbs-hamas-israel-trade-blows -n151836; "LIVE UPDATES: Operation Protective Edge, Day 2," *Haaretz*, July 9, 2014, www .haaretz.com/news/diplomacy-defense/1.603913; "In Two Days, Israeli Bombing in Gaza Exceeds All 2012 Assault," *Times of Israel*, July 10, 2014, www.timesofisrael.com/in-two-days-israeli -bombing-in-gaza-exceeds-all-2012-assault/; "The Victims of Gaza: A List of Palestinians Killed in Israel's Ongoing Assault," *Al-Akhbar English,* October 6, 2014.

347 **"No country would accept such a threat . . ."** "Statement by PM Netanyahu," Israel Ministry of Foreign Affairs, July 8, 2014, http://mfa.gov.il/MFA/PressRoom/2014/Pages/Statement-by-PM -Netanyahu-8-July-2014.aspx.

347 **"We will do more than mow the lawn . . ."** Sheera Frenkel, "Thousands of Israeli Soldiers Called to Border to Begin Long Wait for War," *BuzzFeed*, July 8, 2014, www.buzzfeed.com/sheerafrenkel/ thousands-of-israeli-soldiers-called-to-border-to-begin-long.

347 **This war, Knesset member Ayelet Shaked . . .** Gideon Resnick, "Israeli Politician Declares 'War' on 'the Palestinian People,'" *Daily Beast*, July 7, 2014, www.thedailybeast.com/articles/2014/07/07/ israeli-politician-declares-war-on-the-palestinian-people.html.

347 **(Footnote) Shaked demurred that the words were . . .** Gideon Resnick, "Knesset Member Walks Back on Facebook Post Calling Palestinian Kids 'Little Snakes,'" *Daily Beast*, July 10, 2014, www .thedailybeast.com/articles/2014/07/10/knesset-member-walks-back-on-facebook-post-calling -palestinian-kids-little-snakes.html.

347 **(Footnote) Following elections held eight months later, Netanyahu . . .** Ishaan Tharoor, "Israel's New Justice Minister Considers All Palestinians to Be 'The Enemy,'" *Washington Post*, May 7, 2015, www.washingtonpost.com/news/worldviews/wp/2015/05/07/israels-new-justice-minister -considers-all-palestinians-to-be-the-enemy/.

348 **In the thirteen years between 2001 . . .** Nguyen, "How Many People Have Died from Gaza Rockets?"; "Rocket Fire from Gaza," Israel Ministry of Foreign Affairs; "Road Accidents with Casualties—2013," Israel Central Bureau of Statistics, July 20, 2014, 45, www.cbs.gov.il /publications14/acci13_1572/pdf/t_d.pdf.

348 **Israel's vaunted "Iron Dome" missile defense system . . .** "Israel Deploys 'Iron Dome' Rocket Shield," Al Jazeera, March 27, 2011, www.aljazeera.com/news/middleeast/2011/03 /201132718224159699.html.

348 **On July 8, the official first day . . .** Rabbi Gideon D. Sylvester, "Sorry to Interrupt This Peace Conference, but a Rocket Siren's Sounding," *Haaretz*, July 11, 2014, www.haaretz.com/jewish -world/rabbis-round-table/.premium-1.604510.

349 There were daily clashes in the camps . . . Saeed Bannoura, "Dozens Injured in Clashes with Soldiers Invading Hebron," International Middle East Media Center, July 8, 2014, www.imemc .org/article/68379; "Palestinians Throw Firebombs at Military Camp near Ramallah," Ma'an News Agency, July 8, 2014, www.maannews.com/Content.aspx?id=710825; "Clashes Break Out in Ramallah-Area Village," Ma'an News Agency, July 8, 2014, www.maannews.com/Content .aspx?id=711116; "Palestinians, Israeli Troops Clash near Qalandia Checkpoint," Ma'an News Agency, July 9, 2014, www.maannews.com/Content.aspx?id=711234; "11 Palestinians Hurt in Clashes with Israeli Troops near Ramallah," Ma'an News Agency, July 10, 2014, www.maannews .com/Content.aspx?id=711202; "14 Injured in Clashes in Ramallah, El-Bireh Villages," Ma'an News Agency, July 11, 2014, www.maannews.com/Content.aspx?id=712002; "Palestinians Clash with Israeli Forces Across West Bank," Ma'an News Agency, July 12, 2014, www.maannews.com/ Content.aspx?id=712228.

349 Arrests in the West Bank had reached . . . Amira Hass, "Why the West Bank Isn't Erupting Against Israel," *Haaretz*, July 18, 2014, www.haaretz.com/news/diplomacy-defense/.premium -1.605866.

350 In Gaza, the death toll climbed . . . "The Victims of Gaza," *Al-Akhbar English*.

350 There were clashes still in Jerusalem . . . "Live Updates, July 7, 2014: Rockets Bombard South, Hamas Claims Responsibility," *Haaretz*, July 7, 2014, www.haaretz.com/news/diplomacy-defense/ 1.603472.

350 Leftists demonstrating against the war . . . Ben Hartman, "Following Assaults on Anti-War Protesters in Tel Aviv, Parties on Left Demand Answers," *Jerusalem Post*, July 13, 2014, www .jpost.com/Operation-Protective-Edge/Following-assaults-on-anti-war-protesters-in-Tel-Aviv -parties-on-Left-demand-answers-362602.

350 whole families wiped out, children . . . Jack Khoury, "89 Families Killed in Gaza Since Hostilities Began, Palestinians Say," *Haaretz*, August 24, 2014, www.haaretz.com/news /diplomacy-defense/1.612255; "Israel Bombed 161 Mosques in Gaza," *Middle East Monitor*, August 4, 2014, www.middleeastmonitor.com/news/middle-east/13229-israel-bombed-161 -mosques-in-gaza; "Israel Shells Hospital in Gaza," *Middle East Monitor*, July 16, 2014, www .middleeastmonitor.com/news/middle-east/12830-israel-shells-hospital-in-gaza; "Israel: In-Depth Look at Gaza School Attacks," Human Rights Watch, September 11, 2014, www.hrw.org/news/ 2014/09/11/israel-depth-look-gaza-school-attacks.

350 Hamas offered Israel a ten-year truce . . . Ira Glunts, "Hamas Offers Israel 10 Conditions for a 10 Year Truce," *Mondoweiss*, July 16, 2014, http://mondoweiss.net/2014/07/report-israel -conditions.

350 "I think the Israeli people understand . . ." David Horovitz, "Netanyahu Finally Speaks His Mind," *Times of Israel*, July 13, 2014, www.timesofisrael.com/netanyahu-finally-speaks -his-mind/.

351 Their names were Ismail, Ahed . . . Sheera Frenkel, "Four Children Killed in Attack on Gaza Beach Witnessed by Dozens of Journalists," *BuzzFeed*, July 16, 2014, www.buzzfeed.com/ sheerafrenkel/four-children-killed-in-attack-on-gaza-beach-witnessed-by-do; Peter Beaumont, "Witness to a Shelling: First-Hand Account of Deadly Strike on Gaza Port," *Guardian*, July 16, 2014, www.theguardian.com/world/2014/jul/16/witness-gaza-shelling-first-hand-account.

352 Two nights in, troops and tanks . . . Peter Beaumont and Harriet Sherwood, "'Death and Horror' in Gaza as Thousands Flee Israeli Bombardment," *Guardian*, July 20, 2014, www .theguardian.com/world/2014/jul/20/gaza-thousands-flee-israeli-bombardment; "Report: Shuja'iya Primary School for Girls," Gisha Legal Center for Freedom of Movement, http://gisha .org/gazzamap/401.

352 The IDF lost thirteen soldiers . . . Mark Perry, "Why Israel's Bombardment of Gaza Neighborhood Left US Officers 'Stunned,'" *Al Jazeera America*, August 27, 2014, http://america .aljazeera.com/articles/2014/8/26/israel-bombing-stunsusofficers.html; Mitch Ginsburg, "13 Soldiers Killed Overnight in Fierce Gaza Fighting," *Times of Israel*, July 20, 2014, www

.timesofisrael.com/soldiers-killed-in-gaza/; Sharif Abdel Kaddous, "Massacre in Shejaiya," *Nation*, July 20, 2014, www.thenation.com/article/massacre-shejaiya/; Sara Hussein, "Gaza's Shejaiya: A Moonscape Strewn with Bodies," Agence-France-Presse, July 20, 2014, http://news .yahoo.com/gazas-shejaiya-moonscape-strewn-bodies-145951100.html.

352 **Thousands were protesting** . . . Kim Sengupta, "Israel-Gaza Conflict: Gaza Death Toll Rises as the World Protests," *Independent*, July 20, 2014, www.independent.co.uk/news/world/middle-east/ israelgaza-conflict-gaza-death-toll-rises-as-the-world-protests-9617003.html; "In Pictures: Global Gaza Solidarity Protests," Al Jazeera, July 19, 2014, www.aljazeera.com/indepth/inpictures/2014/ 07/pictures-pro-palestinian-protes-201471811179953166.html.

353 **Hamas's military wing, the al-Qassam Brigades** . . . "Qassam Brigades Says They Have Captured an Israeli Soldier," *Middle East Monitor*, July 20, 2014, www.middleeastmonitor.com/news/middle -east/12937-qassam-brigades-says-held-israeli-soldier-hostage.

354 **The captured soldier, whose name was Oron Shaul** . . . Yoav Zitun, Elior Levy, "Missing Soldier Declared Dead, Another Killed in Gaza on Friday," *Ynet News*, July 25, 2014, www.ynetnews .com/articles/0,7340,L-4549927,00.html; Danny Brenner, "Parents of Soldier Initially Thought Missing Agree to Mourn His Death," *Israel Hayom*, July 28, 2014, www.israelhayom.com/site/ newsletter_article.php?id=19075.

355 **Thousands marched on the checkpoint** . . . "One Killed, Another 'Clinically Dead' from Israeli Fire on Ramallah Demo," Ma'an News Agency, July 24, 2014, www.maannews.com/Content .aspx?id=716030; "Two Palestinians Killed During Clashes with Israeli Occupation Forces in West Bank," *Middle East Monitor*, July 25, 2014, www.middleeastmonitor.com/news/middle-east/13042 -two-palestinians-killed-during-clashes-with-israeli-occupation-forces-in-west-bank; "Six Palestinians Killed in West Bank amid Protests Against Gaza Assault," Ma'an News Agency, July 25, 2014, www.maannews.com/Content.aspx?id=716148.

355 **The Al-Aqsa Brigades later took credit** . . . "Al-Aqsa Brigades Opens Fire on Qalandia, Injuring Israeli Soldiers," Ma'an News Agency, July 24, 2014, www.maannews.com/Content .aspx?id=716264.

355 **the death toll in Gaza had passed** . . . Karen Yourish and Josh Keller, "The Toll in Gaza and Israel, Day by Day," *New York Times*, August 8, 2014, www.nytimes.com/interactive/2014/07/15/ world/middleeast/toll-israel-gaza-conflict.html.

355 **Before it was over, 2,220 Palestinians** . . . "Fragmented Lives: Humanitarian Overview, 2014," United Nations Office for the Coordination of Humanitarian Affairs, March 2015, 4, 8, http:// reliefweb.int/sites/reliefweb.int/files/resources/annual_humanitarian_overview_2014_english _final.pdf.

355 **Much of Gaza's water and sewage** . . . "Gaza: Initial Rapid Assessment," United Nations Office for the Coordination of Humanitarian Affairs, August 27, 2014, 2, 4, 10, 17–19, www.ochaopt .org/documents/gaza_mira_report_9september.pdf.

355 **The one functioning electrical plant** . . . Harriet Sherwood, "Gaza's Only Power Plant Destroyed in Israel's Most Intense Air Strike Yet," *Guardian*, July 29, 2014, www.theguardian.com/world/ 2014/jul/29/gaza-power-plant-destroyed-israeli-airstrike-100 -palestinians-dead.

355 **Half of the Strip's hospitals** . . . "Gaza: Initial Rapid Assessment," UN-OCHA, 3, 4, 15.

356 **as would 278 mosques, including one** . . . "One Third of Gaza's Mosques Destroyed by Israeli Strikes," *Middle East Monitor*, August 20, 2014, www.middleeastmonitor.com/news/middle-east/ 13813-one-third-of-gazas-mosques-destroyed-by-israeli-strikes.

356 **In the West Bank, another 25 people** . . . "Palestinians Killed After Operation Cast Lead," B'Tselem.

356 **Israel would kill more Palestinians** . . . Mairav Zonszein, "Israel Killed More Palestinians in 2014 than in Any Other Year Since 1967," *Guardian*, March 27, 2015, www.theguardian.com/ world/2015/mar/27/israel-kills-more-palestinians-2014-than-any-other-year-since-1967.

356 **According to one poll published** . . . "July 2014 Peace Index," Israel Democracy Institute, July 29, 2014, http://en.idi.org.il/about-idi/news-and-updates/july-2014-peace-index/.

356 In the end, 6 civilians . . . "Unlawful and Deadly Rocket and Mortar Attacks by Palestinian Armed Groups During the 2014 Gaza/Israel Conflict," Amnesty International, March 2015, 3, 14, 19–35, www.amnesty.org/en/documents/mde21/1178/2015/en/; "Israel's Fallen in Operation Protective Edge," *Times of Israel*, August 29, 2014, www.timesofisrael.com/fallen-idf-soldiers-in -operation-protective-edge/.

EPILOGUE

359 "What else is there for any . . ." Doris Lessing, *Shikasta: Re, Colonised Planet 5* (New York: Alfred A. Knopf, 1979), 353.

360 Two months later, Nariman and two others . . . Natasha Roth, "Under Fire in the West Bank," *London Review of Books*, January 28, 2015, www.lrb.co.uk/blog/2015/01/28/natasha-roth/under-fire -in-the-west-bank/.

360 Three weeks after Nariman was shot . . . "Press Release: Military Steps Up Use of Live 0.22 Inch Bullets Against Palestinian Stone-Throwers," B'Tselem, January 18, 2015, www.btselem.org/ press_releases/20150118_use_of_live_ammunition_in_wb.

360 Five months later she too would be shot . . . Anne Paq, "Soldiers Fire Live Ammo, Wound Two in Nabi Saleh Protest," +972, April 5, 2015, http://972mag.com/photos-soldiers-fire-live-ammo -wound-two-in-nabi-saleh-protest/105277/.

361 They destroyed six buildings which . . . Ahmad Jaradat, "Demolitions in South Hebron Hills," *Alternative Information Center*, October 29, 2014, www.alternativenews.org/english/index.php/ news/15-hebron/117-see-demolitions-in-south-hebron-hills.

362 Early in the morning of July 31 . . . Jack Khoury, Chaim Levinson, and Gili Cohen, "Palestinian Infant Burned to Death in West Bank Arson Attack; IDF Blames 'Jewish Terror,'" *Haaretz*, July 31, 2015, www.haaretz.com/israel-news/1.668871; Amira Hass, "Relative of Arson Attack Victims: I Saw Two Masked Men Standing by as They Burned," *Haaretz*, July 31, 2015, www .haaretz.com/israel-news/.premium-1.668947; "Palestinian Mother Wounded in Duma Firebombing Dies," *Times of Israel*, September 7, 2015, www.timesofisrael.com/riham-dawabsha -26-mother-of-ali-has-died/.

362 (Footnote) Amiram Ben-Uliel, the twenty-one-year-old . . . "Jewish Man Charged with July Murders of Palestinian Family in Duma," *Times of Israel*, January 3, 2016, http://www .timesofisrael.com/two-suspected-jewish-extremists-indicted-for-duma-murders/; Roi Yanovsky, "Israeli Hurt in Drive-by Shooting Succumbs to Wounds," *Ynet News*, June 30, 2015, http:// www.ynetnews.com/articles/0,7340,L-4674683,00.html.

362 Israeli restrictions on prayer at the al-Aqsa . . . "Israeli Restrictions on Al-Aqsa Entry Continue for 3rd Week," Ma'an News Agency, September 6, 2015, www.maannews.com/Content .aspx?id=767463; "Palestinians Clash with Israeli Forces in Jerusalem," *Guardian*, September 18, 2015, www.theguardian.com/world/2015/sep/18/palestinians-clash-with-israeli-forces-in -jerusalem; Renee Lewis, "Dozens Wounded in Clashes over Jerusalem's Al-Aqsa Entry Restrictions," Al Jazeera America, September 22, 2015, http://america.aljazeera.com/ articles/2015/9/18/dozens-wounded-in-clashes-over-jerusalems-al-aqsa.html; "Israeli Police, Palestinians Clash at al-Aqsa Compound," Al Jazeera, September 27, 2015, www.aljazeera.com/ news/2015/09/israeli-police-palestinians-clash-al-aqsa-compound-150927132041035.html; "11 Detained, Several Injured in East Jerusalem's Al-Aqsa Clashes," Ma'an News Agency, September 19, 205, www.maannews.com/Content.aspx?id=767705.

362 The clashes spread to the West Bank . . . Patrick Strickland, "Al-Aqsa Tensions Trigger Clashes Across West Bank," Al Jazeera, September 29, 2015, www.aljazeera.com/news/2015/09/al -aqsa-tensions-trigger-clashes-west-bank-150929130038368.html.

362 On September 22, eighteen-year-old Hadeel al-Hashlamoun . . . Amira Hass, "The Execution of Hadeel al-Hashlamoun," *Haaretz*, November 3, 2015, www.haaretz.com/opinion/ .premium-1.684048; "Evidence Indicates West Bank Killing Was Extrajudicial Execution," Amnesty International, September 25, 2015, www.amnesty.org/en/documents/mde15/2529/2015/en/.

362 The first of October brought . . . Chaim Levinson and Barak Ravid, "Israeli Couple Shot Dead in West Bank, Four Kids Unhurt," *Haaretz*, October 1, 2015, www.haaretz.com/israel-news /1.678511.

362 That October, Israeli security forces . . . "Red Crescent: Over 2,600 Shot with Live, Rubber Bullets in October," Ma'an News Agency, November 1, 2015, www.maannews.com/Content .aspx?id=768603; "Wave of Terror 2015/16," Israel Ministry of Foreign Affairs, February 17, 2016, http://mfa.gov.il/MFA/ForeignPolicy/Terrorism/Palestinian/Pages/Wave-of-terror -October-2015.aspx.

363 in several cases, video evidence . . . "Unjustified Use of Lethal Force and Execution of Palestinians Who Stabbed or Were Suspected of Attempted Stabbings," B'Tselem, December 16, 2015, www.btselem.org/gunfire/20151216_cases_of_unjustified_gunfire_and_executions; Mel Frykberg, "The Controversial Killing of Fadi Alloun," Al Jazeera, October 5, 2015, www .aljazeera.com/news/2015/10/controversial-killing-fadi-alloun-151005081834933.html; John Brown, "New Video Shows Accused Stabber Posed No Threat When Shot," +972, October 10, 2015, http://972mag.com/new-video-shows-accused-stabber-posed-no-threat-when-shot/112593/; "Israel Clears Palestinian Woman of Stabbing Charges," *Middle East Eye*, October 29, 2015, www.middleeasteye.net/news/israel-clears-palestinian-woman-stabbing-charges -1415394768#sthash.OzBLn1Aq.dpuf; "Palestinian Shot, Killed in East Jerusalem After Alleged Stab Attack," Ma'an News Agency, October 12, 2015, www.maannews.com/Content .aspx?id=768185; "From Death to Burial: Israel's Failure to Respect International Law, the Cases of Mustafa Al-Khatib and Fadi 'Alloun," Al Haq, January 20, 2016, www.alhaq.org/advocacy/ topics/right-to-life-and-body-integrity/1009-from-death-to-burial-israels-failure-to-respect -international-law-the-cases-of-mustafa-al-khatib-and-fadi-alloun; "Video Footage Raises Questions over Hebron 'Attack,'" Ma'an News Agency, October 17, 2015, www.maannews.com/ Content.aspx?id=768305.

363 The panic was widespread . . . "Watch: When Israeli Man Stabbed Jew He Mistook for an Arab," *Times of Israel*, November 2, 2015, http://www.timesofisrael.com/watch-when-israeli-man-stabbed -jew-he-mistook-for-an-arab/; Tia Goldenberg, "Israeli Man Shot Dead After Being Mistaken for Attacker," Associated Press, October 22, 2015, http://bigstory.ap.org/article/2ebf9b761823497aaaaa 64ecec6e0cf1/police-say-2-arab-attackers-stab-israeli-and-are-shot; Alexandra Sims, "Eritrean Man Shot and Beaten to Death After Being Mistaken for 'Terrorist' in Israeli Bus Station Attack," *Independent*, October 19, 2015, http://www.independent.co.uk/news/world/middle-east/israel -bus-station-attack-innocent-bystander-beaten-to-death-in-beersheba-after-being-mistaken-for -a6699341.html.

363 Fully half of the alleged attackers . . . "Palestinians in the OPT Killed in the OPT and Israel Since 1 October," Al Haq, www.alhaq.org/publications/list.of.palestinians.killed.pdf. Accessed February 18, 2016.

363 kitchen knives, scissors, screwdrivers . . . William Booth and Ruth Eglash, "Israel Calls Palestinian Knife Attacks 'a New Kind of Terrorism,'" *Independent*, December 26, 2015, www .independent.co.uk/news/world/middle-east/israel-calls-palestinian-knife-attacks-a-new-kind -of-terrorism-a6787036.html; "Palestinian Teens Armed with Scissors Shot in Jerusalem," Al Jazeera, November 23, 2015, www.aljazeera.com/news/2015/11/israeli-palestinian-violence -151123101833511.html; "Cops Nab Palestinian Woman on Way to Carry Out Jerusalem Stabbing," *Times of Israel,* December 15, 2015, www.timesofisrael.com/palestinian-woman-nabbed-before -jerusalem-stabbing/.

363 Twenty-four-year-old Rasha Mohammad Oweisi . . . "Palestinian Woman Killed After Alleged Attack at Qalqiliya Checkpoint," Ma'an News Agency, November 9, 2015, www.maannews.com/ Content.aspx?id=768724.

364 (Footnote) In early January, Haaretz would . . . Amos Harel, "Israeli Security Officials: Abbas Cracking Down on Violence, Gestures to PA Are Urgent," *Haaretz*, January 7, 2016, www .haaretz.com/israel-news/.premium-1.695934.

364 Netanyahu cried "incitement," but even . . . Gili Cohen, "Shin Bet: Feelings of Discrimination Driving Palestinian Youth Toward Terror," *Haaretz*, November 11, 2015, www.haaretz.com/ israel-news/.premium-1.685485; Barak Ravid, "IDF Intelligence Chief: Palestinian Despair, Frustration Are Among Reasons for Terror Wave," November 3, 2015, *Haaretz*, www.haaretz .com/israel-news/.premium-1.683860.

364 Shortly before boarding a Jerusalem bus . . . Peter Beaumont, "What's Driving the Young Lone Wolves Who Are Stalking the Streets of Israel?," *Guardian*, October 18, 2015, http://www .theguardian.com/world/2015/oct/18/knife-intifada-palestinian-israel-west-bank.

364 Within three days, footage of the incident . . . Robert Mackey, "Rashomon on the West Bank: Israelis and Palestinians Debate Images of Soldier and Child," *New York Times*, September 1, 2015, www.nytimes.com/2015/09/02/world/middleeast/rashomon-on-the-west-bank-israelis -and-palestinians-debate-images-of-soldier-and-child.html.

365 (Footnote) At that point 151 Palestinians . . . "Palestinians in the OPT Killed," Al Haq; "Wave of Terror 2015/16," Israel Ministry of Foreign Affairs.

365 On October 30, soldiers had informed . . . Alison Deger, "In Hebron 'Even the Kids Have Numbers,'" Al Jazeera, December 16, 2015, www.aljazeera.com/news/2015/12/hebron-kids -numbers-151203091934395.html; "Rights Groups Urge Israel to End Hebron 'Closed Military Zones,'" Ma'an News Agency, January 13, 2016, www.maannews.com/Content.aspx?id=769785.

366 On November 7, soldiers had raided . . . Alison Deger, "Israeli Army Makes Post in Hebron Activist House," Mondoweiss, November 9, 2015, http://mondoweiss.net/2015/11/israeli-hebron -activist/.

366 Two weeks later, they came back . . . "Israeli Settlers Storm Palestinian Activist Center in Hebron," Ma'an News Agency, November 28, 2015, https://www.maannews.com/Content .aspx?id=769073; Michael Salisbury-Corech, "Under Cover of Shabbat, Settlers Invade Palestinian Property in Hebron," *+972*, November 29, 2015, 972mag.com/under-cover-of-shabbat-settlers -invade-palestinian-property-in-hebron/114290/.

366 More Palestinians had been killed . . . "Palestinians in the OPT Killed," Al Haq.

366 After al-Hashlamoun came Fadil al-Qawasmeh . . . "Israeli Authorities Must Protect Palestinian Civilians in Wake of Settler Attacks in Hebron," Amnesty International, October 30, 2015, www .amnesty.org/en/press-releases/2015/10/israel-opt-israeli-authorities-must-protect-palestinian -civilians-in-wake-of-settler-attacks-in-hebron/; "Israeli Settler Shoots Dead Palestinian in Hebron, Two Others Killed in Attempted Stabbings," *Middle East Eye*, October 17, 2015, www.middleeasteye.net/news/israeli-settler-shoots-dead-palestinian-teen-hebron-another -killed-jerusalem-768211142#sthash.JbrWLP8L.dpuf.

366 (Footnote) His name was Tariq Ziad al-Natsha . . . "Protest Called in Hebron as Israel Withholds 11 Palestinians' Bodies," Ma'an News Agency, October 27, 2015, https://www .maannews.com/Content.aspx?id=768500.

366 (Footnote) Houmam Adnan Sa'id was twenty-three . . . "Israeli Forces Erasing Palestinian Lives as If They Never Existed," International Solidarity Movement, October 28, 2015, http:// palsolidarity.org/2015/10/israeli-forces-erasing-palestinian-lives-as-if-they-never-existed-23-year -old-gunned-down-in-hebron/; "Young Unarmed Man Murdered in Cold Blood in Hebron," International Solidarity Movement, October 28, 2015, http://palsolidarity.org/2015/10/young -unarmed-man-murdered-in-cold-blod-in-hebron/.

367 They were cousins, Mustafa and Taher . . . "Two Palestinian Teenagers Killed by IOF, Friday Dawn," Palestine News Network, December 4, 2015, http://english.pnn.ps/2015/12/04/two -palestinian-teenagers-killed-by-iof-friday-dawn/.

367 he left out Farouq 'Abd al-Qadr Sedr . . . "2nd Palestinian Killed in Hebron After Alleged Stabbing Attempt," Ma'an News Agency, October 29, 2015, www.maannews.com/Content .aspx?id=768545; Charlotte Silver and Ali Abunimah, "Israelis Execute Injured Palestinian— Video and Eyewitness," *Electronic Intifada*, October 30, 2015, https://electronicintifada.net/ content/israelis-execute-injured-palestinian-video-and-eyewitness/14966.

368 On the last day of that August, soldiers . . . Isabel Kershner, "Israel Claims Nearly 1,000 Acres of West Bank Land Near Bethlehem," *New York Times*, August 31, 2014, www.nytimes.com/ 2014/09/01/world/middleeast/israel-claims-nearly-1000-acres-of-west-bank-land-near-bethlehem .html?_r=0; Isabel Kershner, "New Emblem of an Elemental Conflict: Seized West Bank Land," *New York Times*, September 9, 2014, www.nytimes.com/2014/09/10/world/middleeast/after-land -seizure-west-bank-villages-symbolize-an-elemental-conflict.html; "Unprecedented Land Confiscation of 4,000 Dunams Near Bethlehem," Peace Now, August 31, 2014, www.peacenow .org.il/eng/GvaotDecleration.

INDEX